THE
WYCLIFFE
NEW TESTAMENT
(1388)

The opening of St John's Gospel (transcribed on p.187 below) in BL Royal MS. I. C. viii, fol. 325v, reproduced at the same size as the original.

putt to hise fadris / And was myche wiþout corupte
dey: hou myche he is foundun cleene fro coruptioun
fleisch / Ierom in his prolog on Ioon: seiþ al þis

In þe bigynnyng was þe word & þe word is
at god · & god was þe word, þis was in þe big-
nyng at god / alle þingis weren maad bi hym
and wiþouten hym was maad no þing / þat
þat was maad in hym was liif · and þe liif was
þe liȝt of men / and liȝt schyneþ in derknessis · a-
derknessis comprehendiden not it / a man was se-
fro god: to whom þe name was Ioon / þis man c-
in to witnessyng · þat he schulde bere witnessi-
of þe liȝt þat alle men schulden bileue bi hym / h-
was not þe liȝt · but þat he schulde bere witnessi-
of þe liȝt / þe was a verri liȝt: which liȝtneþ ech m-
þat comeþ in to þis world / he was in þe world
and þe world was maad bi hym · & þe world knew
hym not / he cam in to hise owne þingis · and hi-
resseyueden hym not · but hou many euere resseyue-

THE
WYCLIFFE
NEW TESTAMENT
(1388)

An edition in modern spelling
with an introduction, the original
prologues and the
Epistle to the Laodiceans

EDITED FOR
THE TYNDALE SOCIETY
BY
W. R. Cooper

The British Library
2002

First published in 2002 by

The British Library
96 Euston Road
London NW1 2DB

in association with The Tyndale Society

Text copyright © 2002 The Tyndale Society

British Library Cataloguing in Publication Data
A CIP record is available from The British Library

ISBN 0 7123 4728 3

Designed and typeset by Justin Howes
Printed in Italy by LEGO

Introduction

THE 'WYCLIFFE' NEW TESTAMENT

Anyone who is not well acquainted with the history of the English Bible may be easily forgiven for assuming that John Wycliffe[1] actually translated the Bible that is named after him. He did not. Instead, his lifetime of preaching and writing inspired a group of his followers to render the Bible into English.

The man who sparked off this translation was an intellectual Augustinian who taught at Oxford University during the 1370s. John Wycliffe lived during a time of upheaval in the Church; the Papal Schism of 1378 gave impetus to those who saw the Church hierarchy as corrupt and removed from the apostolic ideal. Wycliffe used the Bible as the yardstick by which to judge the morality and practice of the Church, and the infallibility of the Church and adoration of its sacraments came to be replaced with the infallibility of Scripture. To Wycliffe, Scripture was 'a divine exemplar conceived in the mind of God before creation, and before the material Scriptures were written down'.[2] The centre of all Christian practice must be the Bible, and every person no matter how unlearned should have access to the Scriptures in their own language.

1. Of the many variations of the spelling of the name, we are here retaining the spelling 'Wycliffe'. It is among the most common spellings of the name in Middle English, and although much modern scholarship uses 'Wyclif', the older spelling still remains the best-known variant for the modern reader.

2. Malcolm Lambert, *Medieval Heresy: Popular Movements from the Gregorian Reform to the Reformation*, 2nd edn (Oxford, 1998) p. 230.

There had been translations of portions of the Bible into the vernacular since Anglo-Saxon times (such as the Gospels, and Aelfric's translation of the Heptateuch). In the medieval period, the bulk of Bible translations were found in sermons, where the preacher would first quote the verses in Latin, and then render them in English for the congregation. Occasionally a significant portion was translated, such as with Richard Rolle's Psalter, but for the most part only small sections were rendered into English. The group that had developed around Wycliffe at Oxford began a massive undertaking: the translation of the entire Bible from the text of the Latin Vulgate into English. The Vulgate was itself a translation from the Greek sources: it took its name from 'vulgare', and was intended for the 'vulgar', or common people. Over the course of the centuries however, the Latin-speaking populace dwindled, and the Vulgate became a text for the privileged. With the Lollards' initial translation - known as the Early Version of the Wycliffe Bible - for the first time, the entire Bible was made available to the people of Britain in their own language.

Although John Wycliffe was forced to retire from Oxford for his controversial views, he enjoyed several powerful supporters during his lifetime, including John of Gaunt (father of King Henry IV), and Sir John Oldcastle, a close friend of Henry V (and a distant inspiration for Shakespeare's Falstaff). However, the work of Wycliffe and the Lollards came to be associated with treason and sedition: Wycliffe's writings were linked (incorrectly) with the Peasant's Revolt of 1381, and Oldcastle himself led a revolt against Henry V. Yet despite increasing pressure from Church and State, Wycliffe's followers persisted: after the (natural) death of John Wycliffe in 1384, they continued to preach his theology, and produced a new translation of the English Bible, known as the Later Version, which came sometime after 1388. This second translation followed the structure of Middle English, rather than the too-literal, latinate translation of the Early Version. It resulted in a superior, powerful rendition of the Scriptures, and the question as to who made this magnificent translation of the Bible has vexed scholarship for two centuries. In this necessarily brief survey of the evidence, we do not have the scope to devote to the characters suspected of being involved: the reader is referred to the bibliography for the in-depth research that has been carried out thus far.

After the initial translation was finished, talented scribes set to work copying out the Lollard text. With the dangerous associations of Lollardy, both Church and State sought its elimination, and in 1401 a statute was issued banning the Later Version upon pain of death. Lollards were prosecuted for their beliefs and their ownership of forbidden texts. The efforts, however, failed to stop the reproduction of the texts, and scribes continued to copy faithfully the Lollard texts, risking great danger to themselves. The Wycliffe Bible was one of many texts produced for distribution, including a sermon cycle, Glossed Gospels, and the compilation work on Wycliffite theology and learning, the *Floretum*. Together, these texts provided a cleric or learned layperson with all the tools necessary to teach and train others.

During this period, Lollardy began to develop away from its intellectual foundation, and spread through the social circles of craftsmen and skilled artisans. People met together to form cells of Lollard reading circles; devoted to the forbidden texts. Although Lollard beliefs varied from place to place, and could include a dislike of all images (including the crucifix), and of all ceremonies (including marriage and baptism), one fundamental tenet of the Lollard faith was always present: the belief in a simple, direct contact between the communicant and God, without intermediaries. This belief survived through the underground artisan reading circles until the English Reformation of the sixteenth century, when the jurisdiction of the Roman Catholic Church was removed totally.

Even after the advent of authorised, printed English Bibles in the sixteenth century, handwritten copies of the Wycliffe Bible were still cherished and read. What finally caused the manuscript Wycliffe Bibles to fall into general disuse was not just their high cost when compared to the new printed Bibles, but the fundamental changes that had so rapidly occurred in the English language from the late 1400s onwards, and which had transformed the language, causing it to pass from an uncertain childhood into a glorious flowering that has often been imitated, but (in the opinion of many) never improved upon.

John Wycliffe, who gave his name to the English Bible that followed him, is considered by many to have been a morning star of the later Reformation, and in many ways he was. Yet it is the English Bible that bears his name that is the real morning star. We must remember that it was no Oxford theologian whose words people memorised and bore in their hearts through persecution, torture and the stake. Wycliffe was certainly the greatest teacher of his age, but even he was quite unable to convert sinners and transform lives. Only the word of God can do that, and it was the appearance of the English Bible from Wycliffe's school that truly heralded the dawning of the great English Reformation that was to follow.

THE TEXT

In spite of the uncertain and sometimes the gangly rough-cut nature of its language, the Wycliffe Bible is still a monument to be read and cherished. Though its idiom and terms of expression are all its own, and may sometimes appear clumsy when compared to William Tyndale's translation from the Greek, it still has power to move and inspire the reader who comes looking for unsuspected and hidden treasures. And these it has aplenty.

After more than 600 years of history, the Wycliffe New Testament has here been printed in modern spelling. The Victorians produced an excellent old-spelling edition of it under Forshall and Madden in 1850, but its four huge volumes are a forbidding and daunting prospect for any modern reader, even when a copy of it may be had.[3] Moreover, to read the old spelling is like reading a foreign language to the modern eye, turning what should be a profound and lasting pleasure into a dolorous and discouraging task. That is why this present edition, published for the benefit of the Tyndale Society, has been rendered into modern spelling and punctuation, so that the modern reader should have no difficulty at all in reading it as it should be read - with enjoyment.

The Wycliffe Bible was intended for the common man, and was written in the everyday language of the merchants, craftsmen and labourers of fourteenth-century England, and it is curious to see how often our modern English so easily reverts to Middle English in its less formal (though still polite) expressions. Listen to any group of children at play, and you will hear them say

3. Josiah Forshall and Frederic Madden (eds), *The Holy Bible containing the Old and New Testaments, in the earliest English versions, made from the Latin Vulgate by John Wycliffe and his followers* (1850).

'went' (for went), 'sold'; 'told'; 'drawed'; 'well good', and so on, with absolutely no idea of the fact that they are speaking what their teachers will quickly tell them is allegedly bad or lazy English. Nor, I dare say, are their teachers in many cases aware that their supposedly way⁄ward charges are speaking the English language just as Chaucer and Wycliffe and other fourteenth⁄century luminaries ⁄ yes, and the common people too ⁄ once spoke it.

In this edition, obsolete words are rendered into mod⁄ern spelling and explained in the glossarial notes, though the context and the reader's own familiarity with the contents of the New Testament generally will often make their meaning clear. What will fascinate most who read it are the native expressions that the Wycliffe New Testament gives to familiar concepts and sayings. For example, in II Thessalonians 2:7, we are used to reading of the 'mystery of iniquity' ⁄ an expression first coined by William Tyndale and carried over (like so much from Tyndale) into the King James Bible. The Wycliffe version renders this phrase, 'the privity of wick⁄edness,' which is far less polished than Tyndale's later rendering from the Greek, but which uses nevertheless the same compulsive rhythm as its successor.

Likewise, where in Luke 21, we are familiar from our King James Bible with the expression 'lest at any time your hearts be overcharged with surfeiting', it is a profound and unexpected delight to encounter in Wycliffe the far more compelling phrase, 'lest peradven⁄ture your hearts be gravid with gluttony' ⁄ an alliterative expression that captures perfectly the turgidity and repul⁄sive nature of greed and self⁄serving.

Surprisingly, more of the Wycliffe Bible has found its way into the King James than at first we might suspect. One example will suffice. Miles Coverdale is credited with one of the most beautiful phrases in the English language, 'Enter thou into the joy of thy Lord' (Matthew 25:21), which he uses in his own revision of Tyndale's New Testament, and which found its way into the Great Bible of 1539 and from there into the King James. But in fact, Coverdale lifted this magnificent rendering straight from the Wycliffe Bible. While it is rightly thought by some that Coverdale had little choice but to translate 'Intra in gaudium domini tui' into English in this way, we must nevertheless note that the Lollards got there first.

Likewise, the Geneva Bible of 1560 was quickly given the nickname of the Breeches Bible, from the famous verse in Genesis in which Adam and Eve made themselves 'breeches' rather than aprons to cover their shame. Yet William Whittingham and his colleagues in Geneva - like Caxton before them when he printed the word in his *Golden Legend* - simply lifted the word 'breeches' once again from the Wycliffe Bible, not being fussy from whichever tree they plucked their fruit, just so long as it was the best.

It is fascinating to encounter the interpolations that have found their way into the Wycliffe New Testament from earlier commentators, but which have been preserved in its text as if they were once part of the Bible. Not all of them are included in this present edition, but amongst those that are, we have in Deeds 21:1 (Acts of the Apostles), 'from thence to Patiram [Patara], *and from thence to Myram*' - that part in italics not being found even in the Vulgate. In II Timothy 1, we read 'that He is mighty for to keep, *that is, to take my keeping*, into that day' - the italicized portion being a gloss on the text. But of special interest is the verse from Apocalypse 9 [Revelation 9:11], which reads, 'And they had on them a king, the angel of deepness, to whom the name by

Hebrew is Abbadon, but by Greek, Apollyon. *And by Latin he has the name Exterminans, that is, a destroyer*'. The italicized portion is not found in the Greek, from which the Latin Bible ⁄ which *does* contain the gloss ⁄ was trans⁄ lated, and is such a curious detail that it is has been retained in this edition without apology, even as it was also retained in the Rheims New Testament of 1582 which, like Wycliffe's, was translated from the Latin.

Another curious anomaly of the Wycliffe New Testament arises in the third chapter of Matthew, which, speaking of John the Baptist, tells us, 'and his meat was honeysuckers and honey of the wood'. Honey of the wood (Lat. Vulg.: *mel silvestre*) is simply wild honey, 'wood' (or *wode*) being merely the fourteenth⁄cen⁄ tury form of 'wild'. But where on earth does 'honeysuck⁄ ers' come from? This is supposed to be a simple translation of the Latin Vulgate's *locustae*, whose mean⁄ ing is plain enough even to those not familiar with the language. Did the idea of a man eating locusts strike the translator of Wycliffe as too repulsive? Who knows? But one is reminded of the early Jewish⁄Christian sect, the Ebionites, who changed their own text of Matthew 3 to suggest that, instead of locusts (Gk. *akrides*), John ate pancakes (*enkrides*).

The literary excellences of the Wycliffe New Test⁄ ament are too numerous to elaborate upon here. Suffice it to say that in all the Middle English literature that has come down to us, there is nothing that even vaguely approaches Paul's speech before Agrippa, to which Agrippa replies, 'In little thing thou counsellest me to be made a Christian man', or the ninth chapter of John's gospel. And to read Luke's account of the angelic annunciation to the shepherds at our Lord's birth, is to experience fourteenth⁄century English at one of its magnificent high points:

And shepherds were in the same country, waking and keeping the watches of the night on their flock. And lo, the angel of the Lord stood beside them, and the clearness of God shined about them, and they dreaded with great dread. And the angel said to them, Nil ye dread, for lo, I preach to you a great joy that shall be to all people. For a Saviour is born today to you that is Christ the Lord in the city of David. And this is a token to you, ye shall find a young child lapped in cloths and laid in a creche. And suddenly there was made with the angel a multitude of heavenly knighthood, herying God and saying, Glory be in the highest things to God, and in earth peace to men of good will.

THE ORDER OF BOOKS

It will be noticed immediately that the order of the New Testament books and epistles in this present edition is not the same as that which appears in more modern translations. In this we have followed exactly the preferred order of the Lollard Bible. Furthermore, among the disordered books will be seen an interloper in the form of the supposed letter of Paul of the Laodiceans that is common to several copies of the Later Version, but which is entirely unknown in modern translations and versions. The Lollards commonly regarded the Epistle as genuine, even though fully aware that it was omitted from the canon and certainly from some of the Latin manuscripts of their day.

We do know that Paul himself refers to a letter of his own to the Laodicean church (Colossians 4:16), though some scholars think that this might be a reference to nothing more than his epistle to the Ephesians. If it is, then it is strange that Paul did not refer to it under its correct name, which he was surely familiar with, but rather incorrectly labelled it as to the Laodiceans. But, barring future archaeological discovery of its Greek text, that is about as far as the surviving evidence can take us.

At best, all we can say is that it is *possible* that the letter to the Laodiceans, as preserved in the Wycliffe New Testament and the Latin Vulgate, is a translation, twice removed, of the letter referred to by Paul, and would, if it could be proven, be a most intriguing and valuable document of the apostolic era.

CONCLUSION

Today's Bible readers can now enjoy reading Wycliffe's New Testament for themselves, rather than just reading about it. Available is a text more splendid (in this writer's opinion, at least) than any of Chaucer's writings, and perhaps of greater historical and literary importance than any other writing that has come down to us from the Middle Ages. Its reappearance, in modern spelling, is an appropriate tribute to those who risked their lives translating the scriptures into English more than 600 years ago.

W. R. COOPER

ACKNOWLEDGEMENTS

My thanks must go to the following, for without their help and contributions this edition might never have seen light of day: Professor David Daniell; Dr Steve Sohmer; Dr Don Brake; Mrs Valerie Offord; Dr Orlaith O'Sullivan; the British Library; and last but by no means least, the always helpful and welcoming staff of Lambeth Palace Library. Thank you all.

A NOTE ON THE TEXT

This modern spelling and grammar edition of the Wycliffe
New Testament is based upon the text of British Library MS.
I. C. viii (Old Royal Library). This manuscript was selected
by Forshall and Madden as the basis of their old spelling edition of the Wycliffe Bible (1850). It is hoped later to produce
the entire Bible from the same text, complete with Prologues
and Apocrypha.

Personal and place names are made in this edition to con-
form to the norms employed in the King James version of the
New Testament. To have produced them in all their Middle
English variations would have spoiled the reader's enjoyment.
Where place names are wrongly given in the Wycliffe text
(which is often), these have been silently corrected.

THE NOTES

The glossarial notes to the text give modern definitions in the
margin. In order to avoid over-burdening the text with notes,
only the first appearance of a difficult word has been glossed:
argument, if one be needed, for reading the text from start to
finish.

SUGGESTIONS FOR FURTHER READING

Bruce, F. F., *A History of the English Bible*, 4th edition
  (Cambridge, 1986)

Hudson, Anne, *The Premature Reformation: Wycliffite Texts
  and Lollard History* (Oxford, 1988)

  — (ed.) *Selections from English Wycliffite Writings*, 2nd
  edition (Toronto, 1997)

  — (ed.) *The Works of a Lollard Preacher* (Oxford, 2001)

Lambert, Malcolm, *Medieval Heresy: Popular Movements from
  the Gregorian Reform to the Reformation*, 2nd edition (Oxford,
  1992; 3rd edition forthcoming 2002)

Smalley, Beryl, *Studies in Medieval Thought and Learning: from
  Abelard to Wyclif* (London, 1981)

The Wycliffe
New Testament
(1388)

Here begins the Prologue on Matthew

Matthew, that was of Judea, as he is set first in order of the gospellers, so he wrote first the gospel in Judea, and from the office of a tollgatherer, he was called to God. When this Matthew had preached first the gospel in Judea, and would go to heathen men, he wrote first the gospel in Hebrew, and left it to mind to christen men of the Jews, from which he departed bodily, for as it was — separated *needful that the gospel were preached to the confirming of faith, so it were needful that it were written also against heretics.*

Though many men have written the gospel, four only, that is, Matthew, Mark, Luke and John, have the witnessing of authority, for they tell the faith of the Trinity by four parts of the world, and they are as four wheels in the four-horsed cart of the Lord that bears Him about by preaching of the gospel. And mankind that was slain by four deaths, should be quickened by the preach- — alive, living *ing of them. And therefore the gospels of other writers fell down and are not received, for the Lord nold that the foresaid number* — would not - contraction of ne wold *were destroyed.*

For the virtue of sacrament, also the four gospellers are understood by four figures of ghostly privity. Matthew is understood by man, for he dwells principally about the manhood of Christ. Mark is understood by a lion, for he treats of Christ's rising again. Luke is understood by a calf, and treats of priesthood. John is understood by an eagle, and writes highlier the sacraments — more particularly *either holy privities of the Godhead.* — private matters, secrets

Forsooth, Christ, whom these gospellers describe, was a Man born of the virgin. He was a calf in offering either dying on the cross. He was a lion in rising again. And He was an eagle in ascension. Either the manhood of Christ is signified in man, priesthood is signified in the calf, realm is signified in the lion, and the sacrament of Godhead is signified in the eagle. That is, by these four beasts it is declared that Jesus Christ is God and Man, King and Priest. Jerome, in his two prologues on Matthew, says plainly thus.

Here begins the book of Matthew

Chapter I

The book of the generation of Jesus Christ, the son of David, the son of Abraham. Abraham begat Isaac. Isaac begat Jacob. Jacob begat Judas and his brethren. Judas begat Phares and Zara of Tamar. Phares begat Esrom. Esrom begat Aram. Aram begat Aminadab. Aminadab begat Naasson. Naasson begat Salmon. Salmon begat Boaz of Rachab. Boaz begat Obed of Ruth. Obed begat Jesse. Jesse begat David the king. David the king begat Solomon of her that was Uriah's wife. Solomon begat Roboam. Roboam begat Abia. Abia begat Asa. Asa begat Josaphat. Josaphat begat Joram. Joram begat Ozias. Ozias begat Joatham. Joatham begat Achaz. Achaz begat Ezekias. Ezekias begat Manasses. Manasses begat Amon. Amon begat Josias. Josias begat Jechonias and his brethren into the transmigration of Babylon. And after the transmigration of Babylon, Jechonias begat Salathiel. Salathiel begat Zorobabel. Zorobabel begat Abiud. Abiud begat Eliakim. Eliakim begat Azor. Azor begat Sadoc. Sadoc begat Achim. Achim begat Eliud. Eliud begat Eleazar. Eleazar begat Matthan. Matthan begat Jacob. Jacob begat Joseph, the husband of Mary of whom Jesus was born that is called Christ. And so all generations from Abraham to David are fourteen generations, and from David to the transmigration of Babylon are fourteen generations, and from the transmigration of Babylon to Christ are fourteen generations.

But the generation of Christ was thus. When Mary, the mother of Jesus, was spoused to Joseph, before they *espoused, betrothed* came together she was found having of the Holy Ghost in the womb. And Joseph, her husband, for he was rightful and would not publish her, he would privily *fair, just* have left her. But while he thought these things, lo, the *behold* angel of the Lord appeared in sleep to him and said, Joseph, the son of David, nil thou dread to take Mary, thy wife, for that thing that is born in her is of the Holy Ghost. And she shall bear a son, and thou shall call his name Jesus, for He shall make His people safe from their sins.

For all this thing was done that it should be fulfilled that was said of the Lord by a prophet, saying, Lo, a virgin shall have in womb, and she shall bear a Son, and they shall call His name Emmanuel, that is to say, God with us. And Joseph rose from sleep and did as the angel of the Lord commanded him, and took Mary his wife. And he knew her not till she had borne her first begotten son, and called His name Jesus.

Chapter II

Therefore, when Jesus was born in Bethlehem of Judea in the days of king Herod, lo, astromiens came from the *astronomers, wise men* east to Jerusalem and said, Where is He that is born King of Jews? For we have seen His star in the east and we come to worship Him.

But king Herod heard and was troubled, and all Jerusalem with him. And he gathered together all the princes of priests and scribes of the people, and enquired *chief priests* of them where Christ should be born. And they said to him, In Bethlehem of Judea, for so it is written by a prophet, And thou, Bethlehem, the land of Judea, art not the least among the princes of Judea, for of thee a duke *leader, prince* shall go out that shall govern My people of Israel.

Then Herod called privily the astromiens and learned busily of them the time of the star that appeared to them. And he sent them into Bethlehem and said, Go ye, and ask ye busily of the child, and when ye have found, tell ye it to me that I also come and worship Him.

And when they had heard the king, they went forth. And lo, the star that they saw in the east went before them, till it came and stood above where the child was. And they saw the star and joyed with full great joy. And they entered into the house and found the child with Mary, His mother. And they fell down and worshipped Him. And when they had opened their treasures, they offered to Him gifts, gold, incense and myrrh. And when they had taken an answer in sleep that they should not turn again to Herod, they turned again by another way into their country.

And when they were gone, lo, the angel of the Lord appeared to Joseph in sleep and said, Rise up, and take the child and His mother, and flee into Egypt, and be thou there till that I say to thee. For it is to come that Herod seek the child to destroy Him.

And Joseph rose and took the child and His mother by night and went into Egypt, and he was there to the death of Herod that it should be fulfilled that was said of the Lord by the prophet, saying, From Egypt I have called My Son.

Then Herod, seeing that he was deceived of the astromiens, was full wroth, and he sent and slew all the children that were in Bethlehem and in all the coasts thereof, from two year age and within after the time that he had enquired of the astromiens. Then it was fulfilled that was said by Jeremiah the prophet, saying, A voice was heard on high, weeping and much wailing, Rachel *crying for, weeping* beweeping her sons. And she would not be comforted, for they are nought.

But when Herod was dead, lo, the angel of the Lord appeared to Joseph in sleep in Egypt, and said, Rise up, and take the child and His mother, and go into the land of Israel. For they that sought the life of the child are dead.

Joseph rose and took the child and His mother, and came into the land of Israel. And he heard that Archelaus reigned in Judea for Herod his father, and dreaded to go thither. And he was warned in sleep, and went into the parties of Galilee, and came and dwelt in a *areas, parts, regions* city that is called Nazareth, that it should be fulfilled that was said by prophets, For He shall be called a Nazarene.

Chapter III

In those days John Baptist came and preached in the desert of Judea, and said, Do ye penance, for the king, dom of heavens shall nigh. For this is he of whom it is said by Isaiah the prophet, saying, A voice of a crier in desert, Make ye ready the ways of the Lord. Make ye right the paths of Him. And this John had clothing of camel's hairs and a girdle of skin about his loins, and *sackcloth* his meat was honeysuckers and honey of the wood. *honey-suckers*

Then Jerusalem went out to him and all Judea, and all the country about Jordan. And they were washed of him in Jordan and acknowledged their sins. But he saw many of the Pharisees and Sadducees coming to his bap, tism, and said to them, Generations of adders, who showed you to flee from the wrath that is to come? Therefore do ye worthy fruit of penance, and nil ye say within you, We have Abraham to father, for I say to you that God is mighty to raise up of these stones the sons of Abraham. And now the axe is put to the root of the tree. Therefore every tree that makes not good fruit, shall be cut down and shall be cast into the fire. I wash you in water into penance, but He that shall come after me is stronger than I, whose shoes I am not worthy to bear. He shall baptize you in the Holy Ghost and fire, whose winnowing-cloth is in His hand. And He shall fully cleanse His corn-floor and shall gather His wheat into His barn. But the chaff He shall burn with fire that may not be quenched.

Then Jesus came from Galilee into Jordan to John, to be baptized of him. And John forbad Him and said, I ought to be baptized of Thee, and Thou comes to me?

But Jesus answered and said to him, Suffer now, for thus it falls to us to fulfill all rightfulness. Then John suffered Him. And when Jesus was baptized, anon He went up from the water, and lo, heavens were opened to Him, and He saw the Spirit of God coming down as a dove and coming on Him. And lo, a voice from hea-vens, saying, This is My loved Son in which I have pleased to Me.

Chapter IV

Then Jesus was led of a Spirit into desert to be tempted of the fiend. And when He had fasted forty days and forty nights, afterward He hungered. And the tempter came nigh and said to Him, If Thou art God's Son, say that these stones are made loaves. Which answered and said to him, It is written, Not only in bread lives man, but in each word that comes of God's mouth.

Then the fiend took Him into the holy city and set Him on the pinnacle of the Temple, and said to Him, If Thou art God's Son, send Thee a-down, for it is writ-ten, That to His angels He commanded of Thee, and they shall take Thee in hands, lest peradventure Thou *again, forthwith* hurt Thy foot at a stone. Eftsoon Jesus said to him, It is written, Thou shall not tempt thy Lord God.

Eftsoon the fiend took Him into a full high hill, and

showed to Him all the realms of the world and the joy of them, and said to Him, All these I shall give to Thee if Thou fall down and worship me. Then Jesus said to him, Go, Satan, for it is written, Thou shall worship thy Lord God, and to Him alone thou shall serve.

Then the fiend left Him, and lo, angels came nigh and served to Him. But when Jesus had heard that John was taken, He went into Galilee. And He left the city of Nazareth, and came and dwelt in the city of Capernaum beside the sea, in the coasts of Zabulon and Nephtalim, that it should be fulfilled that was said by Isaiah the prophet, saying, The land of Zabulon and the land of Nephtalim, the way of the sea over Jordan, of Galilee of heathen men, the people that walked in darkness saw great light, and while men sat in the country of shadow of death, light arose to them.

From that time, Jesus began to preach and say, Do ye penance, for the kingdom of heavens shall come nigh. And Jesus walked beside the sea of Galilee, and saw two brethren, Simon that is called Peter, and Andrew his brother, casting nets into the sea, for they were fishers. And He said to them, Come ye after Me, and I shall *fishermen* make you to be made fishers of men. And anon they left their nets and sued Him. *followed, pursued*

And He went forth from that place and saw twain *two* other brethren, James of Zebedee, and John his brother in a ship with Zebedee their father, mending their nets. And He called them. And anon they left the nets and the father and sued Him.

And Jesus went about all Galilee teaching in the synagogues of them and preaching the gospel of the kingdom, and healing every languor and each sickness *debilitating illness* among the people. And His fame went into all Syria, and they brought to Him all that were at mal ease and *ill ease, malaise, sickness* that were taken with diverse languors and torments, and them that had fiends, and lunatic men, and men in palsy. And He healed them. And there sued Him much people of Galilee and of Decapolis, and of Jerusalem and of Judea, and of beyond Jordan.

Chapter V

And Jesus, seeing the people, went up into an high hill, and when He was sat, His disciples came to Him. And He opened His mouth and taught them, and said, Blessed are poor men in spirit, for the kingdom of heavens is theirs. Blessed are mild men, for they shall wield the earth. Blessed are they that mourn, for they shall be comforted. Blessed are they that hunger and thirst right- *righteousness* wiseness, for they shall be fulfilled. Blessed are merciful men, for they shall get mercy. Blessed are they that are of clean heart, for they shall see God. Blessed are peaceable men, for they shall be called God's children. Blessed are they that suffer persecution for rightfulness, for the kingdom of heavens is theirs.

Ye shall be blessed when men shall curse you and shall pursue you, and shall say all evil against you, *reward* lying, for Me. Joy ye, and be ye glad, for your meed is plenteous in heavens. For so they have pursued also prophets that were before you.

Ye are salt of the earth, that if the salt vanish away, wherein shall it be salted? To nothing is it worth over, *defile, sometimes* no, but that it be cast out and be defouled of men. Ye are *transgress* light of the world. A city set on an hill may not be hid. *basket or pitcher of a* Nor men tend not a lantern and put it under a bushel, *bushel's capacity* but on a candlestick, that it give light to all that are in the house. So shine your light before men, that they see your good works and glorify your Father that is in heavens.

judge Nil ye deem that I came to undo the law or the prophets. I came not to undo the law, but to fulfill. Forsooth, I say to you, till heaven and earth pass, one letter or one tittle shall not pass from the law, till all things are done. Therefore, he that breaks one of these least commandments, and teaches thus men, shall be called the least in the realm of heavens. But he that does and teaches, shall be called great in the kingdom of heavens. And I say to you that but your rightfulness be more plenteous than of scribes and of Pharisees, ye shall not enter into the kingdom of heavens.

Ye have heard that it was said to old men, Thou shall not slay, and he that slays shall be guilty to doom. But I *judgment* say to you that each man that is wroth to his brother, shall be guilty to doom, and he that says to his brother Fie! shall be guilty to the council. But he that says Fool! shall be guilty to the fire of hell. Therefore, if thou offer the gift at the altar, and there thou bethink that thy brother has somewhat against thee, leave there thy gift before the altar and go first to be reconciled to thy brother, and then thou shall come and shall offer thy gift. Be thou consenting to thine adversary soon, while thou art in the way with him, lest peradventure thine adversary take thee to the doomsman, and the dooms- *judge* man take thee to the minister, and thou be sent into prison. Truly I say to thee, thou shall not go out from thence till thou yield the last farthing.

Ye have heard that it was said to old men, Thou shall do no lechery. But I say to you that every man that sees a woman for to covet her, has now done lechery by her in his heart. That if thy right eye sclaunder thee, pull him *offend* out and cast from thee, for it speeds to thee that one of thy *profits, prospers* members perish than that all thy body go into hell. And if thy right hand sclaunder thee, cut him away and cast from thee, for it speeds to thee that one of thy members perish than that all thy body go into hell. And it has been said, Whoever leaves his wife, give he to her a libel of forsaking. But I say to you that every man that leaves his *bill of divorcement*

besides, except, without wife, out-taken cause of fornication, makes her to do lech-
adultery ery. And he that weds the forsaken wife, does advowtry.

Eftsoon ye have heard that it was said to old men, Thou shall not forswear, but thou shall yield thine oaths to the Lord. But I say to you that ye swear not for any-thing, neither by heaven for it is the throne of God, neither by the earth for it is the stool of His feet, neither by Jerusalem for it is the city of a great King. Neither shall thou swear by thine head, for thou may not make one hair white nor black. But be your word Yea, yea, Nay, nay; and that that is more than these is of evil.

Ye have heard that it has been said, Eye for eye and
resist, stand against, tooth for tooth. But I say to you that ye against stand not
withstand an evil man. But if any smite thee in the right cheek, show to him also t'other. And to him that will strive
outer garment with thee in doom and take away thy coat, leave thou to him also thy mantle. And whoever constrains thee a thousand paces, go thou with him other twain. Give thou to him that asks of thee, and turn not away from him that will borrow of thee.

Ye have heard that it was said, Thou shall love thy neighbour and hate thine enemy. But I say to you, love ye your enemies, do ye well to them that hate you, and pray ye for them that pursue and sclaunder you, that ye are the sons of your Father that is in heavens, that makes His sun to rise upon good and evil men, and rains on just men and unjust. For if ye love them that love you, what meed shall ye have? Whether publicans do not this? And if ye greet your brethren only, what shall ye do more? Nor do not heathen men this? Therefore be ye
perfect parfit, as your heavenly Father is parfit.

Chapter VI

Take heed that ye do not your rightwiseness before men to be seen of them, else ye shall have no meed at your

Father that is in heavens. Therefore when thou does alms, nil thou trump tofore thee as hypocrites do in syna- *trumpet before* gogues and streets, that they may be worshipped of men. Soothly I say to you, they have received their meed. But when thou do alms, know not thy left hand what thy right hand does, that thine alms may be in hidles. And *hidy holes or secret places* thy Father that sees in hidles, shall quite thee. *repay, requite*

And when ye pray, ye shall not be as hypocrites that love to pray standing in synagogues and corners of streets to be seen of men. Truly I say you, they have received their meed. But when thou shall pray, enter into thy couch, and when the door is shut, pray thy Father in *chamber, bedroom* hidles. And thy Father that sees in hidles, shall yield to thee.

But in praying, nil ye speak much as heathen men do, for they guess that they are heard in their much *suppose* speech. Therefore, nil ye be made like to them, for your Father wot what is need to you before that ye ask Him. *knows* And thus ye shall pray, Our Father that art in heavens, hallowed be Thy name. Thy kingdom come to. Be Thy will done in earth as in heaven. Give to us this day our bread over other substance, and forgive to us our debts as we forgive to our debtors. And lead us not into temp- *sinner, transgressor* tation, but deliver us from evil. Amen. For if ye forgive to men their sins, your heavenly Father shall forgive to you your trespasses. Soothly, if ye forgive not to men, neither your Father shall forgive to you your sins.

But when ye fast, nil ye be made as hypocrites, sor- rowful. For they deface themselves to seem fasting to men. Truly I say to you, they have received their meed. But when thou fast, anoint thine head and wash thy face, that thou be not seen fasting to men, but to thy Father that is in hidles. And thy Father that sees in privy, shall yield to thee.

Nil ye treasure to you treasures in earth, where rust

dig and moth destroy and where thieves delve out and steal. But gather to you treasures in heaven, where neither rust nor moth destroys, and where thieves delve not out nor steal. For where thy treasure is, there also thine heart is.

The lantern of thy body is thine eye. If thine eye be simple, all thy body shall be lightful. But if thine eye be wayward, all thy body shall be dark. If then the light *darkness* that is in thee be darknesses, how great shall the ilk dar-
the same knesses be?

No man may serve twain lords, for either he shall hate the t'one and love the t'other, either he shall sustain *can, may* the t'one and despise the t'other. Ye moun not serve *riches, treasure, wealth* God and richesses. Therefore I say to you that ye be not *tend to* busy to your life what ye shall eat, neither to your body with what ye shall be clothed. Whether life is not more than meat, and the body more than cloth? Behold the fowls of the air, for they sow not neither reap, neither gather into barns, and your Father of heaven feeds them. Whether ye be not more worthy than they?

But who of you, thinking, may put to his stature one cubit? And of clothing, what are ye busy? Behold ye the lilies of the field, how they wax. They travail not, neither spin, and I say to you, Solomon in all his glory was not covered as one of these. And if God clothes *grass* thus the hay of the field that today is, and tomorrow is cast into an oven, how much more you of little faith? Therefore, nil ye be busy, saying, What shall we eat? or, What shall we drink? or, With what thing shall we be covered? For heathen men seek all these things, and your Father wot that ye have need to all these things. Therefore seek ye first the kingdom of God and His rightfulness, and all these things shall be cast to you. Therefore, nil ye be busy to the morrow, for the morrow shall be busy to himself. For it suffices to the day his own malice.

Chapter VII

Nil ye deem, that ye be not deemed. For in what doom
ye deem, ye shall be deemed, and in what measure ye
mete, it shall be meted again to you. But what see thou a *measure, portion*
little mote in the eye of thy brother, and see not a beam in *particle, speck*
thine own eye? Or how say thou to thy brother, Brother,
suffer I shall do out a mote from thine eye, and lo, a beam
is in thine own eye? Hypocrite! Do thou out first the
beam of thine eye, and then thou shall see to do out the
mote of the eye of thy brother.

Nil ye give holy thing to hounds, neither cast ye your
margarites before swine, lest peradventure they defoul *pearls*
them with their feet and are turned and all to-tear you. *tear in pieces*

Ask ye, and it shall be given to you. Seek ye, and ye
shall find. Knock ye, and it shall be opened to you. For
each that asks, takes; and he that seeks, finds; and it
shall be opened to him that knocks.

What man of you is, that if his son ask him bread,
whether he will take him a stone? Or if he ask fish,
whether he will take him an adder? Therefore if ye,
when ye are evil men, kunnen give good gifts to your *know to, know how to*
sons, how much more your Father that is in heavens
shall give good things to men that ask Him? Therefore
all things, whatever things ye would that men do to you,
do ye to them, for this is the law and the prophets.

Enter ye by the strait gate, for the gate that leads to *narrow*
perdition is large and the way is broad, and there are
many that enter by it. How strait is the gate and narrow
the way that leads to life, and there are few that find it.

Be ye ware of false prophets that come to you in cloth⁄ *wary, prudent*
ings of sheep, but withinforth they are as wolves of
raven. Of their fruits ye shall know them. *avariciousness, greed*

Whether men gather grapes of thorns or figs of briars?
So every good tree makes good fruits. But an evil tree

makes evil fruits. A good tree may not make evil fruits, neither an evil tree make good fruits. Every tree that makes not good fruit, shall be cut down, and shall be cast into the fire. Therefore of their fruits ye shall know them.

Not each man that says to Me, Lord, Lord, shall enter into the kingdom of heavens, but he that does the will of My Father that is in heavens. He shall enter into the kingdom of heavens. Many shall say to Me in that day, Lord, Lord, whether we have not prophesied in Thy name, and have cast out fiends in Thy name, and have done many virtues in Thy name? And then shall I acknowledge to them that, I knew you never. Depart away from Me ye that work wickedness.

Therefore each man that hears these My words and does them, shall be made like to a wise man that has built his house on a stone. And rain fell down and floods came, and winds blew and rushed into that house. And it fell not down, for it was founded on a stone. And every man that hears these My words and does them not, is like to a fool that has built his house on sand gravel. And rain came down and floods came, and winds blew and they hurled against that house. And it fell down, and the falling down thereof was great.

And it was done, when Jesus had ended these words, the people wondered on His teaching, for He taught them as He that had power, and not as the scribes of them and the Pharisees.

Chapter VIII

But when Jesus was come down from the hill, much people sued Him. And lo, a leprous man came and worshipped Him, and said, Lord, if Thou will, Thou may make me clean. And Jesus held forth the hand and touched him, and said, I will, be thou made clean. And anon the leper of Him was cleansed. And Jesus said to him, See, say thou to no man, but go show thee to the priests and offer the gift that Moses commanded in witnessing to them.

And when He had entered into Capernaum, the centurion nighed to Him, and prayed Him and said, Lord, *approached, drew nigh* my child lies in the house sick on the palsy, and is evil tormented. And Jesus said to him, I shall come, and shall heal him.

And the centurion answered and said to Him, Lord, I am not worthy that Thou enter under my roof. But only say Thou by word and my child shall be healed. For why, I am a man ordained under power, and have knights under me. And I say to this, Go, and he goes, *soldiers* and to another, Come, and he comes, and to my servant, Do this, and he does it.

And Jesus heard these things and wondered, and said to men that sued Him, Truly I say to you, I found not so great faith in Israel. And I say to you that many shall come from the east and the west, and shall rest with Abraham and Isaac and Jacob in the kingdom of heavens. But the sons of the realm shall be cast out into utter darknesses. There shall be weeping and grinding of teeth. And Jesus said to the centurion, Go, and as thou has believed be it done to thee. And the child was healed from that hour.

And when Jesus was come into the house of Simon Peter, He saw his wife's mother lying and shaken with fevers. And He touched her hand and the fever left her, and she rose and served them. And when it was evening, they brought to Him many that had devils, and He cast out spirits by word, and healed all that were evil at ease, that it were fulfilled that was said by Isaiah the prophet, saying, He took our infirmities and bore our sicknesses.

And Jesus saw much people about Him, and bade His disciples go over the water. And a scribe nighed and said to Him, Master, I shall sue Thee whitherever Thou shall go. And Jesus said to him, Foxes have dens, and birds of heaven have nests, but Man's Son has not where He shall rest His head.

Another of His disciples said to Him, Lord, suffer me to go first and bury my father. But Jesus said to him, Sue thou me, and let dead men bury their dead men.

And when He was gone up into a little ship, His disciples sued Him. And lo, a great stirring was made *covered, immersed* in the sea so that the ship was hiled with waves. But He slept. And His disciples came to Him and raised Him, and said, Lord, save us. We perish. And Jesus said to them, What are ye of little faith aghast? Then He rose and commanded to the winds and the sea, and a great *peacefulness, quietness* peaceableness was made. And men wondered and said, What manner man is this, for the winds and the sea obey Him?

And when Jesus was come over the water into the country of the men of Gadara, two men met Him that had devils, and came out of graves full wild so that no man might go by that way. And lo, they cried and said, What to us and to Thee, Jesus, the Son of God? Art Thou come hither before the time to torment us? And *grazing, pasturing* not far from them was a flock of many swine, lesewing. And the devils prayed Him and said, If Thou cast us out from hence, send us into the drove of swine. And He said to them, Go ye. And they went out and went into *mad rush, violent attack* the swine, and lo, in a great bire all the drove went heed-*headlong* ling into the sea, and they were dead in the waters. And *shepherds or swineherds* the herds fled away and came into the city and told all these things and of them that had the fiends. And lo, all the city went out against Jesus, and when they had seen Him, they prayed that He would pass from their coasts.

Chapter IX

And Jesus went up into a boat and passed over the water, and came into His city. And lo, they brought to Him a man sick in palsy, lying in a bed. And Jesus saw the faith of them and said to the man sick in palsy, Son, have thou trust. Thy sins are forgiven to thee. And lo, some of the scribes said within themselves, This blas⁄ phemes. And when Jesus had seen their thoughts, He said, Whereto think ye evil things in your hearts? What is lighter to say, Thy sins are forgiven to thee, either to *easier* say, Rise thou and walk? But that ye wit that Man's Son has power to forgive sins in earth, then He said to the sick man in palsy, Rise up, take thy bed and go into thine house. And he rose and went into his house. And the people, seeing, dreaded, and glorified God that gave such power to men.

And when Jesus passed from thence, He saw a man, Matthew by name, sitting in a tolbooth. And He said to *tax collection point* him, Sue thou Me. And he rose and followed Him. And it was done, the while He sat at the meat in the house, lo, many publicans and sinful men came and sat at the meat with Jesus and His disciples. And Pharisees saw and said to His disciples, Why eats your Master with publicans and sinful men? And Jesus heard and said, A leech is not needful to men that fare *doctor, physician* well, but to men that are evil at ease. But go ye and learn what it is, I will mercy and not sacrifice. For I came not to call rightful men, but sinful men.

Then the disciples of John came to Him and said, Why we and Pharisees fast often, but Thy disciples fast not? And Jesus said to them, Whether the sons of the spouse moun mourn as long as the spouse is with them? But days shall come when the spouse shall be taken away from them, and then they shall fast. And no man *rough, rumbustious* puts a clout of bustious cloth into an old clothing, for it does away the fullness of the cloth, and a worse breaking is made. Neither men put new wine into old bottles, else the bottles be to broke and destroyed, and the wine shed out. But men put new wine into new bottles, and both are kept.

Whiles that Jesus spoke these things to them, lo, a prince came and worshipped Him, and said, Lord, my daughter is now dead. But come Thou and put Thine hand on her, and she shall live.

And Jesus rose and His disciples, and sued him. And lo, a woman that had the bloody flux twelve year nighed behind and touched the hem of His cloth. For she said within herself, If I touch only the cloth of Him, *whole* I shall be safe. And Jesus turned and saw her, and said, Daughter, have thou trust. Thy faith has made thee safe. And the woman was whole from that hour.

And when Jesus came into the house of the prince and saw minstrels and the people making noise, He said, Go ye away, for the damsel is not dead but sleeps. And they scorned Him. And when the folk was put out, He went in and held her hand, and the damsel rose. And this fame went out into all that land.

And when Jesus passed from thence, two blind men, crying, sued Him and said, Thou Son of David, have mercy on us. And when He came into the house, the blind men came to Him, and Jesus said to them, What will ye that I do to you? And they said, Lord, that *eyes* our eyes be opened. And Jesus said, Believe ye that I may do this thing to you? They say to Him, Yea, Lord. Then He touched their eyes and said, After your faith be it done to you. And the eyes of them were opened. *admonished, warned* And Jesus threatened them, and said, See ye that no *told about, reported* man wit. But they went out and defamed Him through all that land.

And when they were gone out, lo, they brought to Him a dumb man having a devil. And when the devil was cast out, the dumb man spoke. And the people wondered and said, It has not been seen thus in Israel. But the Pharisees said, In the prince of devils, He casts out devils.

And Jesus went about all the cities and castles, teach- *properly towns and villages* ing in the synagogues of them and preaching the gospel of the kingdom, and healing every languor and every sickness. And He saw the people and had ruth on *compassion, pity* them, for they were travailed and lying as sheep not hav- *burdened or troubled with* ing a shepherd. Then He said to His disciples, Soothly, there is much ripe corn but few workmen. Therefore pray ye the Lord of the ripe corn that He send workmen into His ripe corn.

Chapter X

And when His twelve disciples were called together, He gave to them power of unclean spirits to cast them out of men, and to heal every languor and sickness. And these are the names of the twelve apostles, Simon that is called Peter, and Andrew his brother; James of Zebedee, and John his brother; Philip and Bartholomew; Thomas and Matthew, publican; and James Alphaei, and Thaddaeus; Simon Canaanite and Judas Iscariot that betrayed Christ.

Jesus sent these twelve, and commanded them and said, Go ye not into the way of heathen men, and enter ye not into the cities of Samaritans. But rather go ye to the sheep of the house of Israel that have perished. And go ye and preach ye, and say that the kingdom of hea- vens shall nigh. Heal ye sick men, raise ye dead men, cleanse ye measles, cast ye out devils. Freely ye have *leprosy* taken, freely give ye. Nil ye wield gold, neither silver, nor money in your girdles, not a scrip in the way, neither *wallet, small satchel staff, rod* two coats, neither shoes, neither a yerde. For a workman is worthy his mete.

Into whatever city or castle ye shall enter, ask ye who therein is worthy, and there dwell ye till ye go out. And when ye go into an house, greet ye it and say, Peace to this house. And if the ilk house be worthy, your peace shall come on it. But if that house be not worthy, your peace shall turn again to you. And whoever receives not you, neither hears your words, go ye from that house or *shake off, sprinkle* city and spring off the dust of your feet. Truly I say to you, it shall be more sufferable to the land of men of Sodom and of Gomorrah in the day of judgment than to the ilk city.

Lo, I send you as sheep in the middle of wolves. Therefore be ye sly as serpents and simple as doves. But be ye ware of men, for they shall take you into councils and they shall beat you in their synagogues. And to mayors and to kings ye shall be led for Me, in witnessing to them and to the heathen men. But when they take you, nil ye think how or what thing ye shall speak, for it shall be given to you in that hour what ye shall speak. For it is not ye that speak, but the Spirit of your Father that speaks in you.

And the brother shall take the brother into death, and the father the son, and sons shall rise against father and mother and shall torment them by death. And ye shall be in hate to all men for My name. But he that shall dwell still into the end shall be safe.

And when they pursue you in this city, flee ye into another. Truly I say to you, ye shall not end the cities of Israel tofore that Man's Son comes. The disciple is not above his master, nor the servant above his lord. It is enough to the disciple that he be as his master, and to the servant as his lord. If they have called the husbandman *family, household* Beelzebub, how much more his household meyne?

Therefore dread ye not them, for nothing is hid that shall not be shown, and nothing is privy that shall not be wist. That thing that I say to you in darkness, say ye in the light, and preach ye on houses that thing that ye hear in the ear.

And nil ye dread them that slay the body, for they *fear not, nothing fear* moun not slay the soul. But rather, dread ye Him that may lose both soul and body into hell. Whether two sparrows are not sold for an halfpenny, and one of them shall not fall on the earth without your Father? And all the hairs of your head are numbered. Therefore nil ye dread. Ye are better than many sparrows.

Therefore every man that shall acknowledge Me before men, I shall acknowledge him before my Father that is in heavens. But he that shall deny Me before men, and I shall deny him before my Father that is in heavens. Nil ye deem that I came to send peace into earth. I came not to send peace, but sword. For I came to depart a man against his father and the daughter against her mother, and the son's wife against the husband's mother. And the enemies of a man are they that are homely with him.   *of the same household or family*

He that loves father or mother more than Me, is not worthy to Me. And he that loves son or daughter over Me, is not worthy to Me. And he that takes not his cross and sues Me, is not worthy to Me. He that finds his life, shall lose it, and he that loses his life for Me, shall find it. He that receives you, receives Me. And he that receives Me, receives Him that sent Me. He that receives a prophet in the name of a prophet, shall take the meed of a prophet. And he that receives a just man in the name of a just man, shall take the meed of a just man. And whoever gives drink to one of these least a cup of cold water only in the name of a disciple, truly I say to you, he shall not lose his meed.

Chapter XI

And it was done when Jesus had ended, He commanded to His twelve disciples and passed from thence to teach and preach in the cities of them. But when John, in bonds, had heard the works of Christ, he sent twain of his disciples and said to Him, Art Thou he that shall come, or we abide another? And Jesus answered and said to them, Go ye and tell again to John those things that ye have heard and seen. Blind men see, crooked men go, measles are made clean, deaf men hear, dead men rise again, poor men are taken to preaching of the gospel. And he is blessed that shall not be sclaundered in Me.

And when they were gone away, Jesus began to say of John to the people, What thing went ye out into desert to see? A reed waved with the wind? Or what thing went ye out to see? A man clothed with soft clothes? Lo, they that are clothed with soft clothes are in the houses of kings. But what thing went ye out to see? A prophet? Yea, I say to you, and more than a prophet. For this is he of whom it is written, Lo, I send Mine angel before Thy face, that shall make ready Thy way before Thee. Truly I say to you, there rose none more than John Baptist among the children of women. But he that is less in the kingdom of heavens, is more than he. And from the days of John Baptist till now, the kingdom of heavens suffers violence, and violent men ravish it. For all prophets and the law till to John prophesied, and if ye will receive, he is Elijah that is to come. He that has ears of hearing, hear he.

But to whom shall I guess this generation like? It is *market place* like to children sitting in cheaping, that cry to their peers and say, We have sung to you, and ye have not danced. We have mourned to you, and ye have not wailed. For

John came neither eating nor drinking, and they say, He has a devil. The Son of Man came eating and drinking and they say, Lo, a man, a glutton and a drinker of wine, and a friend of publicans and of sinful men. And wisdom is justified of her sons.

Then Jesus began to say reproof to cities in which full many virtues of Him were done, for they did not penance, Woe to thee, Chorazin! Woe to thee, Bethsaida! For if the virtues that are done in you had been done in Tyre and Sidon, sometime they had done penance in hair and ash. Netheless I say to you, it shall *nevertheless* be less pain to Tyre and Sidon in the day of doom than to you. And thou, Capernaum, whether thou shall be arreared up into heaven? Thou shall go down into hell. *raised, reared* For if the virtues that are done in thee had been done in Sodom, peradventure they should have dwelled into this day. Netheless I say to you, that to the land of Sodom it shall be less pain in the day of doom than to thee.

In the ilk time Jesus answered and said, I acknowledge to Thee, Father, Lord of heaven and of earth, for Thou has hid these things from wise men and ready, and has shown them to little children. So, Father, for so it was pleasing tofore Thee. All things are given to Me of My Father. And no man knew the Son but the Father. Neither any man knew the Father but the Son, and to whom the Son would show. All ye that travail and are charged, come to Me and I shall fulfil you. Take *burdened* ye My yoke on you and learn of Me, for I am mild and meek in heart, and ye shall find rest to your souls. For My yoke is soft, and My charge light.

Chapter XII

In that time, Jesus went by corns in the Sabbath day, and His disciples hungered and began to pluck the ears of corn and to eat. And Pharisees, seeing, said to Him, *lawful, permissible* Lo, thy disciples do that thing that is not leaveful to them to do in Sabbaths. And He said to them, Whether ye have not read what David did when he hungered, and they that were with him, how he entered into *shewbread, or bread kept in the Temple* the house of God and ate loaves of proposition, which loaves it was not leaveful to him to eat, neither to them that were with him, but to priests alone? Or whether ye have not read in the law that in Sabbaths, priests in the Temple defoul the Sabbaths, and they are without blame? And I say to you that here is a greater than the Temple. And if ye wist what it is, I will mercy and not sacrifice, ye should never have condemned innocents. For Man's Son is Lord, yea, of the Sabbath.

And when He passed from thence, He came into the *shrunken, withered* synagogue of them. And lo, a man that had a dry hand. And they asked Him and said, Whether it be leaveful to heal in the Sabbath? that they should accuse Him. And He said to them, What man of you shall be that has one sheep, and if it falls into a ditch in the Sabbaths whether he shall not hold and lift it up? How much more is a man better than a sheep? Therefore it is leaveful to do good in the Sabbaths. Then He said to the man, *stretched* Stretch forth thine hand. And he straught forth and it was restored to health as the t'other.

And the Pharisees went out and made a counsel against Him how they should destroy Him. And Jesus knew it and went away from thence. And many sued Him and He healed them all. And He commanded to them that they should not make Him known, that that thing were fulfilled that was said by Isaiah the prophet, saying, Lo, My child whom I have chosen, My darling in whom it has well pleased to My soul. I shall put My Spirit on Him and He shall tell doom to heathen men. He shall not strive nor cry, neither any man shall hear

His voice in streets. A bruised reed He shall not break, and He shall not quench smoking flax till He cast out doom to victory, and heathen men shall hope in His name.

Then a man, blind and dumb, that had a fiend, was brought to Him, and He healed him so that he spoke and saw. And all the people wondered and said, Whether this be the Son of David? But the Pharisees heard and said, He casts not out fiends but in Beelzebub, prince of fiends.

And Jesus, witting their thoughts, said to them, Each kingdom departed against itself shall be desolated, and each city or house departed against itself shall not stand. And if Satan casts out Satan, he is departed against himself, therefore how shall his kingdom stand? And if I in Beelzebub cast out devils, in whom your sons cast out? Therefore they shall be your doomsmen. But if I, in the Spirit of God, cast out fiends, then the kingdom of God is come into you. Either how may any man enter into the house of a strong man and take away his vessels, but he first bind the strong man, and then he shall spoil his house? He that is not with Me, is against Me, and he that gathers not together with Me, scatters abroad.

Therefore I say to you, all sin and blasphemy shall be forgiven to men, but the spirit of blasphemy shall not be forgiven. And whoever says a word against Man's Son, it shall be forgiven to him. But who that says a word against the Holy Ghost, it shall not be forgiven to him, neither in this world nor in the t'other. Either make ye the tree good, and his fruit good, either make ye the tree evil and his fruit evil. For a tree is known of the fruit.

Ye generation of adders, how moun ye speak good things when ye are evil? For the mouth speaks of plenty *abundance, fulness* of the heart. A good man brings forth good things of good treasure, and an evil man brings forth evil things of evil treasure. And I say to you that of every idle word that men speak, they shall yield reason thereof in the day of doom. For of thy words thou shall be justified, and of *condemned* thy words thou shall be damned.

Then some of the scribes and Pharisees answered to Him and said, Master, we will see a token of Thee. Which answered and said to them, An evil kindred *adultere* and a spouse⁄breakerR seeks a token, and a token shall not be given to it but the token of Jonah the prophet. For as Jonah was in the womb of a whale three days and three nights, so Man's Son shall be in the heart of the earth three days and three nights. Men of Nineveh shall rise in doom with this generation and shall condemn it, for they did penance in the preaching of Jonah, and lo here, a greater than Jonah. The queen of the south shall rise in doom with this generation, and shall condemn it, for she came from the ends of the earth to hear the wis⁄dom of Solomon, and lo here, a greater than Solomon.

When an unclean spirit goes out from a man, he goes by dry places and seeks rest, and finds not. Then he says, I shall turn again into mine house from whence I went out. And he comes and finds it void and cleansed *besoms, brooms* with besoms, and made fair. Then he goes and takes with him seven other spirits worse than himself, and they enter and dwell there. And the last things of that man are made worse than the former. So it shall be to this worst generation.

Yet while He spoke to the people, lo, His mother and His brethren stood withoutforth, seeking to speak with Him. And a man said to Him, Lo, Thy mother and Thy brethren stand withoutforth, seeking Thee. He answered to the man that spoke to Him, and said, Who is My mother? And who are My brethren? And He held forth His hand into His disciples and said, Lo,

My mother and My brethren. For whoever does the will of My Father that is in heavens, he is My brother, and sister, and mother.

Chapter XIII

In that day Jesus went out of the house and sat beside the sea. And much people was gathered to Him so that He went up into a boat and sat, and all the people stood on the brink. And He spoke to them many things in parables, and said, Lo, he that sows went out to sow his seed. And while he sows, some seeds fell beside the way, and birds of the air came and ate them. But other seeds fell into stony places where they had not much earth, and anon they sprang up, for they had not deep ness of earth. But when the sun was risen, they swalled, *dried up, withered* and for they had not root they dried up. And other seeds fell among thorns, and thorns waxed up and strangled them. But other seeds fell into good land and gave fruit, some an hundredfold, another sixtyfold, another thirty fold. He that has ears of hearing, hear he.

And the disciples came nigh and said to Him, Why speaks Thou in parables to them? And He answered and said, For to you it is given to know the privities of the kingdom of heavens. But it is not given to them. For it shall be given to him that has, and he shall have plenty. But if a man has not, also that thing that he has shall be taken away from him. Therefore I speak to them in parables, for they, seeing, see not, and they, hearing, hear not, neither understand, that the prophecy of Isaiah's saying is fulfilled in them, With hearing ye shall hear and ye shall not understand; and ye seeing shall see, and ye shall not see, for the heart of this people is greatly fatted and they heard heavily with ears, and they have closed their eyes lest sometime they see with eyes and with ears hear, and understand in heart, and they be converted and I heal them. But your eyes that see are blessed, and your ears that hear.

Forsooth, I say to you that many prophets and just men coveted to see those things that ye see, and they saw not, and to hear those things that ye hear, and they heard not. Therefore hear ye the parable of the sower. Each that hears the word of the realm and understands not, the evil spirit comes and ravishes that that is sown in his heart. This it is that is sown beside the way. But this that is sown on the stony land, this it is that hears the word of God and anon with joy takes it. And he has not root in himself, but is temporal. For when tribulation and perse- cution is made for the word, anon he is sclaundered. But he that is sown in thorns is this that hears the word, and the business of this world and the fallacy of richesses strangle the word, and it is made without fruit. But he that is sown into good land is this that hears the word and understands, and brings forth fruit. And some make an hundredfold, truly, another sixtyfold, and another thirtyfold.

Another parable Jesus put forth to them, and said, The kingdom of heavens is made like to a man that sowed good seed in his field. And when men slept, his enemy came and sowed above tares in the middle of wheat and went away. But when the herb was grown and made fruit, then the tares appeared. And the ser- vants of the husbandman came and said to him, Lord, whether has thou not sown good seed in thy field? Whereof then has it tares? And he said to them, An enemy has done this thing. And the servants said to him, Will thou that we go and gather them? And he said, Nay, lest peradventure ye, in gathering tares, draw up with them the wheat by the root. Suffer ye them both to wax into reaping time, and in the time of ripe corn I shall say to the reapers, First gather ye together the tares,

and bind them together in knitches to be burnt. But *small bundles*
gather ye wheat into my barn.

Another parable Jesus put forth to them and said,
The kingdom of heavens is like to a corn of senevy *mustard*
which a man took and sowed in his field, which is the
least of all seeds. But when it has waxen, it is the most of
all worts, and is made a tree, so that birds of the air come *herbs*
and dwell in the boughs thereof.

Another parable Jesus spoke to them, The kingdom
of heavens is like to sourdough, which a woman took *leaven, yeast*
and hid in three measures of meal till it were all soured.

Jesus spoke all these things in parables to the people,
and He spoke not to them without parables, that it
should be fulfilled that is said by the prophet, saying, I
shall open My mouth in parables. I shall tell out hid
things from the making of the world.

Then He left the people and came into an house, and
His disciples came to Him and said, Expound to us the
parable of tares of the field. Which answered and said,
He that sows good seed is Man's Son. The field is the
world. But the good seed, these are the sons of the kingdom. But tares, these are evil children. The enemy that
sows them is the fiend, and the ripe corn is the ending of
the world. The reapers are angels. Therefore as tares are
gathered together and are burnt in fire, so it shall be in
the ending of the world. Man's Son shall send His
angels and they shall gather from His realm all sclaunderers and them that do wickedness. And they shall
send them into the chimney of fire. There shall be weep- *fireplace, furnace*
ing and beating together of teeth. Then just men shall
shine as the sun in the realm of their Father. He that has
ears of hearing, hear he.

The kingdom of heavens is like to treasure hid in a
field, which a man that finds hides. And for joy of it he
goes and sells all things that he has, and buys the ilk

field. Eftsoon, the kingdom of heavens is like to a merchant that seeks good margarites. But when he has found one precious margarite, he went and sold all things that he had and bought it. Eft, the kingdom of heavens is like to a net cast into the sea and that gathers together of all kind of fishes. Which when it was full, they drew up and set by the brink, and chose the good into their vessels, but the evil they cast out. So it shall be in the ending of the world. Angels shall go out and shall depart evil men from the middle of just men. And they shall send them into the chimney of fire. There shall be weeping and grinding of teeth.

Have ye understood all these things? They say to Him, Yea. He says to them, Therefore every wise man of law in the kingdom of heavens is like to an husbandman that brings forth of his treasure new things and old.

And it was done, when Jesus had ended these parables, He passed from thence. And He came into His country and taught them in their synagogues, so that they wondered and said, From whence this wisdom and virtues came to this? Whether is not this the son of a carpenter? Whether His mother is not said Mary? And His brethren James and Joseph, and Simon and Judas? And His sisters, whether they all are not among us? From whence then all these things came to this? And so they were sclaundered in Him. But Jesus said to them, A prophet is not without worship but in his own country and in his own house. And He did not there many virtues for the unbelief of them.

Chapter XIV

In that time Herod tetrarch heard the fame of Jesus, and said to his children, This is John Baptist. He is risen from death and therefore virtues work in him. For Herod had held John and bound him, and put him into prison for Herodias, the wife of his brother. For John said to him, It is not leaveful to thee to have her.

And he, willing to slay him, dreaded the people, for they had him as a prophet. But in the day of Herod's birth, the daughter of Herodias danced in the middle and pleased Herod. Wherefore with an oath he behight to give to her whatever thing she had asked of him. And she, beforewarned of her mother, said, Give thou to me here the head of John Baptist in a dish. And the king was sorrowful, but for the oath and for them that sat together at the meat, he commanded to be given. And he sent and beheaded John in the prison. And his head was brought in a dish and it was given to the damsel, and she bore it to her mother.

And his disciples came and took his body and bur⁄ied it, and they came and told to Jesus. And when Jesus had heard this thing, He went from thence in a boat into desert place beside. And when the people had heard, they followed Him on their feet from cities. And Jesus went out and saw a great people and had ruth on them, and healed the sick of them. But when the eventide was come, His disciples came to Him and said, The place is desert, the time is now passed. Let the people go into towns to buy them meat. Jesus said to them, They have not need to go. Give ye them somewhat to eat.

They answered, We have not here but five loaves and two fishes. And He said to them, Bring ye them hither to Me. And when He had commanded the people to sit to meat on the hay, He took five loaves and two fishes, and He beheld into heaven and blessed, and broke, and gave to His disciples, and the disciples gave to the peo⁄ple. And all ate and were fulfilled. And they took the relifs of broken gobbets, twelve coffinsful. And the num⁄ *leftovers, remains* ber of men that ate was five thousand of men, out⁄taken *fragments, pieces* / *baskets, coffers, hampers* women and little children.

And anon Jesus compelled the disciples to go up
into a boat and go before Him over the sea while He left
ascend, go up the people. And when the people were left, He styed
alone into an hill for to pray. But when the evening was
come, He was there alone. And the boat in the middle
thrown about of the sea, was shogged with waves, for the wind was
contrary to them. But in the fourth waking of the night,
He came to them, walking on the sea. And they, seeing
frightened, troubled Him walking on the sea, were disturbed and said that,
ghost, spirit It is a phantom! ✓ and for dread they cried. And anon
Jesus spoke to them and said, Have ye trust. I am. Nil
ye dread.

And Peter answered and said, Lord, if Thou art,
command me to come to Thee on the waters. And He
said, Come thou. And Peter went down from the boat
and walked on the waters to come to Jesus. But he saw
the wind strong and was afeared, and when he began to
drench, he cried and said, Lord, make me safe!

And anon Jesus held forth His hand and took Peter,
and said to him, Thou of little faith, why has thou
feared doubted? And when He had styed into the boat, the
wind ceased. And they that were in the boat came and
worshipped Him, and said, Verily, Thou art God's
Son.

And when they had passed over the sea, they came
into the land of Gennesaret. And when the men of that
place had known Him, they sent into all that country,
and they brought Him all that had sickness. And they
prayed Him that they should touch the hem of His clothing, and whoever touched were made safe.

Chapter XV

Then the scribes and the Pharisees came to Him from
Jerusalem, and said, Why break Thy disciples the traditions of elder men? For they wash not their hands when

they eat bread. He answered and said to them, Why break ye the commandment of God for your traditions? For God said, Honour thy father and thy mother, and he that curses father or mother, die by death. But ye say, Whoever says to father or mother, Whatever gift is of me it shall profit to thee, and he has not worshipped his father or his mother, and ye have made the command⁄ ment of God void for your tradition. Hypocrites! Isaiah the prophet prophesied well of you, and said, These peo⁄ ple honour Me with their lips, but their heart is far from Me, and they worship Me without cause, teaching the doctrines and commandments of men.

And when the people were called together to Him, He said to them, Hear ye, and understand ye. That thing that enters into the mouth defouls not a man, but that thing that comes out of the mouth defouls a man. Then His disciples came and said to Him, Thou knows that if this word be heard, the Pharisees are sclaundered?

And He answered and said, Every planting that My Father of heaven has not planted, shall be drawn up by the root. Suffer ye them. They are blind and leaders of blind men. And if a blind man lead a blind man, both fall down into the ditch.

Peter answered and said to Him, Expound unto us this parable. And He said, Yet ye are also without understanding? Understand ye not that all thing that enters into the mouth goes into the womb and is sent out into the going away? But those things that come forth from the mouth, go out of the heart, and those things defoul a man. For of the heart go out evil thoughts, man⁄ slayings, advowtries, fornications, thefts, false witnes⁄ sings, blasphemies. These things it is that defoul a man. But to eat with hands not washed defouls not a man.

And Jesus went out from thence and went into the

coasts of Tyre and Sidon. And lo, a woman of Canaan went out of those coasts, and cried and said to Him, Lord, the Son of David, have mercy on me. My daughter is evil travailed of a fiend.

And He answered not to her a word. And His disciples came and prayed Him, and said, Leave Thou her, for she cries after us.

He answered and said, I am not sent but to the sheep of the house of Israel that perished. And she came and worshipped Him and said, Lord, help me. Which answered and said, It is not good to take the bread of children and cast it to hounds. And she said, Yes, Lord, for whelps eat of the crumbs that fall down from *table* the board of their lords. Then Jesus answered and said to her, Ah, woman, thy faith is great. Be it done to thee as thou will. And her daughter was healed from that hour.

And when Jesus had passed from thence, He came beside the sea of Galilee. And He went up into an hill and sat there. And much people came to Him, and had with them dumb men and crooked, feeble and blind, and many others. And they cast them down at His feet. And He healed them so that the people wondered, seeing dumb men speaking and crooked going, blind men seeing, and they magnified God of Israel. And Jesus, when His disciples were called together, said to them, I have ruth of the people, for they have abided now three days with Me, and have nothing to eat. And I will not leave them fasting lest they fail in the way.

And the disciples say to Him, Whereof then so many loaves among us in desert to fulfil so great a people? And Jesus said to them, How many loaves have ye? And they said, Seven, and a few small fishes. And He commanded to the people to sit to meat on the earth. And He took seven loaves and five fishes, and did thank ings and broke, and gave to His disciples, and the disciples gave to the people. And all ate and were fulfilled, and they took that that was left of relifs seven leepsful. *baskets, hampers* And they that ate were four thousand of men, without little children and women. And when He had left the people, He went up into a boat and came into the coasts of Magdala.

Chapter XVI

And the Pharisees and the Sadducees came to Him, tempting, and prayed Him to show them a token from heaven. And He answered and said to them, When the eventide is come, ye say, It shall be clear, for heaven is ruddy; and the morrowtide, Today tempest, for heaven *red* shines heavily. Then ye can deem the face of heaven, but ye moun not wit the tokens of times. An evil generation and advowtrous seeks a token, and a token shall not be given to it but the token of Jonah the prophet.

And when he had left them he went forth. And when his disciples came over the sea, they forgot to take loaves. And He said to them, Behold ye, and beware of the sourdough of Pharisees and Sadducees. And they thought among them and said, For we have not taken loaves. But Jesus, witting, said to them, What think ye among you of little faith, for ye have not loaves? Yet understand not ye, neither have mind of five loaves into five thousand of men, and how many coffins ye took? Neither of seven loaves into four thousand of men, and how many leeps ye took? Why understand ye not? For I said not to you of bread, Beware of the sourdough of Pharisees and Sadducees. Then they understood that He said not to beware of sourdough of loaves, but of the teaching of Pharisees and Sadducees.

And Jesus came into the parties of Caesarea of Philippi, and asked His disciples and said, Whom say men to be Man's Son? And they said, Some, John Baptist; others Elijah, and others Jeremiah or one of the prophets. Jesus said to them, But whom say ye Me to be?

Simon Peter answered and said, Thou art Christ, the Son of God Living! Jesus answered and said to him, Blessed art thou, Simon Barjona, for flesh and blood showed not to thee, but My Father that is in heavens. And I say to thee that thou art Peter, and on this stone I shall build My church, and the gates of hell shall not have might against it. And to thee I shall give the keys of the kingdom of heavens. And whatever thou shall bind on earth, shall be bound also in heavens. And whatever thou shall unbind on earth, shall be unbound also in heavens. Then He commanded to His disciples that they should say to no man that He was Christ.

From that time, Jesus began to show to His disciples that it behoved Him go to Jerusalem and suffer many things of the elder men, and of scribes and princes of priests, and be slain, and the third day to rise again. And Peter took Him and began to blame Him, and said, Far be it from Thee, Lord. This thing shall not be to Thee. And He turned and said to Peter, Satan, go after Me. Thou art a sclaunder to Me, for thou savour not those things that are of God, but those things that are of men.

Then Jesus said to His disciples, If any man will come after Me, deny he himself and take his cross, and sue Me. For he that will make his life safe, shall lose it. And he that shall lose his life for Me, shall find it. For what profits it to a man if he win all the world and suffer *damage, destruction, harm* pairing of his soul? Or what changing shall a man give for his soul? For Man's Son shall come in glory of His Father with His angels, and then He shall yield to each

man after his works. Truly I say to you, there are some
of them that stand here which shall not taste death till
they see Man's Son coming in His kingdom.

Chapter XVII

And after six days, Jesus took Peter and James and
John, his brother, and led them aside into an high hill,
and was turned into another likeness before them. And
His face shone as the sun, and His clothes were made
white as snow. And lo, Moses and Elijah appeared to
them and spoke with Him. And Peter answered and
said to Jesus, Lord, it is good us to be here. If Thou will,
make we here three tabernacles, to Thee one, to Moses
one, and one to Elijah. Yet the while he spoke, lo, a
bright cloud overshadowed them, and lo, a Voice out of
the cloud that said, This is My dearworth Son in whom *dearly loved*
I have well pleased to Me. Hear ye Him!

And the disciples heard and fell down on their faces,
and dreaded greatly. And Jesus came and touched
them, and said to them, Rise up, and nil ye dread. And
they lift up their eyes and saw no man, but Jesus alone.

And as they came down of the hill, Jesus commanded to them and said, Say ye to no man the vision
till Man's Son rise again from death. And His disciples
asked Him and said, What then say the scribes that it
behove that Elijah come first? He answered and said to
them, Elijah shall come, and he shall restore all things.
And I say to you that Elijah is now come and they knew
him not, but they did in him whatever things they
would. And so Man's Son shall suffer of them. Then
the disciples understood that He said to them of John
Baptist.

And when He came to the people, a man came to
Him and fell down on his knees before Him, and said,
Lord, have mercy on my son, for he is lunatic and suf-

fers evil. For ofttimes he falls into the fire, and ofttimes into water. And I brought him to Thy disciples and they might not heal him.

Jesus answered and said, Ah, thou generation unbe- *faithless, unbelieving* lieveful and wayward! How long shall I be with you? How long shall I suffer you? Bring ye him hither to Me. And Jesus blamed him, and the devil went out from him, and the child was healed from that hour.

Then the disciples came to Jesus privily, and said to Him, Why might not we cast him out? Jesus says to them, For your unbelief. Truly I say to you, if ye have faith as a corn of senevy, ye shall say to this hill, Pass thou hence, and it shall pass, and nothing shall be *impossible* unpossible to you. But this kind is not cast out but by praying and fasting.

waiting for And whiles they were abiding together in Galilee, Jesus said to them, Man's Son shall be betrayed into the hands of men, and they shall slay Him, and the third day He shall rise again to life. And they were full sorry.

And when they came to Capernaum, they that took tribute came to Peter and said to him, Your Master pays not tribute? And he said, Yes. And when he was come into the house, Jesus came before him and said, Simon, what seems to thee? Kings of earth, of whom take they tribute? Of their sons, either of aliens? And he said, Of aliens. Jesus said to him, Then sons are free. But that we sclaunder them not, go to the sea and cast an hook, and take the ilk fish that first comes up, and when his mouth *coin worth four drachmas* is opened, thou shall find a stater. And give for thee and for Me.

Chapter XVIII

In that hour the disciples came to Jesus and said, Who, guess Thou, is greater in the kingdom of heavens? And Jesus called a little child and put him in the middle of them, and said, I say truth to you, but be ye turned and made as little children, ye shall not enter into the king⁄dom of heavens. Therefore, whoever makes him as this little child, he is greater in the kingdom of heavens. And he that receives one such little child in My name, receives Me. But whoso sclaunders one of these small that believe in Me, it speeds to him that a millstone of asses be hanged in his neck and he be drenched in the deepness of the sea. Woe to the world for sclaunders, for it is need that sclaunders come. Nethless, woe to the ilk man by whom a sclaunder comes. And if thine hand or thy foot sclaunders thee, cut it off and cast away from thee. It is better to thee to enter to life feeble, either crooked, than having twain hands or two feet, to be sent into everlasting fire. And if thine eye sclaunder thee, pull it out and cast away from thee. It is better to thee with one eye to enter into life, than having twain eyes to be sent into the fire of hell.

grinding stone driven round by an ass & V drowned

See ye that ye despise not one of these little, for I say to you that the angels of them in heavens see evermore the face of My Father that is in heavens. For Man's Son came to save that thing that perished.

What seems to you? If there were to some man an hundred sheep, and one of them has erred

wandered off, become lost

But if thy brother sin against thee, go thou and reprove him betwixt thee and him alone. If he hears thee, thou has won thy brother. And if he hears thee not, take with thee one or twain, that every word stand in the mouth of twain or three witnesses. And if he hears not them, say thou to the church. But if he hears not the church, be he as an heathen and a publican to thee.

I say to you truly, whatever things ye bind on earth, those shall be bound also in heaven. And whatever things ye unbind on earth, those shall be unbound also in heaven. Eftsoon I say to you that if twain of you con⁄

destroyed sent on the earth of everything whatever they ask, it shall be done to them of My Father that is in heavens. For where twain or three are gathered in My name, there I am in the middle of them.

Then Peter came to Him and said, Lord, how often shall my brother sin against me and I shall forgive him? *times (as in multiplication)* Whether till seven siths? Jesus says to him, I say not to thee till seven siths, but till seventy siths seven siths. Therefore, the kingdom of heavens is likened to a king that would reckon with his servants. And when he began to reckon, one that owed ten thousand talents was brought to him. And when he had not whereof to yield, his lord commanded him to be sold, and his wife and children and all things that he had, and to be paid. But the ilk servant fell down and prayed him and said, Have patience in me and I shall yield to thee all things. And the lord had mercy on that servant, and suffered him to go and forgave him the debt. But the ilk servant *fellow-servant* went out and found one of his even-servants that owed him an hundred pence. And he held him and strangled him, and said, Yield that that thou owest. And his even-servant fell down and prayed him, and said, Have patience in me and I shall quite all things to thee. But he would not, but went out and put him into prison till he paid all the debt. And his even-servants seeing the things that were done, sorrowed greatly. And they came and told to their lord all the things that were done. Then his lord called him and said to him, Wicked servant, I forgave to thee all the debt, for thou prayed me. Therefore whether it behoved not also thee to have mercy on thine even-servant, as I had mercy on thee? And his lord was wroth, and took him to tormentors till he paid all the debt. So My Father of heaven shall do to you if ye forgive not every man to his brother of your hearts.

Chapter XIX

And it was done, when Jesus had ended these words, He passed from Galilee and came into the coasts of Judea over Jordan. And much people sued Him and He healed them there. And Pharisees came to Him, tempting Him, and said, Whether it be leaveful to a man to leave his wife for any cause? Which answered and said to them, Have ye not read, For He that made men at the beginning, made them male and female? And He said, For this thing, a man shall leave father and mother, and he shall draw to his wife, and they shall be twain in one flesh. And so they are not now twain, but one flesh. Therefore a man depart not that thing that God has joined.

They say to Him, What then commanded Moses to give a libel of forsaking and to leave off? And He said to them, For Moses, for the hardness of your hearts, suffered you leave your wives. But from the beginning it was not so. And I say to you that whoever leaves his wife but for fornication, and weds another, does lechery. And he that weds the forsaken wife, does lechery.

His disciples say to Him, If the cause of a man with a wife is so, it speeds not to be wedded. And He said to them, Not all men take this word, but to which it is given. For there are geldings which are thus born of the *castrati, eunuchs* mother's womb, and there are geldings that are made of men, and there are geldings that have gelded themselves for the kingdom of heavens. He that may take, take he.

Then little children were brought to Him that He should put hands to them and pray. And the disciples blamed them. But Jesus said to them, Suffer ye that little children come to Me, and nil ye forbid them, for of such is the kingdom of heavens. And when He had put to them hands, He went from thence.

And lo, one came and said to Him, Good Master, what good shall I do that I have everlasting life? Which says to him, What asks thou Me of good thing? There is *care, guard, heed, notice* One good, God. But if thou will enter into life, keep the commandments.

He says to Him, Which? And Jesus said, Thou shall not do manslaying; thou shall not do advowtry; thou shall not do theft; thou shall not say false witnessing; worship thy father and thy mother; and thou shall love thy neighbour as thyself.

The young man says to Him, I have kept all these things from my youth. What yet fails to me? Jesus says to him, If thou will be parfit, go and sell all things that thou has and give to poor men, and thou shall have treasure in heaven. And come, and sue Me. And when the young man had heard these words, he went away sorrowful, for he had many possessions. And Jesus said to His disciples, I say to you truth, for a rich man of hard shall enter into the kingdom of heavens. And *again* eftsoon I say to you, it is lighter a camel to pass through a needle's eye than a rich man to enter into the kingdom of heavens.

When these things were heard, His disciples wondered greatly and said, Who then may be safe? Jesus beheld and said to them, Anent men this thing is impossible. *at, with* sible. But anent God, all things are possible.

Then Peter answered and said to Him, Lo, we have forsaken all things and we have sued Thee. What then shall be to us? Jesus said to them, Truly I say to you that ye that have forsaken all things and have sued Me, in the regeneration when Man's Son shall sit in the seat of His Majesty, ye shall sit on twelve seats deeming the twelve *families, tribes* kindreds of Israel. And every man that forsakes house, brethren or sisters, father or mother, wife, either children or fields for My name, he shall take an hundredfold and shall wield everlasting life. But many shall be, the first the last, and the last the first.

Chapter XX

The kingdom of heavens is like to an husbandman that went out first by the morrow to hire workmen into his vineyard. And when the covenant was made with work‑ men of a penny for the day, he sent them into his vine‑ yard. And he went about the third hour and saw others standing idle in the cheaping. And he said to them, Go ye also into mine vineyard, and that that shall be rightful I shall give to you. And they went forth. Eftsoons he went out about the sixth hour, and the ninth, and did in like manner. But about the eleventh hour, he went out and found others standing, and he said to them, What stand ye idle here all day? They say to him, For no man has hired us. He says to them, Go ye also into my vine‑ yard. And when evening was come, the lord of the vine‑ yard said to his procurator, Call the workmen and yield *steward* to them their hire, and begin thou at the last till to the first. And so when they were come that came about the eleventh hour, also they took every each of them a penny. But the first came and deemed that they should take more, but they took each one by themselves a penny, and in the taking grouched against the husbandman *complained, murmured* and said, These last wrought one hour, and thou has *worked* made them even to us that have borne the charge of the day and heat. And he answered to one of them and said, Friend, I do thee no wrong. Whether thou has not accorded with me for a penny? Take thou that that is thine and go, for I will give to this last man as to thee. Whether it is not leaveful to me to do that that I will? Whether thine eye is wicked, for I am good? So the last shall be the first, and the first the last, for many are called but few are chosen.

And Jesus went up to Jerusalem and took His twelve disciples in privity, and said to them, Lo, we go up to Jerusalem, and Man's Son shall be betaken to princes of priests and scribes, and they shall condemn Him to death. And they shall betake Him to heathen men for to be scorned and scourged and crucified. And the third day He shall rise again to life.

Then the mother of the sons of Zebedee came to Him with her sons, honouring and asking something of Him. And He said to her, What will thou? She says to Him, Say that these twain, my sons, sit one at Thy right half, and one at Thy left half in Thy kingdom. Jesus answered and said, Ye wit not what ye ask. Moun ye drink the cup which I shall drink? They say to Him, We moun. He says to them, Ye shall drink My cup, but to sit at My right half or left half, it is not Mine to give to you, but to which it is made ready of My Father.

And the ten, hearing, had indignation of the two brethren. But Jesus called them to Him and said, Ye wit that princes of heathen men are lords of them, and they that are greater use power on them. It shall not be so among you. But whoever will be made greater among you, be he your minister. And whoever among you will be the first, he shall be your servant, as Man's Son came not to be served, but to serve and to give His life redemption for many.

And when they went out of Jericho, much people sued Him. And lo, two blind men sat beside the way and heard that Jesus passed. And they cried and said, Lord, the Son of David, have mercy on us. And the people blamed them that they should be still. And they cried the more and said, Lord, the Son of David, have mercy on us.

And Jesus stood and called them, and said, What will ye that I do to you? They say to Him, Lord, that our eyes be opened. And Jesus had mercy on them and touched their eyes, and anon they saw and sued Him.

Chapter XXI

And when Jesus came nigh to Jerusalem, and came to Bethphage at the mount of Olivet, then sent He His two disciples and said to them, Go ye into the castle that is against you, and anon ye shall find an ass tied and a colt with her. Untie ye and bring to Me. And if any man say to you anything, say ye that the Lord has need to them, and anon he shall leave them. All this was done that that thing should be fulfilled that was said by the prophet, saying, Say ye to the daughter of Zion, Lo, thy King comes to thee, meek, sitting on an ass and a foal of an ass under yoke.

And the disciples went and did as Jesus commanded them. And they brought an ass and the foal, and laid their clothes on them, and made Him sit above. And full much people strewed their clothes in the way. Others cut branches of trees and strewed in the way. And the people that went before and that sued, cried and said, Hosanna to the Son of David! Blessed is He that comes in the name of the Lord. Hosanna in high things!

And when He was entered into Jerusalem, all the city was stirred and said, Who is this? But the people said, This is Jesus, the Prophet of Nazareth, of Galilee. And Jesus entered into the Temple of God and cast out of the Temple all that bought and sold. And He turned upsedown the boards of changers and the chairs of men *upside down* that sold culvers. And He says to them, It is written, Mine house shall be called an house of prayer, but ye have made it a den of thieves!

And blind and crooked came to Him in the Temple, and He healed them. But the princes of priests and scribes, seeing the marvellous things that He did, and children crying in the Temple and saying, Hosanna to the Son of David, had indignation and said to Him, Hear Thou what these say? And Jesus said to them, Yea. Whether ye have never read that of the mouth of *babes* young children and of sucking children, Thou has *praise, worship* made parfit herying?

And when He had left them, He went forth out of the city into Bethany, and there He dwelt and taught them of the kingdom of God. But on the morrow, He, turning again into the city, hungered. And He saw a fig tree beside the way and came to it, and found nothing therein but leaves only. And He said to it, Never fruit come forth of thee into without end. And anon the fig tree was dried up.

And disciples saw and wondered, saying how anon it dried. And Jesus answered and said to them, Truly I say to you, if ye have faith and doubt not, not only ye shall do of the fig tree, but also if ye say to this hill, Take and cast thee into the sea, it shall be done so. And all things whatever ye, believing, shall ask in prayer, ye shall take.

And when He came into the Temple, the princes of priests and elder men of the people came to Him that taught, and said, In what power does Thou these things? And who gave Thee this power? Jesus answered and said to them, And I shall ask you one word, the which if ye tell Me, I shall say to you in what power I do these things. Of whence was the baptism of John, of heaven or of men? And they thought within themselves, saying, If we say of heaven, He shall say to us, Why then believed ye not to him? If we say of men, we dread the people, for all had John as a prophet. And they answered to Jesus and said, We wit not.

And He said to them, Neither I say to you in what

power I do these things. But what seems to you? A man had two sons, and he came to the first and said, Son, go work this day in my vineyard. And he answered and said, I nil. But afterward he forthought and went forth. *reconsidered, thought again* But he came to the t'other and said in like manner. And he answered and said, Lord, I go. And he went not. Who of the twain did the father's will? They say to Him, The first. Jesus says to them, Truly I say to you, for publicans and whores shall go before you into the kingdom of God. For John came to you in the way of rightwiseness, and ye believed not to him. But publicans and whores believed to him. But ye say, and had no forthinking after, that ye believed to him.

Hear ye another parable. There was an husbandman that planted a vineyard and hedged it about, and dalf a *dug* presser therein and built a tower, and hired it to earth‑ *winepress* tillers, and went far in pilgrimage. But when the time of *farmers* fruits nighed, he sent his servants to the earth‑tillers to take fruits of it. And the earth‑tillers took his servants and beat the t'one. They slew another and they stoned another. Eftsoon he sent other servants, more than the first, and in like manner they did to them. And at the last, he sent his son to them and said, They shall dread my son. But the earth‑tillers, seeing the son, said within themselves, This is the heir. Come ye. Slay we him and we shall have his heritage. And they took and cast him out of the vineyard, and slew him. Therefore, when the lord of the vineyard shall come, what shall he do to the ilk earth‑tillers? They say to Him, He shall leese evil the *destroy, lose, make lost* evil men, and he shall set to hire his vineyard to other earth‑tillers which should yield to him fruit in their times.

Jesus says to them, Read ye never in Scriptures, The stone which builders reproved, this is made into the head of the corner? Of the Lord this thing is done, and it is marvellous before our eyes? Therefore I say to you that the kingdom of God shall be taken from you, and shall be given to a folk doing fruits of it. And he that shall fall on this stone, shall be broken. But on whom it *bruise, crush, pound* shall fall, it shall all to-brise him.

And when the princes of priests and Pharisees had heard His parables, they knew that He said of them. And they sought to hold Him, but they dreaded the people, for they had Him as a prophet.

Chapter XXII

And Jesus answered and spoke eftsoon in parables to them, and said, The kingdom of heavens is made like to a king that made weddings to his son. And he sent his *beckoned, bidden, invited* servants for to call men that were bode to the weddings, and they would not come. Eftsoon, he sent other servants and said, Say ye to the men that are bode to the feast, Lo, I have made ready my meat. My bulls and my *birds* volatiles are slain, and all things are made ready. Come ye to the weddings. But they despised and went forth, *goods for bartering* one into his town, another to his merchandise. But others held his servants and tormented them and slew. But the king, when he had heard, was wroth, and he *armies* sent his hosts, and he destroyed those manquellers and *executioners, murderers* burnt their city. Then he said to his servants, The weddings are ready, but they that were called to the feast were not worthy. Therefore go ye to the ends of ways and whomever ye find, call ye to the weddings. And his servants went out into ways and gathered together all that *nuptials, wedding feast* they found, good and evil, and the bridal was fulfilled with men sitting at the meat. And the king entered to see men sitting at the meat. And he saw there a man not clothed with bride-cloth. And he said to him, Friend, how entered thou hither without bride-clothes? And he was dumb. Then the king bade his ministers, Bind him

both hands and feet and send ye him into outer darkness. There shall be weeping and grinding of teeth. For
many are called, but few are chosen.

Then Pharisees went away and took a counsel to take
Jesus in word. And they send to Him their disciples
with Herodians, and say, Master, we wit that Thou art
soothfast and that Thou teaches in truth the way of *truthful*
God. And thou charges not of any man, for Thou
beholds not the person of men. Therefore say to us what
it seems to Thee. Is it leaveful that tribute be given to the
emperor, either nay?

And when Jesus had known the wickedness of
them, He said, Hypocrites! What tempt ye Me? Show
ye to Me the print of the money. And they brought to *impress*
Him a penny. And Jesus said to them, Whose is this
image and the writing above? They say to Him, The
emperor's. Then He said to them, Therefore yield ye to
the emperor those things that are the emperor's, and to
God those things that are of God. And they heard and
wondered, and they left Him and went away.

In that day Sadducees, that say there is no rising
again to life, came to Him and asked Him, and said,
Master, Moses said, If any man is dead, not having a
son, that his brother wed his wife and raise seed to his
brother. And seven brethren were at us, and the first
wedded a wife and is dead. And he had no seed and left
his wife to his brother. Also the second and the third, till
to the seventh. But the last of all, the woman is dead.
Also in the rising again to life, whose wife of the seven
shall she be, for all had her?

Jesus answered and said to them, Ye err and ye know
not the Scriptures, nor the virtue of God. For in the rising again to life, neither they shall wed, neither shall be
wedded. But they are as the angels of God in heaven.
And of the rising again of dead men, have ye not read

that is said of the Lord that says to you, I am God of Abraham, and God of Isaac, and God of Jacob? He is not God of dead men, but of living men. And the people, hearing, wondered in His teaching.

And Pharisees heard that He had put silence to Sadducees, and came together. And one of them, a teacher of the law, asked Jesus and tempted Him, Master, which is a great commandment in the law? Jesus said to him, Thou shall love thy Lord God of all thine heart and in all thy soul, and in all thy mind. This is the first and the most commandment. And the second is like to this, Thou shall love thy neighbour as thyself. In these two commandments hang all the law and the prophets.

And when the Pharisees were gathered together, Jesus asked them and said, What seems to you of Christ? Whose Son is He? They say to Him, Of David. He says to them, How then David, in Spirit, calls Him Lord, and says, The Lord said to my Lord, Sit on my right half till I put Thine enemies a stool of Thy feet? Then if David calls Him Lord, how is He his son? And no man might answer a word to Him, *bold* neither any man was hardy from that day to ask Him more.

Chapter XXIII

Then Jesus spoke to the people and to His disciples, and said, On the chair of Moses scribes and Pharisees have sat. Therefore keep ye and do ye all things, whatever things they say to you. But nil ye do after their works, for they say and do not. And they bind grievous charges and that moun not be borne, and put on shoulders of men. But with their finger they will not move them. Therefore they do all their works that they be seen of men, for they draw abroad their phylacteries and magnify hems. And they love the first sitting-places

in suppers and the first chairs in synagogues, and salutations in cheaping and to be called of men master. But nil
ye be called master, for One is your Master and all ye are
brethren. And nil ye call to you a father on earth, for
One is your Father that is in heavens. Neither be ye
called masters, for One is your Master, Christ.

He that is greatest among you shall be your minister.
For he that highs himself shall be meeked, and he that *exalts, promotes*
meeks himself shall be enhanced. But woe to you, *abased, humbled*
promoted, raised up
scribes and Pharisees, hypocrites, that close the kingdom of heavens before men, and ye enter not, neither
suffer men entering to enter. Woe to you, scribes and
Pharisees, hypocrites, that eat the houses of widows and
pray by long prayer. For this thing ye shall take more
doom.

Woe to you, scribes and Pharisees, hypocrites, that
go about the sea and the land to make one proselyte, and
when he is made ye make him a son of hell double more
than ye are. Woe to you, blind leaders, that say,
Whoever swears by the Temple of God, it is nothing,
but he that swears in the gold of the Temple, is debtor.
Ye fools and blind, for what is greater, the gold, or the
Temple that hallows the gold? And whoever swears in
the altar, it is nothing, but he that swears in the gift that
is on the altar, owes. Blind men, for what is more, the *ought*
gift or the altar that hallows the gift? Therefore, he that
swears in the altar, swears in it and in all things that are
thereon. And he that swears in the Temple, swears in it
and in Him that dwells in the Temple. And he that
swears in heaven, swears in the throne of God and in
Him that sits thereon.

Woe to you, scribes and Pharisees, hypocrites, that
tithe mint, anise and cummin, and have left those things *the herb*
that are of more charge of the law - doom and mercy and *aniseed*
aromatic seeds of the
faith! And it behoved to do these things and not to leave *cummin*

those. Blind leaders, cleansing a gnat but swallowing a camel. Woe to you, scribes and Pharisees, hypocrites, that cleanse the cup and the platter withoutforth, but within ye are full of raven and uncleanness. Thou blind Pharisee, cleanse the cup and the platter withinforth, that that that is withoutforth be made clean.

Woe to you, scribes and Pharisees, hypocrites, that are like to sepulchres whited, which withoutforth seem fair to men, but within they are full of bones of dead men and of all filth. So ye, withoutforth, seem just to men, but within ye are full of hypocrisy and wickedness. Woe to you, scribes and Pharisees, hypocrites, that *monuments, tombs* build sepulchres of prophets and make fair the burials of just men, and say, If we had been in the days of our fathers, we should not have been their fellows in the blood of prophets. And so ye are in witnessing to your-selves that ye are the sons of them that slew the prophets, and fulfil ye the measure of your fathers.

brood of adders Ye adders, and adders' briddis, how shall ye flee from the doom of hell? Therefore lo, I send to you pro-phets and wise men and scribes, and of them ye shall slay and crucify, and of them ye shall scourge in your synagogues and shall pursue from city into city, that all the just blood come upon you that was shed on the earth from the blood of just Abel to the blood of Zacharias, the son of Barachias, whom ye slew betwixt the Temple and the altar. Truly I say to you, all these things shall come on this generation.

Jerusalem, Jerusalem, that slays the prophets and stones them that are sent to thee, how often would I gather together thy children as an hen gathers together her chickens under her wings, and thou would not! Lo, your house shall be left to you desert. And I say to you, ye shall not see Me from henceforth till ye say, Blessed is He that comes in the name of the Lord!

Chapter XXIV

And Jesus went out from the Temple, and His disci╱ples came to Him to show Him the buildings of the Temple. But He answered and said to them, See ye all these things? Truly I say to you, a stone shall not be left here on a stone that nor it shall be destroyed. And when He sat on the hill of Olivet, His disciples came to Him privily and said, Say us when these things shall be, and what token of Thy coming and of the ending of the world.

And Jesus answered and said to them, Look ye, that no man deceive you. For many shall come in My name and shall say, I am Christ, and they shall deceive many. For ye shall hear battles and opinions of battles. See that *reports, rumours* ye be not disturbled, for it behoves these things to be done. But not yet is the end. Folk shall rise together against folk and realm against realm, and pestilences and hungers, and the earthmovings shall be by places, *earthquakes* and all these are beginnings of sorrows. Then men shall betake you into tribulation, and shall slay you, and ye shall be in hate to all folk for My name. And then shall many be sclaundered and betray each other, and they shall hate each other. And many false prophets shall rise and deceive many. And for wickedness shall be plente╱ous, the charity of many shall wax cold. But he that shall dwell stable to the end, shall be safe.

And this gospel of the kingdom shall be preached in all the world in witnessing to all folk, and then the end shall come. Therefore, when ye see the abomination of discomfort that is said of Daniel the prophet, standing in the Holy Place ╱ he that reads understand he ╱ then they that are in Judea flee to the mountains, and he that is in the house╱roof come not down to take anything of his house, and he that is in the field turn not again to take

his coat. But woe to them that are with child and nour-
feed, give suck, nurse ish in those days. Pray ye that your fleeing be not made
in winter or in the Sabbath. For then shall be great tribu-
lation, what manner was not from the beginning of the
world to now, neither shall be made.

shortened   And but those days had been abridged, each flesh
should not be made safe. But those days shall be made
short for the chosen men. Then if any man say to you,
Lo, here is Christ or there, nil ye believe. For false
Christs and false prophets shall rise, and they shall give
great tokens and wonders, so that also the chosen be led
into error if it may be done. Lo, I have before said to you.
Therefore, if they say to you, Lo, He is in desert, nil ye
believe, suppose, trust to go out; Lo, in privy places, nil ye trow. For as light goes
out from the east and appears into the west, so shall be
also the coming of Man's Son. Wherever the body shall
be, also the eagles shall be gathered thither.

And anon after the tribulation of those days, the sun
shall be made dark and the moon shall not give her light.
And the stars shall fall from heaven and the virtues of
heavens shall be moved. And then the token of Man's
Son shall appear in heaven. And then all kindreds of
the earth shall wail, and they shall see Man's Son coming in the clouds of heaven with much virtue and
majesty. And He shall send His angels with a trump
and a great voice, and they shall gather His chosen from
four winds, from the highest things of heavens to the
ends of them. And learn ye the parable of a fig tree.
When his branch is now tender and the leaves are
sprung, ye wit that summer is nigh. So, and ye, when ye
see all these things, wit ye that it is nigh in the gates.
Truly I say to you, for this generation shall not pass till
all things be done. Heaven and earth shall pass, but My
words shall not pass.

But of the ilk day and hour no man wot, neither

angels of heavens, but the Father only. But as it was in the days of Noah, so shall be the coming of Man's Son. For as in the days before the Great Flood, they were eating and drinking, wedding and taking to wedding, to that day that Noah entered into the ship, and they knew not till the Great Flood came and took all men. So shall be the coming of Man's Son. Then two shall be in one field. One shall be taken and another left. Two women shall be grinding in one quern. One shall be taken, and *hand-mill for grinding* the t'other left. Twain in a bed. The t'one shall be taken, *corn* and the t'other left. Therefore wake ye, for ye wit not in what hour the Lord shall come. But wit ye this, that if the husbandman wist in what hour the thief were to come, certes, he would wake and suffer not his house to *certainly* be undermined. And therefore be ye ready, for in what hour ye guess not, Man's Son shall come.

Who, guess thou, is a true servant and prudent, whom his lord ordained on his meyne to give them meat in time? Blessed is that servant whom his lord, when he shall come, shall find so doing. Truly I say to you, for on all his goods he shall ordain him. But if the ilk evil servant say in his heart, My lord tarries to come, and begins to smite his even-servants, and eat and drink with drunken men, the lord of that servant shall come in the day which he hopes not, and in the hour that he knows not, and shall depart him and put his part with hypocrites. There shall be weeping and grinding of teeth.

Chapter XXV

Then the kingdom of heavens shall be like to ten virgins which took their lamps and went out against the husband and the wife, and five of them were fools and five prudent. But the five fools took their lamps and took not oil with them. But the prudent took oil in their vessels with the lamps. And while the husband tarried, all they napped and slept. But at midnight a cry was made, Lo, the spouse comes, go ye out to meet with him! Then all those virgins rise up and arrayed their lamps. And the fools said to the wise, Give ye to us of your oil, for our lamps are quenched. The prudent answered and said, Lest peradventure it suffice not to us and to you, go ye rather to men that sell, and buy to you. And while they went for to buy, the spouse came, and those that were ready entered in with him to the weddings and the gate was shut. And at the last the other virgins came and said, Lord, lord, open to us. And he answered and said, Truly I say to you, I know you not. Therefore wake ye, for ye wit not the day nor the hour.

For as man that goes in pilgrimage, called his servants and betook to them his goods, and to one he gave five talents, and to another twain, and to another one, to each after his own virtue, and went forth anon. And he *gold Byzantine coins* that had five bezants went forth and wrought in them, and won other five also, and he that had taken twain, won other twain. But he that had taken one, went forth and dalf into the earth and hid the money of his lord. But after long time, the lord of those servants came and reckoned with them. And he that had taken five bezants, came and brought other five, and said, Lord, *committed* thou betook to me five bezants. Lo, I have gotten above five other. His lord said to him, Well be thou, good servant and faithful. For on few things thou has been true, I shall ordain thee on many things. Enter thou into the joy of thy lord.

And he that had taken two talents, came and said, Lord, thou betook to me two bezants. Lo, I have won over other two. His lord said to him, Well be thou, good servant and true. For on few things thou has been true, I shall ordain thee on many things. Enter thou into the joy of thy lord. But he that had taken one bezant, came and said, Lord, I wot that thou are an hard man. Thou reaps where thou has not sown, and thou gathers together where thou has not spread abroad, And I, dreading, went and hid thy bezant in the earth. Lo, thou has that that is thine. His lord answered and said to him, Evil servant and slow, wit thou that I reap where I sow not, and gather together where I spread not abroad? Therefore it behoved thee to betake my money to chan⁄gers, that when I came, I should receive that that is mine with usuries. Therefore take away from him the bezant *financial gain by interest* and give ye to him that has ten bezants. For to every man that has, men shall give, and he shall increase. But from him that has not, also that that him seems to have, shall be taken away from him. And cast ye out the unprofita⁄ble servant into outer darkness. There shall be weeping and grinding of teeth.

When Man's Son shall come in His Majesty and all His angels with Him, then He shall sit on the sege of *seat, throne* His Majesty. And all folks shall be gathered before Him, and He shall depart them a⁄twain as a shepherd departs sheep from kids. And He shall set the sheep on His right half, and the kids on the left half. Then the King shall say to them that shall be on His right half, Come ye, the blessed of My Father, take ye in possession the kingdom made ready to you from the making of the world. For I hungered and ye gave Me to eat, I thirsted and ye gave Me to drink, I was harbourless and ye har⁄ *homeless* boured Me, naked and ye hiled Me, sick and ye visited Me, I was in prison and ye came to Me. Then just men shall answer to Him and say, Lord, when saw we Thee hungry and we fed Thee, thirsty and we gave to Thee drink? And when saw we Thee harbourless and we har⁄boured Thee, or naked and we hiled Thee? Or when saw we Thee sick or in prison and we came to Thee?

And the King, answering, shall say to them, Truly I say to you, as long as ye did to one of these my least brethren, ye did to Me.

Then the King shall say also to them that shall be on His left half, Depart from Me, ye cursed, into everlasting fire that is made ready to the devil and his angels. For I hungered and ye gave not Me to eat. I thirsted and ye gave not Me to drink. I was harbourless, and ye harboured not Me, naked and ye covered not Me, sick and in prison and ye visited not Me. Then, and they shall answer to Him and shall say, Lord, when saw we Thee hungering or thirsting, or harbourless or naked, or sick or in prison, and we served not to Thee? Then He shall answer to them and say, Truly I say to you, how long ye did not to one of these least, neither ye did to Me. And these shall go into everlasting torment. But the just men shall go into everlasting life.

Chapter XXVI

And it was done, when Jesus had ended all these words, He said to His disciples, Ye wit that after two *feast of Passover* days Pasch shall be made, and Man's Son shall be betaken to be crucified.

Then the princes of priests and the elder men of the people were gathered into the hall of the prince of priests, that was said Caiaphas, and made a counsel to hold Jesus with guile and slay Him. But they said, Not on the holiday lest peradventure noise were made in the people.

And when Jesus was in Bethany in the house of Simon Leprous, a woman that had a box of alabaster of precious ointment, came to Him and shed out on the *disapproval, indignation* head of Him, resting. And disciples seeing, had dedain and said, Whereto this loss? For it might be sold for much and be given to poor men. But Jesus knew and said to them, What are ye heavy to this woman? For she has wrought in Me a good work. For ye shall ever have poor men with you, but ye shall not algates have Me. *always* This woman sending this ointment into My body, did to bury Me. Truly I say to you, wherever this gospel shall be preached in all the world, it shall be said that she did this in mind of Him.

Then one of the twelve that was called Judas Iscariot, went forth to the princes of priests and said to them, What will ye give to me and I shall betake Him to you? And they ordained to him thirty pence of silver. And from that time, he sought opportunity to betray Him.

And in the first day of therf loaves, the disciples came *unleavened* to Jesus and said, Where will thou we make ready to Thee to eat Pasch? Jesus said, Go ye into the city to some man, and say to him, The Master says, My time is nigh. At thee I make Pasch with My disciples. And the disciples did as Jesus commanded to them, and they made the Pasch ready.

And when eventide was come, He sat to meat with His twelve disciples. And He said to them as they ate, Truly I say to you that one of you shall betray Me. And they, full sorry, began each by himself to say, Lord, whether I am? And He answered and said, He that puts with Me his hand in the platter, shall betray Me. Forsooth, Man's Son goes as it is written of Him. But woe to that man by whom Man's Son shall be betrayed. It were good to him if that man had not been born. But Judas that betrayed Him answered, saying, Master, whether I am? Jesus said to him, Thou has said.

And while they supped, Jesus took bread, and blessed and broke, and gave to His disciples, and said, Take ye and eat. This is My body. And He took the cup and did thankings, and gave to them and said, Drink ye all hereof. This is My blood of the New Testament which shall be shed for many into remission of sins. And I say to you, I shall not drink from this time of this fruit of the vine into that day when I shall drink it new with you in the kingdom of My Father.

hymn   And when the ympne was said, they went out into the mount of Olivet. Then Jesus said to them, All ye shall suffer sclaunder in Me in this night, for it is written, I shall smite the Shepherd and the sheep of the flock shall be scattered. But after that I shall rise again, I shall go before you into Galilee. Peter answered and said to Him, Though all shall be sclaundered in Thee, I shall never be sclaundered. Jesus said to him, Truly I say to thee, for in this night before the cock crow, thrice thou shall deny Me. Peter said to Him, Yea, though it behove that I die with Thee, I shall not deny Thee. Also all the disciples said.

Then Jesus came with them into a town that is said Gethsemane. And He said to His disciples, Sit ye here the while I go thither and pray. And when He had taken Peter and two sons of Zebedee, He began to be heavy and sorry. Then He said to them, My soul is sorrowful to the death. Abide ye here and wake ye with Me. And He went forth a little and fell down on His face, praying, and saying, My Father, if it is possible, pass this cup from Me. Netheless not as I will, but as Thou will.

And He came to His disciples and found them sleeping. And He said to Peter, So, whether ye might not one hour wake with Me? Wake ye, and pray ye that ye enter not into temptation. For the spirit is ready, but the flesh is sick.

Eft the second time He went and prayed, saying, My Father, if this cup may not pass but I drink him, Thy will be done. And eftsoon He came and found them sleeping, for their eyes were heavy. And He left them and went eftsoon and prayed the third time, and said the same

word. Then He came to His disciples and said to them,
Sleep ye now, and rest ye. Lo, the hour has nighed, and
Man's Son shall be taken into the hands of sinners. Rise
ye. Go we. Lo, he that shall take Me is nigh.

Yet the while He spoke, Judas, one of the twelve,
came, and with him a great company with swords and
bats, sent from the princes of priests and from the elder *clubs, cudgels, staves*
men of the people. And he that betrayed Him gave to
them a token and said, Whomever I shall kiss, He it is.
Hold ye Him. And anon he came to Jesus and said,
Hail, Master. And he kissed Him. And Jesus said to
him, Friend, whereto art thou come? Then they came
nigh and laid hands on Jesus, and held Him.

And lo, one of them that were with Jesus, straught
out his hand and drew out his sword, and he smote the
servant of the prince of priests, and cut off his ear. Then
Jesus said to him, Turn thy sword into his place, for all
that take sword, shall perish by sword. Whether guess
thou that I may not pray My Father, and He shall give to
Me now more than twelve legions of angels? How then
shall the Scriptures be fulfilled? For so it behoves to be
done.

In that hour, Jesus said to the people, As to a thief ye
have gone out, with swords and bats to take Me. Day by
day I sat among you and taught in the Temple, and ye
held Me not. But all this thing was done that the
Scriptures of prophets should be fulfilled. Then all the
disciples fled and left Him.

And they held Jesus and led Him to Caiaphas, the
prince of priests, where the scribes and the Pharisees
and the elder men of the people were come together. But
Peter sued Him afar into the hall of the prince of priests.
And he went in and sat with the servants to see the end.
And the prince of priests and all the council sought false
witnessing against Jesus that they should take Him to

death, and they found not when many false witnesses were come. But at the last, two false witnesses came and said, This said, I may destroy the Temple of God, and after the third day build it again.

And the prince of priests rose and said to Him, Answer Thou nothing to those things that these witness against Thee? But Jesus was still. And the prince of priests said to him, I conjure Thee by living God that Thou say to us if Thou art Christ, the Son of God. Jesus said to him, Thou has said. Netheless I say to you, from henceforth ye shall see Man's Son sitting at the right half of the virtue of God, and coming in the clouds of heaven.

Then the prince of priests to-rent his clothes, and said, He has blasphemed! What yet have we need to witnesses? Lo, now ye have heard blasphemy. What seems to you? And they answered and said, He is guilty of death!

Then they spat into His face and smote Him with buffets, and others gave strokes with the palm of their hands in His face, and said, Thou Christ, arede to us, who is he that smote Thee?

declare, prophesy, tell

And Peter sat without in the hall, and a damsel came to him and said, Thou were with Jesus of Galilee. And he denied before all men, and said, I wot not what thou say. And when he went out at the gate, another damsel saw him and said to them that were there, And this was with Jesus of Nazareth. And eftsoon he denied with an oath, For I knew not the Man! And a little after, they that stood came and said to Peter, Truly, thou art of them, for thy speech makes thee known. Then he began to wary and to swear that he knew not the Man. And anon the cock crew. And Peter bethought on the word of Jesus that He had said, Before the cock crow, thrice thou shall deny Me. And he went out and wept bitterly.

Chapter XXVII

But when the morrowtide was come, all the princes of priests and the elder men of the people took counsel against Jesus that they should take Him to the death, and led Him, bound, and betook to Pilate of Pounce, justice. Then Judas that betrayed Him saw that He was damned. He repented and brought again the thirty pence to the princes of priests and to the elder men of the people, and said, I have sinned, betraying rightful blood! And they said, What to us? Busy thee! And when he had cast forth the silver in the Temple, he passed forth and went, and hanged himself with a snare. And the princes of priests took the silver and said, It is not leaveful to put it into the treasury, for it is the price of blood. And when they had taken counsel, they bought with it a field of a potter into burying of pilgrims. Herefore, the ilk field is called Aceldama, that is a field of blood, into this day. Then that was fulfilled that was said by the prophet Jeremiah, saying, And they have taken thirty pence, the price of a man praised, whom *appraised, adjudged, valued* they praised of the children of Israel. And they gave them into a field of a potter, as the Lord has ordained to me.

And Jesus stood before the doomsman, and the justice asked Him and said, Art Thou King of Jews? Jesus says to him, Thou say. And when He was accused of the princes of priests and of the elder men of the people, He answered nothing. Then Pilate says to Him, Hear Thou not how many witnessings they say against Thee? And He answered not to him any word, so that the justice wondered greatly. But for a solemn day, the justice was wont to deliver to the people one bound, whom they would. And he had then a famous man bound that was said Barabbas. Therefore Pilate said to them when they were together, Whom will ye that I deliver to you? Whether Barabbas or Jesus that is said Christ? For he wist that by envy they betrayed Him. And while he sat for doomsman, his wife sent to him and said, Nothing to thee and to that just man, for I have suffered this day many things for Him by a vision.

Forsooth, the princes of priests and the elder men counselled the people that they should ask Barabbas, but they should destroy Jesus. But the justice answered and said to them, Whom of the twain will ye that be delivered to you? And they said, Barabbas! Pilate says to them, What then shall I do of Jesus that is said Christ? All say, Be He crucified! The justice says to them, What evil has He done? And they cried more, and said, Be He crucified! And Pilate, seeing that he profited nothing but that the more noise was made, took water and washed his hands before the people, and said, I am guiltless of the blood of this rightful Man. Busy you! And all the people answered and said, His blood be on us and on our children! Then he delivered to them Barabbas, but he took to them Jesus, scourged, to be crucified.

Then knights of the justice took Jesus in the moot *hall of assembly* hall and gathered to Him all the company of knights. And they unclothed Him and did about Him a red mantle. And they folded a crown of thorns and put on His head, and a reed in His right hand. And they kneeled before Him and scorned Him, and said, Hail, King of Jews! And they spat on Him and took a reed and smote His head. And after that they had scorned Him, they unclothed Him of the mantle, and they clothed Him with His clothes and led Him to crucify Him.

And as they went out, they found a man of Cyrene coming from the town, Simon by name. They con-

strained him to take His cross, and they came into a
place that is called Golgotha, that is the place of
Calvary. And they gave Him to drink wine mingled
with gall. And when He had tasted, He would not
drink.

And after that they had crucified Him, they departed
His clothes and cast lot to fulfil that is said by the pro⟨
phet, saying, They parted to them My clothes, and on
My cloth they cast lot. And they sat and kept Him, and
set above His head his cause, written, This is Jesus of
Nazareth, King of Jews.

Then two thieves were crucified with Him, one on
the right half, and one on the left half. And men that
passed forth blasphemed Him, moving their heads and
saying, Vath to Thee that destroys the Temple of God *fie, faith*
and in the third day builds it again! Save Thou Thyself.
If Thou art the Son of God, come down off the cross!
Also and princes of priests, scorning, with scribes and
elder men, said, He made other men safe. He may not
make Himself safe. If He is King of Israel, come He
now down from the cross and we believe to Him. He
trusted in God, deliver He Him now if He will, for He
said that I am God's Son!

And the thieves that were crucified with Him,
upbraided Him of the same thing. But from the sixth
hour, darknesses were made on all the earth to the ninth
hour. And about the ninth hour, Jesus cried with a
great voice and said, Heli, Heli, lama sabachthani?
That is, My God, My God, why has Thou forsaken
Me?

And some that stood there, hearing, said, This calls
Elijah! And anon, one of them, running, took and
filled a sponge with vinegar, and put on a reed and gave
to Him to drink. But others said, Suffer thou. See
whether Elijah come to deliver Him!

Forsooth, Jesus eftsoon cried with a great voice, and gave up the ghost. And lo, the veil of the Temple was to-rent in two parts, from the highest to the lowest. And the earth shook and stones were clove. And burials were opened and many bodies of saints that had slept, rose up. And they went out of their burials, and after His resurrection they came into the holy city and appeared to many. And the centurion and they that were with him keeping Jesus, when they saw the earth shaking and those things that were done, they dreaded greatly, and said, Verily, this was God's Son!

And there were there many women afar, that sued Jesus from Galilee, and ministered to Him. Among which was Mary Magdalene, and Mary the mother of James, and of Joseph, and the mother of Zebedee's sons. But when evening was come, there came a rich man of Arimathea, Joseph by name, and he was a disciple of Jesus. He went to Pilate and asked the body of Jesus. Then Pilate commanded the body to be given. And *tightly bound, wrapped* when the body was taken, Joseph lapped it in a clean *around* *cotton or muslin cloth,* sendel and laid it in his new burial that he had hewn in a *shroud* stone. And he wallowed a great stone to the door of the *rolled* burial and went away. But Mary Magdalene and another Mary were there, sitting against the sepulchre.

And on the t'other day, that is after Pasch even, the princes of priests and the Pharisees came together to *beguiler, deceiver* Pilate and said, Sir, we have mind that the ilk guiler said, yet living, After three days, I shall rise again to life. Therefore command thou that the sepulchre be kept into the third day, lest His disciples come and steal Him, and say to the people, He has risen from death; and the last error shall be worse than the former.

Pilate said to them, Ye have the keeping. Go ye. Keep ye as ye ken. And they went forth and kept the sepulchre, marking the stone with keepers.

Chapter XXVIII

But in the eventide of the Sabbath that begins to shine in the first day of the week, Mary Magdalene came, and another Mary, to see the sepulchre. And lo, there was made a great earthshaking. For the angel of the Lord *tremor* came down from heaven and nighed, and turned away the stone and sat thereon. And his looking was as light and his clothes as snow, and for dread of him the kee⁄ pers were afeared, and they were made as dead men. But the angel answered and said to the women, Nil ye dread, for I wot that ye seek Jesus that was crucified. He is not here, for He is risen as He said. Come ye and see ye the place where the Lord was laid. And go ye soon, and say to His disciples that He is risen. And lo, He shall go before you into Galilee. There ye shall see Him. Lo, I have beforesaid to you!

And they went out soon from the burials with dread and great joy, running to tell to His disciples. And lo, Jesus met them and said, Hail ye! And they nighed and held His feet and worshipped Him. Then Jesus said to them, Nil ye dread. Go ye. Tell ye to My brethren that they go into Galilee. There they shall see Me.

And when they were gone, lo, some of the keepers came into the city and told to the princes of priests all things that were done. And when they were gathered together with the elder men and had taken their counsel, they gave to the knights much money and said, Say ye that His disciples came by night and have stolen Him while ye slept. And if this be heard of the justice, we shall counsel him and make you secure. And when the *safe* money was taken, they did as they were taught. And this word is published among the Jews into this day. *made public*

And the eleven disciples went into Galilee into an hill where Jesus had ordained to them. And they saw

Him and worshipped. But some of them doubted. And
Jesus came nigh and spoke to them, and said, All
power in heaven and in earth is given to Me. Therefore
go ye and teach all folks, baptizing them in the name of
the Father, and of the Son, and of the Holy Ghost, teaching them to keep all things whatever things I have commanded to you. And lo, I am with you in all days into
the end of the world.

Here ends the book of Matthew, and now begins the Prologue of Mark

*Mark, the gospeller, was the chosen servant of God and the
ghostly son of Peter in baptism, and the disciple in God's word.
He ministered priesthood in Israel, that is, among Jews, and
was of the lineage of Levi by flesh. And he was converted to the*
Attalia *faith of Christ and wrote the gospel in Italy, that is, the country of Rome, and showed in the gospel what he ought to his kin
and to Christ. Mark begins at the sending of John Baptist, and
tells not the nativity of Christ by flesh, but from Christ's baptism when He was full Man. He tells of His fasting by forty
days, and of His tempting in desert, how the devil tempted Him
and how wild beasts were gathered there, and how holy angels
came and served Christ after His temptation and overcoming
thereof.*

*After Christian faith received, he [Mark]cuts off his
thumb that he should be had reprovable to priesthood, that is, be
unable to be priest in the gospel, but choosing, before ordained,
consenting to the faith, might do so much that he lost not in the
work of word, that is, in preaching of God's word that that he
deserved before in kin. That is, as he was a priest by kin in the old
law among Jews, so he was a priest in the gospel among
Christian men, for he was bishop of Alexandria, and by all
things it was his work to ken prophecies and to dispose in himself
the sayings of the gospel, and to know in himself the teaching of*

law and to understand the divine kind of the Lord in flesh, which things it behoves to be sought first in us.

Here begins the gospel of Mark

Chapter I

The beginning of the gospel of Jesus Christ, the Son of God. As it is written in Isaiah the prophet, Lo, I send Mine angel before Thy face, that shall make Thy way ready before Thee. The voice of a crier in desert, Make ye ready the way of the Lord. Make ye His paths right!

John was in desert baptizing and preaching the baptism of repentance into remission of sins. And all the country of Judea went out to him, and all men of Jerusalem. And they were baptized of him in the flom *river* Jordan, and acknowledged their sins. And John was clothed with hairs of camels and a girdle of skin about his loins. And he ate honeysuckers and wild honey, and preached and said, A stronger than I shall come after me, and I am not worthy to kneel down and unlace His shoes. I have baptized you in water. But He shall baptize you in the Holy Ghost.

And it was done in those days, Jesus came from Nazareth of Galilee and was baptized of John in Jordan. And anon He went up of the water and saw heavens opened, and the Holy Ghost coming down as a culver and dwelling in Him. And a Voice was made *dove* from heavens, Thou art My loved Son. In Thee I am pleased.

And anon the Spirit put Him forth into desert, and He was in desert forty days and forty nights and was tempted of Satan. And He was with beasts, and angels ministered to Him. But after that John was taken, Jesus came into Galilee and preached the gospel of the kingdom of God, and said that, The time is fulfilled and the kingdom of God shall come nigh. Do ye penance and believe ye to the gospel.

And as He passed beside the sea of Galilee, He saw Simon and Andrew his brother, casting their nets into the sea, for they were fishers. And Jesus said to them, Come ye after Me. I shall make you to be made fishers of men. And anon they left the nets and sued Him.

And He went forth from thence a little and saw James of Zebedee, and John his brother, in a boat mak⁄ing nets. And anon He called them, and they left Zebedee their father in the boat with hired servants, and they sued Him. And they entered into Capernaum, and anon in the Sabbaths, He went into a synagogue and taught them. And they wondered on His teaching, for He taught them as He that had power, and not as scribes.

And in the synagogue of them was a man in an unclean spirit. And he cried out and said, What to us and to Thee, Thou Jesus of Nazareth? Has Thou come to destroy us? I wot that Thou are the Holy of God. And Jesus threatened him and said, Wax dumb and *plucking to pieces* go out of the man. And the unclean spirit, debraiding him and crying with great voice, went out from him. And all men wondered so that they sought within them⁄selves and said, What thing is this? What new doctrine is this? For in power He commands to unclean spirits, and they obey to Him. And the fame of Him went forth anon into all the country of Galilee.

And anon they went out of the synagogue, and came into the house of Simon and of Andrew, with James and John. And the mother of Simon's wife lay sick in fevers. And anon they say to Him of her. And He came nigh and arreared her, and when He had taken her hand, anon the fever left her and she served them.

But when the eventide was come and the sun was gone down, they brought to Him all that were of mal ease and them that had fiends. And all the city was gathered at the gate. And He healed many that had diverse sicknesses, and He cast out many fiends. And He suffered them not to speak, for they knew Him.

And He rose full early and went out, and went into a desert place and prayed there. And Simon sued Him and they that were with him. And when they had found Him, they said to Him that, All men seek Thee. And He said to them, Go we into the next towns and cities that I preach also there, for hereto I came.

And He preached in the synagogues of them and in all Galilee, and cast out fiends. And a leprous man came to Him, and besought and kneeled, and said, If Thou will, Thou may cleanse me. And Jesus had mercy on him and straught out His hand and touched him, and said to him, I will. Be thou made clean. And when He had said this, anon the leprosy parted away from him, and he was cleansed. And Jesus threatened him, and anon Jesus put him out and said to him, See thou, say to no man, but go show thee to the princes of priests, and offer for thy cleansing into witnessing to them those things that Moses bade. And he went out and began to preach and publish the word, so that now He might not go openly into the city, but be without forth in desert places. And they came to Him on all sides.

Chapter II

And eft He entered into Capernaum after eight days. And it was heard that He was in an house, and many came together, so that they might not be in the house nor at the gate. And He spoke to them the word. And there came to Him men that brought a man sick in palsy

which was borne of four. And when they might not
uncovered bring him to Jesus for the people, they unhiled the roof
where He was and opened it, and they let down the bed
in which the sick man in palsy lay. And when Jesus
had seen the faith of them, He said to the sick man in
palsy, Son, thy sins are forgiven to thee.

But there were some of the scribes, sitting and thinking in their hearts, What speaks He thus? He blasphemes. Who may forgive sins but God alone? And
when Jesus had known this by the Holy Ghost that they
thought so within themselves, He says to them, What
think ye these things in your hearts? What is lighter to
say to the sick man in palsy, Sins are forgiven to thee, or
to say, Rise, take thy bed and walk? But that ye wit that
Man's Son has power in earth to forgive sins, He said to
the sick man in palsy, I say to thee, rise up. Take thy
bed and go into thine house. And anon he rose up.
And when he had taken the bed, he went before all men
so that all men wondered and honoured God, and said,
For we saw never so!

And He went out eftsoon to the sea, and all the people came to Him. And He taught them. And when He
passed, He saw Levi of Alphaeus sitting at the tolbooth, and He said to him, Sue Me. And he rose and
sued Him.

And it was done, when He sat at the meat in His
house, many publicans and sinful men sat together at
the meat with Jesus and His disciples. For there were
many that followed Him. And scribes and Pharisees,
seeing that He ate with publicans and sinful men, said
to His disciples, Why eats and drinks your Master with
publicans and sinners?

When this was heard, Jesus said to them, Whole
men have no need to a leech, but they that are evil at ease.
For I came not to call just men, but sinners.

And the disciples of John and the Pharisees were fasting. And they came and said to Him, Why the disciples of John and the Pharisees fast, but Thy disciples
fast not?

And Jesus said to them, Whether the sons of spou-
sals moun fast as long as the spouse is with them? As *espousals, a wedding*
long time as they have the spouse with them, they moun
not fast. But days shall come when the spouse shall be
taken away from them, and then they shall fast in those
days. No man sews a patch of new cloth to an old cloth,
else he takes away the new patch from the old and a more
breaking is made. And no man puts new wine into old
bottles, else the wine shall brest the bottles, and the wine *burst*
shall be shed out and the bottles shall perish. But new
wine shall be put into new bottles.

And it was done eftsoons, when the Lord walked in
the Sabbaths by the corns, and His disciples began to
pass forth and pluck ears of the corn. And the Pharisees
said to Him, Lo, what Thy disciples do in Sabbaths
that is not leaveful? And He said to them, Read ye never
what David did when he had need, and he hungered
and they that were with him? How he went into the
house of God under Abiathar, prince of priests, and ate
loaves of proposition which it was not leaveful to eat but
to priests alone, and he gave to them that were with him?
And He said to them, The Sabbath is made for man,
and not a man for the Sabbath. And so Man's Son is
Lord also of the Sabbath.

Chapter III

And He entered eftsoon into the synagogue, and there
was a man having a dry hand. And they aspied Him, if *espied, watched*
He healed in the Sabbaths, to accuse Him. And He
said to the man that had a dry hand, Rise into the middle. And He says to them, Is it leaveful to do well in the

Sabbaths either evil? To make a soul safe either to lose? And they were still. And He beheld them about with wrath and had sorrow on the blindness of their hearts, and said to the man, Hold forth thine hand. And he held forth, and his hand was restored to him.

Soothly, Pharisees went out anon and made a counsel with Herodians against Him, how they should leese Him. But Jesus, with His disciples, went to the sea. And much people from Galilee and Judea sued Him, and from Jerusalem, and from Idumea, and from beyond Jordan, and they that were about Tyre and Sidon. A great multitude, hearing the things that He did, came to Him. And Jesus said to His disciples that *crushed, pressed,* the boat should serve Him for the people, lest they thrist *thrusted* Him, for He healed many so that they fell fast to Him to touch Him. And how many ever had sicknesses and unclean spirits, when they saw Him, fell down to Him and cried, saying, Thou art the Son of God! And *admonished, warned* greatly He menaced them that they should not make Him known.

And He went into an hill and called to Him whom He would, and they came to Him. And He made, that there were twelve with Him, to send them to preach. And He gave to them power to heal sicknesses and to cast out fiends. And to Simon, He gave a name, Peter. And He called James of Zebedee and John the brother of James, and He gave to them names, Boanerges, that is, Sons of thundering. And He called Andrew and Philip, and Bartholomew and Matthew, and Thomas and James Alphaei, and Thaddeus and Simon Canaanite, and Judas Iscariot that betrayed Him.

And they came to an house, and the people came together eftsoon so that they might not eat bread. And when His kinsmen had heard, they went out to hold *madness* Him, for they said that He is turned into woodness.

And the scribes that came down from Jerusalem said that he has Beelzebub, and that in the prince of devils He casts out fiends.

And He called them together and He said to them in parables, How may Satan cast out Satan? And if a realm be departed against itself, the ilk realm may not stand. And if an house be disparpled on itself, the ilk *cast asunder, dispersed* house may not stand. And if Satan has risen against himself, he is departed and he shall not more stand, but has an end. No man may go into a strong man's house and take away his vessels but he bind first the strong man, and then he shall spoil his house. Truly I say to you that all sins and blasphemies by which they have blasphemed, shall be forgiven to the sons of men. But he that blasphemes against the Holy Ghost has not remission into without end. But he shall be guilty of everlasting trespass. For they said, He has an unclean spirit.

And His mother and brethren came, and they stood withoutforth and sent to Him, and called Him. And the people sat about Him and they say to Him, Lo, Thy mother and Thy brethren withoutforth seek Thee. And He answered to them and said, Who is My mother and My brethren? And He beheld the ilk that sat about Him, and said, Lo, My mother and My brethren. For who that does the will of God, he is My brother and My sister, and mother.

Chapter IV

And eft Jesus began to teach at the sea. And much people were gathered to Him so that He went into a boat and sat in the sea, and all the people were about the sea on the land. And He taught them in parables many things. And He said to them in His teaching, Hear ye. Lo, a man, sowing, goes out to sow. And the while he sows, some seed fell about the way, and birds of heaven came and ate it. Other fell down on stony places where it had not much earth, and anon it sprung up, for it had not deepness of earth. And when the sun rose up, it wallowed for heat and it dried up, for it had no root. And other fell down into thorns, and thorns sprang up and strangled it, and it gave no fruit. And other fell down into good land, and gave fruit, springing up and waxing. And one brought thirtyfold, and one sixtyfold, and one an hundredfold. And He said, He that has ears of hearing, hear he.

And when He was by Himself, the twelve that were with Him asked Him to expound the parable. And He said to them, To you it is given to know the privity of the kingdom of God. But to them that are withoutforth, all things be made in parables, that they, seeing, see and see not, and they, hearing, hear and understand not, lest some time they be converted and sins be forgiven to them.

And He said to them, Know not ye this parable? And how ye shall know all parables? He that sows, sows a word. But these it is that are about the way where the word is sown. And when they have heard, anon comes Satan and takes away the word that is sown in their hearts. And in like manner are these that are sown on stony places, which when they have heard the word, anon they take it with joy. And they have not root in themselves, but they are lasting a little time. Afterward, when tribulation rises and persecution for the word, anon they are sclaundered. And there are others that are sown in thorns. These it is that hear the word, and dis-

discomfort, unease ease of the world and deceit of richesses and other charge

covetousness, greed, envy of covetise, enters and strangles the word, and it is made without fruit. And these it is that are sown on good land, which hear the word and take, and make fruit, one thirtyfold, one sixtyfold, and one an hundredfold.

And He said to them, Where a lantern comes, that it be put under a bushel or under a bed? Nay, but that it be put on a candlestick. There is nothing hid that shall not be made open, neither anything is privy that shall not come into open. If any man have ears of hearing, hear he. And He said to them, See ye what ye hear. In what measure ye mete, it shall be meted to you again and be cast to you. For it shall be given to him that has, and it shall be taken away from him that has not, also that that he has.

And He said, So the kingdom of God is as if a man cast seed into the earth and he sleeps, and it rises up night and day and brings forth seed and waxes fast while he wot not. For the earth makes fruit, first the grass, afterward the ear, and after, full fruit in the ear. And when of itself it has brought forth fruit, anon he sends a sickle, for reaping time is come.

And He said, To what thing shall we liken the kingdom of God? Or to what parable shall we comparison *compare* it? As a corn of senevy, which when it is sown in the earth, is less than all seeds that are in the earth. And when it is sprung up, it waxes into a tree and is made greater than all herbs. And it makes great branches so that birds of heaven moun dwell under the shadow thereof.

And in many such parables He spoke to them the word, as they might hear. And He spoke not to them without parable. But He expounded to His disciples all things by Himself. And He said to them in that day when evening was come, Pass we againward. And they left the people and took Him, so that He was in a boat. And other boats were with Him. And a great storm of wind was made, and cast waves into the boat so that the boat was full. And He was in the hinder part of the boat and slept on a pillow. And they raise Him and say to

Him, Master, pertains it not to Thee that we perish? And He rose up and menaced the wind, and said to the sea, Be still. Wax dumb! And the wind ceased and great peaceableness was made. And He said to them, What dread ye? Ye have no faith yet? And they dreaded with great dread, and said each to other, Who, guess thou, is this? For the wind and the sea obey to Him!

Chapter V

And they came over the sea into the country of Gaderenes. And after that He was gone out of the boat, anon a man in an unclean spirit ran out of burials to Him. Which man had an house in burials, and neither with chains now might any man bind him. For ofttimes he was bound in stocks and chains, and he had broken the chains and had broken the stocks to small gobbets, and no man might make him tame. And evermore, night and day, in burials and in hills, he was crying and beating himself with stones. And he saw Jesus afar, and ran and worshipped Him. And he cried with a great voice and said, What to me and to Thee, Thou Jesus, the Son of the highest God? I conjure Thee by God that Thou torment me not!

And Jesus said to him, Thou unclean spirit, go out from the man. And Jesus asked him, What is thy name? And he says to Him, A Legion is my name, for we are many. And he prayed Jesus much that He should not put him out of the country. And there was there about the hill a great flock of swine lesewing. And the spirits prayed Jesus and said, Send us into the swine that we enter into them. And anon, Jesus granted to them, and the unclean spirits went out and entered into the swine, and with a great bire the flock was cast down into the sea, a two thousand, and they were drowned in the sea.

And they that kept them, fled, and told into the city and into the fields, and they went out to see what was done. And they came to Jesus and saw him that had been travailed of the fiend, sitting, clothed and of a whole mind. And they dreaded. And they that saw how it was done to him that had a fiend, and of the swine, told to them. And they began to pray Him that He should go away from their coasts. And when He went up into a boat, he that was travailed of the devil, began to pray Him that he should be with Him. But Jesus received him not, but said to him, Go thou into thine house, to thine, and tell to them how great things the Lord has done to thee, and had mercy of thee. And he went forth, and began to preach in Decapolis how great things Jesus had done to him. And all men won-dered.

And when Jesus had gone up into the boat eftsoon over the sea, much people came together to Him and were about the sea. And one of the princes of synago-gues, by name Jairus, came and saw Him, and fell down at His feet and prayed Him much and said, My daughter is nigh dead. Come Thou, put Thine hand on her that she be safe and live. And He went forth with him, and much people sued Him and thrust Him. And a woman had been in the bloody flux twelve year, and had received many things of full many leeches and had spent all her good, and was nothing amended but was rather the worse. When she had heard of Jesus, she came among the people behind and touched His cloth. For she said that, If I touch, yea, His cloth, I shall be safe. And anon the well of her blood was dried up, and she felt in body that she was healed of the sickness.

And anon Jesus knew in Himself the virtue that was gone out of Him, and turned to the people and said, Who touched My clothes? And His disciples said to

Him, Thou see the people thristing Thee, and say,
Who touched Me? And Jesus looked about to see her
that had done this thing. And the woman dreaded and
quaked, witting that it was done in her, and came and
fell down before Him, and said to Him all the truth.
And Jesus said to her, Daughter, thy faith has made
thee safe. Go in peace, and be thou whole of thy sick‑
ness.

Yet while He spoke, messengers came to the prince
of the synagogue and say, Thy daughter is dead. What
travail thou the Master further? But when the word was
heard that was said, Jesus said to the prince of the syna‑
gogue, Nil thou dread. Only believe thou. And He
took no man to sue Him but Peter and James and John,
the brother of James. And they came into the house of
the prince of the synagogue. And He saw noise and
men weeping and wailing much. And He went in and
said to them, What are ye troubled and weep? The dam‑
sel is not dead, but sleeps. And they scorned Him. But
when all were put out, He takes the father and the
mother of the damsel, and them that were with Him,
and they enter where the damsel lay. And He held the
hand of the damsel and said to her, Tabitha cumi, that
is to say, Damsel, I say to thee, arise. And anon the
damsel rose and walked, and she was of twelve year.
amazed, astounded And they were abashed with great stonying. And He
astonishment, wonder commanded to them greatly that no man should wit it.
And He commanded to give her meat.

Chapter VI

And He went out from thence and went into His own
country, and His disciples followed Him. And when
the Sabbath was come, Jesus began to teach in a synago‑
gue. And many heard and wondered in His teaching,
and said, Of whence to this all things? And what is the

wisdom that is given to Him, and such virtues which
are made by His hands? Whether this is not a carpenter,
the son of Mary, the brother of James and of Joseph, and
of Judas and of Simon? Whether His sisters are not here
with us? And they were sclaundered in Him.

And Jesus said to them that, A prophet is not without honour but in his own country, and among his kin
and in his house. And He might not do there any virtue,
save that He healed a few sick men, laying on them His
hands. And He wondered for the unbelief of them.

And He went about castles on each side, and taught.
And He called together twelve, and began to send them
by two together, and gave to them power of unclean spirits, and commanded them that they should not take anything in the way but a yard only; not a scrip nor bread,
neither money in the girdle, but shod with sandals, and
that they should not be clothed with two coats. And He
said to them, Whitherever ye enter into an house, dwell
ye there till ye go out from thence. And whoever receives
you not, nor hears you, go ye out from thence and shake
away the powder from your feet into witnessing to them. *dust*

And they went forth and preached that men should
do penance. And they cast out many fiends and
anointed with oil many sick men, and they were healed.
And king Herod heard, for His name was made open,
and said that John Baptist has risen again from death,
and therefore virtues work in him. Others said that it is
Elijah. But others said that it is a prophet, as one of prophets.

And when this thing was heard, Herod said, This
John, whom I have beheaded, is risen again from death.
For the ilk Herod sent and held John, and bound him
into prison for Herodias, the wife of Philip, his brother,
for he had wedded her. For John said to Herod, It is not
leaveful to thee to have the wife of thy brother. And

Herodias laid aspies to him, and would slay him and might not. And Herod dreaded John, and knew him a just man and holy, and kept him. And Herod heard him, and he did many things and gladly heard him.

fit, convenient, suitable   And when a covenable day was fallen, Herod in his birthday made a supper to the princes and tribunes, and to the greatest of Galilee. And when the daughter of the ilk Herodias was come in, and danced and pleased to Herod, and also to men that sat at the meat, the king said to the damsel, Ask thou of me what thou will, and I shall give to thee. And he swore to her that, Whatever thou ask, I shall give to thee though it be half my kingdom.

And when she had gone out, she said to her mother, What shall I ask? And she said, The head of John Baptist. And when she was come in anon with haste to the king, she asked and said, I will that anon thou give to me in a dish the head of John Baptist. And the king *true* was very sorry for the oath. And for men that sat together at the meat he would not make her sorry, but sent a manqueller and commanded that John's head were brought in a dish. And he beheaded him in the prison and brought his head in a dish, and gave it to the damsel, and the damsel gave to her mother. And when this thing was heard, his disciples came and took his body, and laid it in a burial.

And the apostles came together to Jesus and told to Him all things that they had done and taught. And He said to them, Come ye by yourselves into a desert place and rest ye a little. For there were many that came and went again, and they had not space to eat. And they went into a boat and went into a desert place by themselves. And they saw Him go away and many knew, and they went afoot from all cities and ran thither, and came before them. And Jesus went out and saw much people, and had ruth on them, for they were as sheep not having a shepherd. And He began to teach them many things.

And when it was forth-days, His disciples came and *late in the day* said, This is a desert place and the time is now passed. Let them go into the next towns and villages to buy them meat to eat. And He answered and said to them, Give ye to them to eat. And they said to Him, Go we, and buy we loaves with two hundred pence, and we shall give to them to eat? And He says to them, How many loaves have ye? Go ye and see. And when they had known, they say, Five, and two fishes. And He commanded to them that they should make all men sit to meat by companies on green hay. And they sat down by parties, by hundreds and by fifties. And when He had taken the five loaves and two fishes, He beheld into heaven and blessed, and broke loaves, and gave to His disciples that they should set before them. And He departed two fishes to all, and all ate and were fulfilled. And they took the relifs of broken meats twelve coffins-ful, and of the fishes. And they that ate were five thou-sand of men.

And anon He made His disciples to go up into a boat to pass before Him over the sea to Bethsaida the while He left the people. And when He had left them, He went into an hill to pray. And when it was evening, the boat was in the middle of the sea, and He alone in the land. And He saw them travailing in rowing, for the wind was contrary to them. And about the fourth waking of the night, He wandered on the sea and came *walked* to them, and would pass them. And as they saw Him wandering on the sea, they guessed that it were a phan-tom and cried out, for all saw Him and they were afraid. And anon He spoke with them, and said to them, Trust ye, I am. Nil ye dread. And He came up to them into the boat, and the wind ceased. And they wondered more within themselves, for they understood not of the loaves, for their heart was blinded.

And when they were passed over the sea, they came into the land of Gennesaret and set to land. And when they were gone out of the boat, anon they knew Him, and they ran through all that country and began to bring sick men in beds on each side where they heard that He was. And whitherever He entered into villages, either into towns or into cities, they set sick men in streets and prayed Him that they should touch namely the hem of His cloth. And how many that touched Him were made safe.

Chapter VII

And the Pharisees and some of the scribes came from Jerusalem together to Him. And when they had seen some of His disciples eat bread with unwashed hands, they blamed. The Pharisees and all the Jews eat not but they wash often their hands, holding the traditions of elder men. And when they turn again from cheaping, they eat not but they wash. And many other things are, that are taken to them to keep, washing of cups and of water vessels, and of vessels of brass and of beds. And Pharisees and scribes asked Him and said, Why go not Thy disciples after the tradition of elder men, but with unwashed hands they eat bread?

And He answered and said to them, Isaiah prophesied well of you hypocrites. As it is written, These people worship Me with lips, but their heart is far from Me. And in vain they worship Me, teaching the doctrines *behests, precepts* and the hests of men. For ye leave the commandment of God and hold the traditions of men, washing of water vessels and of cups. And many other things like to these ye do. And He said to them, Well, ye have made the commandment of God void to keep your tradition. For Moses said, Worship thy father and thy mother, and he that curses father or mother, die he by death. But ye say, If a man say to father or mother, Corban, that is, Whatever gift is of me, it shall profit to thee. And over ye suffer not him to do anything to father or mother. And ye break the word of God by your tradition that ye have given. And ye do many such things.

And He eftsoon called the people, and said to them, Ye all hear Me and understand. Nothing that is without a man that enters into him, may defoul him. But those things that come forth of a man, those it is that defoul a man. If any man have ears of hearing, hear he.

And when He was entered into an house from the people, His disciples asked Him the parable. And He said to them, Ye are unwise also? Understand ye not that all thing withoutforth that enters into a man may not defoul him? For it has not entered into his heart, but into his womb, and beneath it goes out, purging all meats. But He said, The things that go out of a man, those defoul a man. For from within of the heart of men come forth evil thoughts, advowtries, fornications, man-slayings, thefts, avarice, wickednesses, guile, unchas-tity, evil eye, blasphemies, pride, folly. All these evils come forth from within and defoul a man.

And Jesus rose up from thence and went into the coasts of Tyre and Sidon. And He went into an house and would that no man wist. And He might not be hid, for a woman, anon as she heard of Him, whose daugh-ter had an unclean spirit, entered and fell down at His feet. And the woman was heathen, of the generation of Syro-Phoenicia. And she prayed Him that He would cast out a devil from her daughter. And He said to her, Suffer thou that the children be fulfilled first. For it is not good to take the bread of children and give to hounds.

And she answered and said to Him, Yes, Lord, for little whelps eat under the board of the crumbs of children.
And Jesus said to her, Go thou. For this word, the fiend
went out of thy daughter. And when she was gone into
her house, home, she found the damsel lying on the bed,
and the devil gone out of her.

And eftsoons Jesus went out from the coasts of Tyre,
and came through Sidon to the sea of Galilee, betwixt
the middle of the coasts of Decapolis. And they bring to
Him a man deaf and dumb, and prayed Him to lay His
hand on him. And He took him asides from the people
and put His fingers into his ears, and He spat and
touched his tongue. And He beheld into heaven and
sorrowed within, and said, Ephphasa! That is, Be thou
opened! And anon his ears were opened and the bond
of his tongue was unbound, and he spoke rightly. And
He commanded to them that they should say to no man.
But how much He commanded to them, so much more
they preached, and by so much more they wondered
and said, He did well all things, and He made deaf men
to hear and dumb men to speak!

Chapter VIII

In those days, eft, when much people were with Jesus
and had not what they should eat, when His disciples
were called together He said to them, I have ruth on the
people, for lo, now the third day they abide Me and have
not what to eat. And if I leave them fasting into their
house, they shall fail in the way, for some of them came
from far. And His disciples answered to Him,
be able to Whereof shall a man mow fill them with loaves here in
wilderness? And He asked them, How many loaves
have ye? Which said, Seven.

And He commanded the people to sit down on the
earth. And He took the seven loaves and did thankings,

and broke and gave to His disciples that they should set forth. And they set forth to the people. And they had a few small fishes, and He blessed them and commanded that they were set forth. And they ate and were fulfilled, and they took up that that left of relifs, seven leeps. And they that ate were as four thousand men, and He left them.

And anon He went up into a boat with His disciples, and came into the coasts of Dalmanutha. And the Pharisees went out and began to dispute with Him, and asked a token of Him from heaven, and tempted Him. And He, sorrowing within spirit, said, What seeks this generation a token? Truly I say to you, a token shall not be given to this generation. And He left them and went up eftsoon into a boat, and went over the sea.

And they forgot to take bread, and they had not with them but one loaf in the boat. And He commanded them and said, See ye and beware of the sourdough of Pharisees and of the sourdough of Herod. And they thought and said one to another, For we have not loaves. And when this thing was known, Jesus said to them, What think ye, for ye have not loaves? Yet ye know not, nor understand. Yet ye have your hearts blinded. Ye, having eyes, see not, and ye, having ears, hear not. Neither ye have mind when I broke five loaves among five thousand. And how many coffinsful of broken meat ye took up? They say to Him, Twelve. When also seven loaves among four thousand of men, how many leeps of broken meat took ye up? And they say to Him, Seven. And He said to them, How understand ye not yet?

And they came to Bethsaida, and they bring to Him a blind man. And they prayed Him that He should touch him. And when He had taken the blind man's hand, He led him out of the street and spat into his eyes, and set His hands on him, and He asked him if he saw anything. And he beheld and said, I see men as trees walking. Afterward eftsoons He set His hands on his eyes and he began to see, and he was restored so that he saw clearly all things. And He sent him into his house and said, Go into thine house, and if thou goes into the street, say to no man.

And Jesus entered, and His disciples, into the castles of Caesarea of Philip. And in the way He asked His disciples and said to them, Whom say men that I am? Which answered to Him and said, Some say John Baptist, others say Elijah, and others say as one of the prophets. Then He says to them, But whom say ye that I am? Peter answered and said to Him, Thou art Christ. And He charged them that they should not say of Him to any man. And He began to teach them that it behoves Man's Son to suffer many things and to be reproved of the elder men and of the highest priests and the scribes, and to be slain and after three days to rise again. And He spoke plainly the word. And Peter took Him and began to blame Him, and said, Lord, be Thou merciful to Thee, for this shall not be. And He turned and saw His disciples and menaced Peter, and said, Go after Me, Satan, for thou savours not those things that are of God, but those things that are of man.

And when the people were called together with His disciples, He said to them, If any man will come after Me, deny he himself and take his cross, and sue he Me. For he that will make safe his life, shall leese it. And he that leeses his life for Me, shall make it safe. For what profits it to a man if he win all the world and do pairing to his soul? Or what changing shall a man give for his soul? But who that acknowledges Me and My words in this generation advowtrous and sinful, also Man's Son shall acknowledge him when He shall come in the glory of His Father with His angels. And He said to them, Truly I say to you that there are some standing here which shall not taste death till they see the realm of God coming in virtue.

Chapter IX

And after six days, Jesus took Peter and James and John, and led them by Himself alone into an high hill, and He was transfigured before them. And His clothes were made full shining and white as snow, which manner white clothes a fuller may not make on earth. And Elijah with Moses appeared to them, and they spoke with Jesus. And Peter answered and said to Jesus, Master, it is good us to be here. And make we here three tabernacles, one to Thee, one to Moses and one to Elijah. For he wist not what he should say, for they were aghast by dread. And there was made a cloud overshadowing them, and a Voice came of the cloud, and said, This is My most dearworth Son. Hear ye Him. And anon they beheld about, and saw no more any man, but Jesus only with them.

And when they came down from the hill, He commanded them that they should not tell to any man those things that they had seen but when Man's Son has risen again from death. And they held the word at themselves seeking what this should be, when He had risen again from death. And they asked Him and said, What then say the Pharisees and scribes, for it behoves Elijah to come first? And He answered and said to them, When Elijah comes, he shall first restore all things, and, as it is written of Man's Son, that he suffer many things and be despised. And I say to you that Elijah is come and they did to him whatever things they would, as it is written of him.

And He, coming to His disciples, saw a great com-

pany about them, and scribes disputing with them.
And anon, all the people, seeing Jesus, were astonied,
and they dreaded. And they, running, greeted Him.
And He asked them, What dispute ye among you?
And one of the company answered and said, Master, I
have brought to Thee my son that has a dumb spirit.
And wherever he takes him, he hurtles him down and
he foams, and beats together with teeth and waxes dry.
And I said to Thy disciples that they should cast him
out, and they might not.

And He answered to them and said, Ah, thou generation out of belief! How long shall I be among you?
How long shall I suffer you? Bring ye him to Me. And
they brought him. And when He had seen him, anon
the spirit troubled him and was thrown down to
ground, and wallowed and foamed. And He asked his
since father, How long is it sith this has fallen to him? And
he said, From childhood. And often he has put him
into fire and into water to leese him. But if Thou may
anything, help us, and have mercy on us! And Jesus
said to him, If thou may believe, all things are possible
to man that believes. And anon the father of the child
cried with tears, and said, Lord, I believe. Lord, help
Thou mine unbelief.

And when Jesus had seen the people running
together, He menaced the unclean spirit and said to
him, Thou deaf and dumb spirit, I command thee. Go
out from him and enter no more into him! And he, crying and much tobraiding him, went out from him, and
he was made as dead so that many said that he was dead.
And Jesus held his hand and lifted him up, and he rose.
And when He had entered into an house, His disciples
asked Him privily, Why might not we cast him out?
And He said to them, This kind in no thing may go
out, but in prayer and fasting.

And they went from thence and went forth into Galilee, and they would not that any man wist. And He taught His disciples and said to them, For Man's Son shall be betrayed into the hands of men, and they shall slay Him. And He, slain, shall rise again on the third day. And they knew not the word and dreaded to ask Him.

And they came to Capernaum. And when they were in the house, He asked them, What treated ye in the way? And they were still, for they disputed among them in the way who of them should be greatest. And He sat and called the twelve, and said to them, If any man will be the first among you, he shall be the last of all and the minister of all. And He took a child, and set him in the middle of them. And when He had beclipped him, He *cuddled, embraced* said to them, Whoever receives one of such children in My name, he receives Me. And whoever receives Me, he receives not Me alone, but Him that sent Me.

John answered to Him and said, Master, we saw one casting out fiends in Thy name, which sues not us, and we have forbidden him. And Jesus said, Nil ye forbid him, for there is no man that does virtue in My name and may soon speak evil of Me. He that is not against us, is for us. And whoever gives you a cup of cold water to drink in My name for ye are of Christ, truly I say to you, he shall not leese his meed. And whoever shall sclaunder one of these little that believes in Me, it were better to him that a millstone of asses were done about his neck and he were cast into the sea. And if thine hand sclaunder thee, cut it away. It is better to thee to enter feeble into life than have two hands and go into hell, into fire that never shall be quenched, where the worm of them dies not and the fire is not quenched. And if thy foot sclaunder thee, cut it off. It is better to thee to enter crooked into everlasting life, than have two feet and be

sent into hell of fire that never shall be quenched, where
the worm of them dies not and the fire is not quenched.
That if thine eye sclaunder thee, cast it out. It is better to
half blind thee to enter goggle-eyed into the realm of God than have
two eyes and be sent into hell of fire, where the worm of
them dies not and the fire is not quenched. And every
man shall be salted with fire, and every slain sacrifice
shall be made savoury with salt. Salt is good. If salt be
unsavoury, in what thing shall ye make it savoury?
Have ye salt among you, and have ye peace among you.

Chapter X

And Jesus rose up from thence and came into the coasts
of Judea over Jordan. And eftsoons the people came
together to Him, and as He was wont, eftsoon He
taught them. And the Pharisees came and asked Him
whether it be leaveful to a man to leave his wife. And
they tempted Him. And He answered and said to them,
What commanded Moses to you? And they said,
Moses suffered to write a libel of forsaking, and to forsake. To which Jesus answered and said, For the hardness of your heart Moses wrote to you this
commandment. But from the beginning of creature
God made them male and female, and said, For this
thing a man shall leave his father and mother and shall
draw to his wife, and they shall be twain in one flesh.
And so now they are not twain, but one flesh. Therefore
that thing that God joined together, no man depart.

And eftsoon in the house, His disciples asked Him
of the same thing, and He said to them, Whoever leaves
his wife and weds another, he does advowtry on her.
And if the wife leave her husband and be wedded to
another man, she does lechery.

And they brought to Him little children, that He
should touch them. And the disciples threatened the

men that brought them. And when Jesus had seen them, He bore heavy and said to them, Suffer ye little children to come to Me and forbid them not, for of such is the kingdom of God. Truly I say to you, whoever receives not the kingdom of God as a little child, he shall not enter into it. And He beclipped them and laid His hands on them, and blessed them.

And when Jesus was gone out in the way, a man ran before and kneeled before Him, and prayed Him and said, Good Master, what shall I do that I receive everlasting life? And Jesus said to him, What say thou that I am good? There is no man good but God Himself. Thou knows the commandments, Do thou none advowtry; slay not; steal not; say not false witnessing; do no fraud; worship thy father and thy mother. And he answered and said to Him, Master, I have kept all these things from my youth. And Jesus beheld him and loved him, and said to him, One thing fails thee. Go thou, and sell all things that thou has and give to poor men, and thou shall have treasure in heaven. And come, sue thou Me. And he was full sorry in the word, and went away mourning, for he had many possessions.

And Jesus beheld about and said to His disciples, How hard they that have richesses shall enter into the kingdom of God. And the disciples were astonied in His words. And Jesus eftsoon answered and said to them, Ye little children, how hard it is for men that trust in richesses to enter into the kingdom of God. It is lighter a camel to pass through a needle's eye than a rich man to enter into the kingdom of God. And they wondered more, and said among themselves, And who may be saved? And Jesus beheld them and said, Anents men it is impossible, but not anents God, for all things be possible anents God.

And Peter began to say to Him, Lo, we have left all

things and have sued Thee. Jesus answered and said, Truly I say to you, there is no man that leaves house or brethren, or sisters, or father or mother, or children or fields for Me and for the gospel, which shall not take an hundredfold so much now in this time, houses and brethren, and sisters and mothers, and children and fields with persecutions, and in the world to coming, everlasting life. But many shall be, the first the last and the last the first.

And they were in the way going up to Jerusalem, and Jesus went before them, and they wondered, and followed, and dreaded. And eftsoon Jesus took the twelve and began to say to them what things were to come to Him. For lo, we stye to Jerusalem, and Man's Son shall be betrayed to the princes of priests and to scribes, and to the elder men. And they shall damn Him by death, and they shall take Him to heathen men. *spit at* And they shall scorn Him and bespit Him and beat Him, and they shall slay Him. And in the third day, He shall rise again.

And James and John, Zebedee's sons, came to Him and said, Master, we will that whatever we ask, Thou does to us. And He said to them, What will ye that I do to you? And they said, Grant to us that we sit the t'one at Thy right half and the t'other at Thy left half, in Thy glory. And Jesus said to them, Ye wit not what ye ask. Moun ye drink the cup which I shall drink? Or be washed with the baptism in which I am baptized? And they said to Him, We moun. And Jesus said to them, Ye shall drink the cup that I drink, and ye shall be washed with the baptism in which I am baptized. But to sit at My right half or left half is not Mine to give to you, but to which it is made ready.

And the ten heard and began to have indignation of James and John. But Jesus called them and said to

them, Ye wit that they that seem to have princehood of
folks, are lords of them, and the princes of them have *rulers of the people*
power of them. But it is not so among you. But whoever
will be made greater, shall be your minister. And whoever will be the first among you, shall be servant of all.
For why, Man's Son came not that it should be ministered to Him, but that He should minister, and give His
life again-buying for many.   *ransom, redemption*

And they came to Jericho. And when He went forth
from Jericho, and His disciples and a full much people,
Bartimaeus, a blind man, the son of Timaeus, sat beside
the way and begged. And when he heard that it is Jesus
of Nazareth, he began to cry and say, Jesus, the Son of
David, have mercy on me! And many threatened him
that he should be still. And he cried much the more,
Jesus, the Son of David, have mercy on me! And Jesus
stood, and commanded him to be called. And they
called the blind man and said to him, Be thou of better
heart. Rise up. He calls thee. And he cast away his cloth
and skipped and came to Him. And Jesus answered
and said to him, What will thou that I shall do to thee?
The blind man said to him, Master, that I see! Jesus
said to him, Go thou. Thy faith has made thee safe.
And anon he saw, and sued Him in the way.

Chapter XI

And when Jesus came nigh to Jerusalem and to
Bethany, to the mount of Olives, He sends twain of His
disciples and says to them, Go ye into the castle that is
against you, and anon as ye enter there ye shall find a colt
tied on which no man has sat yet. Untie ye and bring
him. And if any man say anything to you, What do ye?
say ye that he is needful to the Lord, and anon he shall
leave him hither.

And they went forth and found a colt tied before the

gate withoutforth, in the meeting of two ways. And they untied him. And some of them that stood there said to them, What do ye, untying the colt? And they said to them as Jesus commanded them, and they left it to them. And they brought the colt to Jesus, and they laid on him their clothes, and Jesus sat on him. And many strewed their clothes in the way. Other men cut down branches from trees, and strewed in the way. And they that went before and that sued, cried and said, Hosanna! Blessed is He that comes in the name of the Lord. Blessed be the kingdom of our father David that is come. Hosanna in the highest things!

And He entered into Jerusalem into the Temple, and when He had seen all thing about, when it was eve‑ning He went out into Bethany with the twelve. And another day, when He went out of Bethany, He hun‑gered. And when He had seen a fig tree afar, having *by chance* leaves, He came, if happily He should find anything thereon. And when He came to it, He found nothing, out‑taken leaves, for it was not time of figs. And Jesus answered and said to it, Now never eat any man fruit of thee more. And His disciples heard, and they came to Jerusalem.

And when He was entered into the Temple, He began to cast out sellers and beggars in the Temple. And He turned upsedown the boards of changers and the chairs of men that sold culvers. And He suffered not that any man should bear a vessel through the Temple. And He taught them and said, Whether it is not written that Mine house shall be called the house of praying to all folks? But ye have made it a den of thieves! And when this thing was heard, the princes of priests and scribes sought how they should leese Him, for they dreaded Him, for all the people wondered on His teaching.

And when evening was come, He went out of the city. And as they passed forth early, they saw the fig tree made dry from the roots. And Peter bethought him, and said to Him, Master, lo, the fig tree whom Thou cursed is dried up. And Jesus answered and said to him, Have ye the faith of God. Truly I say to you that whoever says to this hill, Be thou taken and cast into the sea, and doubts not in his heart but believes that what'ever he says shall be done, it shall be done to him. Therefore I say to you, all things, whatever things ye praying shall ask, believe ye that ye shall take, and they shall come to you. And when ye shall stand to pray, forgive ye if ye have anything against any man, that your Father that is in heavens forgive to you your sins. And if ye forgive not, neither your Father that is in heavens shall forgive to you your sins.

And eftsoon they came to Jerusalem. And when He walked in the Temple, the highest priests and scribes, and the elder men, came to Him and say to Him, In what power does Thou these things? Or who gave to Thee this power that Thou does these things? Jesus answered and said to them, And I shall ask you one word, and answer ye to Me, and I shall say to you in what power I do these things. Whether was the baptism of John, of heaven or of men? Answer ye to Me. And they thought within themselves, saying, If we say of hea'ven, He shall say to us, Why then believe ye not to him? If we say of men, we dread the people, for all men had John that he was verily a prophet. And they answered and said to Jesus, We wit never. And Jesus answered and said to them, Neither I say to you in what power I do these things.

Chapter XII

And Jesus began to speak to them in parables. A man

planted a vineyard and set an hedge about it, and dalf a
farmers, growers lake and built a tower, and hired it to tillers and went
forth in pilgrimage. And he sent to the earth⁄tillers in
time a servant to receive of the earth⁄tillers of the fruit of
the vineyard. And they took him and beat, and left him
void. And eftsoon he sent to them another servant, and
they wounded him in the head and tormented him.
And eftsoon he sent another and they slew him, and
others more, beating some and slaying others. But yet he
had a most dearworth son, and he sent him last to them,
and said, Peradventure they shall dread my son. But the
earth⁄tillers said together, This is the heir. Come ye, slay
we him, and the heritage shall be ours. And they took
him and killed, and cast out without the vineyard.
Then what shall the lord of the vineyard do? He shall
come and leese the tillers and give the vineyard to others.
Whether ye have not read this Scripture, The stone
which the builders have despised, this is made into the
head of the corner? This thing is done of the Lord, and
is wonderful in our eyes.

And they sought to hold Him, and they dreaded the
people, for they knew that to them He said this parable.
And they left Him and they went away. And they sent
to Him some of the Pharisees and Herodians to take
Him in word. Which came and say to Him, Master, we
wit that Thou are soothfast and reckon not of any man.
For neither Thou beholds into the face of man, but
Thou teaches the way of God in truth. Is it leaveful that
tribute be given to the emperor, or we shall not give?
Which, witting their privy falseness, said to them,
What tempt ye Me? Bring ye to Me a penny that I see.
And they brought to Him. And He said to them,
Whose is this image and the writing? They say to Him,
The emperor's. And Jesus answered and said to them,
Then yield ye to the emperor those things that are of the

emperor's, and to God those things that are of God. And they wondered of Him.

And Sadducees, that say that there is no resurrection, came to Him and asked Him, and said, Master, Moses wrote to us that if the brother of a man were dead, and left his wife, and had no sons, his brother take his wife and raise up seed to his brother. Then seven brethren there were, and the first took a wife and died, and left no seed. And the second took her and he died, and neither this left seed. And the third also. And in like manner the seven took her, and left not seed. And the woman, the last of all, is dead. Then in the resurrection, when they shall rise again, whose wife of these shall she be? For seven had her to wife.

And Jesus answered and said to them, Whether ye err not therefore, that ye know not Scriptures neither the virtue of God? For when they shall rise again from death, neither they shall wed neither shall be wed, but they shall be as angels of God in heavens. And of dead men that they rise again, have ye not read in the book of Moses on the bush, how God spoke to him and said, I am God of Abraham, and God of Isaac, and God of Jacob? He is not God of dead men, but of living men. Therefore ye err much.

And one of the scribes that had heard them disputing together, came nigh and saw that Jesus had well answered them, and asked Him which was the first commandment of all. And Jesus answered to him that the first commandment of all is, Hear, thou Israel, thy Lord God is one God, and thou shall love thy Lord God of all thine heart, and of all thy soul, and of all thy mind, and of all thy might. This is the first commandment. And the second is like to this, Thou shall love thy neighbour as thyself. There is none other commandment greater than these.

And the scribe said to Him, Master, in truth Thou has well said, for one God is, and there is none other out-taken Him. That He be loved of all the heart and of all the mind, and of all the understanding and of all the soul, and of all strength, and to love the neighbour as himself, is greater than all burnt offerings and sacrifices. And Jesus, seeing that he had answered wisely, said to him, Thou are not far from the kingdom of God. And then no man dared ask Him no more anything.

And Jesus answered and said, teaching in the Temple, How say scribes that Christ is the Son of David? For David himself said in the Holy Ghost, The Lord said to my Lord, Sit on My right half till I put Thine enemies the stool of Thy feet. Then David himself calls Him Lord. How then is He his Son? And much people gladly heard Him. And He said to them in His teaching, Be ye ware of scribes that will wander in stoles and be saluted in cheaping, and sit in synagogues in the first chairs and the first sitting-places in suppers, which devour the houses of widows under colour of long prayer. They shall take the longer doom.

And Jesus, sitting against the treasury, beheld how the people cast money into the treasury, and many rich men cast many things. But when a poor widow was *coins of very small value, mites* come, she cast two minutes, that is, a farthing. And He called together His disciples and said to them, Truly I say to you that this poor widow cast more than all that cast into the treasury. For all cast of that thing that they had plenty of. But this of her poverty cast all things that she had, all her livelihood.

Chapter XIII

And when He went out of the Temple, one of His disciples said to Him, Master, behold what manner stones, and what manner buildings! And Jesus answered and said to him, See thou all these great buildings? There shall not be left a stone on a stone which shall not be destroyed.

And when He sat in the mount of Olives against the Temple, Peter and James and John and Andrew asked Him by themselves, Say Thou to us when these things shall be done, and what token shall be when all these things shall begin to be ended.

And Jesus answered and began to say to them, Look ye that no man deceive you. For many shall come in My name saying that, I am, and they shall deceive many. And when ye hear battles and opinions of battles, dread ye not, for it behoves these things to be done, but not yet anon is the end. For folk shall rise on folk and realm on realm, and earthmovings and hunger shall be by places. These things shall be beginnings of sorrows. But see ye yourselves, for they shall take you in councils and ye shall be beaten in synagogues, and ye shall stand before kings and doomsmen for Me, in witnessing to them. And it behoves that the gospel be first preached among all folk.

And when they take you and lead you forth, nil ye before think what ye shall speak. But speak ye that thing that shall be given to you in that hour, for ye are not the speakers, but the Holy Ghost. For a brother shall betake the brother into death, and the father the son. And sons shall rise together against fathers and mothers, and punish them by death. And ye shall be in hate to all men for My name. But he that lasts into the end shall be safe.

But when ye shall see the abomination of discomfort standing where it owes not, he that reads understand, then they that are in Judea flee into hills. And he that is above the roof, come not down into the house, neither enter he to take anything of his house. And he that shall be in the field turn not again behind to take his cloth.

But woe to them that are with child and nourish in those days. Therefore pray ye that they be not done in winter. But the ilk days of tribulation shall be such, which manner were not from the beginning of creature, which God has made, till now, neither shall be. And but the Lord had abridged those days, all flesh had not been safe. But for the chosen which He chose, the Lord has made short the days.

And then, if any man say to you, Lo, here is Christ, lo there, believe ye not. For false Christs and false prophets shall rise and shall give tokens and wonders to deceive, if it may be done, yea, them that are chosen. Therefore take ye keep. Lo, I have before said to you all things. But in those days, after that tribulation, the sun shall be made dark and the moon shall not give her light, and the stars of heaven shall fall down, and the virtues that are in heavens shall be moved. And then they shall see Man's Son coming in clouds of heaven with great virtue and glory. And then He shall send His angels, and shall gather His chosen from the four winds, from the highest thing of earth till to the highest thing of heaven. But of the fig tree learn ye the parable. When now his branch is tender and leaves are sprung out, ye know that summer is nigh. So when ye see these things be done, wit ye that it is nigh in the doors. Truly I say to you that this generation shall not pass away till all these things be done. Heaven and earth shall pass, but My words shall not pass.

But of that day or hour no man wot, neither angels in heaven, neither the Son, but the Father. See ye. Wake ye. And pray ye, for ye wit not when the time is. For as a man that is gone far in pilgrimage, left his house and gave to his servants power of every work, and commanded to the porter that he wake. Therefore wake ye, for ye wit not when the Lord of the house comes, in the eventide or at midnight, or at cock's crowing, or in the morning. Lest when He comes suddenly, He find you sleeping. Forsooth, that that I say to you, I say to all. Wake ye!

Chapter XIV

Pasch, and the feast of therf loaves, was after two days. And the highest priests and scribes sought how they should hold Him with guile, and slay. But they said, Not in the feast day, lest peradventure a noise were made among the people.

And when He was at Bethany, in the house of Simon Leprous, and rested, a woman came that had a box of alabaster of precious ointment, spikenard. And when the box of alabaster was broken, she held it on His head. But there were some that bore it heavily within themselves, and said, Whereto is this loss of ointment made? For this ointment might have been sold more than for three hundred pence, and be given to poor men. And they groaned against her.

But Jesus said, Suffer ye her. What are ye heavy to her? She has wrought a good work in Me. For evermore ye shall have poor men with you, and when ye will, ye moun do well to them. But ye shall not evermore have Me. She did that that she had. She came before to anoint My body into burying. Truly I say to you, wherever this gospel be preached in all the world, and that that this woman has done, shall be told into mind of him.

And Judas Iscariot, one of the twelve, went to the highest priests to betray Him to them. And they heard and joyed, and behight to give him money. And he sought how he should betray Him covenably.

And the first day of therf loaves, when they offered Pasch, the disciples say to Him, Whither will Thou that we go and make ready to Thee, that Thou eat the

Pasch? And He sends twain of His disciples and says to them, Go ye into the city, and a man bearing a gallon of water shall meet you. Sue ye him. And whitherever he enters, say ye to the lord of the house, Where is Mine eating-place where I shall eat Pasch with My disciples? And he shall show you to a great supping-place arrayed, and there make ye ready to us. And His disciples went forth and came into the city, and found as He had said to them. And they made ready the Pasch.

And when the eventide was come, He came with the twelve. And when they sat at the meat and ate, Jesus said, Truly I say to you that one of you that eats with Me shall betray Me. And they began to be sorry and to say to Him, each by himself, Whether I? Which said to them, One of twelve that puts the hand with Me in the *truly* platter. And soothly, Man's Son goes as it is written of Him. But woe to that man by whom Man's Son shall be betrayed. It were good to him if the ilk man had not been born.

And while they ate, Jesus took bread and blessed, and broke and gave to them, and said, Take ye. This is My body. And when He had taken the cup, He did thankings and gave to them, and all drank thereof. And He said to them, This is My blood of the New Testament which shall be shed for many. Truly I say to you, for now I shall not drink of this fruit of vine into that day when I shall drink it new in the realm of God.

And when the hymn was said, they went out into the hill of Olives. And Jesus said to them, All ye shall be sclaundered in Me this night, for it is written, I shall smite the Shepherd, and the sheep of the flock shall be disparpled. But after that I shall rise again, I shall go before you into Galilee. And Peter said to Him, Though all shall be sclaundered, but not I. And Jesus said to him, Truly I say to thee that today, before the cock in this night crow twice, thou shall thrice deny Me. But he said more, Though it behoves that I die together with Thee, I shall not forsake Thee! And in like manner, all said.

And they came into a place whose name is Gethsemane. And He said to His disciples, Sit ye here while I pray. And He took Peter and James and John with Him, and began to dread and to be annoyed. And *hurt, trouble* He said to them, My soul is sorrowful to the death. Abide ye here and wake ye with Me. And when He was gone forth a little, He fell down on the earth and prayed that, if it might be, that the hour should pass from Him. And He said, Abba, Father, all things are possible to Thee. Bear over from Me this cup. But not that I will, but that Thou will be done.

And He came and found them sleeping. And He said to Peter, Simon, sleeps thou? Might thou not wake with Me one hour? Wake ye and pray ye, that ye enter not into temptation. For the spirit is ready, but the flesh is sick. And eftsoon He went and prayed and said the same word, and turned again eftsoon and found them sleeping, for their eyes were heavied. And they knew not what they should answer to Him. And He came the third time and said to them, Sleep ye now and rest ye. It suffices. The hour is come. Lo, Man's Son shall be betrayed into the hands of sinful men. Rise ye. Go we. Lo, he that shall betray Me is nigh!

And yet while He spoke, Judas Iscariot, one of the twelve, came, and with him much people with swords and staves, sent from the highest priests and the scribes, and from the elder men. And His traitor had given to them a token, and said, Whomever I kiss, He it is. Hold ye Him and lead ye warily. And when he came, anon he came to Him and said, Master! And he kissed Him. And they laid hands on Him and held Him.

But one of the men that stood about, drew out a sword and smote the servant of the highest priest, and cut off his ear. And Jesus answered and said to them, As to a thief ye have gone out with swords and staves to take Me. Day by day I was among you and taught in the Temple, and ye held not Me, but that the Scriptures be fulfilled. Then all His disciples forsook Him and fled. But a young man, clothed with linen cloth on the bare, sued Him, and they held him. And he left the linen clothing and fled naked away from them.

And they led Jesus to the highest priest, and all the priests and scribes and elder men came together. But Peter sued Him afar into the hall of the highest priest, and he sat with the ministers and warmed him at the fire.

And the highest priests and all the council sought witnessing against Jesus to take Him to the death, but they found not. For many said false witnessing against Him, and the witnesses were not covenable. And some rise up and bore false witnessing against Him, and said, For we have heard Him saying, I shall undo this Temple made with hands, and after the third day I shall build another not made with hands. And the witnessing of them was not covenable.

And the highest priest rose up into the middle, and asked Jesus and said, Answer Thou nothing to those things that are put against Thee of these? But He was still and answered nothing. Eftsoon the highest priest asked Him and said to Him, Are Thou Christ, the Son of the blessed God? And Jesus said to him, I am, and ye shall see Man's Son sitting on the right half of the virtue of God and coming in the clouds of heaven. And the highest priest to rent his clothes and said, What yet desire we witnesses? Ye have heard blasphemy! What seems to you? And they all condemned Him to be guilty of death. And some began to bespit Him and to hile

His face, and to smite Him with buffets and say to Him, Arede Thou! And the ministers beat Him with strokes.

And when Peter was in the hall beneath, one of the damsels of the highest priest came. And when she had seen Peter warming him, she beheld him and said, And thou were with Jesus of Nazareth. And he denied and said, Neither I wot, neither I know what thou say! And he went withoutforth before the hall, and anon the cock crew. And eftsoon, when another damsel had seen him, she began to say to men that stood about, That this is of them. And he eftsoon denied. And after a little, eftsoon, they that stood nigh said to Peter, Verily, thou are of them, for thou are of Galilee also. But he began to curse and to swear, For I know not this Man whom ye say! And anon, eftsoons, the cock crew. And Peter bethought on the word that Jesus had said to him, Before the cock crow twice, thrice thou shall deny Me. And he began to weep.

Chapter XV

And anon in the morrowtide, the highest priests made a counsel with the elder men and the scribes and with all the council, and bound Jesus, and led and betook Him to Pilate. And Pilate asked Him, Are Thou King of Jews? And Jesus answered and said to him, Thou say. And the highest priests accused Him in many things. But Pilate eftsoon asked Him and said, Answer Thou nothing? See Thou in how many things they accuse Thee? But Jesus answered no more, so that Pilate wondered.

But by the feast day he was wont to leave to them one of men bound, whomever they asked. And one there was that was said Barabbas, that was bound with men of dissension that had done manslaughter in sedition.

And when the people were gone up, he began to pray as he evermore did to them. And Pilate answered to them and said, Will ye that I leave to you the King of Jews? For he wist that the highest priests had taken Him by envy. But the bishops stirred the people that he should rather leave to them Barabbas. And eftsoon Pilate answered and said to them, What then will ye that I shall do to the King of Jews? And they eftsoon cried, Crucify Him! But Pilate said to them, What evil has He done? And they cried the more, Crucify Him! And *appeasement, satisfaction* Pilate, willing to make aseeth to the people, left to them Barabbas, and betook to them Jesus, beaten with scourges, to be crucified.

And knights led Him withinforth, into the porch of the moot hall. And they called together all the company of knights, and clothed Him with purple. And they writhed a crown of thorns and put on Him. And they began to greet Him, and said, Hail, Thou King of Jews! And they smote His head with a reed and bespat Him, and they kneeled and worshipped Him. And after that they had scorned Him, they unclothed Him of purple and clothed Him with His clothes, and led out Him to crucify Him.

And they compelled a man that passed the way that came from the town, Simon of Cyrene, the father of Alexander and of Rufus, to bear His cross. And they led Him into a place, Golgotha, that is to say, the place of Calvary. And they gave to Him to drink wine *mixed* meddled with myrrh, and He took not. And they crucified Him and departed His clothes, and cast lot on those, who should take what. And it was the third hour, and they crucified Him. And the title of His cause was written, King of Jews.

And they crucified with Him two thieves, one at the right half and one at His left half. And the Scripture was fulfilled that says, And He is ordained with wicked men. And as they passed forth, they blasphemed Him, moving their heads and saying, Vath, Thou that destroys the Temple of God and in three days builds it again! Come a-down from the cross and make Thyself safe! Also the highest priests scorned Him, each to other with the scribes, and said, He made other men safe. He may not save Himself! Christ, King of Israel, come down now from the cross, that we see and believe! And they that were crucified with Him, despised Him.

And when the sixth hour was come, darknesses were made on all the earth till into the ninth hour. And in the ninth hour Jesus cried with a great voice, and said, Eloi, Eloi, lama sabachthani? That is to say, My God, My God, why has Thou forsaken Me? And some men that stood about, heard and said, Lo, He calls Elijah. And one ran and filled a sponge with vinegar, and put about a reed and gave to Him drink, and said, Suffer ye. See we if Elijah come to do Him down. And Jesus gave out a great cry, and died.

And the veil of the Temple was rent a two, from the highest to beneath. But the centurion that stood forn-against, saw that He so crying had died, and said, *opposite, over against* Verily, this Man was God's Son. And there were also women beholding from afar, among which was Mary Magdalene, and Mary the mother of James the less, and of Joseph and of Salome. And when Jesus was in Galilee, they followed Him and ministered to Him, and many other women that came up together with Him to Jerusalem.

And when eventide was come, for it was the eventide which is before the Sabbath, Joseph of Arimathea, the noble decurion, came, and he abode the realm of God. *colonial senator* And boldly he entered to Pilate and asked the body of Jesus. But Pilate wondered if He were now dead. And when the centurion was called, he asked him if He were dead, and when he knew of the centurion, he granted the body of Jesus to Joseph.

And Joseph bought linen cloth and took Him down and lapped in the linen cloth, and laid Him in a sepulchre that was hewn of a stone, and wallowed a stone to the door of the sepulchre. And Mary Magdalene and Mary of Joseph beheld where He was laid.

Chapter XVI

And when the Sabbath was passed, Mary Magdalene and Mary of James, and Salome, bought sweet-smel-
unguents ling ointments to come to anoint Jesus. And full early in one of the week days, they came to the sepulchre when the sun was risen. And they said together, Who shall move away to us the stone from the door of the sepulchre? And they beheld and see the stone wallowed away, for it was full great. And they went into the sepulchre, and saw a youngling hiled with a white stole, sitting at the right half. And they were afraid. Which says to them, Nil ye dread. Ye seek Jesus of Nazareth crucified. He is risen. He is not here. Lo, the place where they laid Him! But go ye, and say to His disciples, and to Peter, that He shall go before you into Galilee. There ye shall see Him, as He said to you.

And they went out and fled from the sepulchre, for dread and quaking had assailed them, and to no man they said anything, for they dreaded. And Jesus rose early the first day of the week and appeared first to Mary Magdalene, from whom He had cast out seven devils. And she went and told to them that had been with Him, which were wailing and weeping. And they, hear-ing that He lived and was seen of her, believed not. But after these things, when twain of them wandered, He was shown in another likeness to them going into a town. And they went and told to the others, and neither they believed to them.

But at the last, when the eleven disciples sat at the meat, Jesus appeared to them and reproved the unbelief of them and the hardness of heart, for they believed not to them that had seen that He was risen from death. And He said to them, Go ye into all the world and preach the gospel to each creature. Who that believes and is baptized shall be safe. But he that believes not shall be damned. And these tokens shall sue them that believe. In My name they shall cast out fiends. They shall speak with new tongues. They shall do away serpents. And if they drink any venom, it shall not noy *hurt, harm* them. They shall set their hands on sick men, and they shall wax whole.

And the Lord Jesus, after He had spoken to them, was taken up into heaven, and He sits on the right half of God. And they went forth and preached everywhere, for the Lord wrought with them and confirmed the word with signs following.

Here begins the Prologue on Luke

Luke was a man of Syria by nation and of Antioch, and was a leech in craft and a disciple of apostles. Afterward he sued Paul till to his ending and served God, and was without great sin, for neither he had a wife in any time neither children. And he died in Bethany at three score year and fourteen, and was full of the Holy Ghost. And when the gospels were written by Matthew in Judea and by Mark in Italy, Luke, by stirring of the Holy Ghost, wrote this gospel in the countries of Achaia. The most need of his travail was this, that the manhood of Christ should be open to faithful Greeks by all prophets that God should come in flesh, that is, to show by all prophets that Christ should be God and Man together, lest Christian Greeks took heed to the fables of Jews and were held in desire a love of Moses' law. And Luke travailed lest ere they were deceived by fables of heretics and fond stealths and fell away from truth.

This Luke begins at the conception and nativity of John Baptist, and describes the nativity and baptism and preaching of Christ, and His death and rising again, and ascension.

Here begins the gospel of Luke

Chapter I

determined, intended Forsooth, for many men enforced to ordain the telling of things which are fulfilled in us, as they that saw at the beginning and were ministers of the word betaken, it is seen also to me, having all things diligently by order to write to thee, thou best Theophilus, that thou know the truth of those words of which thou art learned.

In the days of Herod, king of Judea, there was a priest, Zacharias by name, of the sort of Abia, and his wife was of the daughters of Aaron, and her name was Elizabeth. And both were just before God, going in all the commandments and justifyings of the Lord without *complaint, fault* plaint. And they had no child, for Elizabeth was barren, and both were of great age in their days. And it befell that when Zacharias should do the office of priesthood in the order of his course tofore God after the custom of the priesthood, he went forth by lot and entered into the Temple to incense. And all the multitude of the people was withoutforth, and prayed in the hour of incensing. And an angel of the Lord appeared to him and stood on the right half of the altar of incense. And Zacharias was afraid and dread fell upon him.

And the angel said to him, Zacharias, dread thou not, for thy prayer is heard, and Elizabeth thy wife shall bear to thee a son, and his name shall be called John. And joy and gladding shall be to thee, and many shall *rejoicing* have joy in his nativity. For he shall be great before the Lord, and he shall not drink wine and cider, and he shall be fulfilled with the Holy Ghost yet of his mother's womb. And he shall convert many of the children of Israel to their Lord God, and he shall go before Him in the spirit and virtue of Elijah. And he shall turn the hearts of the fathers into the sons, and men out of belief to the prudence of just men, to make ready a perfect people to the Lord.

And Zacharias said to the angel, Whereof shall I wit this? For I am old, and my wife has gone far into her days.

And the angel answered and said to him, For I am Gabriel that stands nigh before God, and I am sent to thee to speak and to evangelise to thee these things. And lo, thou shall be dumb, and thou shall not more speak till into the day in which these things shall be done, for thou has not believed to my words which shall be fulfilled in their time.

And the people were abiding Zacharias, and they wondered that he tarried in the Temple. And he went out and might not speak to them, and they knew that he had seen a vision in the Temple. And he beckoned to them and he dwelled still dumb. And it was done, when the days of his office were fulfilled, he went into his house.

And after these days, Elizabeth his wife conceived and hid her five months, and said, For so the Lord did to me in the days in which He beheld to take away my reproof among men.

But in the sixth month, the angel Gabriel was sent from God into a city of Galilee whose name was Nazareth, to a maiden wedded to a man whose name was Joseph, of the house of David. And the name of the maiden was Mary. And the angel entered to her and said, Hail, full of grace. The Lord be with thee. Blessed be thou among women.

And when she had heard, she was troubled in his word, and thought what manner salutation this was. And the angel said to her, Nor dread thou not, Mary, for thou has found grace anent God. Lo, thou shall conceive in womb and shall bear a Son, and thou shall call His name Jesus. This shall be great, and He shall be called the Son of the Highest. And the Lord God shall give to Him the seat of David His father, and He shall reign in the house of Jacob without end, and of His realm shall be none end. And Mary said to the angel, On what manner shall this thing be done? For I know not man.

And the angel answered and said to her, The Holy Ghost shall come from above into thee, and the virtue of the Highest shall overshadow thee. And therefore that holy thing that shall be born of thee shall be called the Son of God. And lo Elizabeth thy cousin, and she also has conceived a son in her eld, and this month is the sixth to her that is called barren. For every word shall not be impossible anent God.

And Mary said, Lo, the handmaiden of the Lord. Be it done to me after thy word. And the angel departed from her.

And Mary rose up in those days and went with haste into the mountains, into a city of Judea. And she entered into the house of Zacharias and greeted Elizabeth. And it was done, as Elizabeth heard the salu *was glad, rejoiced* tation of Mary, the young child in her womb gladded. And Elizabeth was fulfilled with the Holy Ghost and cried with a great voice, and said, Blessed be thou among women, and blessed be the fruit of thy womb.

And whereof is this thing to me, that the mother of my Lord come to me? For lo, as the voice of thy salutation was made in mine ears, the young child gladded in joy in my womb. And blessed be thou that has believed, for the ilk things that be said of the Lord to thee shall be parfitly done.   *perfectly*

And Mary said, My soul magnifies the Lord, and my spirit has gladded in God mine health. For He has beheld the meekness of His handmaiden. For lo, of this all generations shall say I am blessed. For He that is mighty has done to me great things, and His name is holy. And His mercy is from kindred into kindreds to men that dread Him. He made might in His arm. He scattered proud men with the thought of His heart. He set down mighty men from seat, and enhanced meek men. He has fulfilled hungry men with goods, and He has left rich men void. He, having mind of His mercy, took Israel His child, as He has spoken to our fathers, to Abraham and to his seed into worlds.

And Mary dwelled with her, as it were, three months and turned again into her house. But the time of bearing child was fulfilled to Elizabeth, and she bore a son. And the neighbours and cousins of her heard that the Lord had magnified His mercy with her, and they thanked Him. And it was done in the eighth day, they came to circumcise the child, and they called his name Zacharias by the name of his father. And his mother answered and said, Nay, but he shall be called John.

And they said to her, For no man is in thy kindred that is called this name. And they beckoned to his father what he would that he were called.

And he, asking a poyntil, wrote, saying, John is his   *stylus*
name. And all men wondered. And anon his mouth was opened and his tongue, and he spoke and blessed God. And dread was made on all their neighbours, and

all these words were published on all the mountains of Judea. And all men that heard, put in their heart and said, What manner child shall this be? For the hand of the Lord was with him.

And Zacharias, his father, was fulfilled with the Holy Ghost, and prophesied and said, Blessed be the Lord God of Israel, for He has visited and made redemption of His people. And He has reared to us an horn of health in the house of David His child, as He spoke by the mouth of His holy prophets that were from the world. Health from our enemies, and from the hand of all men that hated us. To do mercy with our fathers and to have mind of His holy testament. The great oath that He swore to Abraham our father, to give Himself to us. That we without dread, delivered from the hand of our enemies, serve to Him in holiness and rightwise‚ness before Him in all our days. And thou, child, shall be called the prophet of the Highest, for thou shall go before the face of the Lord to make ready His ways. To *knowledge* give science of health to His people into remission of their sins, by the inwardness of the mercy of our God, in the which He springs up from on high has visited us. To give light to them that sit in darkness and in shadow of death, to dress our feet into the way of peace.

And the child waxed and was comforted in spirit, and was in desert places till to the day of his showing to Israel.

Chapter II

And it was done in those days, a commandment went out from the emperor Augustus that all the world should be described. This first describing was made of Cyrenius, justice of Syria. And all men went to make profession, each into his own city. And Joseph went up from Galilee, from the city Nazareth into Judea, into a city of David that is called Bethlehem, for that he was of the house and of the meyne of David, that he should acknowledge with Mary his wife that was wedded to him and was great with child. And it was done, while they were there the days were fulfilled that she should bear child. And she bore her first born son and lapped Him in cloths and laid Him in a cratche, for there was *fodder stall, crib* no place to Him in no chamber.

And shepherds were in the same country, waking and keeping the watches of the night on their flock. And lo, the angel of the Lord stood beside them, and the clearness of God shone about them, and they *brightness, glory* dreaded with great dread. And the angel said to them, Nil ye dread, for lo, I preach to you a great joy that shall be to all people. For a Saviour is born today to you that is Christ the Lord in the city of David. And this is a token to you, ye shall find a young child lapped in cloths and laid in a cratche.

And suddenly there was made with the angel a multitude of heavenly knighthood, herying God and saying, Glory be in the highest things to God, and in earth peace to men of good will.

And it was done, as the angels passed away from them into heaven, the shepherds spoke together and said, Go we over to Bethlehem and see we this word that is made, which the Lord has made and shown to us.

And they, hyeing, came and found Mary and Joseph and the young child laid in a cratche. And they seeing, knew of the word that was said to them of this child. And all men that heard, wondered and of those things that were said to them of the shepherds. But Mary kept all these words bearing together in her heart. And the shepherds turned again, glorifying and herying God in all things that they had heard and seen, as it was said to them.

And after that the eight days were ended that the child should be circumcised, His name was called Jesus, which was called of the angel before that He was conceived in the womb. And after that the days of purgation of Mary were fulfilled after Moses' law, they took Him into Jerusalem to offer Him to the Lord, as it is written in the law of the Lord, Every male-kind opening the womb shall be called holy to the Lord, and that they shall give an offering, after that it is said in the law of the Lord, A pair of turtles or twain culver birds.

turtle doves

And lo, a man was in Jerusalem whose name was Simeon, and this man was just and virtuous, and abided the comfort of Israel, and the Holy Ghost was in him. And he had taken an answer of the Holy Ghost that he should not see death but he saw first the Christ of the Lord. And he came in Spirit into the Temple. And when his father and mother led the child Jesus to do after the custom of the law for Him, he took Him into his arms and he blessed God, and said, Lord, now thou leaves Thy servant after Thy word in peace, for mine eyes have seen Thine health which Thou has made ready before the face of all peoples, light to the showing of heathen men and glory of Thy people Israel.

And His father and mother were wondering on these things that were said of Him. And Simeon blessed them and said to Mary his mother, Lo, this is set into the falling down and into the rising again of many men in Israel, and into a token to whom it shall be againsaid. And a sword shall pass through thine own soul, that the thoughts are shown of many hearts.

And Anna was a prophetess, the daughter of Phanuel of the lineage of Aser. And she had gone forth in many days, and had lived with her husband seven year from her maidenhood. And this was a widow to four score year and four, and she departed not from the Temple but served to God night and day in fastings and prayers. And this came upon them in the ilk hour, and acknowledged to the Lord, and spoke of Him to all that abide the redemption of Israel. And as they had full done all things after the law of the Lord, they turned again into Galilee in their city, Nazareth.

And the child waxed and was comforted, full of wisdom, and the grace of God was in Him. And His father and mother went each year into Jerusalem in the solemn day of Pasch. And when Jesus was twelve year old, they went up to Jerusalem after the custom of the feast day. And when the days were done, they turned again, and the child abode in Jerusalem and His father and mother knew it not. For they, guessing that He had been in the fellowship, came a day's journey and sought Him among his cousins and His knowledge. And when they found Him not, they turned again into Jerusalem and sought Him.

And it befell that after the third day they found Him in the Temple, sitting in the middle of the doctors, hearing them and asking them. And all men that heard Him, wondered on the prudence and the answers of Him. And they saw and wondered. And His mother said to Him, Son, what has Thou done to us thus? Lo, Thy father and I, sorrowing, have sought Thee.

And He said to them, What is it that ye sought Me? Wist ye not that in those things that are of my Father, it behoves Me to be?

And they understood not the word which He spoke to them. And He came down with them, and came to Nazareth, and was subject to them. And his mother *liable to obey* kept together all these words and bore them in her heart. And Jesus profited in wisdom, age and grace anent God and men.

Chapter III

In the fifteenth year of the empire of Tiberius the emperor, when Pilate of Pounce governed Judea and Herod was prince of Galilee, and Philip his brother was prince of Iturea and of the country of Trachonitis, and Lysanias was prince of Abilene under the princes of priests, Annas and Caiaphas, the word of the Lord was made on John the son of Zacharias in desert. And he came into all the country of Jordan and preached baptism of repentance into remission of sins. As it is written in the book of the words of Isaiah the prophet, The voice of a crier in desert, Make ye ready the way of the Lord, make ye His paths right. Each valley shall be fulfilled, and every hill and little hill shall be made low, and *depraved, perverse* shrewd things shall be into dressed things, and sharp things into plain ways, and every flesh shall see the health of God.

Therefore he said to the people which went out to be baptized of him, Kindlings of adders, who showed to you to flee from the wrath to coming? Therefore, do ye worthy fruits of penance, and begin ye not to say, We have a father, Abraham. For I say to you that God is mighty to raise of these stones the sons of Abraham. And now an axe is set to the root of the tree, and therefore every tree that makes no good fruit shall be cut down, and shall be cast into the fire.

And the people asked him and said, What then shall we do? He answered and said to them, He that has two coats, give to him that has none. And he that has meats, do in like manner. And publicans came to be baptized, and they said to him, Master, what shall we do? And he said to them, Do ye nothing more than that that is ordained to you. And knights asked him and said, What shall also we do? And he said to them, Smite ye wrongfully no man, neither make ye false challenge, and be ye appayed with your sowdes.

content, satisfied
salary, wages

When all the people guessed, and all men thought in their hearts of John lest peradventure he were Christ, John answered and said to all men, I baptize you with water, but a stronger than I shall come after me of whom I am not worthy to unbind the lace of His shoes. He shall baptize you in the Holy Ghost and fire, whose winnowing tool in His hand, and He shall purge His floor of corn and shall gather the wheat into His barn. But the chaffs shall He burn with fire unquenchable.

And many other things also he spoke and preached to the people. But Herod tetrarch, when he was blamed of John for Herodias, the wife of his brother, and for all the evils that Herod did, increased this over all and shut John in prison. And it was done, when all the people were baptized, and when Jesus was baptized and prayed, heaven was opened. And the Holy Ghost came down in bodily likeness as a dove on Him, and a voice was made from heaven, Thou art my dearworth Son. In Thee it has pleased to Me.

And Jesus himself was beginning as of thirty year, that He was guessed the son of Joseph, which was of Heli, which was of Matthat, which was of Levi, which was of Melchi, that was of Janna, that was of Joseph, that was of Mattathias, that was of Amos, that was of Naum, that was of Esli, that was of Nagge, that was of Maath, that was of Mattathias, that was of Semei, that was of Joseph, that was of Juda, that was of Joanna, that was of Rhesa, that was of Zerubbabel, that was of Salathiel, that was of Neri, that was of Melchi, that was of Addi, that was of Cosam, that was of Elmodam, that was of Er, that was of Jose, that was of Eliezer, that was of Jorim, that was of Matthat, that was of Levi, that was of Simeon, that was of Juda, that was of Joseph, that was of Jonan, that was of Eliakim, that was of Meliea, that was of Menan, that was of Mattatha, that was of Nathan, that was of David, that was of Jesse, that was of Obed, that was of Boaz, that was of Salmon, that was of Naasson, that was of Aminadab, that was of Aram, that was of Esrom, that was of Phares, that was of Juda, that was of Jacob, that was of Isaac, that was of Abraham, that was of Thara, that was of Nachor, that was of Saruch, that was of Ragau, that was of Phalec, that was of Heber, that was of Sala, that was of Cainan, that was of Arphaxad, that was of Shem, that was of Noah, that was of Lamech, that was of Methuselah, that was Enoch, that was Jared, that was of Mahalaleel, that was of Cainan, that was of Enos, that was of Seth, that was of Adam, that was of God.

Chapter IV

And Jesus, full of the Holy Ghost, turned again from Jordan and was led by the Spirit into desert forty days, and was tempted of the devil and ate nothing in those days. And when those days were ended, He hungered. And the devil said to Him, If Thou art God's Son, say to this stone that it be made bread.

And Jesus answered to him, It is written that a man lives not in bread alone, but in every word of God.

And the devil led Him into an high hill and showed to Him all the realms of the world in a moment of time, and said to Him, I shall give to Thee all this power and the glory of them, for to me they are given, and to whom I will I give them. Therefore, if Thou fall down and worship before me, all things shall be Thine.

And Jesus answered and said to him, It is written, Thou shall worship thy Lord God, and to Him alone thou shall serve.

And he led Him into Jerusalem, and set Him on the

pinnacle of the Temple and said to Him, If Thou art God's Son, send Thyself from hence down, for it is written, For He has commanded to His angels of Thee, that they keep Thee in all Thy ways, and that they shall take Thee in hands lest peradventure Thou hurt Thy foot at a stone.

And Jesus answered and said to him, It is said, Thou shall not tempt thy Lord God. And when every temptation was ended, the fiend went away from Him for a time. And Jesus turned again in the virtue of the Spirit into Galilee, and the fame went forth of Him through all the country. And He taught in the synagogues of them, and was magnified of all men.

And He came to Nazareth where He was nourished, and entered after His custom in the Sabbath day into a synagogue and rose to read. And the book of Isaiah the prophet was taken to Him, and as He turned the book He found a place where it was written, The Spirit of the Lord on Me, for which thing He anointed Me. He sent Me to preach to poor men, to heal contrite men in heart and to preach remission to prisoners and sight to blind men, and to deliver broken men into remission, to preach the year of the Lord pleasant, and the day of yielding again.

And when He had closed the book, He gave again to the minister and sat, and the eyes of all men in the synagogue were beholding into Him. And He began to say to them, For in this day this Scripture is fulfilled in your ears.

And all men gave witnessing to Him and wondered in the words of grace that came forth of His mouth. And they said, Whether this is not the son of Joseph? And He said to them, Soothly, ye shall say to Me in this likeness, Leech, heal Thyself.

The Pharisees said to Jesus, How great things have

we heard done in Capernaum, do Thou also here in Thy country.

And He said, Truly I say to you that no prophet is received in his own country. In truth I say to you that many widows were in the days of Elijah the prophet in Israel, when heaven was closed three year and six months, when great hunger was made in all the earth. And to none of them was Elijah sent but into Sarepta of Sidon, to a widow. And many measles were in Israel under Elisha the prophet, and none of them was cleansed but Naaman of Syria.

And all in the synagogue, hearing these things, were filled with wrath. And they rose up and drove Him out without the city, and led Him to the top of the hill on which their city was built to cast Him down. But Jesus passed and went through the middle of them, and came down into Capernaum, a city of Galilee, and there He taught them in Sabbaths. And they were astonied at His teaching, for His word was in power.

And in their synagogue was a man having an unclean fiend, and he cried with great voice and said, Suffer! What to us and to Thee, Jesus of Nazareth? Art Thou come to leese us? I know that Thou art the holy of God. And Jesus blamed him and said, Wax dumb, and go out from him. And when the fiend had cast him forth into the middle, he went away from him and he *annoyed, tormented* noyed him nothing. And dread was made in all men, and they spoke together and said, What is this word, for in power and virtue He commands to unclean spirits and they go out?

And the fame was published of Him into each place of the country. And Jesus rose up from the synagogue and entered into the house of Simon. And the mother of Simon's wife was held with great fevers, and they prayed Him for her. And Jesus stood over her and com⁄

manded to the fever, and it left her. And anon she rose up and served them.

And when the sun went down, all that had sick men with diverse languors led them to Him, and He set His hands on each by himself, and healed them. And fiends went out from many, and cried and said, For Thou art the Son of God.

And He blamed and suffered them not to speak, for they wist Him that He was Christ. And when the day was come, He went out and went into a desert place. And the people sought Him, and they came to Him and they held Him, that He should not go away from them. To which He said, For also to other cities it behoves Me to preach the kingdom of God, for therefore I am sent. And He preached in the synagogues of Galilee.

Chapter V

And it was done, when the people came fast to Jesus to hear the word of God, He stood beside the pool of Gennesaret, and saw two boats standing beside the pool, and the fishers were gone down and washed their nets. And He went up into a boat that was Simon's, and prayed him to lead it a little from the land. And He sat and taught the people out of the boat. And as He ceased to speak, he said to Simon, Lead thou into the depth and slake your nets to take fish.   *slacken, let down*

And Simon answered and said to Him, Commander, we travailed all the night and took nothing, but in Thy word I shall lay out the net. And when they had done this thing, they closed together a great multitude of fishes, and their net was broken. And they beckoned to fellows that were in another boat that they should come and help them. And they came and filled both the boats so that they were almost drenched. And when Simon Peter saw this thing, he fell down to the knees of Jesus and said, Lord, go from me, for I am a sinful man. For he was on each side astonied and all that were with him in the taking of fishes which they took.. Soothly in like manner, James and John, the sons of Zebedee that were fellows of Simon Peter. And Jesus said to Simon, Nil thou dread. Now from this time thou shall take men.

And when the boats were led up to the land, they left all things and they sued Him. And it was done, when He was in one of the cities, lo, a man full of leprosy, and seeing Jesus fell down on his face and prayed Him, and said, Lord, if Thou will, Thou may make me clean.

And Jesus held forth His hand and touched him, and said, I will, be thou made clean. And anon the leprosy passed away from him. And Jesus commanded to him that he should say to no man. But go, show thou thee to a priest and offer for thy cleansing as Moses bade into witnessing of them.

And the word walked about the more of Him, and much people came together to hear and to be healed of their sicknesses. And He went into desert and prayed.

And it was done in one of the days, He sat and taught, and there were Pharisees sitting and doctors of the law that came of each castle of Galilee and of Judea and of Jerusalem, and the virtue of the Lord was to heal sick men. And lo, men bore in a bed a man that was sick in the palsy, and they sought to bear him in and set before Him. And they found not in what part they should bear him in for the people, and they went on the *slates, roof-tiles* roof and by the slates they let him down with the bed into the middle before Jesus.

And when Jesus saw the faith of them, He said, Man, thy sins are forgiven to thee. And the scribes and Pharisees began to think, saying, Who is this that speaks blasphemies? Who may forgive sins but God alone? And as Jesus knew the thoughts of them, He answered and said to them, What think ye evil things in your hearts? What is lighter to say, Sins are forgiven to thee, or to say, Rise up and walk? But that ye wit that Man's Son has power in earth to forgive sins, He said to the sick man in palsy, I say to thee, rise up, take thy bed and go into thine house. And anon, he rose up before them and took the bed in which he lay, and went into his house and magnified God. And great wonder took all, and they magnified God, and they were fulfilled with great dread and said, For we have seen marvellous things today.

And after these things Jesus went out and saw a publican, Levi by name, sitting at the tolbooth. And He said to him, Sue thou Me. And when he had left all things, he rose up and sued Him. And Levi made to him a great feast in his house, and there was a great company of publicans and of others that were with them sitting at the meat. And Pharisees and the scribes of them grouched, and said to His disciples, Why eat ye and drink with publicans and sinful men? And Jesus answered and said to them, They that are whole have no need to a leech, but they that are sick, for I came not to call just men, but sinful men to penance.

And they said to Him, Why the disciples of John fast often and make prayers, also and of Pharisees, but Thine eat and drink? To which He said, Whether ye moun make the sons of the spouse to fast while the spouse is with them? But days shall come when the spouse shall be taken away from them, and then they shall fast in those days. And He said to them also a likeness, For no man takes a piece from a new cloth and puts it into an old clothing, else both he breaks the new and the piece of the new accords not to the old. And no man puts new wine into old bottles, else the new wine shall break the bottles and the wine shall be shed out, and the bottles shall perish. But new wine ought to be put into new bottles, and both are kept. And no man drinking the old will anon the new, for he says, The old is the better.

Chapter VI

And it was done in the second first Sabbath, when He passed by corns, His disciples plucked ears of corn, and *rubbing* they, froting with their hands, ate. And some of the Pharisees said to them, What do ye that that is not leaveful in the Sabbaths? And Jesus answered and said to them, Have ye not read what David did when he hungered, and they that were with him, how he entered into the house of God and took loaves of proposition and ate, and gave to them that were with them, which loaves it was not leaveful to eat but only to priests? And He said to them, For Man's Son is Lord, yea, of the Sabbath.

And it was done in another Sabbath that He entered into a synagogue and taught. And a man was there, and his right hand was dry. And the scribes and Pharisees aspied Him if He would heal him in the Sabbath, that they should find cause whereof they should accuse Him. And He wist the thoughts of them, and He said to the man that had a dry hand, Rise up and stand into the middle. And Jesus said to them, I ask you if it is leaveful to do well in the Sabbath, or evil? To make a soul safe, or to loose? And when He had beheld all men about, He said to the man, Hold forth thine hand. And he held forth, and his hand was restored to health. And they were fulfilled with unwisdom, and spoke together what they should do of Jesus.

And it was done in those days, He went out into an hill to pray, and He was all night dwelling in the prayer of God. And when the day was come, He called His disciples and chose twelve of them which He called also apostles: Simon, whom He called Peter; and Andrew his brother; James and John; Philip and Bartholomew; Matthew and Thomas; James Alphaeus, and Simon that is called Zelotes; Judas of James, and Judas Iscariot that was traitor.

And Jesus came down from the hill with them and stood in a fieldy place, and the company of His disciples *open space, as of meadows* and a great multitude of people of all Judea and Jerusalem, and of the sea coasts and of Tyre and Sidon that came to hear Him and to be healed of their sicknesses, and they that were travailed of unclean spirits, were healed. And all people sought to touch Him, for virtue went out of Him and healed all.

And when His eyes were cast up into His disciples, He said, Blessed be ye poor men, for the kingdom of God is yours. Blessed be ye that now hunger, for ye shall be fulfilled. Blessed be ye that now weep, for ye shall laugh. Ye shall be blessed when men shall hate you and depart you away, and put shenship to you, and cast out *isolation, shunning,* your name as evil for Man's Son. Joy ye in that day and *disgrace* be ye glad, for lo, your meed is much in heaven, for after these things the fathers of them did to prophets. Netheless, woe to you, rich men, that have your comfort. Woe to you that are fulfilled, for ye shall hunger. Woe to you that now laugh, for ye shall mourn and weep. Woe to you when all men shall bless you. After these things the fathers of them did to prophets. But I say to you that hear, love ye your enemies, do ye well to them that hated you. Bless ye men that curse you, pray ye for men that defame you. And to him that smites thee on one cheek, show also the t'other, and from him that takes away from thee a cloth, nil ye forbid the coat. And give to each that asks thee. And if a man takes away those things that are thine, ask thou not again. And as ye will that men do to you, do ye also to them in like manner. And if ye love them that love you, what thank is to you? For sinful men love men that love them. And if ye do well to them that do well to you, what grace is to you? Sinful men do this thing. And if ye lend to them of which ye hope to take again, what thank is to you? For sinful men lend to sinful men, to take again as much. Netheless, love ye your enemies, and do ye well, and lend ye, hoping nothing thereof, and your meed shall be much, and ye shall be the sons of the Highest, for He is benign on unkind men and evil men. Therefore, be ye merciful, as your Father is merciful. Nil ye deem, and ye shall not be deemed. Nil ye condemn, and ye shall not be condemned. Forgive ye, and it shall be forgiven to you. Give ye, and it shall be given to you. They shall give into your bosom a good measure and well filled, and shaken together and overflowing. For by the same measure that ye mete, it shall be meted again to you.

And He said to them a likeness, Whether the blind may lead the blind? Nor fall they not both into the ditch? A disciple is not above the master. But each shall be parfit if he be as his master. And what see thou in thy brother's eye a mote, but thou beholds not a beam that is in thine own eye? Or how may thou say to thy brother, Brother, suffer, I shall cast out the mote of thine eye, and thou beholds not a beam in thine own eye? Hypocrite, first take out the beam of thine eye, and then shall thou see to take the mote of thy brother's eye.

It is not a good tree that makes evil fruits, neither an evil tree that makes good fruits. For every tree is known of his fruit. And men gather not figs of thorns, neither men gather a grape of a bush of briars. A good man, of the good treasure of his heart, brings forth good things, and an evil man, of the evil treasure, brings forth evil

things. For of the plenty of the heart, the mouth speaks.
And what call ye Me, Lord, Lord, and do not those
things that I say? Each that comes to Me and hears My
words, and does them, I shall show to you to whom he
is like. He is like to a man that builds an house, that
digged deep and set the fundament on a stone. And *foundation*
when great flood was made, the flood was hurtled to that
house and it might not move it, for it was founded on a
sad stone. But he that hears and does not, is like to a *firm, solid*
man building his house on earth without fundament,
into which the flood was hurled and anon it fell down,
and the falling down of that house was made great.

Chapter VII

And when He had fulfilled all His words into the ears
of the people, He entered into Capernaum. But a servant
of a centurion, that was precious to him, was sick and
drawing to the death. And when he had heard of Jesus,
he sent to Him the elder men of Jews, and prayed Him
that He would come and heal his servant. And when
they came to Jesus, they prayed Him busily and said to
Him, For he is worthy that Thou grant to him this
thing, for he loves our folk and he built to us a synagogue.

And Jesus went with them. And when He was not
far from the house, the centurion sent to Him friends,
and said, Lord, nil Thou be travailed, for I am not
worthy that Thou enter under my roof. For which thing
I deemed not myself worthy that I come to Thee. But
say Thou by word and my child shall be healed. For I
am a man ordained under power, and have knights
under me. And I say to this, Go, and he goes, and to
another, Come, and he comes, and to my servant, Do
this thing, and he does. And when this thing was
heard, Jesus wondered, and said to the people suing

Him, Truly I say to you, neither in Israel I found so great faith. And they that were sent, turned again home and found the servant whole which was sick.

And it was done afterward, Jesus went into a city that is called Nain and His disciples. And full great people went with Him. And when He came nigh to the gate of the city, lo, the son of a woman that had no more children, was borne out dead. And this was a widow and much people of the city with her. And when the Lord Jesus had seen her, He had ruth on her, and said to her, Nil thou weep. And He came nigh and touched the bier, and they that bore, stood. And He said, Young man, I say to thee, rise up. And he that was dead, sat up again and began to speak, and He gave him to his mother. And dread took all men, and they magnified God and said, For a great prophet is risen among us, and, For God has visited his people.

And this word went out of Him into all Judea and into all the country about. And John's disciples told him of all these things. And John called twain of his disciples and sent them to Jesus, and said, Art Thou He that is to come, or abide we another? And when the men came to Him, they said, John Baptist sent us to thee, and he said, Art Thou He that is to come, or we abide another? And in that hour He healed many men of their sicknesses and wounds and evil spirits. And He gave sight to many blind men. And Jesus answered and said to them, Go ye again and tell John those things that ye have heard and seen. Blind men see. Crooked men go. Measles are made clean. Deaf men hear. Dead men rise again. Poor men are taken to preaching of the gospel. And he that shall not be sclaundered in Me, is blessed.

And when the messengers of John were gone forth, He began to say of John to the people, What went ye out into desert to see? A reed wagged with the wind? But what went ye out to see? A man clothed with soft clothes? Lo, they that are in precious cloth and in deli⁄ cies, are in kings' houses. But what went ye out to see? *delicacies, luxuries* A prophet? Yea, I say to you, and more than a prophet. This is he of whom it is written, Lo, I send mine angel before Thy face which shall make Thy way ready before Thee. Certes, I say to you, there is no man more prophet among children of women than is John. But he that is less in the kingdom of heavens is more than he.

And all the people hearing, and publicans that had been baptized with baptism of John, justified God. But the Pharisees and the wise men of the law that were not baptized of him, despised the counsel of God against themselves. And the Lord said, Therefore to whom shall I say men of this generation like, and to whom are they like? They are like to children sitting in cheaping, and speaking together and saying, We have sung to you with pipes, and ye have not danced. We have made mourning, and ye have not wept. For John Baptist came neither eating bread nor drinking wine, and ye say he has a fiend. Man's Son came eating and drinking, and ye say, Lo, a man, a devourer and drinking wine, a friend of publicans and of sinful men. And wisdom is justified of her sons.

But one of the Pharisees prayed Jesus that He should eat with him. And He entered into the house of the Pharisee and sat at the meat. And lo, a sinful woman that was in the city, as she knew that Jesus sat at the meat in the house of the Pharisee, she brought an alabaster box of ointment, and she stood behind beside His feet, and began to moist His feet with tears and wiped with the hairs of her head, and kissed His feet and anointed with ointment. And the Pharisee seeing that had called Him, said within himself, saying, If this were a pro⁄

phet, He should wit who and what manner woman it were that touched Him, for she is a sinful woman.

And Jesus answered and said to him, Simon, I have something to say to thee. And he said, Master, say Thou. And He answered, Two debtors were to one len, der, and one owed five hundred pence, and the other fifty. But when they had not whereof they should yield, he forgave to both. Who then loves him more? Simon answered and said, I guess that he to whom he forgave more. And He answered to him, Thou has deemed rightly. And He turned to the woman and said to Simon, See thou this woman? I entered into thine house. Thou gave no water to My feet. But this has *moistened, watered* moisted My feet with tears, and wiped with her hairs. Thou has not given to Me a kiss. But this, since she entered, ceased not to kiss My feet. Thou anointed not Mine head with oil, but this anointed My feet with oint, ment. For the which thing I say to thee, many sins be forgiven to her, for she has loved much. And to whom is less forgiven, he loves less. And Jesus said to her, Thy sins are forgiven to thee. And they that sat together at the meat, began to say within themselves, Who is this that forgives sins? But He said to the woman, Thy faith has made thee safe. Go thou in peace.

Chapter VIII

And it was done afterward, and Jesus made journey by cities and castles, preaching and evangelising the realm of God, and twelve with Him and some women that were healed of wicked spirits and sicknesses, Mary, that is called Magdalene, of whom seven devils went out, and Joanna the wife of Chusa, the procurator of Herod, and Susanna and many others that ministered to Him of their riches. And when much people were come *hurried* together, and men hyed to Him from the cities, He said

by a similitude, He that sows, went out to sow his seed.
And while he sows, some fell beside the way and was
defouled, and birds of the air ate it. And other fell on a
stone and it sprung up and dried, for it had not moist-
ure. And other fell among thorns, and the thorns
sprung up together and strangled it. And other fell into
good earth, and it, sprung, made an hundredfold fruit.
He said these things and cried, He that has ears of hearing, hear he.

But His disciples asked Him what this parable was.
And He said to them, To you it is granted to know the
privity of the kingdom of God. But to other men in parables, that they, seeing, see not, and they, hearing, understand not. And this is the parable. The seed is God's
word, and they that are beside the way are these that
hear, and afterward the fiend comes and takes away the
word from their heart, lest they believing be made safe.
But they that fell on a stone are these that when they have
heard, receive the word with joy. But these have not
roots, for at a time they believe, and in time of temptation
they go away. But that that fell among thorns are these
that heard, and of business, and riches, and lusts of life,
they go forth and are strangled, and bring forth no fruit.
But that that fell into good earth are these that, in a good
heart, and best hear the word, and hold, and bring forth
fruit in patience.

No man lights a lantern and heleth it with a vessel, or *covers, hides*
puts it under a bed, but on a candlestick, that men that
enter see light. For there is no privy thing which shall
not be opened, neither hid thing which shall not be
known and come into open. Therefore see ye how ye
hear. For it shall be given to him that has, and whoever
has not, also that that he weens that he have, shall be
taken away from him.

And His mother and brethren came to Him, and

they might not come to Him for the people. And it was told to Him, Thy mother and Thy brethren stand without-forth, willing to see Thee. And He answered and said to them, My mother and My brethren are these that hear the word of God and do it.

And it was done in one of days, He went up into a boat and His disciples. And He said to them, Pass we over the sea. And they went up. And while they rowed, He slept. And a tempest of wind came down into the water, and they were driven hither and thither with waves, and were in peril. And they came nigh and raised Him and said, Commander, we perish! And He rose and blamed the wind and the tempest of water, and it ceased and peaceability was made. And He said to them, Where is your faith? Which, dreading, wondered and said together, Who, guess thou, is this? For He commands to winds and to the sea and they obey to Him.

And they rowed to the country of Gadarenes that is against Galilee. And when He went out to the land, a man ran to Him that had a devil long time. And he was not clothed with cloth, neither dwelled in house, but in sepulchres. This, when he saw Jesus, fell down before Him, and he, crying with a loud voice, said, What to me and to Thee, Jesus, the Son of the highest God? I beseech Thee that Thou torment me not. For He commanded the unclean spirit that he should go out from the man. For he took him often times, and he was bound with chains and kept in stocks, and when the bonds were broken, he was led of devils into desert. And Jesus asked him and said, What name is to thee? And he said, A legion. For many devils were entered into him. And they prayed Him that He should not command them that they should go into hell. And there was a flock of many swine lesewing in an hill, and they prayed

Him that He should suffer them to enter into them. And He suffered them. And so the devils went out from the man and entered into the swine, and with a bire the flock went heedling into the pool and was drenched.

And when the herds saw this thing done, they flew and told into the city and into the towns. And they went out to see that thing that was done. And they came to Jesus, and they found the man sitting, clothed, from whom the devils went out, and in whole mind at His feet. And they dreaded. And they that saw, told to them how he was made whole of the legion. And all the multitude of the country of Gadarenes prayed Him that He should go from them, for they were held with great dread.

He went up into a boat and turned again. And the man of whom the devils were gone out, prayed Him that he should be with Him. Jesus left him and said, Go again into thine house and tell how great things God has done to thee. And he went through all the city and preached how great things Jesus had done to him.

And it was done, when Jesus was gone again the people received Him and all were abiding Him. And lo, a man to whom the name was Jairus, and he was prince of a synagogue. And he fell down at the feet of Jesus and prayed Him that He should enter into his house, for he had but one daughter almost of twelve year old, and she was dead.

And it befell the while He went, He was thronged of the people. And a woman that had a flux of blood twelve year, and had spent all her chattels in leeches and she might not be cured of any. And she came nigh behind and touched the hem of His cloth, and anon the flux of her blood ceased. And Jesus said, Who is it that touched Me? And when all men denied, Peter said, and they that were with him, Commander, the people thrust and disease Thee, and Thou say, Who touched Me?

And Jesus said, Someone has touched Me, for that virtue went out of Me. And the woman, seeing that it was not hid from Him, came trembling and fell down at His feet, and for what cause she had touched Him she showed before all the people, and how anon she was healed. And He said to her, Daughter, thy faith has made thee safe. Go thou in peace.

And yet while He spoke, a man came from the prince of the synagogue, and said to him, Thy daughter is dead. Nil thou travail the Master. And when this word was heard, Jesus answered to the father of the damsel, Nil thou dread, but believe thou only and she shall be safe. And when He came to the house, He suffered no man to enter with him but Peter and John and James, and the father and the mother of the damsel. And all wept and bewailed her. And He said, Nil ye weep, for the damsel is not dead but sleeps. And they scorned Him and wist that she was dead. But He held her hand, and cried and said, Damsel, rise up. And her spirit turned again and she rose anon. And He commanded to give to her to eat. And her father and mother wondered greatly, and He commanded them that they should not say to any that thing that was done.

Chapter IX

And when the twelve apostles were called together, Jesus gave to them virtue and power on all devils, and that they should heal sicknesses. And He sent them for to preach the kingdom of God and to heal sick men. And He said to them, Nothing take ye in the way, neither yard nor scrip, neither bread nor money, and neither have ye two coats. And into what house that ye enter, dwell ye there, and go ye not out from thence. And whosoever receive not you, go ye out of that city and shake ye of the powder of your feet into witnessing on them.

And they went forth and went about by castles, preaching and healing everywhere. And Herod tetrarch heard all these things that were done of Him, and he doubted for that it was said of some men that John was risen from death, and of some that Elijah had appeared, but of others that one of the old prophets was risen. And Herod said, I have beheaded John. And who is this of whom I hear such things? And he sought to see Him.

And the apostles turned again and told to Him all things that they had done. And He took them, and went beside into a desert place that is Bethsaida. And when the people knew this, they followed Him. And He received them and spoke to them of the kingdom of God. And He healed them that had need of cure.

And the day began to bow down, and the twelve came and said to Him, Leave the people, that they go and turn into castles and towns that are about, that they find meat, for we are here in a desert place. And He said to them, Give ye to them to eat. And they said, There are not to us more than five loaves and two fishes, but peradventure that we go and buy meats to all these people. And the men were almost five thousand.

And He said to His disciples, Make ye them sit to meat by companies, a fifty together. And they did so, and they made all men sit to meat. And when He had taken the five loaves and two fishes, He beheld into heaven and blessed them, and broke, and dealt to His disciples that they should set forth before the companies. And all men ate and were fulfilled, and that that left to them of broken meats was taken up, twelve coffins.

And it was done, when He was alone praying, His disciples were with him, and He asked them and said, Whom say the people that I am? And they answered and said, John Baptist, others say Elijah, and others say one prophet of the former is risen. And He said to them, But who say ye that I am? Simon Peter answered and said, The Christ of God.

And He, blaming them, commanded that they should say to no man, and said these things, For it behoves Man's Son to suffer many things and to be reproved of the elder men and of the princes of priests and of scribes, and to be slain and the third day to rise again. And He said to all, If any will come after Me, deny he himself and take he his cross every day, and sue he Me. For he that will make his life safe, shall lose it. And he that loses his life for Me, shall make it safe. And what profits it to a man if he win all the world and lose himself, and do pairing of himself? For whoso shames Me and My words, Man's Son shall shame him when He comes in His majesty, and of the Father's and of the holy angels. And I say to you, verily, there are some standing here which shall not taste death till they see the realm of God.

And it was done after these words almost eight days, and He took Peter and James and John, and He styed into an hill to pray. And while He prayed, the likeness *countenance, face* of His cheer was changed, and His clothing was white shining. And lo, two men spoke with Him, and Moses and Elijah were seen in majesty, and they saw His going out which he should fulfil in Jerusalem.

And Peter and they that were with Him, were heavy of sleep. And they, waking, saw His majesty and the two men that stood with Him. And it was done, when they departed from Him, Peter said to Jesus, Commander, it is good that we are here, and make we here three tabernacles, one to Thee, and one to Moses, and one to Elijah. And he wist not what he should say. But while he spoke these things, a cloud was made and overshadowed them, and they dreaded when they entered into the cloud. And a voice was made out of the cloud, and said, This is my dearworth Son. Hear ye Him. And while the voice was made, Jesus was found alone. And they were still, and to no man said in those days aught of those things that they had seen.

But it was done in the day suing, when they came down of the hill, much people met them. And lo, a man of the company cried and said, Master, I beseech Thee, behold my son, for I have no more. And lo, a spirit takes him and suddenly he cries and hurtles down, and to-draws him with foam, and unneth he goes away all to-drawing him. And I prayed Thy disciples that they should cast him out, and they might not.

pulls in pieces, rends barely, hardly, scarcely

And Jesus answered and said to them, Ah, unfaithful generation and wayward, how long shall I be at you and suffer you? Bring hither thy son. And when he came nigh, the devil hurtled him down and to-braided him. And Jesus blamed the unclean spirit and healed the child, and yielded him to his father. And all men wondered greatly in the greatness of God.

bruised, tore

And when all men wondered in all things that He did, He said to His disciples, Put ye these words in your hearts, for it is to come that Man's Son be betrayed into the hands of men. And they knew not this word, and it was hid before them that they felt it not, and they dreaded to ask Him of this word. But a thought entered into them who of them should be greatest. And Jesus, seeing the thoughts of the heart of them, took a child and set him beside him, and said to them, Whoever receives this child in My name, receives Me. And who ever receives Me, receives Him that sent Me. For he that is least among you all, is the greatest.

And John answered and said, Commander, we saw a man casting out fiends in Thy name, and we have forbidden him, for he sues not Thee with us. And Jesus said to him, Nil ye forbid, for he that is not against us, is for us.

And it was done, when the days of His taking up were fulfilled, He set fast his face to go to Jerusalem, and sent messengers before His sight. And they went and entered into a city of Samaritans to make ready to Him. And they received not Him, for the face was of Him going into Jerusalem. And when James and John, His disciples, saw, they said, Lord, will Thou that we say that fire come down from heaven and waste them? And He turned and blamed them, and said, Ye wit not whose Spirit ye are, for Man's Son came not to lose men's souls, but to save. And they went into another castle.

And it was done, when they walked in the way, a man said to him, I will sue Thee whitherever Thou go. And Jesus said to him, Foxes have dens, and birds of the air have nests, but Man's Son has not where He rest His head. And He said to another, Sue thou Me. And he said, Lord, suffer me first to go and bury my father. And Jesus said to him, Suffer that dead men bury their dead men. But go thou and tell the kingdom of God.

And another said, Lord, I shall sue Thee, but first suffer me to leave all things that are at home.

And Jesus said to him, No man that puts his hand to the plough and beholding backward, is able to the realm of God.

Chapter X

And after these things, the Lord Jesus ordained also other seventy and twain, and sent them by twain and twain before His face into every city and place whither He was to come. And He said to them, There is much ripe corn and few workmen. Therefore pray ye the Lord of the ripe corn that He send workmen into His ripe corn. Go ye. Lo, I send you as lambs among wolves. Therefore nil ye bear a satchel, neither scrip, neither shoes, and greet ye no man by the way. Into what house that ye enter, first say ye, Peace to this house. And if a son of peace be there, your peace shall rest on him. But if none, it shall turn again to you. And dwell ye in the same house, eating and drinking those things that are at them, for a workman is worthy of his hire. Nil ye pass from house into house. And into whatever city ye enter, and they receive you, eat ye those things that are set to you, and heal ye the sick men that are in that city. And say ye to them, The kingdom of God shall nigh into you.

Into what city ye enter, and they receive you not, go ye out into the streets of it, and say ye, We wipe off against you the powder that cleaved to us of your city. Netheless, wit ye this thing, that the realm of God shall come nigh. I say to you that to Sodom it shall be easier than to that city in that day. Woe to thee, Chorazin. Woe to thee, Bethsaida. For if in Tyre and Sidon the virtues had been done which have been done in you, some time they would have sat in hair and ashes, and have done penance. Netheless, to Tyre and Sidon it shall be easier in the doom than to you. And thou, Capernaum, art enhanced till to heaven. Thou shall be drenched till into hell. He that hears you, hears Me. And he that despises you, despises Me. And he that despises Me, despises Him that sent Me.

And the two and seventy disciples turned again with joy, and said, Lord, also devils are subject to us in Thy name. And He said to them, I saw Satan falling down from heaven as light. And lo, I have given to you power to tread on serpents and on scorpions, and on all the virtue of the enemy, and nothing shall annoy you.

Netheless, nil ye joy on this thing that spirits are subject to you. But joy ye that your names are written in heavens.

In the ilk hour He gladded in the Holy Ghost, and said, I acknowledge to Thee, Father, Lord of heaven and of earth, for Thou has hid these things from wise men and prudent, and has showed them to small children. Yea, Father, for so it pleased before Thee. All things are given to Me of My Father, and no man wot who is the Son but the Father, and who is the Father but the Son, and to whom the Son will show. And He turned to His disciples and said, Blessed are the eyes that see those things that ye see. For I say to you that many prophets and kings would have seen those things that ye see, and they saw not, and hear those things that ye hear, and they heard not.

And lo, a wise man of the law rose up, tempting Him and saying, Master, what thing shall I do to have everlasting life? And He said to him, What is written in the law? How reads thou? He answered and said, Thou shall love the Lord God of all thine heart, and of all thy soul, and of all thy strengths, and of all thy mind, and thy neighbour as thyself. And Jesus said to him, Thou has answered rightly. Do this thing and thou shall live. But he, willing to justify himself, said to Jesus, And who is my neighbour?

And Jesus beheld and said, A man came down from Jerusalem into Jericho and fell among thieves. And they robbed him and wounded him, and went away and left the man half alive. And it befell that a priest came down the same way and passed forth when he had seen him. *minister* Also a deacon, when he was beside the place and saw him, passed forth. But a Samaritan going the way, came beside him, and he saw him and had ruth on him, and *pour* came to him and bound together his wounds, and heled in oil and wine, and laid him on his beast and led into an hostry and did the cure of him. And another day he *hostelry, hotel* brought forth two pence, and gave to the hostellerR and *hotel or inn-keepe* said, Have the cure of him, and whatever thou shall give over, I shall yield to thee when I come again. Who of these three, seems to thee, was neighbour to him that fell among thieves? And he said, He that did mercy into him. And Jesus said to him, Go thou, and do thou on like manner.

And it was done, while they went, He entered into a castle, and a woman, Martha by name, received Him into her house. And to this was a sister, Mary by name, which also sat beside the feet of the Lord and heard His word. But Martha busied about the oft service, and she stood and said, Lord, takes Thou no keep that my sister has left me alone to serve? Therefore say Thou to her that she help me. And the Lord answered and said to her, Martha, Martha, thou art busy and art troubled about full many things. But one thing is necessary. Mary has chosen the best part, which shall not be taken away from her.

Chapter XI

And it was done when He was praying in a place, as He ceased, one of His disciples said to Him, Lord, teach us to pray, as John taught his disciples. And He said to them, When ye pray, say ye, Father, hallowed be Thy name. Thy kingdom come to. Give to us today our each day's bread. And forgive to us our sins as we forgive to each man that owes to us. And lead us not into temptation.

And He said to them, Who of you shall have a friend and shall go to him at midnight, and shall say to him, Friend, lend to me three loaves, for my friend comes to me from the way and I have not what I shall set before him? And he, withinforth answer and say, Nil thou be heavy to me, the door is now shut and my children are with me in bed. I may not rise and give to thee. And if he shall dwell still knocking, I say to you though he shall not rise and give to him for that he is his friend, *nevertheless,* netheless for his continual asking he shall rise and give *notwithstanding* to him as many as he has need to. And I say to you, ask ye and it shall be given to you. Seek ye, and ye shall find. Knock ye, and it shall be opened to you. For each that asks, takes, and he that seeks, finds, and to a man that knocks it shall be opened.

Therefore, who of you asks his father bread, whether he shall give him a stone? Or if he asks fish, whether he shall give him a serpent for the fish? Or if he asks an egg, whether he shall a-reach him a scorpion? Therefore if ye, when ye are evil, ken give good gifts to your children, how much more your Father of heaven shall give a good Spirit to men that ask Him?

And Jesus was casting out a fiend, and he was dumb. And when He had cast out the fiend, the dumb man spoke and the people wondered. And some of them said, In Beelzebub, prince of devils, He casts out devils. And others, tempting, asked of Him a token from heaven. And as He saw the thoughts of them, He said to them, Every realm departed against itself, shall be desolate, and an house shall fall on an house. And if Satan be departed against himself, how shall his realm stand? For ye say that I cast out fiends in Beelzebub. And if I in Beelzebub cast out fiends, in whom cast out your sons? Therefore they shall be your doomsmen. But if I cast out fiends in the finger of God, then the realm of God is come among you. When a strong armed man keeps his house, all thing that he wields are in peace. But if a stronger than he come upon him and overcome him, he shall take away all his armour in which he tristed, and shall deal abroad his robberies. He that is not with Me, is against Me. And he that gathers not together with Me, scatters abroad.

When an unclean spirit goes out of a man, he wanders by dry places and seeks rest. And he, finding not, says, I shall turn again into mine house from whence I came out. And when he comes, he finds it cleansed with besoms and fair arrayed. Then he goes and takes with him seven other spirits worse than himself, and they enter and dwell there. And the last things of that man are made worse than the former.

And it was done, when He had said these things, a woman of the company reared her voice and said to Him, Blessed be the womb that bore Thee, and blessed are the teats that Thou has sucked! And He said, But yea, blessed are they that hear the word of God and keep it.

And when the people ran together, He began to say, This generation is a wayward generation. It seeks a token, and a token shall not be given to it but the token of Jonah the prophet. For as Jonah was a token to men of Nineveh, so Man's Son shall be to this generation. The queen of the south shall rise in doom with men of this generation and shall condemn them, for she came from the ends of the earth for to hear the wisdom of Solomon. And lo, here is a greater than Solomon. Men of Nineveh shall rise in doom with this generation and shall condemn it, for they did penance in the preaching of Jonah, and lo, here is a greater than Jonah.

No man tends a lantern and puts in hidles, neither under a bushel, but on a candlestick, that they that go in, see light. The lantern of thy body is thine eye. If thine eye be simple, all thy body shall be lighty. But if it be *full of light* wayward, all thy body shall be darkful. Therefore see thou, lest the light that is in thee be darknesses.

Therefore, if all thy body be bright, and have no part of darknesses, it shall be all bright, and as a lantern of brightness it shall give light to thee.

And when He spoke, a Pharisee prayed Him that He should eat with him. And He entered and sat to the meat. And the Pharisee began to say, guessing within himself, why He was not washed before meat. And the Lord said to him, Now ye Pharisees cleanse that that is withoutforth of the cup and the platter. But that thing that is within of you is full of raven and wickedness. Fools. Whether He that made that that is withoutforth made not also that that is within? Netheless, that that is overplus, give ye alms, and lo, all things are clean to you.

But woe to you, Pharisees, that tithe mint and rue and each herb, and leave doom and the charity of God. For it behoved to do these things and not leave those.

Woe to you, Pharisees, that love the first chairs in synagogues and salutations in cheaping. Woe to you that are as sepulchres that are not seen, and men walking above wit not.

But one of the wise men of the law answered and said to Him, Master, Thou saying these things also to us dost despite.

And He said, Also woe to you, wise men of law, for *burdens* ye charge men with burthens which they moun not bear, and ye yourselves with your one finger touch not the heavinesses. Woe to you that build tombs of pro- phets, and your fathers slew them. Truly ye witness that ye consent to the works of your fathers, for they slew them but ye build their sepulchres. Therefore the wis- dom of God said, I shall send to them prophets and apostles, and of them they shall slay and pursue, that the blood of all prophets that was shed from the making of the world, be sought of this generation, from the blood of the just Abel to the blood of Zacharias that was slain betwixt the altar and the house. So I say to you, it shall be sought of this generation.

Woe to you, wise men of the law, for ye have taken away the key of kunning, and ye yourselves entered not, *knowledge* and ye have forbidden them that entered.

And when He had said these things to them, the Pharisees and wise men of law began grievously to againstand and stop His mouth of many things, aspy-ing Him and seeking to take something of His mouth to accuse Him.

Chapter XII

And when much people stood about so that they trod each on other, He began to say to His disciples, Be ye ware of the sourdough of the Pharisees that is hypocrisy. For nothing is hiled that shall not be showed, neither hid that shall not be wist. For why, those things that ye have said in darknesses, shall be said in light. And that that ye have spoken in ear in the couches, shall be preached in roofs. And I say to you, My friends, be ye not afeared of them that slay the body, and after these things have no more what they shall do. But I shall show to you whom ye shall dread. Dread ye Him that after He has slain, He has power to send into hell. And so I say to you, dread ye Him.

Whether five sparrows are not sold for two halfpence, and one of them is not in forfeiting before God? But also all the hairs of your head are numbered. Therefore nil ye dread. Ye are of more price than many sparrows.

Truly I say to you, each man that acknowledges Me before men, Man's Son shall acknowledge him before the angels of God. But he that denies Me before men, shall be denied before the angels of God. And each that says a word against Man's Son, it shall be forgiven to him. But it shall not be forgiven to him that blasphemes against the Holy Ghost. And when they lead you into *powers, rulers* synagogues and to magistrates and potentates, nil ye be busy how or what ye shall answer, or what ye shall say. For the Holy Ghost shall teach you in that hour what it behoves you to say.

And one of the people said to Him, Master, say to my brother that he depart with me the heritage.

And He said to him, Man, who ordained Me a doomsman or a departer on you? And He said to them, See ye, and be ye ware of all covetise, for the life of a man is not in the abundance of those things which he wields. And He told to them a likeness, and said, The field of a rich man brought forth plenteous fruits. And he thought within himself and said, What shall I do, for I have not whither I shall gather my fruits? And he said, This thing I shall do. I shall throw down my barns and I shall make greater, and thither I shall gather all things that grow to me, and my goods. And I shall say to my soul, Soul, thou has many goods kept into full many years. Rest thou. Eat, drink and make feast. And God said to him, Fool. In this night they shall take thy life from thee. And whose shall those things be that thou has arrayed? So is he that treasures to himself, and is not rich in God.

And He said to His disciples, Therefore I say to you, nil ye be busy to your life, what ye shall eat, neither to your body, with what ye shall be clothed. The life is more than meat, and the body more than clothing. Behold ye crows, for they sow not neither reap, to which is no cellar nor barn, and God feeds them. How much more ye are of more price than they? And who of you, *taking thought* bethinking, may put to one cubit to his stature? Therefore, if ye moun not that that is least, what are ye busy of other things?

Behold ye the lilies of the field, how they wax. They travail not, neither spin. And I say to you that neither Solomon in all his glory was clothed as one of these. And if God clothes thus the hay that today is in the field and tomorrow is cast into an oven, how much more you of little faith? And nil ye seek what ye shall eat or what ye shall drink. And nil ye be raised on high. For folks of the world seek all these things, and your Father wot that ye need all these things. Netheless, seek ye first the kingdom of God, and all these things shall be cast to you. Nil ye, little flock, dread, for it pleased to your Father to give you a kingdom. Sell ye those things that ye have in possession, and give ye alms. And make to you satchels *money bags, wallets* that wax not old, treasure that fails not in heavens, whither a thief nighs not, neither moth destroys. For where is thy treasure, there thine heart shall be.

Be your loins girded above, and lanterns burning in your hands. And be ye like to men that abide their lord when he shall turn again from the weddings, that when he shall come and knock, anon they opened to him. Blessed be those servants that when the Lord shall come, He shall find waking. Truly I say to you that He shall gird Himself and make them sit to meat, and He shall go and serve them. And if He come in the second waking, and if He come in the third waking and find so, those servants be blessed. And wit ye this thing, for if an husbandman wist in what hour the thief would come, soothly he should wake and not suffer his house to be mined. And be ye ready, for in what hour ye guess not, *broken into, dug through* Man's Son shall come.

And Peter said to Him, Lord, say Thou this parable to us, or to all? And the Lord said, Who, guess thou, is a true dispender and a prudent, whom the lord has *steward* ordained on his meyne to give him in time measure of wheat? Blessed is that servant that the lord, when he comes, shall find so doing. Verily I say to you that on all things that he wields, he shall ordain him.

That if that servant say in his heart, My lord tarries to come, and begin to smite children and handmaidens, and eat and drink, and be fulfilled over measure, the lord of that servant shall come in the day that he hopes not, and the hour that he wot not, and shall depart him and put his part with unfaithful men. But the ilk servant that knew the will of his lord and made not him ready, and did not after his will, shall be beaten with many beat⁄ings. But he that knew not, and did worthy things of strokes, shall be beaten with few. For to each man to whom much is given, much shall be asked of him. And they shall ask more of him to whom they betook much.

I came to send fire into the earth, and what will I but that it be kindled? And I have to be baptized with a baptism, and how am I constrained till that it be parfitly done? Ween ye that I came to give peace into earth? Nay, I say to you, but departing. For from this time there shall be five departed in one house. Three shall be departed against twain, and twain shall be departed against three, the father against the son and the son against the father, the mother against the daughter and the daughter against the mother, the husband's mother against the son's wife, and the son's wife against her husband's mother.

And he said also to the people, When ye see a cloud rising from the sun going down, anon ye say, Rain comes, and so it is done. And when ye see the south blowing, ye say that heat shall be. And it is done. Hypocrites! Ye ken prove the face of heaven and of earth, but how prove ye not this time? But what and of yourselves ye deem not that it is just? But when thou goes with thine adversary in the way to the prince, do business to be delivered from him, lest peradventure he take thee to the doomsman, and the doomsman betake thee to the masterful asker, and the masterful asker send thee into prison. I say to thee, thou shall not go from thence till thou yield the last farthing.

authorized or powerful judge

Chapter XIII

And some men were present in that time that told to Him of the Galileans whose blood Pilate mingled with the sacrifices of them. And He answered and said to them, Ween ye that these men of Galilee were sinners more than all Galileans for they suffered such things? I say to you nay. All ye shall perish in like manner but ye have penance. And as those eighteen on which the tower in Siloam fell down and slew them, guess ye for they were debtors more than all men that dwell in Jerusalem? I say to you nay, but also ye all shall perish if ye do not penance.

And He said this likeness, A man had a fig tree planted in his vineyard, and he came seeking fruit in it and found none. And he said to the tiller of the vineyard, Lo, three years are since I come seeking fruit in this fig tree, and I find none. Therefore cut it down. Whereto occupies it the earth? And he, answering, said to him, Lord, suffer it also this year the while I delve it about, and I shall dung it if it shall make fruit. If nay, in time coming thou shall cut it down.

And He was teaching in their synagogues in the Sabbaths, and lo, a woman that had a spirit of sickness eighteen years, and was crooked and neither any manner might look upward. Whom, when Jesus had seen, He called to Him and said to her, Woman, thou art delivered of thy sickness. And He set on her His hands, and anon she stood upright and glorified God. And the prince of the synagogue, having disdain for Jesus had healed in the Sabbath, and he said to the people, There are six days in which it behoves to work. Therefore come ye in these and be ye healed, and not in the day of Sabbath. But the Lord answered to him and said, Hypocrite! Whether each of you unties not in the Sabbath his ox or ass from the creche and leads to water? Behoved it not this daughter of Abraham, whom Satan has bound, lo, eighteen years, to be unbound of this bond in the day of the Sabbath?

And when He had said these things, all His adversaries were ashamed, and all the people joyed in all things that were gloriously done of Him. Therefore He said, To what thing is the kingdom of God like? And to what thing shall I guess it to be like? It is like to a corn of senevy which a man took and cast into his yard. And it waxed and was made into a great tree, and fowls of the air rested in the branches thereof.

And eftsoon He said, To what thing shall I guess the kingdom of God like? It is like to sourdough that a woman took, and hid it into three measures of meal till all were soured.

And He went by cities and castles, teaching and making a journey into Jerusalem. And a man said to Him, Lord, if there are few that are saved? And He said to them, Strive ye to enter by the strait gate, for I say to you, many seek to enter, and they shall not mow. For when the Husbandman is entered and the door is closed, ye shall begin to stand withoutforth and knock at the door, and say, Lord, open to us! And He shall answer and say to you, I know you not of whence ye are. Then ye shall begin to say, We have eaten before Thee and drunken, and in our streets Thou has taught. And He shall say to you, I know you not of whence ye are. Go away from Me all ye workers of wickedness! There *gnashing, grinding* shall be weeping and grunting of teeth when ye shall see

Abraham and Isaac and Jacob and all the prophets in the kingdom of God, and you to be put out. And they shall come from the east and west, and from the north and south, and shall sit at the meat in the realm of God. And lo, they that were the first are the last, and they that were the last, are the first.

In that day, some of the Pharisees came nigh and said to Him, Go out, and go from hence, for Herod will slay Thee. And He said to them, Go ye, and say to that fox, Lo, I cast out fiends and I make parfitly healths today and tomorrow, and the third day I am ended. Netheless, it behoves Me today and tomorrow and the day that sues, to walk. For it falls not a prophet to perish out of Jerusalem.

Jerusalem, Jerusalem, that slays the prophets and stones them that are sent to thee, how often would I gather together thy sons as a bird gathers his nest under feathers, and thou would not? Lo, your house shall be left to you desert. And I say to you that ye shall not see Me till it come when ye shall say, Blessed is He that comes in the name of the Lord!

Chapter XIV

And it was done, when He had entered into the house of a prince of Pharisees in the Sabbath to eat bread, they aspied Him. And lo, a man sick in the dropsy was before Him. And Jesus, answering, spoke to the wise men of law and to the Pharisees, and said, Whether it is leaveful to heal in the Sabbath? And they held their peace. And Jesus took and healed him, and let him go. And He answered to them and said, Whose ass or ox of you shall fall into a pit and he shall not anon draw him out in the day of the Sabbath? And they might not answer to Him to these things.

He said also a parable to men bidden to a feast, and

beheld how they chose the first sitting-places, and said to them, When thou art bidden to a bridal's, sit not at the meat in the first place, lest peradventure a worthier than thou be bidden of him, and lest he come that called thee and him and say to thee, Give place to this. And then thou shall begin with shame to hold the lowest place. But when thou art bidden to a feast, go, and sit in the last place, that when he comes that bade thee to the feast, he say to thee, Friend, come higher. Then worship shall be to thee before men that sit at the meat. For each that enhances him, shall be lowed, and he that meeks him shall be highed.

And He said to him that had bidden Him to the feast, When thou makes a meat or a supper, nil thou call thy friends neither thy brethren, neither cousins, neither neighbours nor rich men, lest peradventure they bid thee again to the feast and it be yielded again to thee. But when thou makes a feast, call poor men, feeble, crooked and blind, and thou shall be blessed, for they have not whereof to yield thee. For it shall be yielded to thee in the rising again of just men.

And when one of them that sat together at the meat had heard these things, he said to Him, Blessed is he that shall eat bread in the realm of God. And He said to him, A man made a great supper and called many. And he sent his servant in the hour of supper to say to men that were bidden to the feast that they should come, for now all things are ready. And all began together to excuse them. The first said, I have bought a farm and I have need to go out and see it. I pray thee have me excused. And the t'other said, I have bought five yokes of oxen, and I go to prove them. I pray thee, have me excused. And another said, I have wedded a wife, and therefore I may not come. And the servant turned again and told these things to his lord. Then the husbandman was wroth and said to his servant, Go out swithy into *quickly* the great streets and small streets of the city, and bring in hither poor men and feeble, blind and crooked. And the servant said, Lord, it is done as thou has commanded, and yet there is a void place. And the lord said to the servant, Go out into ways and hedges and constrain men to enter, that mine house be fulfilled. For I say to you that none of those men that are called, shall taste my supper.

And much people went with Him, and He turned and said to them, If any man comes to Me and hates not his father and mother, and wife and sons, and brethren and sisters, and yet his own life, he may not be My disciple. And he that bears not his cross and comes after Me, may not be My disciple. For who of you, willing to build a tower, whether he first sit not and counts the spenses that are needful if he have to perform? Lest after *cost, expenses* that he has set the fundament and may not perform, all that see begin to scorn him and say, For this man began to build and might not make an end. Or what king that will go to do a battle against another king, whether he sits not first and bethinks if he may, with ten thousand, go against him that comes against him with twenty thousand? Else yet while he is afar, he, sending a messenger, prays those things that are of peace. So therefore each of you that forsakes not all things that he has, may not be My disciple. Salt is good. But if salt vanish, in what thing shall it be savoured? Neither in earth, neither in a dunghill it is profitable, but it shall be cast out. He that has ears of hearing, hear he.

Chapter XV

And publicans and sinful men were nighing to Him to hear Him. And the Pharisees and scribes grouched, saying, For this receives sinful men and eats with them.

And He spoke to them this parable, and said, What man of you that has an hundred sheep, and if he has lost one of them, whether he leaves not ninety and nine in desert, and goes to it that perished till he find it? And when he has found it, he joys and lays it on his shoulders, and he comes home and calls together his friends and neighbours, and says to them, Be ye glad with me, for I have found my sheep that had perished. And I say to you, so joy shall be in heaven on one sinful man doing penance, more than on ninety and nine just that have no need to penance.

Or what woman, having ten bezants, and if she has lost one bezant, whether she tends not a lantern and turns upsedown the house and seeks diligently, till that she find it? And when she has found, she calls together friends and neighbours and says, Be ye glad with me, for I have found the bezant that I had lost. So I say to you, joy shall be before angels of God on one sinful man doing penance.

And He said, A man had two sons, and the younger of them said to the father, Father, give me the *chattels* portion of cattle that falls to me. And he departed to them the cattle. And not after many days, when all things were gathered together, the younger son went forth in pilgrimage into a far country, and there he wasted his goods in living lecherously. And after that he had ended all things, a strong hunger was made in that country and he began to have need. And he went and drew him to one of the citizens of that country, and he sent him into his farm to feed swine. And he coveted *pods* to fill his womb of the cods that the hogs ate, and no man gave him. And he turned again to himself and said, How many hired men in my father's house have plenty of loaves, and I perish here through hunger? I shall rise up and go to my father, and I shall say to him,

Father, I have sinned into heaven and before thee, and now I am not worthy to be called thy son. Make me as one of thine hired men. And he rose up and came to his father. And when he was yet afar, his father saw him and was stirred by mercy. And he ran and fell on his neck, and kissed him. And the son said to him, Father, I have sinned into heaven and before thee, and now I am not worthy to be called thy son. And the father said to his servants, Swithy, bring ye forth the first stole and clothe ye him, and give ye a ring in his hand and shoes on his feet. And bring ye a fat calf and slay ye, and eat we and make we feast. For this my son was dead, and has lived again. He perished, and is found. And all men began to eat. But his elder son was in the field, and when he came and nighed to the house, he heard a symphony and a crowd. And he called one of the ser- *music-making* vants, and asked what these things were. And he said to him, Thy brother is come, and thy father slew a fat calf, for he received him safe. And he was wroth and would not come in. Therefore his father went out and began to pray to him. And he answered to his father and said, Lo, so many years I serve thee and I never broke thy commandment. And thou never gave to me a kid that I with my friends should have eaten. But after that this thy son, that has devoured his substance with whores, came, thou has slain to him a fat calf. And he said to him, Son, thou art evermore with me, and all my things are thine. But it behoved for to make feast and to have joy, for this thy brother was dead and lived again. He perished, and is found.

Chapter XVI

He said also to His disciples, There was a rich man that had a bailiff, and this was defamed to him as he had *estate manager, magistrate* wasted his goods. And he called him, and said to him,

What hear I this thing of thee? Yield reckoning of thy bailey, for thou might not now be bailiff. And the bailiff said within himself, What shall I do, for my lord takes away from me the bailey? Delve may I not. I shame to beg. I wot what I shall do, that when I am removed from the bailey, they receive me into their house. Therefore, when all the debtors of his lord were called together, he said to the first, How much owes thou to my lord? And he said, An hundred barrels of oil. And he said to him, *bill, invoice* Take thy caution and sit soon, and write fifty. Afterward he said to another, And how much owes *measures* thou? Which answered, And hundred cores of wheat. And he said to him, Take thy letters and write four score. And the lord praised the bailiff of wickedness, for he had done prudently. For the sons of this world are more prudent in their generation than the sons of light. And I say to you, make ye to you friends of the riches of wickedness, that when ye shall fail they receive you into everlasting tabernacles.

He that is true in the least thing, is true also in the more. And he that is wicked in a little thing, is wicked also in the more. Therefore, if ye were not true in the wicked thing of riches, who shall betake to you that that is very? And if ye were not true in other men's thing, who shall give to you that that is yours? No servant may serve to two lords. For either he shall hate the t'one and love the t'other, either he shall draw to the t'one and shall despise the t'other. Ye moun not serve to God and to riches.

But the Pharisees that were covetous, heard all these things and they scorned Him. And He said to them, Ye it be that justify you before men, but God has known your hearts, for that that is high to men is abomination before God. The law and prophets till to John, from that time the realm of God is evangelised, and each man does violence into it. Forsooth, it is lighter heaven and earth to pass, than that one tittle fall from the law. Every man that forsakes his wife and weds another, does lech￾ery. And he that weds the wife forsaken of the husband, does advowtry.

There was a rich man and was clothed in purple and white silk, and ate every day shiningly. And there *splendidly, sumptuously* was a beggar, Lazarus by name, that lay at his gate full of boils, and coveted to be fulfilled of the crumbs that *ulcers* fell down from the rich man's board. And no man gave to him, but hounds came and licked his boils. And it was done that the beggar died and was borne of angels into Abraham's bosom. And the rich man was dead also, and was buried in hell. And he raised his eyes when he was in torments, and saw Abraham afar and Lazarus in his bosom. And he cried and said, Father Abraham, have mercy on me and send Lazarus, that he dip the end of his finger in water to cool my tongue, for I am tormented in this flame. And Abraham said to him, Son, have mind, for thou has received good things in thy life, and Lazarus also evil things. But he is now comforted, and thou art tormen￾ted. And in all these things, a great dark place is estab￾lished betwixt us and you, that they that will from hence pass to you, moun not, neither from thence pass over hither. And he said, Then I pray thee, father, that thou send him into the house of my father, for I have five brethren, that he witness to them, lest also they come into this place of torments. And Abraham said to him, They have Moses and the prophets. Hear they them. And he said, Nay, father Abraham, but if any of dead men go to them, they shall do penance. And he said to him, If they hear not Moses and prophets, neither if any dead man rise again they shall believe to him.

Chapter XVII

And Jesus said to His disciples, It is impossible that sclaunders come not. But woe to that man by whom they come. It is more profitable to him if a millstone be put about his neck and he be cast into the sea, than that he sclaunder one of these little. Take ye heed yourself. If thy brother has sinned against thee, blame him, and if he do penance, forgive him. And if seven siths in the day he do sin against thee, and seven siths in the day he *reconsiders, repents* be converted to thee and say, It forthinks me, forgive thou him.

And the apostles said to the Lord, Increase to us faith. And the Lord said, If ye have faith as the corn of *mulberry tree* senevy, ye shall say to this more tree, Be thou drawn up by the root and be overplanted into the sea, and it shall obey to you. But who of you has a servant ering or lesew⁄ ing oxes, which says to him when he turns again from the field, Anon go, and sit to meat, and says not to him, Make ready that I sup, and gird thee and serve me while I eat and drink, and after this thou shall eat and drink. Whether he has grace to that servant for he did that that he commanded him? Nay, I guess. So ye, when ye have done all things that are commanded to you, say ye, We are unprofitable servants. We have done that that we ought to do.

And it was done the while Jesus went into *midst* Jerusalem, He passed through the middes of Samaria and Galilee. And when He entered into a castle, ten leprous men came against Him, which stood afar and raised their voice, and said, Jesus, Commander, have mercy on us! And as He saw them, He said, Go ye. Show ye to the priests. And it was done the while they went, they were cleansed. And one of them, as he saw that he was cleansed, went again, magnifying God with

great voice. And he fell down on the face before His feet
and did thankings. And this was a Samaritan. And
Jesus answered and said, Whether ten are not cleansed?
And where are the nine? There is none found that
turned again and gave glory to God, but this alien. And
He said to him, Rise up. Go thou, for thy faith has made
thee safe.

And He was asked of Pharisees when the realm of
God comes. And He answered to them and said, The
realm of God comes not with aspying. Neither they
shall say, Lo here, or, lo there. For lo, the realm of God
is within you. And He said to His disciples, Days shall
come when ye shall desire to see one day of Man's Son,
and ye shall not see. And they shall say to you, Lo here,
and, lo there. Nil ye go, neither sue ye. For as light shin‑
ing from under heaven shines into those things that are
under heaven, so shall Man's Son be in His day. But
first it behoves Him to suffer many things and to be
reproved of this generation. And as it was done in the
days of Noah, so it shall be in the days of Man's Son.
They ate and drank, wedded wives and were given to
weddings, till into the day in the which Noah entered
into the ship and the Great Flood came, and lost all.
Also as it was done in the days of Lot, they ate and
drank, bought and sold, planted and built. But the day
that Lot went out of Sodom, the Lord rained fire and
brimstone from heaven, and lost all. Like this thing it *burning sulphur*
shall be in what day Man's Son shall be shown. In that
hour, he that is in the roof and his vessels in the house,
come he not down to take them away. And he that shall
be in the field, also turn not again behind. Be ye mindful
of the wife of Lot. Whoever seeks to make his life safe,
shall lose it. And whoever loses it, shall quicken it. But
I say to you, in that night two shall be in one bed. One
shall be taken and the t'other forsaken. Two women

shall be grinding together. The t'one shall be taken, and the t'other forsaken. Two in a field. The t'one shall be taken, and the t'other left.

They answer and say to Him, Where, Lord? Which said to them, Wherever the body shall be, thither shall be gathered together also the eagles.

Chapter XVIII

And He said to them also a parable that it behoves to pray evermore and not fail, and said, There was a judge in a city that dreaded not God neither shamed of men. And a widow was in that city, and she came to him and said, Venge me of mine adversary. And he would not, long time. But after these things he said within himself, Though I dread not God and shame not of man, nethe- *avenge* less, for this widow is heavy to me, I shall venge her, lest at the last she, coming, condemn me. And the Lord said, Hear ye what the doomsman of wickedness says, and whether God shall not do vengeance of His chosen crying to Him day and night, and shall have patience in them? Soothly I say to you, for soon He shall do ven- geance of them. Netheless, guess thou that Man's Son, coming, shall find faith in earth?

And He said also to some men that tristed in them- selves as they were rightful and despised others, this para- ble, saying, Two men went up into the Temple to pray, the t'one a Pharisee and the t'other a publican. And the Pharisee stood and prayed by himself these things, and said, God, I do thankings to Thee for I am not as other *money-grabbers, robbers* men, raveners, unjust, advowtrers, as also this publi- can. I fast twice in the week, I give tithes of all things that I have in possession. And the publican stood afar and would neither raise his eyes to heaven, but smote his breast and said, God be merciful to me, sinner. Truly I say to you, this went down into his house, and was justi-

fied from the other. For each that enhances him, shall be
made low, and he that meeks him, shall be enhanced.

And they brought to Him young children that He
should touch them. And when the disciples saw this
thing, they blamed them. But Jesus called together them
and said, Suffer ye children to come to Me and nil ye
forbid them, for of such is the kingdom of heavens.
Truly I say to you, whoever shall not take the kingdom
of God as a child, he shall not enter into it.

And a prince asked Him and said, Good Master, in
what thing doing shall I wield everlasting life? And
Jesus said to him, What say thou Me good? No man is
good but God alone. Thou knows the commandment
is, Thou shall not slay, thou shall not do lechery, thou
shall not do theft, thou shall not say false witnessing,
worship thy father and thy mother. Which said, I have
kept all these things from my youth. And when this
thing was heard, Jesus said to him, Yet one thing fails to
thee. Sell thou all things that thou has and give to poor
men, and thou shall have treasure in heaven. And
come, sue thou Me. When these things were heard, he
was sorrowful, for he was full rich. And Jesus, seeing
him made sorry, said, How hard they that have money
shall enter into the kingdom of God. For it is lighter a
camel to pass through a needle's eye than a rich man to
enter into the kingdom of God. And they that heard
these things, said, Who may be made safe? And He
said to them, Those things that are impossible anents
men, are possible anents God.

But Peter said, Lo, we have left all things and have
sued Thee. And He said to him, Truly I say to you,
there is no man that shall forsake house, or father,
mother, or brethren, or wife, or children, or fields, for
the realm of God and shall not receive many more things
in this time, and in the world to come, everlasting life.

And Jesus took His twelve disciples and said to them, Lo, we go up to Jerusalem, and all things shall be ended that are written by the prophets of Man's Son. For He shall be betrayed to heathen men. And He shall be scorned and scourged and bespat. And after that they have scourged, they shall slay Him, and the third day He shall rise again. And they understood nothing of these. And this word was hidden from them, and they understood not those things that were said.

But it was done, when Jesus came nigh to Jericho, a blind man sat beside the way and begged. And when he heard the people passing, he asked what this was. And they said to him that Jesus of Nazareth passed. And he cried and said, Jesus, the Son of David, have mercy on me! And they that went before, blamed him that he should be still. But he cried much the more, Thou Son of David, have mercy on me! And Jesus stood and commanded him to be brought forth to Him. And when he came nigh, He asked him and said, What will thou that I shall do to thee? And he said, Lord, that I see! And Jesus said to him, Behold, thy faith has made thee safe. And anon he saw and sued Him, and magnified God. And all the people as it saw, gave herying to God.

Chapter XIX

And Jesus, going in, walked through Jericho. And lo, a man, Zacchaeus by name. And this was a prince of publicans, and he was rich. And he sought to see Jesus who He was, and he might not for the people, for he was little in stature. And he ran before and styed into a sycamore tree to see Him, for He was to pass from thence. And Jesus beheld up when He came to the place, and saw him, and said to him, Zacchaeus, haste thee and come down, for today I must dwell in thine house. And he, hying, came down, and joying received Him. And when all men saw, they grouched, saying, For He had turned to a sinful man. But Zacchaeus stood and said to the Lord, Lo, I give the half of my goods to poor men, and if I have anything defrauded any man, I yield four so much. Jesus says to him, For today health is made to this house, for that he is Abraham's son. For Man's Son came to seek and make safe that thing that perished.

When they heard these things, He added and said a parable for that He was nigh Jerusalem, and for they guessed that anon the kingdom of God should be shown. Therefore He said, A worthy man went into a far country to take to him a kingdom and to turn again. And when his ten servants were called, he gave to them ten bezants, and said to them, Chaffare ye till I come. But his citizens hated him and sent a messenger after him, and said, We will not that he reign on us. And it was done that he turned again when he had taken the kingdom, and he commanded his servants to be called to which he had given money, to wit how much each had won by chaffaring. And the first came and said, Lord, thy bezant has won ten bezants. He said to him, Well be, thou good servant, for in little thing thou has been true. Thou shall be having power on ten cities. And the t'other came and said, Lord, thy bezant has made five bezants. And to this he said, And be thou on five cities. And the third came and said, Lo, thy bezant that I had put up in a sudary, for I dreaded thee. For *napkin, sweat-cloth* thou art a stern man. Thou takes away that that thou set not, and thou reaps that that thou has not sown. He says to him, Wicked servant! Of thy mouth I deem thee. Wit thou that I am a stern man, taking away that thing that I set not, and reaping that thing that I sowed not? And why has thou not given my money to the board, and I, coming, should have asked it with usuries? And he said to men standing nigh, Take ye away from him the bezant, and give ye to him that has ten bezants. And they said to him, Lord, he has ten bezants! And I say to you, to each man that has, it shall be given and he shall increase. But from him that has not, also that thing that he has shall be taken off him. Netheless, bring ye hither those mine enemies that would not that I reigned on them, and slay ye before me.

And when these things were said, He went before and went up to Jerusalem. And it was done, when Jesus came nigh to Bethphage and Bethany, at the mount that is called of Olivet, He sent His two disciples and said, Go ye into the castle that is against you, into which as ye enter, ye shall find a colt of an ass tied, on which never man sat. Untie ye him and bring ye to Me. And if any man ask you why ye untie, thus ye shall say to him, For the Lord desires his work.

And they that were sent, went forth and found as He said to them, a colt standing. And when they untied the colt, the lords to him said to them, What untie ye the colt? And they said, For the Lord has need of him. And they led him to Jesus, and they, casting their clothes on the colt, set Jesus on him. And when He went, they strewed their clothes in the way.

And when He came nigh to the coming down of the mount of Olivet, all the people that came down began to joy and to hery God with great voice on all the virtues that they had seen, and said, Blessed be the King that comes in the name of the Lord. Peace in heaven and glory in high things. And some of the Pharisees of the people said to Him, Master, blame Thy disciples! And He said to them, I say to you, for if these are still, stones shall cry.

And when He nighed, He saw the city and wept on

it, and said, If thou had known, thou should weep also, for in this day the things are in peace to thee. But now they are hidden from thine eyes. But days shall come in thee, and thine enemies shall environ thee with a pale. *surround* And they shall go about thee and make thee strait on all *fence, palisade* sides, and cast thee down to the earth and thy sons that are in thee. And they shall not leave in thee a stone on a stone, for thou has not known the time of thy visitation.

And He entered into the Temple and began to cast out men selling therein and buying, and said to them, It is written that Mine house is an house of prayer, but ye have made it a den of thieves! And He was teaching every day in the Temple. And the princes of priests, and the scribes and the princes of the people sought to leese Him, and they found not what they should do to Him, for all the people were occupied and heard Him.

Chapter XX

And it was done in one of the days, when He taught the people in the Temple and preached the gospel, the princes of priests and scribes came together with the elder men, and they said to Him, Say to us in what power Thou does these things, or who is He that gave to Thee this power? And Jesus answered and said to them, And I shall ask you one word. Answer ye to Me. Was the baptism of John of heaven or of men? And they thought within themselves, saying, For if we say, Of heaven, He shall say, Why then believe ye not to him? And if we say, Of men, all the people shall stone us, for they are certain that John is a prophet. And they answered that they knew not of whence it was. And Jesus said to them, Neither I say to you in what power I do these things.

And He began to say to the people this parable: A man planted a vineyard and hired it to tillers, and he

was in pilgrimage long time. And in the time of gather‑
ing of grapes, he sent a servant to the tillers, that they
should give to him of the fruit of the vineyard, which
beat him and let him go void. And he thought yet to
send another servant, and they beat this and tormented
him sore, and let him go. And he thought yet to send the
third, and him also they wounded and cast out. And
the lord of the vineyard said, What shall I do? I shall
send my dearworth son. Peradventure when they see
him, they shall dread. And when the tillers saw him,
they thought within themselves and said, This is the
heir. Slay we him, that the heritage be ours. And they
cast him out of the vineyard and killed him. What then
shall the lord of the vineyard do to them? He shall come
and destroy these tillers, and give the vineyard to others.

And when this thing was heard, they said to Him,
God forbid. But He beheld them and said, What then
is this that is written, The stone which men building
reproved, this is made into the head of the corner? Each
that shall fall on that stone, shall be to‑brised, but on
whom it shall fall, it shall all to‑break him.

And the princes of priests and scribes sought to lay
on Him hands in that hour, and they dreaded the peo‑
ple, for they knew that to them He said this likeness.
spies, watchers And they aspied and sent aspiers that feigned them just,
that they should take Him in word and betake Him to
the power of the prince and to the power of the justice.
And they asked Him and said, Master, we wit that
rightly Thou says and teaches, and Thou takes not the
person of man, but Thou teaches in truth the way of
God. Is it leaveful to us to give tribute to the emperor, or
nay? And He beheld the deceit of them, and said to
them, What tempt ye Me? Show ye to Me a penny.
Whose image and superscription has it? They
answered and said to Him, The emperor's. And He

said to them, Yield ye therefore to the emperor those things that are the emperor's, and those things that are of God, to God. And they might not reprove His word before the people, and they wondered in His answer and held peace.

Some of the Sadducees that denied the again⁄rising *resurrection* from death to life, came and asked Him, and said, Master, Moses wrote to us, If the brother of any man have a wife and is dead, and he was without heirs, that his brother take his wife and raise seed to his brother. And so there were seven brethren. The first took a wife and is dead without heirs, and the brother suing took her, and he is dead without son. And the third took her also and all seven, and left not seed but are dead. And the last of all, the woman is dead. Therefore, in the ris⁄ing again, whose wife of them shall she be? For seven had her to wife.

And Jesus said to them, Sons of this world wed and are given to weddings, but they that shall be had worthy of that world and of the rising again from death, neither are wedded, neither wed wives, neither shall mow die more. For they are even with angels and are the sons of God, since they are the sons of rising again from death. And that dead men rise again, also Moses showed beside the bush. As he says, The Lord God of Abraham, and God of Isaac, and God of Jacob. And God is not of dead men, but of living men, for all men live to Him.

And some of scribes answering, said, Master, Thou has well said. And they dared no more ask Him any⁄thing. But He said to them, How say men, Christ to be the Son of David, and David himself says in the book of Psalms, The Lord said to my Lord, Sit Thou on My right half till that I put Thine enemies a stool of Thy feet? Therefore David calls Him Lord, and how is He his son? And in hearing of all the people, He said to His disciples, Be ye ware of scribes that will wander in stoles, and love salutations in cheaping and the first chairs in synagogues, and the first sitting-places in feasts, that devour the houses of widows and feign long praying. These shall take the more damnation.

Chapter XXI

And He beheld and saw those rich men that cast their gifts into the treasury. But He saw also a little poor widow casting two farthings. And He said, Truly I say to you that this poor widow cast more than all men. For why, all these of thing that was plenteous to them, cast into the gifts of God. But this widow of that thing that failed to her, cast all her livelihood that she had.

And when some men said of the Temple that it was apparelled with good stones and gifts, He said, These things that ye see, days shall come in which a stone shall not be left on a stone which shall not be destroyed. And they asked Him and said, Commander, when shall these things be? And what token shall be when they shall begin to be done? And He said, See ye that ye be not deceived. For many shall come in My name saying, For I am. And the time shall nigh. Therefore, nil ye go after them. And when ye shall hear battles and strifes within, nil ye be afeared. It behoves first these things to be done, but not yet anon is an end.

Then He said to them, Folk shall rise against folk, and realm against realm. Great movings of earth shall be by places, and pestilences and hungers, and dreads from heaven and great tokens shall be. But before all these things, they shall set their hands on you and shall pursue, betaking into synagogues and keepings, drawing to kings and to justices for My name. But it shall fall to you into witnessing. Therefore, put ye in your hearts

not to think before how ye shall answer. For I shall give
to you mouth and wisdom to which all your adversaries
shall not mow againstand and againsay. And ye shall *contradict, gainsay*
be taken of father and mother, and brethren and cousins
and friends, and by death they shall torment of you, and
ye shall be in hate of all men for My name. And an hair
of your head shall not perish. In your patience ye shall
wield your souls.

But when ye shall see Jerusalem be environed with
an host, then wit ye that the desolation of it shall nigh.
Then they that are in Judea flee to the mountains, and
they that are in the middle of it go away, and they that
are in the countries, enter not into it. For these are days of
vengeance, that all things that are written, be fulfilled.
And woe to them that are with child and nourish in
those days, for a great disease shall be on the earth and
wrath to this people. And they shall fall by the sharp-
ness of the sword, and they shall be led prisoners into all
folks. And Jerusalem shall be defouled of heathen men
till the times of nations be fulfilled. And tokens shall be
in the sun and the moon and in the stars, and in the earth
overlaying of folks for confusion of sound of the sea and *overthrowing*
of floods. For men shall wax dry for dread and abiding
that shall come to all the world, for virtues of heavens
shall be moved. And then they shall see Man's Son coming in a cloud with great power and majesty. And when
these things begin to be made, behold ye, and raise ye
your heads, for your redemption nighs.

And He said to them a likeness: See ye the fig tree
and all trees. When they bring forth now of themselves
fruit, ye wit that summer is nigh. So ye, when ye see
these things to be done, wit ye that the kingdom of God
is nigh. Truly I say to you that this generation shall not
pass till all things be done. Heaven and earth shall pass,
but My words shall not pass. But take ye heed to your-

distended, swollen selves, least peradventure your hearts be gravid with gluttony and drunkenness and business of this life, and the
ilk day come sudden on you, for as a snare it shall come
on all men that sit on the face of all earth. Therefore
wake ye, praying in each time, that ye be had worthy to
flee all these things that are to come, and to stand before
Man's Son.

And in days He was teaching in the Temple, but in
nights He went out and dwelled in the mount that is
called of Olivet. And all the people rose early to come to
Him in the Temple and to hear Him.

Chapter XXII

And the holiday of therf loaves that is said Pasch,
nighed. And the princes of priests and the scribes
sought how they should slay Jesus, but they dreaded the
people. And Satan entered into Judas that was called
Iscariot, one of the twelve. And he went and spoke with
the princes of priests and with the magistrates, how he
should betray Him to them. And they joyed and made
covenant to give him money. And he behight, and he
sought opportunity to betray Him without people.

But the days of therf loaves came, in which it was
need that the sacrifice of Pasch were slain. And He sent
Peter and John, and said, Go ye, and make ye ready to
us the Pasch, that we eat. And they said, Where will
Thou that we make ready? And He said to them, Lo,
when ye shall enter into the city, a man bearing a vessel
of water shall meet you. Sue ye him into the house into
which he enters. And ye shall say to the husbandman of
the house, The Master says to thee, Where is a chamber
where I shall eat the Pasch with My disciples? And he
shall show to you a great souping-place strewed, and
there make ye ready. And they went and found as He
said to them, and they made ready the Pasch.

And when the hour was come, He sat to the meat and the twelve apostles with Him. And He said to them, With desire I have desired to eat with you this Pasch before that I suffer. For I say to you that from this time I shall not eat it till it be fulfilled in the realm of God. And when He had taken the cup, He did graces, and said, Take ye, and depart ye among you. For I say to you that I shall not drink of the kind of this vine till the realm of God come.

And when He had taken bread, He did thankings and broke, and gave to them, and said, This is My body which shall be given for you. Do this thing in mind of Me. He took also the cup after that He had supped, and said, This cup is the New Testament in My blood that shall be shed for you. Netheless lo, the hand of him that betrays Me is with Me at the table. And Man's Son goes after that it is determined. Netheless, woe to that man by whom He shall be betrayed. And they began to seek among them who it was of them that was to do this thing.

And strife was made among them which of them should be seen to be greatest. But He said to them, Kings of heathen men are lords of them, and they that have power on them are called good-doers. But ye not so. But he that is greatest among you be made as younger, and he that is before-goer, as a servant. For who is greater, he that sits at the meat, or he that ministers? Whether not he that sits at the meat? And I am in the middle of you as He that ministers. And ye are that have dwelled with Me in My temptations, and I dispose to you as My Father has disposed to Me a realm, that ye eat and drink on My board in My realm, and sit on thrones and deem the twelve kindreds of Israel.

And the Lord said to Simon, Simon, lo, Satan has asked you, that he should riddle as wheat. But I have *sift* prayed for thee that thy faith fail not. And thou some-time converted, confirm thy brethren. Which said to Him, Lord, I am ready to go into prison and into death with Thee! And He said, I say to thee, Peter, the cock shall not crow today till thou thrice forsake that thou knows Me.

And He said to them, When I sent you without satchel and scrip and shoes, whether anything failed to you? And they said, Nothing. Therefore He said to them, But now he that has a satchel, take also and a scrip. And he that has none, sell his coat and buy a sword. For I say to you that yet it behoves that thing that is written to be fulfilled in Me, And He is a-retted with wicked men. For those things that are of Me have end. And they said, Lord, lo, two swords here! And He said to them, It is enough.

And He went out and went after the custom into the hill of Olives. And the disciples sued Him. And when He came to the place, He said to them, Pray ye, lest ye enter into temptation. And He was taken away from them so much as is a stone's cast, and He kneeled and prayed, and said, Father, if Thou will, do away this cup from Me. Netheless, not My will be done, but Thine. And an angel appeared to Him from heaven and com-forted Him. And He was made in agony and prayed the longer, and His sweat was made as drops of blood running down into the earth. And when He was risen from prayer, and was come to His disciples, He found them sleeping for heaviness. And He said to them, What sleep ye? Rise ye and pray ye, that ye enter not into temptation.

Yet while He spoke, lo, a company, and he that was called Judas, one of the twelve, went before them. And he came to Jesus to kiss Him. And Jesus said to him, Judas, with a kiss thou betrays Man's Son?

And they that were about Him and saw that that was to come, said to Him, Lord, whether we smite with sword? And one of them smote the servant of the prince of priests, and cut off his right ear. But Jesus answered and said, Suffer ye till hither. And when He had touched his ear, He healed him.

And Jesus said to them that came to Him, the princes of priests and magistrates of the Temple and elder men, As to a thief ye have gone out with swords and staves? When I was each day with you in the Temple, ye straught not out hands into Me. But this is your hour and the power of darknesses.

And they took Him and led to the house of the prince of priests, and Peter sued Him afar. And when a fire was kindled in the middle of the great house and they sat about, Peter was in the middle of them. Whom, when a damsel had seen sitting at the light and had beholden him, she said, And this was with Him. And he denied Him and said, Woman, I know Him not! And after a little, another man saw him and said, And thou art of them. But Peter said, Ah, man, I am not! And when a space was made as of one hour, another affirmed and said, Truly this was with Him, for also he is of Galilee. And Peter said, Man, I noot what thou say! And anon, *know not* yet while he spoke, the cock crowed. And the Lord turned again and beheld Peter, and Peter had mind on the word of Jesus as He had said, For before that the cock crows, thrice thou shall deny Me. And Peter went out and wept bitterly.

And the men that held Him, scorned Him and smote Him. And they blindfolded Him and smote His *blindfolded* face, and asked Him and said, Arede, Thou Christ, to us, who is he that smote Thee? Also they, blaspheming, said against Him many other things.

And as the day was come, the elder men of the people

and the princes of priests and the scribes came together
and led Him to their council, and said, If Thou art
Christ, say to us! And He said to them, If I say to you,
ye shall not believe to Me. And if I ask, ye shall not
answer to Me, neither ye shall deliver Me. But after this
time, Man's Son shall be sitting on the right half of the
virtue of God. Therefore all said, Then art Thou the
Son of God? And He said, Ye say that I am. And they
said, What yet desire we witnessing? For we ourselves
have heard of His mouth!

Chapter XXIII

And all the multitude of them arose and led Him to
Pilate. And they began to accuse Him and said, We
have found this turning upsedown our folk and forbidding tributes to be given to the emperor, and saying that
Himself is Christ and King! And Pilate asked Him
and said, Art Thou King of Jews? And He answered
and said, Thou say. And Pilate said to the princes of
priests and to the people, I find nothing of cause in this
Man.

And they waxed stronger and said, He moves the
people, teaching through all Judea, beginning from
Galilee till hither! And Pilate, hearing Galilee, asked if
He were a man of Galilee. And when he knew that He
was of the power of Herod, he sent Him to Herod,
which was at Jerusalem in those days. And when
Herod saw Jesus, he joyed full much, for long time he
coveted to see Him, for he heard many things of Him
and hoped to see some token to be done of Him. And he
asked Him in many words, and He answered nothing
to him. And the princes of priests and the scribes stood,
steadfastly accusing Him. But Herod and his host
despised Him and scorned Him, and clothed with a
white cloth and sent Him again to Pilate. And Herod

and Pilate were made friends from that day, for before they were enemies together.

And Pilate called together the princes of priests and the magistrates of the people, and said to them, Ye have brought to me this Man as turning away the people, and lo, I, asking before you, find no cause in this Man of these things in which ye accuse Him. Neither Herod, for he has sent Him again to us, and lo, nothing worthy of death is done to Him. And therefore I shall amend Him and deliver Him.

But he must need deliver to them one by the feast day. And all the people cried together, and said, Do away Him, and deliver to us Barabbas! ⁄ which was sent into prison for disturbling made in the city and for manslay⁄ing. And eftsoon Pilate spoke to them and would deli⁄ver Jesus. And they undercried and said, Crucify! *cried out* Crucify Him! And the third time he said to them, For what evil has this done? I find no cause of death in Him. Therefore I shall chastise Him and I shall deliver! And they continued with great voices, asking that He should be crucified. And the voices of them waxed strong, and Pilate deemed their asking to be done. And he delivered to them him that for manslaying and sedition was sent into prison, whom they asked. But he betook Jesus to their will.

And when they led Him, they took a man, Simon of Cyrene, coming from the town, and they laid on him the cross to bear after Jesus. And there sued Him much people and women that wailed and bemourned Him. *lamented* And Jesus turned to them and said, Daughters of Jerusalem, nil ye weep on Me, but weep ye on yourselves and on your sons. For lo, days shall come in which it shall be said, Blessed be barren women and wombs that have not borne children, and the teats that have not given suck! Then they shall begin to say to mountains,

Fall ye down on us, and to small hills, Cover ye us! For if in a green tree they do these things, what shall be done in a dry?

Also, other two wicked men were led with Him to be slain. And after that they came into a place that is called of Calvary, there they crucified Him and the thieves, one on the right half and the t'other on the left half. But Jesus said, Father, forgive them, for they wit not what they do. And they departed His clothes and cast lots.

And the people stood abiding, and the princes scorned Him with them, and said, Other men He made safe. Make He Himself safe if this be Christ, the Chosen of God! And the knights nighed and scorned Him, and proffered vinegar to Him and said, If Thou art King of Jews, make Thee safe! And the superscrip-tion was written over Him with Greek letters and of Latin and of Hebrew: This is the King of Jews.

And one of these thieves that hanged, blasphemed Him and said, If Thou art Christ, make Thyself safe and us! But the t'other, answering, blamed him and said, Neither thou dreads God that art in the same dam-nation? And truly we justly, for we have received worthy things to works. But this did nothing of evil. And he said to Jesus, Lord, have mind of me when Thou comes into Thy kingdom. And Jesus said to him, Truly I say to thee, this day thou shall be with Me in Paradise.

And it was almost the sixth hour, and darknesses were made in all the earth into the ninth hour. And the sun was made dark, and the veil of the Temple was rent a-two. And Jesus, crying with a great voice, said, Father, into Thine hands I betake My spirit! And He, saying these things, gave up the ghost. And the centur-ion, seeing that thing that was done, glorified God and said, Verily, this Man was just.

And all the people of them that were there together at this spectacle and saw those things that were done, smote their breasts and turned again. But all His known stood afar and women that sued Him from Galilee, see⁄ ing these things. And lo, a man, Joseph by name, of Arimathea, a city of Judea, that was a decurion, a good man and a just, this man consented not to the counsel and to the deeds of them, and he abode the kingdom of God. This Joseph came to Pilate and asked the body of Jesus and took it down, and lapped it in a clean linen cloth, and laid Him in a grave hewn, in which not yet any man had been laid. And the day was the even of the holiday, and the Sabbath began to shine.

And the women, suing, that came with Him from Galilee, saw the grave and how His body was laid. And they turned again and made ready sweet smelling spices and ointments. But in the Sabbath they rested, *appearance, species* after the commandment.

Chapter XXIV

But in one day of the week, full early, they came to the grave and brought sweet smelling spices that they had arrayed. And they found the stone turned away from the grave. And they went in and found not the body of the Lord Jesus. And it was done, the while they were aston⁄ ied in thought of this thing, lo, two men stood beside them in shining cloth. And when they dreaded and bowed their semblant into the earth, they said to them, *face, features* What seek ye Him that lives with dead men? He is not here, but is risen. Have ye mind how He spoke to you when He was yet in Galilee and said, For it behoves Man's Son to be betaken into the hands of sinful men and to be crucified, and the third day to rise again. And they bethought on His words.

And they went again from the grave and told all these

things to the eleven and to all others. And there was Mary Magdalene, and Joanna, and Mary of James, and other women that were with them that said to apostles these things. And these words were seen before them as madness, and they believed not to them. But Peter rose up and ran to the grave, and he bowed down and saw the linen clothes lying alone. And he went by himself, wondering on that that was done.

And lo, twain of them went in that day into a castle *eighths of a mile* that was from Jerusalem the space of sixty furlongs, by name Emmaus. And they spoke together of all these things that had befallen. And it was done, the while they talked and sought by themselves, Jesus Himself nighed and went with them. But their eyes were held that they knew Him not. And He said to them, What are these words that ye speak together, wandering, and ye are sorrowful? And one, whose name was Cleopas, answered and said, Thou thyself art a pilgrim in Jerusalem and has Thou not known what things are done in it in these days? To whom He said, What things?

And they said to Him, Of Jesus of Nazareth that was a Man, Prophet, mighty in work and word before God and all the people, and how the highest priests of our princes betook Him into damnation of death, and crucified Him. But we hoped that He should have *redeemed* again-bought Israel. And now on all these things the third day is today that these things were done. But also some women of ours made us afeared, which before day were at the grave. And when His body was not found, they came and said that they saw also a sight of angels which say that He lives. And some of ours went to the grave and they found so as the women said, but they found not Him!

And He said to them, Ah, fools and slow of heart to believe in all things that the prophets have spoken.

Whether it behoved not Christ to suffer these things and so to enter into His glory? And He began at Moses and at all the prophets, and declared to them in all Scriptures that were of Him. And they came nigh the castle whither they went, and He made countenance that He would go further. And they constrained Him and said, Dwell with us, for it draws to night and the day is now bowed down. And He entered with them.

And it was done, while He sat at the meat with them, He took bread and blessed and broke, and took to them. And the eyes of them were opened and they knew Him, and He vanished from their eyes. And they said *became vain* together, Whether our heart was not burning in us while He spoke in the way and opened to us Scriptures? And they rose up in the same hour and went again into Jerusalem, and found the eleven gathered together and them that were with them, saying that, The Lord is risen verily, and appeared to Simon! And they told what things were done in the way and how they knew Him in breaking of bread.

And the while they spoke these things, Jesus stood in the middle of them and said to them, Peace to you. I am. Nil ye dread. But they were afraid and aghast, and guessed Him to be a spirit. And He said to them, What are ye troubled and thoughts come up into your hearts? See ye My hands and My feet, for I Myself am! Feel ye and see ye, for a spirit has not flesh and bones as ye see that I have. And when He had said this thing, He showed hands and feet to them.

And yet while they believed not and wondered for joy, He said, Have ye here anything that shall be eaten? And they proffered Him a part of a fish roasted and an honeycomb. And when He had eaten before them, He took that that left and gave to them, and said to them,

These are the words that I spoke to you when I was yet with you, for it is need that all things are fulfilled that are written in the law of Moses and in prophets and in psalms of Me. Then He opened to them wit, that they should understand the Scriptures.

And He said to them, For thus it is written and thus it behoved Christ to suffer and rise again from death in the third day, and penance and remission of sins to be preached in His name into all folks, beginning at Jerusalem. And ye are witnesses of these things. And I *promise* shall send the behest of My Father into you. But sit ye in the city till that ye are clothed with virtue from on high.

And He led them forth into Bethany. And when His hands were lift up, He blessed them. And it was done the while He blessed them, He departed from them and was borne into heaven. And they worshipped and went again into Jerusalem with great joy, and were evermore in the Temple, herying and blessing God.

Here begins the Prologue
on the gospel of John

This is John Evangelist, one of the disciples of the Lord, the which, as a virgin chosen of God, whom God called from the spousals when he would be wedded. And double witness of virginity is given to him in the gospel in this, that he is said loved of God before other disciples. And God, hanging in the cross, betook His mother in keeping to him, that a virgin should keep a virgin.

This John, in the gospel, begins alone the work of uncorrupti- naturally *ble word, and witnessing that the kindly Son of God is made Man, and that the Light was not taken of darkness. And he shows the first miracle which God did at the weddings to show where the Lord is prayed to the feast, the wine of the weddings ought to fail, that when old things are changed, all new things that are ordained of Christ appear.*

John wrote this gospel in Asia after that he had written the Apocalypse in the Isle of Patmos. Netheless, he wrote the gospel after all the gospellers, that also an uncorruptible end by a virgin in the Apocalypse to Him to whom an uncorruptible beginning is given in Genesis in the beginning of holy scripture. For Christ in the Apocalypse, I am the beginning and the end. And this John was he that knew that the day of his departing was come, and he called together his disciples in Ephesus, and showed Christ by many provings of miracles, and went down into a dolven place of his burying. And when he had made prayer, he was   *dug, excavated* *put to his fathers, and was much without sorrow of death. How much he is found clean from corruption of flesh, Jerome in his Prologue on John says all this.*

Here ends the Prologue, and now begins the gospel of John.

Chapter I

In the beginning was the Word, and the Word was at God, and God was the Word. This was in the beginning at God. All things were made by Him, and without Him was made nothing, that thing that was made. In Him was life, and the life was the light of men. And the light shines in darknesses, and darknesses comprehended not it.

A man was sent from God to whom the name was John. This man came into witnessing, that he should bear witnessing of the light, that all men should believe by him. He was not the light, but that he should bear witnessing of the light. There was a very light which lights each man that comes into this world. He was in the world, and the world was made by Him, and the world knew Him not. He came into His own things, and His received Him not. But how many ever received

Him, He gave to them power to be made the sons of God, to them that believed in His name. The which, not of bloods, neither of the will of flesh, neither of the will of man, but are born of God.

And the Word was made Man and dwelled among us, and we have seen the glory of Him, as the glory of the one begotten Son of the Father, full of grace and of truth. John bears witnessing of Him, and cries and says, This is whom I said, He that shall come after me is made before me, for He was tofore me. And of the plenty of Him we all have taken, and grace for grace. For the law was given by Moses, but grace and truth is made by Jesus Christ. No man saw ever God. No. But the one begotten Son that is in the bosom of the Father, He has told out.

And this is the witnessing of John. When Jews sent from Jerusalem priests and deacons to him, that they should ask him, Who art thou?, he acknowledged and denied not, and he acknowledged, For I am not Christ. And they asked him, What then? Art thou Elijah? And he said, I am not. Art thou a prophet? And he answered, Nay. Therefore they said to him, Who art thou, that we give an answer to these that sent us. What say thou of thyself? He said, I am a voice of a crier in desert. Dress ye the way of the Lord, as Isaiah the pro- phet said. And they that were sent, were of the Pharisees. And they asked him, and said to him, What then baptizes thou if thou art not Christ, neither Elijah, neither a prophet? John answered to them and said, I baptize in water, but in the middle of you has stood One that ye know not. He it is that shall come after me, that was made before me, of whom I am not *shoelace* worthy to loose the thong of His shoe. These things were done in Bethabara beyond Jordan where John was baptizing.

Another day, John saw Jesus coming to him, and he said, Lo, the Lamb of God. Lo, He that does away the sins of the world! This is He that I said of, After me is come a man which was made before me. For He was rather than I. And I knew Him not but that He be shown in Israel. Therefore I came baptizing in water. And John bore witnessing and said that, I saw the Spirit coming down as a culver from heaven, and dwelled on Him. And I knew Him not. But He that sent me to baptize in water, said to me, On whom thou see the Spirit coming down and dwelling on Him, this is He that baptizes in the Holy Ghost. And I saw, and bear witnessing, that this is the Son of God!

Another day, John stood and twain of his disciples. And he beheld Jesus walking, and says, Lo, the Lamb of God! And two disciples heard him speaking and followed Jesus. And Jesus turned and saw them suing Him, and says to them, What seek ye? And they said to Him, Rabbi, that is to say, Master, where dwells Thou? And He says to them, Come ye and see. And they came and saw where He dwelled, and dwelt with Him that day. And it was as the tenth hour.

And Andrew, the brother of Simon Peter, was one of the twain that heard of John and had sued Him. This found first his brother Simon, and he said to him, We have found Messiah! ⁄ that is to say, Christ, and he led him to Jesus. And Jesus beheld him and said, Thou art Simon, the son of Jona. Thou shall be called Cephas ⁄ that is to say, Peter.

And on the morrow, He would go out into Galilee. And He found Philip. And He says to him, Sue thou Me. Philip was of Bethsaida, the city of Andrew and Peter.

Philip found Nathaniel, and said to him, We have found Jesus, the Son of Joseph of Nazareth, whom

Moses wrote in the law and prophets. And Nathaniel said to him, Of Nazareth may some good thing be? Philip said to him, Come and see. Jesus saw Nathaniel coming to Him, and said to him, Lo, verily a man of Israel in whom is no guile. Nathaniel said to Him, Whereof has Thou known me? Jesus answered and said to him, Before that Philip called thee, when thou were under the fig tree I saw thee. Nathaniel answered to Him and said, Rabbi, Thou art the Son of God, Thou art King of Israel. Jesus answered and said to him, For I said to thee, I saw thee under the fig tree, thou believe? Thou shall see more than these things. And He said to them, Truly, truly I say to you, ye shall see heaven opened and the angels of God stying up and coming down on Man's Son.

Chapter II

And the third day, weddings were made in the Cana of Galilee, and the mother of Jesus was there. And Jesus was called and His disciples to the weddings. And when wine failed, the mother of Jesus said to Him, They have not wine. And Jesus says to her, What to Me and to thee, woman? Mine hour came not yet. His mother says to the ministers, Whatever thing He say to you, do ye. And there were six stone cans after the cleans-ing of the Jews, holding each twain either three metretes. And Jesus says to them, Fill ye the pots with water. And they filled them up to the mouth. And Jesus said to them, Draw ye now, and bear ye to the architricline. And they bore. And when the architricline had tasted the water made wine, and wist not whereof it was ⁄ but the ministers wist that drew the water ⁄ the architricline called the spouse and says to him, Each man sets first good wine, and when men are fulfilled, then that that is worse. But thou has kept the good wine into this time!

water-jugs

measures equal to firkins

master of the festive board

Jesus did this, the beginning of signs, in the Cana of Galilee and showed His glory. And His disciples believed in Him.

After these things, He came down to Capernaum, and His mother and His brethren and His disciples. And they dwelled there not many days. And the Pasch of Jews was nigh, and Jesus went up to Jerusalem. And He found in the Temple men selling oxen and sheep and culvers, and changers sitting. And when He had made as it were a scourge of small cords, He drove out all of the Temple, and oxen and sheep, and He shed the money of changers and turned upsedown the boards. And He said to them that sold culvers, Take away from hence these things, and nil ye make the house of My Father an house of merchandise! And His disciples had mind, for it was written, The fervent love of Thine house has eaten Me!

Therefore the Jews answered and said to Him, What token shows Thou to us that Thou does these things? Jesus answered and said to them, Undo ye this temple, and in three days I shall raise it! Therefore the Jews said to Him, In forty and six year this Temple was built, and shall Thou in three days raise it? But He said of the temple of His body. Therefore when He was risen from death, His disciples had mind that He said these things of His body, and they believed to the Scripture and to the word that Jesus said.

And when Jesus was at Jerusalem in Pasch, in the feast day, many believed in His name, seeing His signs that He did. But Jesus trowed not Himself to them, for He knew all men, and for it was not need to Him that any man should bear witnessing, for He wist what was in man.

Chapter III

And there was a man of the Pharisees, Nicodemus by name, prince of the Jews. And he came to Jesus by night and said to Him, Rabbi, we wit that Thou art come from God, Master, for no man may do these signs that Thou does but God be with him. Jesus answered and said to Him, Truly, truly, I say to thee, but a man be born again, he may not see the kingdom of God. Nicodemus said to Him, How may a man be born when he is old? Whether he may enter again into his mother's womb and be born again? Jesus answered, Truly, truly, I say to thee, but a man be born again of water and of the Holy Ghost, he may not enter into the kingdom of God. That that is born of the flesh, is flesh, and that that is born of spirit, is spirit. Wonder thou not for I said to thee, It behoves you to be born again. The Spirit breathes where He will, and thou hears His voice, but thou wist not from whence He comes nor whither He goes. So is each man that is born of the Spirit.

Nicodemus answered and said to Him, How moun these things be done? Jesus answered and said to him, Thou art a master in Israel and knows not these things? Truly, truly, I say to thee, for we speak that we wit, and we witness that that we have seen, and ye take not our witnessing. If I have said to you earthly things and ye believe not, how, if I say to you heavenly things, shall ye believe? And no man styes into heaven but He that came down from heaven, Man's Son that is in heaven. And as Moses arreared a serpent in desert, so it behoves Man's Son to be raised, that each man that believes in Him perish not, but have everlasting life. For God loved so the world that He gave His one begotten Son, that each man that believes in Him perish not, but have everlasting life. For God sent not His Son into the world that He judge the world, but that the world be saved by Him. He that believes in Him is not deemed. But he that believes not, is now deemed, for he believes not in the name of the one begotten Son of God. And this is the doom, for light came into the world, and men loved more darknesses than light, for their works were evil. For each man that does evil, hates the light, and he comes not to the light, that his works be not reproved. But he that does truth, comes to the light, that his works be showed that they are done in God.

After these things, Jesus came and His disciples into the land of Judea, and there He dwelled with them, and baptized. And John was baptizing in Aenon beside Salim, for many waters were there, and they came and were baptized. And John was not yet sent into prison. Therefore a question was made of John's disciples with the Jews of the purification. And they came to John and said to him, Master, He that was with thee beyond Jordan, to whom thou has borne witnessing, lo, He baptizes and all men come to Him.

John answered and said, A man may not take anything but it be given to him from heaven. Ye yourselves bear witnessing to me that I said, I am not Christ, but that I am sent before Him. He that has a wife, is the husband. But the friend of the spouse that stands and hears him, joys with joy for the voice of the spouse. Therefore in this thing my joy is fulfilled. It behoves Him to wax, but me to be made less. He that came from above, is above all. He that is of the earth, speaks of the earth. He that comes from heaven, is above all. And He witnesses that thing that He has seen and heard, and no man takes His witnessing. But he that takes His witnessing, has confirmed that God is soothfast. But He whom God has sent, speaks the words of God, for not to measure God gives the Spirit. The Father loves the Son, and He has given all things in His hand. He that believes in the Son, has everlasting life. But he that is unbelieveful to the Son, shall not see everlasting life, but the wrath of God dwells on him.

Chapter IV

Therefore, as Jesus knew that the Pharisees heard that Jesus makes and baptizes more disciples than John, though Jesus baptized not but His disciples, He left Judea and went again into Galilee. And it behoved Him to pass by Samaria. Therefore Jesus came into a city of Samaria that is said Sychar, beside the place that Jacob gave to Joseph, his son. And the well of Jacob was there. And Jesus was weary of the journey and sat thus upon the well.

And the hour was, as it were, the sixth, and a woman came from Samaria to draw water. And Jesus says to her, Give Me drink. And His disciples were gone into the city to buy meat. Therefore the ilk woman of Samaria says to Him, How Thou, when Thou art a Jew, asks of me drink that am a woman of Samaria? ˒ for Jews used not to deal with Samaritans. Jesus answered and said to her, If thou wist the gift of God, and who He is that says to thee, Give Me drink, thou peradventure would have asked of Him, and He should *living water* have given to thee quick water.

The woman says to Him, Sire, Thou has not wherein to draw, and the pit is deep. Whereof has Thou quick water? Whether Thou art greater than our father Jacob that gave to us the pit, and he drank thereof, and his sons and his beasts? Jesus answered and said to her, Each man that drinks of this water, shall thirst eft˒ soon. But he that drinks of the water that I shall give him, shall not thirst without end. But the water that I shall give him shall be made in him a well of water, springing up into everlasting life.

The woman says to him, Sire, give me this water that I thirst not, neither come hither to draw. Jesus says to her, Go, call thine husband and come hither. The woman answered and said, I have none husband. Jesus says to her, Thou said well that I have none husband, for thou has had five husbands, and he that thou has is not thine husband. This thing thou said soothly. The woman says to Him, Lord, I see that Thou art a pro-phet. Our fathers worshipped in this hill, and ye say that at Jerusalem is a place where it behoves to worship. Jesus says to her, Woman, believe thou to Me, for the hour shall come when neither in this hill, neither in Jerusalem, ye shall worship the Father. Ye worship that ye know not. We worship that we know, for health is of the Jews. But the time is come, and now it is, when true worshippers shall worship the Father in spirit and truth. For also the Father seeks such that worship Him. God is a Spirit, and it behoves them that worship Him to worship in spirit and truth. The woman says to Him, I wot that Messiah is come that is said Christ. Therefore when He comes, He shall tell us all things. Jesus says to her, I am He that speaks with thee.

And anon His disciples came and wondered that He spoke with the woman. Netheless no man said to Him, What seeks Thou? or, What speaks Thou with her? Therefore the woman left her water pot and went into the city and said to those men, Come ye, and see ye a Man that said to me all things that I have done, whether He be Christ. And they went out of the city and came to Him.

In the meanwhile His disciples prayed Him and said, Master, eat. But He said to them, I have meat to eat that ye know not. Therefore disciples said together,

Whether any man has brought Him meat to eat? Jesus says to them, My meat is that I do the will of Him that sent Me, that I perform the work of Him. Whether ye say not that yet four months are and ripe corn comes? Lo, I say to you, lift up your eyes and see ye the fields, for now they are white to reap. And he that reaps, takes hire and gathers fruit into everlasting life, that both he that sows and he that reaps have joy together. In this thing is the word true, For another is that sows, and another that reaps. I sent you to reap that that ye have not travailed. Other men have travailed, and ye have entered into their travails.

And of that city many Samaritans believed in Him, for the word of the woman that bore witnessing that, He said to me all things that I have done. Therefore, when Samaritans came to Him, they prayed Him to dwell there, and He dwelt there two days. And many more believed for His word, and said to the woman that, Now not for thy speech we believe, for we have heard and we wit that this is verily the Saviour of the world.

And after two days, He went out from thence and went into Galilee. And He bore witnessing that a prophet in his own country has none honour. Therefore, when He came into Galilee, men of Galilee received Him when they had seen all things that He had done in Jerusalem in the feast day, for also they had come to the feast day. Therefore He came eftsoon into the Cana of Galilee where He made the water wine.

And a little king was, whose son was sick at Capernaum. When this had heard that Jesus should come from Judea into Galilee, he went to Him and prayed Him that He should come down and heal his son, for he began to die. Therefore Jesus said to him, But ye see tokens and great wonders, ye believe not. The little king says to Him, Lord, come down before that my son die! Jesus says to him, Go, thy son lives. The man believed to the word that Jesus said to him, and he went. And now when he came down, the servants came against him, and told to him and said that his son lived. And he asked of them the hour in which his son was amended. And they said to him, For yesterday, in the seventh hour, the fever left him. Therefore the father knew that the ilk hour it was in which Jesus said to him, Thy son lives. And he believed, and all his house. Jesus did eft this second token when He came from Judea into Galilee.

Chapter V

After these things there was a feast day of Jews, and Jesus went up to Jerusalem. And in Jerusalem is a wash⁄ing⁄place that in Hebrew is named Bethesda, and has five porches. In these lay a great multitude of sick men, blind, crooked, and dry, abiding the moving of the water. For the angel of the Lord came down certain times into the water, and the water was moved. And he that first came down into the cistern after the moving of the water, was made whole of whatever sickness he was held. And a man was there, having eight and thirty year in his sickness. And when Jesus had seen him lying, and had known that he had much time, He says to him, Will thou be made whole? The sick man answered to Him, Lord, I have no man that when the water is moved, to put me into the cistern. For the while I come, another goes down before me. Jesus says to him, Rise up. Take thy bed and go.

And anon the man was made whole, and took up his bed and went forth. And it was Sabbath in that day. Therefore the Jews said to him that was made whole, It is Sabbath! It is not leaveful to thee to take away thy bed! He answered to them, He that made me whole, said to me, Take thy bed and go. Therefore they asked him, What man is that that said to thee, Take up thy bed and go? But he that was made whole, wist not who it was. And Jesus bowed away from the people that were set in the place. Afterward Jesus found him in the Temple, and said to him, Lo, thou art made whole. Now nil thou do sin, lest any worse thing befall to thee.

The ilk man went and told to the Jews that it was Jesus that made him whole. Therefore the Jews pursued Jesus, for He did this thing in the Sabbath. And Jesus answered to them, My Father works till now, and I work. Therefore the Jews sought more to slay Him, for not only He broke the Sabbath, but He said that God was His Father, and made Him even to God.

Therefore Jesus answered and said to them, Truly, truly, I say to you, the Son may not of Himself do anything but that thing that He sees the Father doing. For whatever things He does, the Son does in like manner those things. For the Father loves the Son, and shows to Him all things that He does. And He shall show to Him greater works than these that ye wonder. For as the Father raises dead men and quickens, so the Son quickens whom He will. For neither the Father judges any man, but has given each doom to the Son, that all men honour the Son as they honour the Father. He that honours not the Son, honours not the Father that sent Him.

Truly, truly, I say to you that he that hears My word and believes to Him that sent Me, has everlasting life. And he comes not into doom, but passes from death into life. Truly, truly, I say to you, for the hour comes and now it is, when dead men shall hear the voice of God's Son, and they that hear shall live. For as the Father has life in Himself, so He gave to the Son to have life in Himself. And He gave to Him power to make doom, for He is Man's Son. Nil ye wonder this, for the hour comes in which all men that are in burials, shall hear the voice of God's Son. And they that have done good things, shall go into again-rising of life. But they that have done evil things, into again-rising of doom.

I may nothing do of Myself. But as I hear, I deem. And My doom is just, for I seek not My will, but the will of the Father that sent Me. If I bear witnessing of Myself, My witnessing is not true. Another is that bears witnessing of Me, and I wot that His witnessing is true that He bears of Me. Ye sent to John, and he bore witnessing to truth. But I take not witnessing of man, but I say these things that ye be safe. He was a lantern burning and shining, but ye would glad at an hour in his light. But I have more witnessing than John, for the works that My Father gave to Me to perform them, the ilk works that I do bear witnessing of Me that the Father sent Me. And the Father that sent Me, He bore witnessing of Me. Neither ye heard ever His voice. Neither ye see His likeness. And ye have not His word dwelling in you, for ye believe not to Him whom He sent.

Seek ye Scriptures in which ye guess to have everlasting life, and those they are that bear witnessing of Me. And ye will not come to Me that ye have life. I take not clearness of men. But I have known you, that ye have not the love of God in you. I came in the name of My Father, and ye took not Me. If another come in his own name, ye shall receive him. How moun ye believe, that receive glory of each other, and ye seek not the glory that is of God alone?

Nil ye guess that I am come to accuse you anents the Father. It is Moses that accuses you, in whom ye hope. For if ye believed to Moses, peradventure ye should believe also to Me, for he wrote of Me. But if ye believe not to his letters, how shall ye believe to My words?

Chapter VI

After these things, Jesus went over the sea of Galilee, that is Tiberias. And a great multitude sued Him, for they saw the tokens that He did on them that were sick. Therefore Jesus went into an hill, and sat there with His disciples. And the Pasch was full nigh, a feast day of the Jews. Therefore when Jesus had lifted up His eyes and had seen that a great multitude came to Him, He says to Philip, Whereof shall we buy loaves, that these men eat? But He said this thing, tempting him, for He wist what He was to do. Philip answered to Him, The loaves of twain hundred pence suffice not to them, that each man take little what. One of His disciples, Andrew, the brother of Simon Peter, says to Him, A child is here that has five barley loaves and two fishes. But what are these among so many? Therefore Jesus says, Make ye them sit to the meat. And there was much hay in the place. And so men sat to the meat as five thousand in number.

And Jesus took five loaves, and when He had done thankings, He departed to men that sat to the meat, and also of the fishes as much as they would. And when they were filled, He said to His disciples, Gather ye the relifs that be left, that they perish not. And so they gathered, and filled twelve coffins of relif of the five barley loaves and two fishes that left to them that had eaten. Therefore those men, when they had seen the sign that He had done, said, For this is verily the Prophet that is to come into the world.

And when Jesus had known that they were to come to take Him and make Him king, He fled alone into an hill. And when eventide was come, His disciples went down to the sea. And they went up into a boat, and they came over the sea into Capernaum. And darknesses were made then, and Jesus was not come to them. And for a great wind blew, the sea rose up. Therefore, when they had rowed as five and twenty furlongs, or thirty, they see Jesus walking on the sea and to be nigh the boat. And they dreaded. And He said to them, I am. Nil ye dread. Therefore they would take Him into the boat, and anon the boat was at the land to which they went.

On the t'other day, the people that stood over the sea, saw that there was none other boat there but one, and that Jesus entered not with His disciples into the boat, but His disciples alone went. But other boats came from Tiberias beside the place where they had eaten bread and did thankings to God. Therefore, when the people had seen that Jesus was not there, neither His disciples, they went up into boats and came to Capernaum, seeking Jesus. And when they had found Him over the sea, they said to Him, Rabbi, how came Thou hither? Jesus answered to them and said, Truly, truly, I say to you, ye seek Me not for ye saw the miracles, but for ye ate of loaves and were filled. Work ye not meat that perishes, but that dwells into everlasting life, which meat Man's Son shall give to you, for God the Father has marked Him.

Therefore they said to Him, What shall we do that we work the works of God? Jesus answered and said to them, This is the work of God, that ye believe to Him whom He has sent. Therefore they said to Him, What token, then, does Thou that we see and believe to Thee? What works Thou? Our fathers ate manna in desert. As it is written, He gave to them bread from heaven to eat. Therefore Jesus says to them, Truly, truly, I say to you, Moses gave you not bread from heaven, but My Father gives you very bread from heaven. For it is very bread that comes down from heaven and gives life to the

world. Therefore they said to Him, Lord, ever give us
this bread. And Jesus said to them, I am bread of life.
He that comes to Me shall not hunger. He that believes
in Me shall never thirst. But I said to you that ye have
seen Me and ye believed not. All thing that the Father
gives to Me shall come to Me, and I shall not cast him
out that comes to Me. For I came down from heaven not
that I do My will, but the will of Him that sent Me.
And this is the will of the Father that sent Me, that all
thing that the Father gave Me, I lose not of it, but again-
resurrect raise it in the last day. And this is the will of My Father
that sent Me, that each man that sees the Son and
believes in Him, have everlasting life. And I shall again-
raise him in the last day.

Therefore Jews grouched of Him, for He had said, I
am bread that came down from heaven. And they said,
Whether this is not Jesus, the son of Joseph, whose
father and mother we have known? How then says this
that, I came down from heaven? Therefore Jesus
answered and said to them, Nil ye grouch together. No
man may come to Me but if the Father that sent Me draw
him, and I shall again-raise him in the last day. It is
written in the prophets, And all men shall be able for to
be taught of God. Each man that heard of the Father
and has learned, comes to Me. Not for any man has seen
the Father. But this that is of God has seen the Father.
Soothly, soothly, I say to you, he that believes in Me has
everlasting life. I am bread of life. Your fathers ate
manna in desert, and are dead. This is bread coming
down from heaven that if any man eat thereof, he die
not. I am living bread that came down from heaven. If
any man eat of this bread, he shall live without end.
And the bread that I shall give is My flesh for the life of
the world.

Therefore the Jews chid together and said, How may

this give to us His flesh to eat? Therefore Jesus says to them, Truly, truly, I say to you, but ye eat the flesh of Man's Son and drink His blood, ye shall not have life in you. He that eats My flesh and drinks My blood, has everlasting life, and I shall again/raise him in the last day. For My flesh is very meat, and My blood is very drink. He that eats My flesh and drinks My blood, dwells in Me and I in him. As My Father, living, sent Me, and I live for the Father, and he that eats Me, he shall live for Me. This is bread that came down from heaven. Not as your fathers ate manna and are dead. He that eats this bread, shall live without end.

He said these things in the synagogue, teaching in Capernaum. Therefore many of His disciples, hearing, said, This word is hard. Who may hear it? But Jesus, witting at Himself that His disciples grouched of this thing, said to them, This thing sclaunders you? Therefore, if ye see Man's Son stying where He was before? It is the Spirit that quickens. The flesh profits nothing. The words that I have spoken to you are Spirit and life. But there are some of you that believe not. For Jesus wist from the beginning which were believing and who was to betray Him. And He said, Therefore I said to you that no man may come to Me but it were given to him of My Father.

From this time many of His disciples went aback, and went not now with Him. Therefore Jesus said to the twelve, Whether ye will also go away? And Simon Peter answered to Him, Lord, to whom shall we go? Thou has words of everlasting life, and we believe and have known that Thou art Christ, the Son of God. Therefore Jesus answered to them, Whether I chose not you twelve, and one of you is a fiend? And He said this of Judas of Simon of Iscariot, for this was to betray Him when he was one of the twelve.

Chapter VII

After these things, Jesus walked into Galilee, for He would not walk into Judea for the Jews sought to slay Him. And there was nigh a feast day of the Jews, *feast of Tabernacles* Scenophegia. And His brethren said to Him, Pass from hence and go into Judea, that also Thy disciples see Thy works that Thou does. For no man does any⸗ thing in hidles and himself seeks to be open. If Thou does these things, show Thyself to the world. ⸗ for neither His brethren believed in Him. Therefore Jesus says to them, My time came not yet, but your time is ever⸗ more ready. The world may not hate you. Soothly, it hates Me, for I bear witnessing thereof that the works of it are evil. Go ye up to this feast day. But I shall not go up to this feast day, for My time is not yet fulfilled.

When He had said these things, He dwelt in Galilee. And after that His brethren were gone up, then He went up to the feast day, not openly, but as in privity. Therefore the Jews sought Him in the feast day and said, Where is He? And much grouching was of Him among the people, for some said that He is good, and other said, Nay, but He deceives the people. Netheless, no man spoke openly of Him for dread of the Jews.

But when the middle feast day came, Jesus went up into the Temple and taught. And the Jews wondered and said, How can this Man letters since He has not learned? Jesus answered to them and said, My doctrine is not Mine, but His that sent Me. If any man will do His will, he shall know of the teaching whether it be of God or I speak of Myself. He that speaks of himself seeks his own glory, but He that seeks the glory of Him *evil, unrighteousness* that sent Him, is soothfast, and unrightwiseness is not in Him. Whether Moses gave not to you a law, and none of you does the law? What seek ye to slay Me?

And the people answered and said, Thou has a devil. Who seeks to slay Thee? Jesus answered, I have done one work, and all ye wonder. Therefore Moses gave to you circumcision, not for it is of Moses, but of the fathers, and in the Sabbath ye circumcise a man. If a man take circumcision in the Sabbath that the law of Moses be not broken, have ye indignation to Me for I made all a man whole in the Sabbath? Nil ye deem after the face, but deem ye a rightful doom.

Therefore some of Jerusalem said, Whether this is not He whom the Jews seek to slay, and lo, He speaks openly and they say nothing to Him! Whether the princes knew verily that this is Christ? But we know this Man of whence He is. But when Christ shall come, no man wot of whence He is. Therefore Jesus cried in the Temple, teaching, and said, Ye know Me, and ye know of whence I am. And I came not of Myself, but He that is true sent Me, whom ye know not. I know Him, and if I say that I know Him not, I shall be like to you, a liar! But I know Him, for of Him I am, and He sent Me.

Therefore they sought to take Him, and no man set on Him hands, for His hour came not yet. And many of the people believed in Him, and said, When Christ shall come, whether He shall do more tokens than those that this does? Pharisees heard the people musing of Him these things, and the princes and Pharisees sent ministers to take Him. Therefore Jesus said to them, Yet a little time I am with you, and I go to the Father that sent Me. Ye shall seek Me and ye shall not find, and where I am ye may not come. Therefore the Jews said to themselves, Whither shall this go for we shall not find Him? Whether He will go into the scattering of heathen men, and will teach the heathen? What is this word *Jews of the Diaspora* which He said, Ye shall seek Me and ye shall not find? And where I am, ye moun not come?

But in the last day of the great feast, Jesus stood and cried, and said, If any man thirsts, come he to Me, and drink. He that believes in Me, as the Scripture says, Floods of quick water shall flow from his womb. But He said this thing of the Spirit whom men that believed in Him should take. For the Spirit was not yet given, for Jesus was not yet glorified.

Therefore of that company, when they had heard these words of Him, they said, This is verily a prophet! Others said, This is Christ! But some said, Whether Christ comes from Galilee? Whether the Scripture says not that of the seed of David, and of the castle of Bethlehem where David was, Christ comes? Therefore dissension was made among the people for Him, for some of them would have taken Him. But no man set hands on Him.

Therefore the ministers came to bishops and Pharisees, and they said to them, Why brought ye not Him? The ministers answered, Never man spoke so as this Man speaks! Therefore the Pharisees answered to them, Whether ye are deceived also? Whether any of the princes or of the Pharisees believed in Him? But these people that know not the law, are cursed!

Nicodemus said to them, he that came to Him by night that was one of them, Whether our law deems a man but it have first heard of him and know what he does? They answered and said to him, Whether thou art a man of Galilee also? Seek thou the Scriptures and see thou that a prophet rises not of Galilee! And they turned again, each to his house.

Chapter VIII

But Jesus went into the mount of Olivet. And early eft He came into the Temple, and all the people came to Him, and He sat and taught them. And scribes and

Pharisees bring a woman taken in advowtry, and they set her in the middle and said to Him, Master, this woman is now taken in advowtry. And in the law, Moses commanded us to stone such. Therefore, what say Thou? And they said this thing, tempting Him, that they might accuse Him. And Jesus bowed Himself down and wrote with His finger in the earth. And when they abide asking Him, He raised Himself and said to them, He of you that is without sin, first cast a stone into her. And eft He bowed Himself and wrote in the earth. And they, hearing these things, went away, one after another, and they begin from the elder men. And Jesus dwelt alone and the woman standing in the middle. And Jesus raised Himself and said to her, Woman, where are they that accused thee? No man has damned thee? She said, No man, Lord. Jesus said to her, Neither I shall damn thee. Go thou, and now afterward nil thou sin more.

Therefore eft Jesus spoke to them and said, I am the light of the world. He that sues Me, walks not in darknesses, but shall have the light of life! Therefore the Pharisees said, Thou bears witnessing of Thyself. Thy witnessing is not true. Jesus answered and said to them, And if I bear witnessing of Myself, My witnessing is true, for I wot from whence I came and whither I go. But ye wit not from whence I came, nor whither I go. For ye deem after the flesh, but I deem no man. And if I deem, My doom is true, for I am not alone, but I and the Father that sent Me. And in your law it is written that the witnessing of two men is true. I am, that bear witnessing of Myself. And the Father that sent Me bears witnessing of Me.

Therefore they said to Him, Where is Thy Father? Jesus answered, Neither ye know Me, neither ye know My Father. If ye knew Me, peradventure ye should know also My Father. Jesus spoke these words in the treasury, teaching in the Temple, and no man took Him, for His hour came not yet. Therefore eft Jesus said to them, Lo, I go, and ye shall seek Me. And ye shall die in your sin. Whither I go, ye moun not come.

Therefore the Jews said, Whether He shall slay Himself, for He says, Whither I go, ye moun not come? And He said to them, Ye are of beneath. I am of above. Ye are of this world. I am not of this world. Therefore I said to you that ye shall die in your sins, for if ye believe not that I am, ye shall die in your sin. Therefore they said to Him, Who art Thou? Jesus said to them, The beginning, which also speak of you. I have many things to speak and deem of you. But He that sent Me is soothfast, and I speak in the world these things that I heard of Him. And they knew not that He called His Father, God. Therefore Jesus says to them, When ye have a-raised Man's Son, then ye shall know that I am, and of Myself I do nothing. But as My Father taught Me, I speak these things. And He that sent Me is with Me, and left Me not alone, for I do evermore those things that are pleasing to Him!

When He spoke these things, many believed in Him. Therefore Jesus said to the Jews that believed in Him, If ye dwell in My word, verily ye shall be My disciples. And ye shall know the truth, and the truth shall make you free. Therefore the Jews answered to Him, We are the seed of Abraham, and we served never to man! How say Thou that ye shall be free? Jesus answered to them, Truly, truly, I say to you, each man that does sin, is servant of sin. And the servant dwells not in the house without end. But the Son dwells without end. Therefore, if the Son make you free, verily ye shall be free. I wot that ye are Abraham's sons. But ye seek to slay Me, for My word takes not in you. I speak those things that I saw at My Father, and ye do those things that ye saw at your father. They answered and said to Him, Abraham is our father! Jesus says to them, If ye are the sons of Abraham, do ye the works of Abraham. But now ye seek to slay Me, a Man that have spoken to you truth that I heard of God. Abraham did not this thing. Ye do the works of your father!

Therefore they said to Him, We are not born of fornication! We have one Father, God! But Jesus says to them, If God were your Father, soothly ye should love Me, for I passed forth of God and came. For neither I came of Myself, but He sent Me. Why know ye not My speech? For ye moun not hear My word. Ye are of the father, the devil, and ye will do the desires of your father. He was a manslayer from the beginning, and he stood not in truth, for truth is not in him. When he speaks leasing, he speaks of his own, for he is a liar *falsehood, lying* and father of it. But for I say the truth, ye believe not to Me. Who of you shall reprove Me of sin? If I say truth, why believe ye not to Me? He that is of God, hears the words of God. Therefore ye hear not, for ye are not of God.

Therefore the Jews answered and said, Whether we say not well that Thou art a Samaritan and has a devil? Jesus answered and said, I have not a devil. But I honour My Father and ye have unhonoured Me, for I seek *dishonoured, insulted* not My glory. There is He that seeks, and deems. Truly, truly, I say to you, if any man keep My word, he shall not taste death without end. Therefore the Jews said, Now we have known that Thou has a devil. Abraham is dead, and the prophets, and Thou say, If any man keep My word he shall not taste death without end? Whether Thou art greater than our father, Abraham, that is dead, and the prophets are dead? Whom makes Thou Thyself?

Jesus answered, If I glorify Myself, My glory is nought. My Father is that glorifies Me, whom ye say that He is your God. And ye have not known Him. But I have known Him, and if I say that I know Him not, I shall be a liar like to you. But I know Him, and I keep His word. Abraham, your father, gladded to see My day, and he saw and joyed. Then the Jews said to Him, Thou has not yet fifty year, and Thou has seen Abraham? Therefore Jesus said to them, Truly, truly, I say to you, before that Abraham should be, I am! Therefore they took stones to cast at Him. But Jesus hid Him, and went out of the Temple.

Chapter IX

And Jesus, passing, saw a man blind from the birth. And His disciples asked Him, Master, what sinned, this man or his elders that he should be born blind? Jesus answered, Neither this man sinned, neither his elders, but that the works of God be showed in him. It behoves Me to work the works of Him that sent me as long as the day is. The night shall come when no man may work. As long as I am in the world, I am the light of the world.

When He had said these things, He spit into the _mud_ earth and made clay of the spittle, and anointed the clay on his eyes, and said to him, Go, and be thou washed in the water of Siloam ⁄ that is to say, Sent. Then he went and washed, and came seeing. And so neighbours and they that had seen him before, for he was a beggar, said, Whether this is not he that sat and begged? Other men said that, This it is. Other men said, Nay, but he is like him. But he said, That I am. Therefore they said to him, How are thine eyes opened? He answered, The ilk Man that is said Jesus, made clay and anointed mine eyes, and said to me, Go thou to the water of Siloam and wash. And I went and washed ⁄ and saw! And they said to him, Where is He? He said, I wot not.

They led him that was blind to the Pharisees. And it was Sabbath when Jesus made clay and opened his eyes. Eft the Pharisees asked him how he had seen. And he said to them, He laid to me clay on the eyes, and I washed, and I see! Therefore some of the Pharisees said, This Man is not of God that keeps not the Sabbath. Other men said, How may a sinful man do these signs? And strife was among them. Therefore they say eftsoons to the blind man, What say thou of Him that opened thine eyes? And he said that, He is a prophet.

Therefore Jews believed not of him that he was blind and had seen, till they had called his father and mother that had seen. And they asked them and said, Is this your son which ye say was born blind? How then sees he now? His father and mother answered to them and said, We wit that this is our son and that he was born blind. But how he sees now we wit never, or who opened his eyes we wit never. Ask ye him. He has age. Speak he of himself. His father and mother said these things for they dreaded the Jews. For then the Jews had conspired that if any man acknowledge Him Christ, he should be done out of the synagogue. Therefore his father and mother said that, He has age. Ask ye him.

Therefore eftsoon they called the man that was blind, and said to him, Give thou glory to God. We wit that this Man is a sinner. Then he said, If He is a sinner, I wot never. One thing I wot, that when I was blind, now I see! Therefore they said to him, What did He to thee? How opened He thine eyes? He answered to them, I said to you now and ye heard. What, will ye eftsoon hear? Whether ye will be made His disciples? Therefore they cursed him, and said, Be thou His disciple! We are disciples of Moses. We wit that God spoke to Moses. But we know not this, of whence He is! The ilk man answered and said to them, For in this is a wonderful thing that ye wit not of whence He is, and He has opened mine eyes. And we wit that God hears not sinful men, but if any man is worshipper of God, and does His will, He hears him. From the world it is not heard that any man opened the eyes of a blind-born man. But this were of God, He might not do anything! They answered and said to him, Thou art all born in sin, and teaches thou us? And they put him out.

Jesus heard that they had put him out, and when He had found him, He said to him, Believe thou in the Son of God? He answered and said, Lord, who is He that I believe in Him? And Jesus said to him, And thou has seen Him, and He it is that speaks with thee. And he said, Lord, I believe. And he fell down and worshipped Him. Therefore Jesus said to him, I came into this world into doom, that they that see not, see, and they that see, be made blind. And some of the Pharisees heard that were with Him, and they said to Him, Whether we are blind? Jesus said to them, If ye were blind, ye should not have sin. But now ye say that we see, your sin dwells still.

Chapter X

Truly, truly, I say to you, he that comes not in by the door into the fold of sheep, but styes by another way, is a night-thief and a day-thief. But He that enters by the door, is the Shepherd of the sheep. To this the porter opens, and the sheep hear His voice. And He calls His own sheep by name, and leads them out. And when He has done out His own sheep, He goes before them and the sheep sue Him, for they know His voice. But they sue not an alien, but flee from him, for they have not

known the voice of aliens. Jesus said to them this pro⁄
verb, but they knew not what He spoke to them.
Therefore Jesus said to them eftsoon, Truly, truly, I say
to you that I am the Door of the sheep. As many as have
come were night⁄thieves and day⁄thieves, but the sheep
heard not them. I am the Door. If any man shall enter by
Me, he shall be saved, and he shall go in and shall go
out, and he shall find lesewes. A night⁄thief comes not   *pasture*
but that he steal, slay and leese. And I came that they
have life, and have more plenteously.

I am a Good Shepherd. A Good Shepherd gives
His life for His sheep. But an hired hand, and that is not
the shepherd, whose are not the sheep his own, sees a
wolf coming, and he leaves the sheep and flees. And the
wolf ravishes and disparples the sheep. And the hired
hand flees for he is an hired hand, and it pertains not to
him of the sheep. I am a Good Shepherd, and I know
My sheep, and My sheep know Me. As the Father has
known Me, I know the Father, and I put My life for My
sheep. I have other sheep that are not of this fold, and it
behoves Me to bring them together. And they shall hear
My voice, and it shall be made one fold and one
Shepherd. Therefore the Father loves Me, for I put My
life, that eftsoon I take it. No man takes it from me, but I
have put it of myself. I have power to put it, and I have
power to take it again. This commandment I have taken
of My Father.

Eft dissension was made among the Jews for these
words, and many of them said, He has a devil and mad⁄
deth! What hear ye Him? Other men said, These   *acts insanely*
words are not of a man that has a fiend. Whether the
devil may open the eyes of blind men? But the feasts of
hallowing of the Temple were made in Jerusalem, and
it was winter. And Jesus walked in the Temple, in the
porch of Solomon. Therefore the Jews came about Him

and said to Him, How long takes Thou away our soul? If Thou art Christ, say Thou to us openly.

Jesus answered to them, I spoke to you and ye believed not. The works that I do in the name of My Father, bear witnessing of Me. But ye believed not, for ye are not of My sheep. My sheep hear My voice, and I know them, and they sue Me. And I give to them everlasting life, and they shall not perish without end, and none shall ravish them from Mine hand. That thing that My Father gave to Me is more than all things, and no man may ravish from My Father's hand. I and the Father are One!

The Jews took up stones to stone Him. Jesus answered to them, I have showed to you many good works of My Father. For which of them stone ye Me? The Jews answered to Him, We stone Thee not of good work, but of blasphemy, and for Thou, since Thou art a man, make Thyself God! Jesus answered to them, Whether it is not written in your law that I said ye are gods? If He said that they were gods, to which the word of God was made, and Scripture may not be undone, the ilk that the Father has hallowed and has sent into the world, ye say that, Thou blasphemes, for I said I am God's Son? If I do not the works of My Father, nil ye believe to Me. But if I do, though ye will not believe to Me, believe ye to the works, that ye know and believe that the Father is in Me, and I in the Father.

Therefore they sought to take Him, and He went out of their hands. And He went eftsoon over Jordan, into that place where John was first baptizing, and He dwelt there. And many came to Him and said, For John did no miracle, and all things whatever John said of this, were sooth. And many believed in Him.

Chapter XI

And there was a sick man, Lazarus of Bethany, of the castle of Mary and Martha, his sisters. And it was Mary which anointed the Lord with ointment and wiped His feet with her hairs, whose brother Lazarus was sick. Therefore his sisters sent to Him and said, Lord, lo, he whom Thou loves is sick. And Jesus heard and said to them, This sickness is not to the death, but for the glory of God, that Man's Son be glorified by Him. And Jesus loved Martha and her sister Mary, and Lazarus. Therefore when Jesus heard that he was sick, then He dwelled in the same place two days.

And after these things, He said to His disciples, Go we eft into Judea. The disciples say to Him, Master, now the Jews sought for to stone Thee, and eft goes Thou thither? Jesus answered, Whether there are not twelve hours in the day? If any man wander in the day, he hurts not, for he sees the light of this world. But if he wander in the night, he stumbles, for light is not in him.

He says these things, and after these things He says to them, Lazarus, our friend, sleeps, but I go to raise him from sleep. Therefore His disciples said, Lord, if he sleeps, he shall be safe. But Jesus had said of his death, but they guessed that He said of sleeping of sleep. Then therefore Jesus said to them openly, Lazarus is dead. And I have joy for you that ye believe, for I was not there. But we go to him. Therefore Thomas, that is said Didymus, said to even-disciples, Go we also, that we *fellow-disciples* die with him!

And so Jesus came and found him having then four days in the grave. And Bethany was beside Jerusalem, as it were, fifteen furlongs. And many of the Jews came to Mary and Martha, to comfort them of their brother. Therefore as Martha heard that Jesus came, she ran to

Him. But Mary sat at home. Therefore Martha said to Jesus, Lord, if Thou had been here, my brother had not been dead. But now I wot that whatever things Thou shall ask of God, God shall give to Thee.

Jesus says to her, Thy brother shall rise again. Martha says to Him, I wot that he shall rise again in the again-rising in the last day. Jesus says to her, I am again-rising and life. He that believes in Me, yea, though he be dead, he shall live. And each that lives and believes in Me, shall not die without end. Believe thou this thing? She says to Him, Yea, Lord, I have believed that Thou art Christ, the Son of the living God that has come into this world. And when she had said this thing, she went and called Mary, her sister, in silence, and said, The Master comes, and calls thee!

She, as she heard, arose anon, and came to Him. And Jesus came not yet into the town, but He was yet in that place where Martha had come against Him. Therefore the Jews that were with her in the house and comforted her, when they saw Mary that she rose swithy and went out, they sued her and said, For she goes to the grave to weep there! But when Mary was come where Jesus was, she, seeing Him, fell down to His feet and said to Him, Lord, if Thou had been here, my brother had not been dead.

And therefore, when Jesus saw her weeping, and the Jews weeping that were with her, He made noise in spirit and troubled Himself, and said, Where have ye laid him? They say to Him, Lord, come and see! And Jesus wept. Therefore the Jews said, Lo, how He loved him! And some of them said, Whether this Man that opened the eyes of the born-blind man, might not make that this should not die?

Therefore Jesus, eft making noise in Himself, came to the grave. And there was a den, and a stone was laid thereon. And Jesus says, Take ye away the stone. Martha, the sister of him that was dead, says to Him, Lord, he stinks now, for he has lain four days! Jesus says to her, Have I not said to thee that if thou believe, thou shall see the glory of God? Therefore they took away the stone. And Jesus lifted up His eyes and said, Father, I do thankings to Thee, for Thou has heard Me. And I wist that Thou evermore hears Me. But for the people standing about I said, that they believe that Thou has sent Me.

When He had said these things, He cried with a great voice, Lazarus! Come thou forth! And anon, he that was dead, came out, bound the hands and feet with bonds, and his face bound with a sudary. And Jesus says to them, Unbind ye him, and suffer him to go forth. Therefore many of the Jews that came to Mary and Martha and saw what things Jesus did, believed in Him. But some of them went to the Pharisees, and said to them what things Jesus had done.

Therefore the bishops and the Pharisees gathered a council against Jesus, and said, What do we, for this Man does many miracles? If we leave Him thus, all men shall believe in Him. And Romans shall come and shall take our place and our folk. But one of them, Caiaphas by name, when he was bishop of that year, said to them, Ye wit nothing, nor think that it speeds to you that one man die for the people, and that all folk perish not. But he said not this thing of himself, but when he was bishop of that year he prophesied that Jesus was to die for the folk, and not only for the folk, but that He should gather into one the sons of God that were scattered. Therefore from that day, they sought for to slay Him.

Therefore Jesus walked not then openly among the Jews. But He went into a country beside desert, into a city that is said Ephraim, and there He dwelled with His disciples. And the Pasch of the Jews was nigh, and many of the country went up to Jerusalem before the Pasch to hallow themselves. Therefore they sought Jesus, and spoke together standing in the Temple, What guess ye, for He comes not to the feast day? For the bishops and Pharisees had given a commandment that if any man know where He is, that he show, that they take Him.

Chapter XII

Therefore Jesus, before six days of Pasch, came to Bethany where Lazarus had been dead, whom Jesus raised. And they made to Him a supper there, and Martha ministered to Him. And Lazarus was one of men that sat at the meat with Him. Therefore Mary took a pound of ointment or true nard, precious, and anointed the feet of Jesus, and wiped His feet with her hairs, and the house was fulfilled of the savour of the ointment. Therefore Judas Iscariot, one of the twelve that was to betray Him, said, Why is not this ointment sold for three hundred pence, and is given to needy men? But he said this thing not for it pertained to him of needy men, but for he was a thief, and he had the purses and bore those things that were sent. Therefore Jesus said, Suffer ye her, that into the day of My burying she kept that. For ye shall evermore have poor men with you, but ye shall not evermore have Me.

Therefore much people of Jews knew that Jesus was there, and they came not only for Jesus, but to see Lazarus whom He had raised from death. But the princes of priests thought to slay Lazarus, for many of the Jews went away for him and believed in Jesus.

But on the morrow, a much people that came together to the feast day, when they had heard that Jesus came to Jerusalem, took branches of palms and came forth against Him, and cried, Hosanna! Blessed is the King of Israel that comes in the name of the Lord! And Jesus found a young ass and sat on him. As it is written, The daughter of Zion, nil thou dread! Lo, thy King comes, sitting on an ass's foal. His disciples knew not first these things, but when Jesus was glorified, then they had mind for these things that were written of Him, and these things they did to Him.

Therefore the people bore witnessing that were with Him when He called Lazarus from the grave and raised him from death. And therefore the people came and met with Him, for they heard that He had done this sign. Therefore the Pharisees said to themselves, Ye see that we profit nothing. Lo, all the world went after Him.

And there were some heathen men of them that had come up to worship in the feast day. And these came to Philip that was of Bethsaida of Galilee, and prayed him and said, Sire, we will see Jesus! Philip comes and says to Andrew, eft Andrew and Philip said to Jesus. And Jesus answered to them and said, The hour comes that Man's Son be clarified. Truly, truly, I say to you, but a corn of wheat fall into the earth and be dead, it dwells alone. But if it be dead, it brings much fruit. He that loves his life shall leese it, and he that hates his life in this world, keeps it into everlasting life. If any serve Me, sue he Me, and where I am, there My minister shall be. If any man serve Me, My Father shall worship him. Now my soul is troubled, and what shall I say? Father, save Me from this hour? But therefore I came into this hour. Father, clarify Thy name! And a voice came from heaven and said, And I have clarified and eft I shall clarify!

glorified, made plain to the mind

Therefore the people that stood and heard, said that thunder was made. Other men said, An angel spoke to

Him! Jesus answered and said, This voice came not for Me, but for you. Now is the doom of the world. Now the prince of this world shall be cast out. And if I shall be enhanced from the earth, I shall draw all things to Myself. And He said this thing, signifying by what death He was to die. And the people answered to Him, We have heard of the law that Christ dwells without end. And how say Thou, It behoves Man's Son to be arreared? Who is this Man's Son? And Jesus says to them, Yet a little light is in you. Walk ye the while ye have light, that darknesses catch you not. He that wan⁄ders in darknesses wot ne'er whither he goes. While ye have light, believe ye in light, that ye be the children of light!

Jesus spoke these things and went and hid Him from them. And when He had done so many miracles before them, they believed not into Him, that the word of Isaiah the prophet should be fulfilled, which he said, Lord, who believed to our hearing, and to whom is the arm of the Lord shown? Therefore they might not believe, for eft Isaiah said, He has blinded their eyes, and He has made hard the heart of them, that they see not with eyes and understand with heart, and that they be converted and I heal them. Isaiah said these things when he saw the glory of Him and spoke of Him. Netheless, of the princes many believed on Him, but for the Pharisees they acknowledged not, that they should not be put out of the synagogue. For they loved the glory of men more than the glory of God.

And Jesus cried and said, He that believes in Me, believes not in Me, but in Him that sent Me! He that sees Me, sees Him that sent Me. I, Light, came into the world, that each that believes in Me dwells not in dar⁄knesses. And if any man hear My words and keeps them, I deem him not. For I came not that I deem the

world, but that I make the world safe. He that despises
Me, and takes not My words, has Him that shall judge
him. The ilk word that I have spoken, shall deem him
in the last day. For I have not spoken of Myself, but the
ilk Father that sent Me, gave to Me a commandment
what I shall say and what I shall speak. And I wot that
His commandment is everlasting life. Therefore, those
things that I speak, as the Father said to Me, so I speak!

Chapter XIII

Before the feast day of Pasch, Jesus, witting that His
hour is come that He pass from this world to the Father,
when He had loved His that were in the world, into the
end He loved them. And when the supper was made,
when the devil had put then into the heart that Judas of
Simon Iscariot should betray Him, He, witting that the
Father gave all things to Him into His hands, and that
He went out from God and goes to God, He rises from
the supper and does off His clothes. And when He had
taken a linen cloth, He girded Him. And afterward, He
put water into a basin and began to wash the disciples
feet, and to wipe with the linen cloth with which He
was girt.

And so He came to Simon Peter, and Peter says to
Him, Lord, wash Thou my feet? Jesus answered and
said to him, What I do, thou wost not now. But thou
shall wit afterward. Peter says to Him, Thou shall never
wash my feet! Jesus answered to him, If I shall not wash
thee, thou shall not have part with Me. Simon Peter says
to Him, Lord, not only my feet, but both the hands and
the head. Jesus said to him, He that is washed, has no
need but that he wash the feet. But he is all clean. And
ye are clean, but not all. For He wist who was he that
should betray Him. Therefore He said, Ye are not all
clean.

And so, after that He had washed the feet of them, He took His clothes. And when He was sat to meat again, eft He said to them, Ye wit what I have done to you. Ye call Me Master and Lord, and ye say well, for I am. Therefore if I, Lord and Master, have washed your feet, and ye shall wash one another's feet. For I have given example to you, that as I have done to you, so do ye. Truly, truly, I say to you, the servant is not greater than his lord, neither an apostle greater than He that sent him. If ye wit these things, ye shall be blessed if ye do them. I say not of all you. I wot which I have chosen. But that the Scripture be fulfilled, He that eats My bread, shall raise his heel against Me. Truly, I say to you before it be done, that when it is done ye believe that I am. Truly, truly, I say to you, he that takes whomever I shall send, receives Me. And he that receives Me, receives Him that sent Me.

When Jesus had said these things, He was troubled in spirit, and witnessed and said, Truly, truly, I say to you, that one of you shall betray Me. Therefore the disci-ples looked together, doubting of whom He said. And so one of His disciples was resting in the bosom of Jesus, whom Jesus loved. Therefore Simon Peter beck-ons to him and says to him, Who is it of whom He says? And so, when he had rested again on the breast of Jesus, he says to Him, Lord, who is it? Jesus answered, He it is to whom I shall a-reach a sop of bread. And when He had wet bread, He gave to Judas of Simon Iscariot. And after the morsel, then Satan entered into him. And Jesus says to him, That thing that thou does, do thou swithy.

And none of them that sat at the meat wist whereto He said to him. For some guessed, for Judas had purses, that Jesus had said to him, Buy thou those things that are needful to us to the feast day ⸍ or that he should give something to needy men. Therefore when he had taken the morsel, he went out anon, and it was night.

And when he was gone out, Jesus said, Now Man's Son is clarified, and God is clarified in Him. If God is clarified in Him, God shall clarify Him in Himself, and anon He shall clarify Him. Little sons, yet a little I am with you. Ye shall seek Me, and, as I said to the Jews, whither I go ye moun not come. And to you I say now. I give to you a new commandment, that ye love together, as I loved you, and that ye love together. In this thing all men shall know that ye are My disciples if ye have love together.

Simon Peter says to Him, Lord, whither goes Thou? Jesus answered, Whither I go, thou may not sue Me now. But thou shall sue afterward. Peter says to Him, Why may I not sue Thee now? I shall put my life for Thee. Jesus answered, Thou shall put thy life for Me? Truly, truly, I say to thee, the cock shall not crow till thou shall deny Me thrice. And He says to His disciples,

Chapter XIV

Be not your heart afeared, nor dread it. Ye believe in God, and believe ye in Me. In the house of My Father are many dwellings. If anything less, I had said to you, for I go to make ready to you a place. And if I go and make ready to you a place, eftsoons I come, and I shall take you to Myself, that where I am, ye are. And whither I go, ye wit, and ye wit the way. Thomas says to Him, Lord, we wit not whither Thou goes, and how moun we wit the way? Jesus says to him, I am way, truth and life. No man comes to the Father but by Me. If ye had known Me, soothly ye had known also My Father. And afterward ye shall know Him, and ye have seen Him.

Philip says to Him, Lord, show to us the Father and it suffices to us. Jesus says to him, So long time I am with you, and have ye not known Me, Philip? He that sees Me, sees also the Father. How say thou, show to us the Father? Believe thou not that I am in the Father, and the Father is in Me? The words that I speak to you, I speak not of Myself. But the Father Himself, dwelling in Me, does the works. Believe ye not that I am in the Father, and the Father is in Me? Else believe ye for the ilk works. Truly, truly, I say to you, if a Man believe in Me, also he shall do the works that I do. And he shall do greater works than these, for I go to the Father. And whatever thing ye ask the Father in My name, I shall do this thing, that the Father be glorified in the Son. If ye ask anything in My name, I shall do it.

If ye love Me, keep ye My commandments. And I shall pray the Father, and He shall give to you another Comforter, the Spirit of Truth, to dwell with you without end. Which Spirit the world may not take, for it sees Him not, neither knows Him. But ye shall know Him, for He shall dwell with you and He shall be in you. I shall not leave you fatherless. I shall come to you. Yet a little, and the world sees not now Me. But ye shall see Me. For I live, and ye shall live. In that day, ye shall know that I am in My Father, and ye in Me, and I in you. He that has My commandments and keeps them, he it is that loves Me. And he that loves Me, shall be loved of My Father, and I shall love him, and I shall show to him Myself.

Judas says to Him, not he of Iscariot, Lord, what is done that Thou shall show Thyself to us and not to the world? Jesus answered and said to him, If any man loves Me, he shall keep My word, and My Father shall love him, and We shall come to him, and We shall dwell with him. He that loves Me not, keeps not My words, and the word which ye have heard is not Mine, but the Father's that sent Me. These things I have spoken to you, dwelling among you, but the ilk Holy Ghost, the Comforter, whom the Father shall send in My name, He shall teach you all things, and shall show to you all things, whatever things I shall say to you.

Peace I leave to you. My peace I give to you. Not as the world gives I give to you. Be not your heart afraid, nor dread it. Ye have heard that I said to you, I go and come to you. If ye loved Me, forsooth ye should have joy, for I go to the Father, for the Father is greater than I. And now I have said to you before that it be done, that when it is done, ye believe. Now I shall not speak many things with you, for the prince of this world comes, and has not in Me anything. But that the world know that I love the Father, and as the Father gave a commandment to Me, so I do. Rise ye. Go we hence.

Chapter XV

I am a very vine, and My Father is an earth-tiller. Each branch in Me that bears not fruit, He shall take away it. And each that bears fruit, He shall purge it that it bear the more fruit. Now ye are clean for the word that I have spoken to you. Dwell ye in Me and I in you. As a branch may not make fruit of itself but it dwell in the vine, so neither ye, but ye dwell in Me. I am a vine, ye are the branches. Who that dwells in Me, and I in him, this bears much fruit, for without Me ye moun nothing do. If any man dwells not in Me, he shall be cast out as a branch and shall wax dry. And they shall gather him, and they shall cast him into the fire, and he burns. If ye dwell in Me and My words dwell in you, whatever thing ye will, ye shall ask, and it shall be done to you. In this thing My Father is clarified, that ye bring forth full much fruit, and that ye be made My disciples.

As My Father loved Me, I have loved you. Dwell ye in My love. If ye keep My commandments, ye shall dwell in My love, as I have kept the commandments of My Father, and I dwell in His love. These things I spoke to you, that my joy be in you and your joy be fulfilled. This is My commandment, that ye love together as I loved you. No man has more love than this, that a man put his life for his friends. Ye are My friends if ye do those things that I command to you. Now I shall not call you servants, for the servant wot not what his lord shall do. But I have called you friends, for all things whatever I heard of My Father, I have made known to you.

Ye have not chosen Me, but I chose you, and I have put you, that ye go and bring forth fruit, and your fruit dwell, that whatever thing ye ask the Father in My name, He give to you. These things I command to you, that ye love together. If the world hates you, wit ye that it had Me in hate rather than you. If ye had been of the world, the world should love that thing that was his. But for ye are not of the world, but I chose you from the world, therefore the world hates you. Have ye mind of My word which I said to you, The servant is not greater than his lord. If they have pursued Me, they shall pursue you also. If they have kept My word, they shall keep yours also. But they shall do to you all these things for My name, for they know not Him that sent Me.

If I had not come, and had not spoken to them, they should not have sin. But now they have none excusing of their sin. He that hates Me, hates also My Father. If I had not done works in them which none other man did, they should not have sin. But now both they have seen and hated Me and My Father. But that the word be ful- filled that is written in their law, For they had Me in hate without cause. But when the Comforter shall come, which I shall send to you from the Father, a Spirit of

Truth which comes of the Father, He shall bear witnessing of Me. And ye shall bear witnessing, for ye are with Me from the beginning.

Chapter XVI

These things I have spoken to you that ye be not sclaundered. They shall make you without synagogues, but the hour comes that each man that slays you, deems that he does service to God. And they shall do to you these things, for they have not known the Father, neither Me. But these things I spoke to you that when the hour of them shall come, ye have mind that I said to you.

I said not to you these things from the beginning, for I was with you. And now I go to Him that sent Me, and no man of you asks Me, Whither Thou goes? But for I have spoken to you these things, heaviness has fulfilled your heart. But I say to you truth. It speeds to you that I go, for if I go not forth, the Comforter shall not come to you. But if I go forth, I shall send Him to you. And when He comes, He shall reprove the world of sin, and of rightwiseness and of doom. Of sin, for they have not believed in Me. And of rightwiseness, for I go to the Father and now ye shall not see Me. But of doom, for the prince of this world is now deemed.

Yet I have many things for to say to you, but ye moun not bear them now. But when the ilk Spirit of Truth is come, He shall teach you all truth. For He shall not speak of Himself, but whatever things He shall hear, He shall speak, and He shall tell to you those things that are to come. He shall clarify Me, for of Mine He shall take and shall tell to you. All things which ever the Father has, are Mine. Therefore I said to you, For of Mine He shall take and shall tell to you. A little, and then ye shall not see Me. And eftsoon a little, and ye shall see Me, for I go to the Father.

Therefore some of His disciples said together, What is this thing that He says to us, A little, and ye shall not see Me, and eftsoon a little, and ye shall see Me, for I go to the Father? Therefore they said, What is this that He says to us? We wit not what He speaks!

And Jesus knew that they would ask Him, and He said to them, Of this thing ye seek among you, for I said, A little, and ye shall not see Me, and eftsoon a little, and ye shall see Me? Truly, truly, I say to you that ye shall mourn and weep, but the world shall have joy. And ye shall be sorrowful, but your sorrow shall be turned into joy. A woman, when she bears child, has heaviness, for her time is come. But when she has borne a son, now she thinks not on the pain for joy, for a man is born into the world. And therefore ye have now sorrow. But eftsoon I shall see you, and your heart shall have joy, and no man shall take from you your joy. And in that day ye shall not ask Me anything. Truly, truly, I say to you, if ye ask the Father anything in My name, He shall give to you. Till now, ye asked nothing in My name. Ask ye, and ye shall take, that your joy be full.

I have spoken to you these things in proverbs. The hour comes when now I shall not speak to you in proverbs, but openly of My Father I shall tell to you. In that day, ye shall ask in My name, and I say not to you that I shall pray the Father of you, for the Father Himself loves you. For ye have loved Me, and have believed that I went out from God. I went out from the Father, and I came into the world. Eftsoon I leave the world, and I go to the Father.

His disciples said to Him, Lo, now Thou speaks openly, and Thou says no proverb. Now we wit that Thou wost all things, and it is not need to Thee that any man ask Thee. In this thing we believe, that Thou went out from God.

Jesus answered to them, Now ye believe? Lo, the hour comes, and now it comes, that ye be disparpled, each to his own things, and that ye leave Me alone. And I am not alone, for the Father is with Me. These things I have spoken to you that ye have peace in Me. In the world ye shall have disease. But trust ye. I have over‑come the world.

Chapter XVII

These things Jesus spoke. And when He had cast up His eyes into heaven, He said, Father, the hour comes. Clarify Thy Son, that Thy Son clarify Thee. As Thou has given to Him power on each flesh, that all things that Thou has given to Him, He give to them everlast‑ing life. And this is everlasting life, that they know Thee, very God alone, and whom Thou has sent, Jesus Christ. I have clarified Thee on the earth. I have ended the work that Thou has given to Me to do. And now, Father, clarify Thou Me at Thyself, with the clearness that I had at Thee before the world was made. I have showed Thy name to those men which Thou has given to Me of the world. They were Thine, and Thou has given them to Me, and they have kept Thy word. And now they have known that all things that Thou has given to Me, are of Thee. For the words that Thou has given to Me, I gave to them. And they have taken, and have known verily, that I went out from Thee. And they believed that Thou sent Me. I pray for them. I pray not for the world, but for them that Thou has given to Me. For they are Thine. And all My things are Thine, and Thy things are Mine, and I am clarified in them.

And now I am not in the world. And these are in the world, and I come to Thee. Holy Father, keep them in Thy name which Thou gave to Me, that they are one as We are. While I was with them, I kept them in Thy name. The ilk that Thou gave to Me, I kept, and none of them perished but the son of perdition, that the Scripture be fulfilled. But now I come to Thee, and I speak these things in the world, that they have My joy fulfilled in themselves.

I gave to them Thy word, and the world had them in hate. For they are not of the world, as I am not of the world. I pray not that Thou take them away from the world, but that Thou keep them from evil. They are not of the world, as I am not of the world. Hallow Thou them in truth. Thy word is truth. As Thou sent Me into the world, also I sent them into the world. And I hallow Myself for them, that also they are hallowed in truth. And I pray not only for them, but also for them that should believe into Me by the word of them, that all are one, as Thou, Father, in Me, and I in Thee, that also they in Us are one, that the world believe that Thou has sent Me. And I have given to them the clearness that Thou has given to Me, that they are one as We are one, I in them and Thou in Me, that they be ended into one, and that the world know that Thou sent Me, and has loved them as Thou has loved Me.

Father, they which Thou gave to me, I will that where I am, that they are with Me, that they see My clearness that Thou has given to Me. For Thou loved Me before the making of the world. Father, rightfully the world knew Thee not. But I knew Thee, and these knew that Thou sent Me. And I have made Thy name known to them, and shall make known, that the love by which Thou has loved Me, be in them, and I in them.

Chapter XVIII

When Jesus had said these things, He went out with His disciples over the strand of Cedron, where was a garden into which He entered with His disciples. And

Judas, that betrayed Him, knew the place, for often Jesus came thither with His disciples. Therefore, when Judas had taken a company of knights and ministers of the bishops and of the Pharisees, he came thither with lanterns and brands and arms. And so Jesus, witting all things that were to come on Him, went forth and said to them, Whom seek ye?

They answered to Him, Jesus of Nazareth! Jesus says to them, I am. And Judas that betrayed Him, stood with them. And when He said to them, I am, they went aback and fell down on the earth.

And eft He asked them, Whom seek ye? And they said, Jesus of Nazareth! He answered to them, I said to you that I am. Therefore, if ye seek Me, suffer ye these to go away ⁄ that the word which He said should be fulfilled, For I lost not any of them which Thou has given to Me.

Therefore Simon Peter had a sword and drew it out, and smote the servant of the bishop and cut off his right ear. And the name of the servant was Malchus. Therefore Jesus said to Peter, Put thou thy sword into thy sheath. Will thou not that I drink of the cup that My Father gave to Me?

Therefore the company of knights and the tribune, and the ministers of the Jews, took Jesus and bound Him, and led Him first to Annas, for he was father of Caiaphas' wife that was bishop of that year. And it was Caiaphas that gave counsel to the Jews that it speeds that one man die for the people. But Simon Peter sued Jesus, and another disciple, and the ilk disciple was known to the bishop. And he entered with Jesus into the hall of the bishop, but Peter stood at the door, withoutforth. Therefore the t'other disciple that was known to the bishop, went out and said to the woman that kept the door, and brought in Peter. And the damsel, keeper of the door, said to Peter, Whether thou art also of this Man's disciples? He said, I am not. And the servants and ministers stood at the coals, for it was cold and they warmed them. And Peter was with them, standing and warming him.

And the bishop asked Jesus of His disciples and of His teaching. Jesus answered to him, I have spoken openly to the world. I taught evermore in the synagogue and in the Temple whither all Jews came together, and in hidles I spoke nothing. What asks thou Me? Ask them that heard what I have spoken to them. Lo, they wit what things I have said.

When He had said these things, one of the ministers standing nigh, gave a buffet to Jesus and said, Answers Thou so to the bishop? Jesus answered to him, If I have spoken evil, bear thou witnessing of evil. But if I said well, why smites thou Me? And Annas sent Him bound to Caiaphas, the bishop.

And Simon Peter stood and warmed him, and they said to him, Whether also thou art His disciple? He denied and said, I am not. One of the bishop's servants, cousin of him whose ear Peter cut off, said, Saw I thee not in the garden with Him? And Peter eftsoon denied, and anon the cock crew.

Then they led Jesus to Caiaphas, into the moot hall, and it was early. And they entered not into the moot hall, that they should not be defouled, but that they should eat Pasch. Therefore Pilate went out without forth to them, and said, What accusing bring ye against this Man? They answered and said to him, If this were not a misdoer, we had not betaken Him to thee. Then Pilate says to them, Take ye Him, and deem ye Him after your law. And the Jews said to him, It is not leaveful to us to slay any man ⁄ that the word of Jesus should be fulfilled which He said, signifying by what death He should die. Therefore eftsoon Pilate entered into the moot hall and called Jesus, and said to Him, Art Thou King of Jews?

Jesus answered and said to him, Says thou this thing of thyself, either others have said to thee of Me? Pilate answered and said, Whether I am a Jew? Thy folk and bishops betook Thee to me. What has Thou done? Jesus answered, My kingdom is not of this world. If My kingdom were of this world, My ministers should strive that I should not be taken to the Jews. But now My kingdom is not here. And so Pilate said to Him, Then Thou art a King? Jesus answered, Thou say that I am a King. To this thing I am born, and to this I am come into the world to bear witnessing to truth. Each that is of truth, hears My voice. Pilate says to Him, What is truth? And when he had said this thing, eft he went out to the Jews and said to them, I find no cause in Him. But it is a custom to you that I deliver one to you in Pasch. Therefore will ye that I deliver to you the King of Jews? All cried eftsoon, and said, Not this, but Barabbas! And Barabbas was a thief.

Chapter XIX

Therefore Pilate took then Jesus, and scourged. And knights writhed a crown of thorns and set on His head, and did about Him a cloth of purple, and came to Him and said, Hail, King of Jews! And they gave to Him buffets. Eftsoon, Pilate went out and said to them, Lo, I bring Him out to you that ye know that I find no cause in Him! And so Jesus went out, bearing a crown of thorns and a cloth of purple. And he says to them, Lo, the Man!

But when the bishops and ministers had seen Him, they cried and said, Crucify! Crucify Him! Pilate says to them, Take ye Him and crucify ye, for I find no cause in Him! The Jews answered to him, We have a law, and by the law He owes to die, for He made Himself God's Son! Therefore when Pilate had heard this word, he dreaded the more. And he went into the moot hall eftsoon, and said to Jesus, Of whence art Thou? But Jesus gave none answer to him. Pilate says to Him, Speaks Thou not to me? Wist Thou not that I have power to crucify Thee, and I have power to deliver Thee? Jesus answered, Thou should not have any power against Me but it were given to thee from above. Therefore he that betook Me to thee has the more sin.

From that time Pilate sought to deliver Him. But the Jews cried and said, If thou delivers this Man, thou art not the emperor's friend, for each man that makes himself king, says against the emperor! And Pilate, when he had heard these words, led Jesus forth and sat for doomsman in a place that is said Lithostrotos, but in Hebrew Gabbatha. And it was Pasch eve, as it were the sixth hour. And he says to the Jews, Lo, your King! But they cried and said, Take away! Take away! Crucify Him! Pilate says to them, Shall I crucify your King? The bishops answered, We have no king but the emperor!

And then Pilate betook Him to them, that He should be crucified. And they took Jesus and led Him out. And He bore to Himself a cross, and went out into that place that is said of Calvary, in Hebrew Golgotha, where they crucified Him and other twain with Him, one on this side and one on that side, and Jesus in the middle. And Pilate wrote a title and set on the cross, and it was written, Jesus of Nazareth, King of Jews. Therefore many of the Jews read this title, for the place where Jesus was crucified was nigh the city, and it was written in Hebrew, Greek and Latin. Therefore the bishops of the Jews said to Pilate, Nil thou write, King of Jews, but for He said, I am King of Jews! Pilate answered, That that I have written, I have written.

Therefore the knights, when they had crucified Him, took His clothes and made four parts, to each knight a part, and a coat. And the coat was without seam, and woven all about. Therefore they said together, Cut we not it, but cast we lot whose it is ⸱ that the Scripture be fulfilled, saying, They parted My clothes to them, and on My cloth they cast lot. And the knights did these things. But beside the cross of Jesus, stood His mother and the sister of His mother, Mary Cleophas, and Mary Magdalene. Therefore when Jesus had seen His mother and the disciple standing whom He loved, He says to His mother, Woman, lo, thy son. Afterward He says to the disciple, Lo, thy mother. And from that hour the disciple took her into his mother.

Afterward Jesus, witting that now all things are ended, that the Scripture be fulfilled, He says, I thirst! And a vessel was set full of vinegar, and they laid in hyssop about the sponge full of vinegar, and put it to His mouth. Therefore when Jesus had taken the vine⸗ gar, He said, It is ended! And when His head was bowed down, He gave up the ghost. Therefore, for it was the Pasch eve that the bodies should not abide on the cross in the Sabbath, for that was a great Sabbath day, the Jews prayed Pilate that the hips of them should be broken, and they taken away. Therefore knights came, and they broke the thighs of the first and of the t'other that was crucified with Him. But when they were come to Jesus, as they saw Him dead then, they broke not His thighs. But one of the knights opened His side with a spear, and anon blood and water went out. And he that saw, bore witnessing, and his witnessing is true. And he wot that he says true things, that ye believe. And these things were done that the Scripture should

be fulfilled, Ye shall not break a bone of Him. And eftsoon another Scripture says, They shall see in whom
pierced they pighted through.

But after these things, Joseph of Arimathea prayed
Pilate that he should take away the body of Jesus for that
he was a disciple of Jesus, but privy for dread of the
Jews. And Pilate suffered. And so he came and took
away the body of Jesus. And Nicodemus came also that
mixture had come to Him first by night, and brought a meddling
of myrrh and aloes, as it were an hundred pound. And
they took the body of Jesus and bound it in linen clothes
with sweet smelling ointments, as it is custom to Jews
for to bury. And in the place where He was crucified,
was a garden, and in the garden a new grave in which
yet no man was laid. Therefore there they put Jesus for
the vigil of the Jews' feast, for the sepulchre was nigh.

Chapter XX

And in one day of the week, Mary Magdalene came
early to the grave when it was yet dark. And she saw the
stone moved away from the grave. Therefore she ran
and came to Simon Peter, and to another disciple whom
Jesus loved, and says to them, They have taken the
Lord from the grave, and we wit not where they have
laid Him! Therefore Peter went out and the ilk other
disciple, and they came to the grave. And they twain
ran together, and the ilk other disciple ran before Peter
and came first to the grave. And when he stooped, he
saw the sheets lying. Netheless, he entered not.
Therefore Simon Peter came suing him, and he entered
into the grave and he saw the sheets laid, and the sudary
that was on His head, not laid with the sheets, but by
itself lapped into a place. Therefore then, the ilk disciple
that came first to the grave, entered and saw, and
believed. For they knew not yet the Scripture that it

behoved Him to rise again from death. Therefore the disciples went eftsoon to themselves.

But Mary stood at the grave withoutforth, weeping. And the while she wept, she bowed her and beheld forth into the grave. And she saw two angels sitting, in white, one at the head and one at the feet where the body of Jesus was laid. And they say to her, Woman, what weeps thou? She said to them, For they have taken away my Lord, and I wot not where they have laid Him. When she had said these things, she turned backward and saw Jesus standing, and wist not that it was Jesus.

Jesus says to her, Woman, what weeps thou? Whom seeks thou? She, guessing that He was a gardener, says to Him, Sire, if Thou has taken Him up, say to me where Thou has laid Him, and I shall take Him away. Jesus says to her, Mary. She turned and says to Him, Rabboni! that is to say, Master. Jesus says to her, Nil ye touch Me, for I have not yet styed to My Father. But go to My brethren and say to them, I stye to My Father and to your Father, to My God and to your God.

Mary Magdalene came, telling to the disciples that, I saw the Lord, and these things He said to me! Therefore, when it was eve in that day, one of the Sabbaths, and the gates were shut where the disciples were gathered for dread of the Jews, Jesus came and stood in the middle of the disciples, and He says to them, Peace to you. And when He had said this, He showed to them hands and side. Therefore the disciples joyed, for the Lord was seen. And He says to them eft, Peace to you. As the Father sent Me, I send you. When He had said this, He blew on them and said, Take ye the Holy Ghost. Whose sins ye forgive, those are forgiven to them. And whose sins ye withhold, those are withheld.

But Thomas, one of the twelve that is said Didymus, was not with them when Jesus came. Therefore the other disciples said, We have seen the Lord! And he said to them, But I see in His hands the fitching of the nails, and put my finger into the places of the nails, and put mine hand into His side, I shall not believe! And after eight days, eftsoon His disciples were within, and Thomas with them. Jesus came while the gates were shut, and stood in the middle, and said, Peace to you. Afterward He says to Thomas, Put in here thy finger and see Mine hands, and put hither thine hand and put into My side, and nil thou be unbelieveful, but faithful. Thomas answered and said to Him, My Lord and my God. Jesus says to him, Thomas, for thou has seen Me thou believes. Blessed are they that see not, and have believed.

fixing

And Jesus did many other signs in the sight of His disciples which are not written in this book. But these are written that ye believe that Jesus is Christ, the Son of God, and that ye, believing, have life in His name.

Chapter XXI

Afterward, Jesus eftsoon showed Him to His disciples at the sea of Tiberias. And He showed Him thus. There were together Simon Peter and Thomas that is said Didymus, and Nathaniel that was of the Cana of Galilee, and the sons of Zebedee, and twain other of His disciples. Simon Peter says to them, I go to fish. They say to him, And we come with thee. And they went out, and went into a boat. And in that night, they took nothing. But when the morrow was come, Jesus stood in the brink. Netheless, the disciples knew not that it was Jesus. Therefore Jesus says to them, Children, whether ye have any souping thing? They answered to Him, Nay! He said to them, Put ye the net into the right half of the rowing, and ye shall find. And they put the net. And then they might not draw it for multitude of fishes. Therefore the ilk disciple whom Jesus loved, said to Peter, It is the Lord! Simon Peter, when he had heard that it is the Lord, girt him with a coat, for he was naked, and went into the sea. But the other disciples came by boat, for they were not far from the land, but as a two hundred cubits, drawing the net of fishes.

And as they came down into the land, they saw coals lying and a fish laid on, and bread. Jesus says to them, Bring ye of the fishes which ye have taken now. Simon Peter went up and drew the net into the land, full of great fishes, an hundred, fifty and three. And when they were so many, the net was not broken.

Jesus says to them, Come ye. Eat ye. And no man of them that sat at the meat dared ask Him, Who art Thou? ˒ witting that it was the Lord. And Jesus came and took bread, and gave to them. And fish also. Now this third time Jesus was shown to His disciples when He had risen again from death. And when they had eaten, Jesus says to Simon Peter, Simon of Jonas, loves thou Me more than these? He says to Him, Yea, Lord, Thou wot that I love Thee. Jesus says to him, Feed thou My lambs.

Eft He says to him, Simon of Jonas, loves thou Me? He says to Him, Yea, Lord, Thou wot that I love Thee. He says to him, Feed thou My lambs. He says to him the third time, Simon of Jonas, loves thou Me? Peter was heavy for He says to him the third time, Loves thou Me? And he says to Him, Lord, Thou knows all things. Thou wot that I love Thee! Jesus says to him, Feed My sheep. Truly, truly, I say to thee, when thou were younger, thou girded thee and wandered where thou would. But when thou shall wax elder, thou shall hold forth thine hands and another shall gird thee, and shall lead thee whither thou would not. He said this thing, signifying by what death he should glorify God. And when He had said these things, He says to him, Sue thou Me.

Peter turned and saw the ilk disciple suing, whom Jesus loved, which also rested in the supper on His breast, and he said to Him, Lord, who is it that shall betray Thee? Therefore, when Peter had seen this, he says to Jesus, Lord, but what this? Jesus says to him, So I will that he dwell till that I come, what to thee? Sue thou Me. Therefore the word went out among the brethren that the ilk disciple dies not. And Jesus said not to him that he dies not, but, So I will that he dwell till I come, what to thee?

This is the ilk disciple that bears witnessing of these things and wrote them, and we wit that his witnessing is true. And there are also many other things that Jesus did, which if they are written by each by himself, I deem that the world himself shall not take those books that are to be written.

Here ends the gospel of John

Here begins a Prologue on the Pistle to the Romans

Romans are they that, of Jews and heathen men gathered together, believed in Christ. And the cause of the sending of the pistle of Paul is this, that when strife was among themselves, they desired to set themselves each above other in worship. For the Jews said, We are the people of God which He has loved and nourished from the beginning. We are circumcised and we come by descent of Abraham's kind and holy lineage. And herefore God was only known at Judah. We were delivered out of Egypt with tokens and virtues of God, and passed the sea with dry foot when most heavy floods drenched our enemies. To us also God rained down angel's meat in desert, and ministered an heavenly food to us as to His own sons. And a pillar of cloud and of fire went before us day and night, for it should show to us our passage, there was no way used. Also, though we are still of all benefits wrought about us, we were only worthy to take the law of God and to hear the voice of God speaking and to know His will. In which law, Christ was behoot to us, to whom He Himself wit- *promised* nessed to come, and said, I came not but to the sheep that have perished of the house of Israel. And since He calls you hounds rather than men, therefore is it good equity that ye, that this day first have forsaken your mawmets to whom ye have served from *idol, image (from 'Mahomet')* the beginning, are made now even to us in worship ? But rather be ye ordained in the stead of proselytes and underlings, both by authority of law and of custom. And yet ye deserved never this worship, but for He, of His plenteous goodness, would receive you to our sect.

And then the heathen men answered againward, and said, Ever the greater benefits of God that ye tell that God has done to you, ever the more ye should show you guilty of the greater tres- passes, for in all these benefits that ye tell, ye were evermore unkind. For with the same feet that ye passed the dry sea, ye played and danced before your mawmets that ye made. And with the same mouth that a little before ye worshipped God with song for slaughter of your enemies, ye asked your mawmets to be made. And with the ilk eyes that ye were wont to behold God in cloud or in fire, ye beheld inwardly in your mawmets. Also angel's meat was to you abominable, and ever ye grouched against the Lord in desert, desiring to turn again into Egypt from the which God had brought you out with strong hand. What more ? Thus your fathers, with oft-terring, stirred God to wrath, so that all died in desert, and no more of the elder men but twain entered into the land of behest. But whereto rehearse we old things ? Since though ye had never done these things, yet of this alone no man would deem you worthy forgiveness, that ye would not receive only our Lord Jesus Christ that was ever behoot to you by the *voice of prophets, but also ye destroyed Him with most dispiteous death. And on Him we believed as soon as we heard of Him, and yet there was nothing prophesied to us before. Wherefore it is* counted among, reckoned *well proved that it should not be aretted to a rotted malice of our* ignorance, not knowing *will that we served to mawmets, but to our uncunning. For the ilk same God that we follow now, sikerly we would have followed before if we had rather known as we know now. And truly, if ye boast of nobility of kind, as though following of good manners made you not rather God's sons than fleshly birth, sikerly Esau and Ishmael, though they are of Abraham's lineage, they are not reckoned among sons.*

And while they strive thus, the apostle put him between as a mean, destroying all their questions as a good umpire, stretching forth the hand to them and speaking, brought them all to one accord, showing none of them to be saved through his own merits. But he proved both the peoples that they had grievously trespassed.

The Jews had trespassed, for they dishonoured God by breaking of the law. And the heathen men trespassed that sith knowingly they worshipped a creature as maker of the world. For they changed God's worship into mawmets made with hand. Also he proves ever either people to have forgiveness, and to be even in worship by a full true reason. And namely sith he shows that it was prophesied in their own law that both of Jews and of heathen men should be called to the faith of Christ. Wherefore by diverse admonished, taught *times, Paul meeked them and monested them to come to peace and accord.*

Here ends the Prologue to the Romans

Another prologue to the Romans

Romans are in the country of Italy. They were first deceived of false prophets, that is, false teachers, and under the name of our Lord Jesus Christ they were brought into the law and prophets, that is, into ceremonies and fleshly keeping of Moses' law and of

prophets according with those ceremonies which using is con-
trary now to the truth and freedom of Christ's gospel. Paul
again-calls these Romans to very faith and truth of the gospel,
and writes to them this epistle from Corinth. Jerome says this in
his prologue to the Romans.

Here begins the pistle of Paul to the Romans

Chapter I

Paul, the servant of Jesus Christ, called an apostle, departed into the gospel of God, which He had behoot by His prophets in holy Scriptures of His Son, which is made to Him of the seed of David by the flesh. And He was before ordained the Son of God in virtue by the Spirit of hallowing of the again-rising of dead men, of Jesus Christ our Lord, by whom we have received grace and the office of apostle to obey to the faith in all folks for His name, among which ye are also called of Jesus Christ, to all that are at Rome, darlings of God and called holy, grace to you and peace of God our Father, and of the Lord Jesus Christ.

First, I do thankings to my God by Jesus Christ for all you, for your faith is shown in all the world. For God is a witness to me, to whom I serve in my spirit in the gospel of His Son, that without ceasing I make mind of you ever in my prayers, and beseech if, in any manner some time, I have a speedy way in the will of God to come to you. For I desire to see you, to part somewhat of spiritual grace, that ye be confirmed, that is, to be com-forted together in you by faith that is both yours and mine together.

And, brethren, I nile that ye unknow, that often I *do not, will not* purposed to come to you, and I am let to this time, that I have some fruit in you as in other folks. To Greeks and to barbarians, to wise men and to unwise men, I am debtor, so that that is in me is ready to preach the gospel also to you that are at Rome. For I shame not the gospel, for it is the virtue of God into health of each man that believes, to the Jew first and to the Greek. For the right wiseness of God is shown in it, of faith into faith, as it is written, For a just man lives of faith.

For the wrath of God is shown from heaven on all unpiety and wickedness of those men that withhold the truth of God in unrightwiseness. For that thing of God that is known, is shown to them, for God has shown to them. For the invisible things of Him that are understood, are beheld of the creature of the world by those things that are made, yea, and the everlasting virtue of Him and the Godhead, so that they mow not be excused. For when they had known God, they glorified Him not as God, neither did thankings. But they vanished in their thoughts and the unwise heart of them was darked. For, they saying that themselves were wise, they were made fools.

And they changed the glory of God uncorruptible into the likeness of an image of a deadly man, and of birds, and of four footed beasts, and of serpents. For which thing God betook them into the desires of their heart, into uncleanness, that they punish with wrongs their bodies in themselves. The which changed the truth *falsehood, lie* of God into leesing, and heryed and served a creature rather than to the Creator that is blessed into worlds of worlds. Amen. Therefore God betook them into passions of shenship. For the women of them changed the kindly use into that use that is against kind. Also the men forsook the kindly use of woman, and burned in their desires together, and men into men wrought filthihood and received into themselves the meed that behoved of their error.

And as they proved that they had not God in knowing, God betook them into a reprovable wit, that they do those things that are not covenable, that they are fulfilled with all wickedness, malice, fornication, covetise, waywardness, full of envy, manslayings, strife, guile, evil will, privy backbiters, detractors, hateful to God, debaters, proud and high over measure, finders of evil things, not obeying to father and mother, unwise, unmannerly, without love, without bond of peace, without mercy. The which, when they had known the rightwiseness of God, understood not that they that do such things are worthy the death ⁄ not only they that do those things, but also they that consent to the doers!

Chapter II

Wherefore thou art inexcusable, each man that deems, for in what thing thou deems another man, thou condemns thyself, for thou does the same things which thou deems. And we wit that the doom of God is, after truth, against them that do such things. But guess thou, man, that deems them that do such things and thou does those things, that thou shall escape the doom of God? Whether despises thou the richesses of His goodness, and the patience and the long abiding? Know thou not that the benignity of God leads thee to forthinking? But after thine hardness and unrepentant heart, thou treasures to thee wrath in the day of wrath, and of showing of the rightful doom of God that shall yield to each man after his works ⁄ soothly to them that are by patience of good work, glory and honour and uncorruption to them that seek everlasting life. But to them that are of strife and that assent not to truth, but believe to wickedness, wrath and indignation, tribulation and anguish, into each soul of man that works evil, to the Jew first and to the Greek. But glory and honour and peace to each man that works good things, to the Jew first and to the Greek.

receiving of, respect for

For acception of persons is not anents God, for whoever have sinned without the law, shall perish without the law. And whoever have sinned in the law, they shall be deemed by the law. For the hearers of the law are not just anents God, but the doers of the law shall be made just. For when heathen men that have not law, do kindly those things that are of the law, they not having such manner law, are law to themselves that show the work of the law written in their hearts. For the conscience of them yields to them a witnessing betwixt themselves of thoughts that are accusing or defending in the day when God shall deem the privy things of men, after my gospel, by Jesus Christ.

But if thou art named a Jew and rests in the law, and has glory in God and has known His will, and thou, learned by law, proves the more profitable things, and trusts thyself to be a leader of blind men, the light of them that are in darknesses, a teacher of unwise men, a master of young children, that has the form of kunning and of truth in the law, what then teaches thou another and teaches not thyself? Thou that preaches that men shall steal not, steals? Thou that teaches that men shall do no lechery, do lechery? Thou that loathes mawmets, do sacrilege? Thou that has glory in the law, unworships God by breaking of the law?

For the name of God is blasphemed by you among heathen men, as it is written. For circumcision profits if thou keep the law. But if thou be a trespasser against the law, thy circumcision is made prepucy. Therefore, if prepucy keep the rightwiseness of the law, whether his prepucy shall not be aretted into circumcision? And the prepucy of kind that fulfils the law, shall deem thee that by letter and circumcision art trespasser against the law.

For he that is in open is not a Jew, neither it is circumci⁄sion that is openly in the flesh. But he that is a Jew is hidden, and the circumcision of heart, in spirit, not by the letter whose praising is not of men, but of God.

Chapter III

What then is more to a Jew, or what profit of circumci⁄sion? Much by all wise, first, for the speakings of God were betaken to them. And what if some of them believed not? Whether the unbelief of them has avoided the faith of God? God forbid. For God is soothfast but each man a liar, as it is written that, Thou be justified in Thy words, and overcomes when Thou art deemed. But if our wickedness commend the rightwiseness of God, what shall we say? Whether God is wicked that brings in wrath? ⁄ (after man I say). God forbid. Else how shall God deem this world? For if the truth of God has abounded in my leesing into the glory of Him, what yet am I deemed as a sinner? And not as we are blas⁄phemed and as some say that we say, Do we evil things that good things come' (whose damnation is just).

What then? Pass we them? Nay, for we have shown by skill that all, both Jews and Greeks, are under sin. As it is written, For there is no man just. There is no man understanding, neither seeking God. All bowed away. Together they are made unprofitable. There is none that does good thing. There is none till to one. The throat of them is an open sepulchre. With their tongues they did guilefully. The venom of snakes is under their lips. The mouth of which is full of cursing and bitter⁄ness. The feet of them are swift to shed blood. Sorrow and cursedness are in the ways of them, and they knew not the way of peace. The dread of God is not before their eyes.

And we wit that whatever things the law speaks, it

speaks to them that are in the law, that each mouth be
stopped and each world be made subject to God. For of
the works of the law, each flesh shall not be justified
before Him. For by the law there is knowing of sin. But
now, without the law the rightwiseness of God is
shown that is witnessed of the law and the prophets.
And the rightwiseness of God is by the faith of Jesus
Christ, into all men and on all men that believe in Him,
for there is no departing. For all men sinned and have
need to the glory of God, and are justified freely by His
grace, by the again‑buying that is in Christ Jesus.
Whom God ordained forever by faith in His blood to
the showing of His rightwiseness, for remission of
before‑going sins in the bearing up of God, to the show‑
ing of His rightwiseness in this time, that He be just,
and justifying him that is of the faith of Jesus Christ.

Where then is thy glorying? It is excluded. By what
law? Of deeds doing? Nay, but by the law of faith. For
we deem a man to be justified by the faith without works
of the law. Whether of Jews is God only? Whether He
is not also of heathen men. Yes, and of heathen men.
For one God is that justifies circumcision by faith, and
prepucy by faith. Destroy we therefore the law by the
faith? God forbid, but we stablish the law.

Chapter IV

What then shall we say? That Abraham, our father,
after the flesh found? For if Abraham is justified of
works of the law, he has glory ‑ but not anents God. For
what says the Scripture? Abraham believed to God,
and it was aretted to him to rightwiseness. And to him
that works, meed is not aretted to him by grace, but by
debt. Soothly, to him that works not, but believes into
Him that justifies a wicked man, his faith is aretted to
rightwiseness, after the purpose of God's grace. As

David says, the blessedness of a man whom God accepts, He gives to him rightwiseness without works of the law. Blessed are they whose wickednesses are forgiven and whose sins are hidden. Blessed is that man to whom God aretted not sin.

Then whether dwells this blissfulness? Only in circumcision, or also in prepucy? For we say that the faith was aretted to Abraham to rightwiseness. How then was it aretted? In circumcision, or in prepucy? Not in circumcision, but in prepucy. And he took a sign of circumcision, a tokening of rightwiseness of the faith which is in prepucy, that he be father of all men believing by prepucy, that it be aretted also to them to rightwiseness, and that he be father of circumcision not only to them that are of circumcision, but also to them that sue the steps of the faith, which faith is in prepucy of our father Abraham. For not by the law is behest to Abraham, or to his seed that he should be heir of the world, but by the rightwiseness of faith. For if they that are of the law, are heirs, faith is destroyed. Behest is done away! For the law works wrath. For where there is no law, there is no trespass, neither is trespassing.

Therefore rightfulness is of the faith, that by grace behest be stable to each seed, not to that seed only that is of the law, but to that that is of the faith of Abraham, which is father of us all. As it is written, For I have set thee father of many folks before God, to whom thou has believed. Which God quickens dead men, and calls those things that are not, as those that are. Which Abraham, against hope, believed into hope, that he should be made father of many folks, as it was said to him, Thus shall thy seed be as the stars of heaven, and as the gravel that is in the brink of the sea.

And he was not made unsteadfast in the belief, neither he beheld his body then nigh dead when he was almost of an hundred year, nor the womb of Sarah nigh dead. Also in the behest of God, he doubted not with untrust, but he was comforted in belief, giving glory to God, witting most fully that whatever things God has behight, He is mighty also to do. Therefore it was aretted to him to rightwiseness. And it is not written only for him that it was aretted to him to rightwiseness, but also for us, to which it shall be aretted that believe in Him that raised our Lord Jesus Christ from death. Which was betaken for our sins, and rose again for our justifying.

Chapter V

Therefore we, justified of faith, have we peace at God by our Lord Jesus Christ. By whom we have nigh going to by faith into this grace in which we stand, and have glory in the hope of the glory of God's children. And not this only, but also we glory in tribulations, witting that tribulation works patience, and patience proving, and proving hope. And hope confounds not, for the charity of God is spread abroad in our hearts by the Holy Ghost that is given to us.

And while that we were sick after the time, what died Christ for wicked men? For unneths dies any man for the just man, and yet for a good man peradventure some dare die. But God commends His charity in us, for if when we were yet sinners after the time Christ was dead for us, then much more now we, justified in His blood, shall be safe from wrath by Him. For if when we were enemies, we are reconciled to God by the death of His Son, much more we, reconciled, shall be safe in the life of Him. And not only this, but also we glory in God by our Lord Jesus Christ, by whom we have received now reconciling.

Therefore, as by one man, sin entered into this world,

and by sin death, and so death passed forth into all men. In which man, all men sinned. For till to the law, sin was in the world. But sin was not aretted when law was not. But death reigned from Adam till to Moses also into them that sinned not in likeness of the trespassing of Adam, the which is likeness of Christ to coming. But not as the guilt, so the gift. For if through the guilt of one many are dead, much more the grace of God and the gift in the grace of one man, Jesus Christ, has abounded into many men.

And not as by one sin, so by the gift. For the doom of one into condemnation, but grace of many guilts into justification. For if, in the guilt of one, death reigned through one, much more men that take plenty of grace, and of giving, and of rightwiseness, shall reign in life by one Jesus Christ. Therefore, as by the guilt of one into all men into condemnation, so by the rightwiseness of one into all men into justifying of life. For as by inobedience of one man, many are made sinners, so by the obedience of one, many shall be just. And the law entered that guilt should be plenteous. But where guilt was plenteous, grace was more plenteous. That as sin reigned into death, so grace reigns by rightwiseness into everlasting life by Christ Jesus our Lord.

Chapter VI

Therefore what shall we say? Shall we dwell in sin that grace be plenteous? God forbid. For how shall we that are dead to sin, live yet therein? Whether, brethren, ye know not that whichever we are baptized in Christ Jesus, we are baptized in His death? For we are together buried with Him by baptism into death, that as Christ arose from death by the glory of the Father, so walk we in a newness of life. For if we, planted together, are made to the likeness of His death, also we shall be of the likeness of His rising again, witting this thing, that our old man is crucified together that the body of sin be destroyed, that we serve no more to sin.

For he that is dead, is justified from sin. And if we are dead with Christ, we believe that also we shall live together with Him, witting for Christ, rising again from death, now dies not, death shall no more have lordship on Him. For that He was dead to sin, He was dead once. But that He lives, He lives to God.

So ye deem yourselves to be dead to sin, but living to God in Jesus Christ our Lord. Therefore, reign not sin in your deadly body, that ye obey to his covetings. Neither give ye your members arms of wickedness to sin. But give ye yourselves to God as they that live of dead men, and your members arms of rightwiseness to God. For sin shall not have lordship on you, for ye are not under the law but under grace.

What therefore? Shall we do sin, for we are not under the law but under grace? God forbid. Wit ye not that to whom ye give you servants to obey to, ye are servants of that thing to which ye have obeyed, either of sin to death, either of obedience to rightwiseness? But I thank God that ye were servants of sin, but ye have obeyed of heart into that form of teaching in which ye are betaken. And ye, delivered from sin, are made servants of rightwiseness. I say that thing that is of man for the unsteadfastness of your flesh. But as ye have given your members to serve to uncleanness, and to wickedness into wickedness, so now give ye your members to serve to rightwiseness into holiness. For when ye were servants of sin, ye were free of rightfulness. Therefore, what fruit had ye then in those things in which ye shame now? For the end of them is death. But now ye are delivered from sin and made servants to God, have your fruit into holiness and the end, everlasting life. For the wages of sin is death. The grace of God is everlasting life in Christ Jesus our Lord.

Chapter VII

Brethren, whether ye know not, for I speak to men that know the law, for the law has lordship in a man as long time as it lives? For that woman that is under an husband, is bound to the law while the husband lives. But if her husband is dead, she is delivered from the law of her husband. Therefore she shall be called advowtress if she be with another man while the husband lives. But if her husband is dead, she is delivered from the law of the husband, that she be not advowtress if she be with another man. And so, my brethren, ye are made dead to the law by the body of Christ, that ye are of another that rose again from death, that ye bear fruit to God. For when we were in flesh, passions of sins that were by the law, wrought in our members to bear fruit to death. But now we be unbound from the law of death in which we were held, so that we serve in newness of spirit, and not in oldness of letter.

What, therefore, shall we say? The law is sin? God forbid. But I knew not sin but by law. For I wist not that coveting was sin but for the law said, Thou shall not covet. And through occasion taken, sin, by the commandment, has wrought in me all covetise, for without the law sin was dead. And I lived without the law sometime. But when the commandment was come, sin lived again.

But I was dead, and this commandment that was to life, was found to me to be to death. For sin, through occasion taken by the commandment, deceived me, and by that it slew me. Therefore the law is holy, and the commandment is holy, and just, and good. Is then that thing that is good, made death to me? God forbid. But sin, that it seem sin, through good things wrought death to me, that me sin over manner through the commandment.

And we wit that the law is spiritual. But I am fleshly, sold under sin. For I understand not that that I work. For I do not the good thing that I will, but I do the ilk evil thing that I hate. And if I do that thing that I will not, I consent to the law that it is good. But now I work not it now, but the sin that dwells in me.

But and I wot that in me, that is in my flesh, dwells no good. For will lies to me, but I find not to perform good thing. For I do not the ilk good thing that I will, but I do the ilk evil thing that I will not. And if I do that evil thing that I will not, I work not it, but the sin that dwells in me. Therefore I find the law to me willing to do good thing, for evil thing lies to me. For I delight together to the law of God after the inner man.

fighting against   But I see another law in my members, again-fighting the law of my soul, and making me captive in the law of *unhappy, unlucky,* sin that is in my members. I am an uncely man! Who *wretched* shall deliver me from the body of this sin? The grace of God, by Jesus Christ our Lord! Therefore, I myself, by the soul, serve to the law of God, but by flesh to the law of sin.

Chapter VIII

Therefore now, nothing of condemnation is to them that are in Christ Jesus, which wander not after the flesh. For the law of the Spirit of life in Christ Jesus has delivered me from the law of sin and of death. For that that was unpossible to the law in what thing it was sick by flesh, God sent His Son into the likeness of flesh of sin, and of sin damned sin in flesh, that the justifying of the law were fulfilled in us that go not after the flesh, but after the Spirit. For they that are after the flesh, savour those things that are of the flesh. But they that are after the Spirit, feel those things that are of the Spirit. For the prudence of flesh is death, but the prudence of Spirit is life and peace. For the wisdom of the flesh is enemy to God, for it is not subject to the law of God, for neither it may. And they that are in flesh moun not please to God.

But ye are not in flesh, but in Spirit, if netheless the Spirit of God dwells in you. But if any has not the Spirit of Christ, this is not His. For if Christ is in you, the body is dead for sin. But the Spirit lives for justifying. And if the Spirit of Him that raised Jesus Christ from death dwells in you, He that raised Jesus Christ from death, shall quicken also your deadly bodies for the Spirit of Him that dwells in you.

Therefore, brethren, we are debtors, not to the flesh that we live after the flesh. For if ye live after the flesh, ye shall die. But if ye, by the Spirit, slay the deeds of the flesh, ye shall live. For whoever are led by the Spirit of God, these are the sons of God. For ye have not taken eftsoon the spirit of servage in dread, but ye have taken *bondage, slavery* the Spirit of adoption of sons, in which we cry, Abba, Father. And the ilk Spirit yields witnessing to our spirit, that we are the sons of God. If sons and heirs, and heirs of God, and heirs together with Christ ⁄ if, netheless, we suffer together, that also we are glorified together.

And I deem that the passions of this time are not worthy to the glory to coming that shall be shown in us. For the abiding of creature abides the showing of the sons of God. But the creature is subject to vanity, not willing, but for Him that made it subject in hope. For the ilk creature shall be delivered from servage of corruption into liberty of the glory of the sons of God. And we wit that each creature sorrows and travails in pain till yet. And not only it, but also we ourselves that have the first-fruits of the Spirit. And we ourselves sorrow within us for the adoption of God's sons, abiding the again-buying of our body.

But by hope we are made safe. For hope that is seen, is not hope, for who hopes that thing that he sees? And if we hope that thing that we see not, we abide by patience. And also the Spirit helps our infirmity, for what we shall pray as it behoves, we wit not. But the ilk Spirit asks for us with sorrowings that moun not be told out. For He that seeks the hearts, wot what the Spirit desires, for by God He asks for holy men. And we wit that to men that love God, all things work together into good to them that after purpose are called saints. For the ilk that He knew before, He before ordained by grace to be made like to the image of His Son, that He be the first begotten among many brethren. And the ilk that He before ordained to bliss, them He called, and which He called, them He justified, and which He justified, and them He glorified.

What then shall we say to these things? If God for us, who is against us? The which also spared not His own Son, but for us all betook Him, how also gave He not to us all things with Him? Who shall accuse against the chosen men of God? It is God that justifies. Who is it that condemns? It is Jesus Christ that was dead, yea, the which rose again, the which is on the right half of God, and the which prays for us.

Who then shall depart us from the charity of Christ? Tribulation? Or anguish? Or hunger? Or nakedness? Or persecution? Or peril? Or sword? As it is written, For we are slain all day for Thee. We are guessed as sheep of slaughter. But in all these things, we overcome for Him that loved us. But I am certain that neither death, neither life, neither angels, neither principalities, neither virtues, neither present things, neither things to coming, neither strength, neither height, neither deepness, neither none other creature may depart us from the charity of God that is in Christ Jesus our Lord.

Chapter IX

I say truth in Christ Jesus, I lie not, for my conscience bears witnessing to me in the Holy Ghost, for great heaviness is to me, and continual sorrow to my heart. For I myself desired to be departed from Christ for my brethren that are my cousins after the flesh, that are men of Israel, whose is adoption of sons and glory and testament, and giving of the law, and service and behests, whose are the fathers and of which is Christ after the flesh, that is God above all things, blessed into worlds. Amen.

But not that the word of God has fallen down. For not all that are of Israel, these are Israelites. Neither they that are seed of Abraham, all are sons. But in Isaac shall be called to thee, that is to say, not they that are sons of the flesh are sons of God, but they that are sons of behest are deemed in the seed. For why, this is the word of behest, After this time I shall come, and a son shall be to Sarah. And not only she, but also Rebecca had two sons of one lying by of Isaac, our father. And when they were not yet born, neither had done anything of good either of evil, that the purpose of God should dwell by election, not of works, but of God calling, it was said, to Him, that the more should serve the less, as it is written, I loved Jacob, but I hated Esau.

What, therefore, shall we say? Whether wickedness be anents God? God forbid. For He says to Moses, I shall have mercy on whom I have mercy, and I shall give mercy on whom I shall have mercy. Therefore it is not neither of man willing, neither running, but of God having mercy. And the Scripture says to Pharaoh, For to this thing I have stirred thee, that I show in thee My virtue, and that My name be told in all earth. Therefore of whom God will, He has mercy. And whom He will, he endures.

Then say thou to me, What is sought yet, for who withstands His will? Oh man, who art thou that answers to God? Whether a made thing says to him that made it, What has thou made me so? Whether a potter of clay has not power to make of the same gobbet one vessel into honour, another into despite? That if God, willing to show His wrath and to make His power known, has suffered in great patience vessels of wrath able into death, to show the richesses of His glory into vessels of mercy which He made ready into glory. Which also He called not only of Jews, but also of heathen men. As He says in Hosea, I shall call not My people, My people, and not My loved, My loved, and not getting mercy, getting mercy. And it shall be in the place where it is said to them, Not ye, My people, there they shall be called the sons of God living.

But Isaiah cries for Israel, If the number of Israel shall be as gravel of the sea, the relifs shall be made safe. Forsooth, a word making an end and abridging in equity, for the Lord shall make a word bridged on all the earth. And as Isaiah before said, But God of hosts had left to us seed, we had been made as Sodom, and we had been like as Gomorrah.

Therefore, what shall we say? That heathen men that sued not rightwiseness, have got rightwiseness? Yea, the rightwiseness that is of faith. But Israel, suing the law of rightwiseness, came not perfectly into the law of rightwiseness. Why? For not of faith, but as of works. And they spurned against the stone of offension, as it is written, Lo, I put a stone of offence in Zion, and a stone of sclaunder. And each that shall believe in it, shall not be confounded.

Chapter X

Brethren, the will of mine heart and my beseeching is made to God for them into health. But I bear witnessing to them that they have love of God, but not after kun/ning. For they, unknowing God's rightwiseness, and seeking to make steadfast their own rightfulness, are not subject to the rightwiseness of God. For the end of the law is Christ to rightwiseness to each man that believes. For Moses wrote, For the man that shall do rightwise/ness that is of the law, shall live in it.

But the rightwiseness that is of belief says thus, Say thou not in thine heart, Who shall stye into heaven?, That is to say, to lead down Christ. Or, who shall go down into hell? That is, to again/call Christ from death. But what says the Scripture? The word is nigh in thy mouth and in thine heart. This is the word of belief which we preach, that if thou acknowledges in thy mouth the Lord Jesus Christ, and believes in thine heart that God raised Him from death, thou shall be safe. For by heart, men believe to rightwiseness. But by mouth, acknowledging is made to health. For why, the Scripture says, Each that believes in Him shall not be confounded.

And there is no distinction of Jew and of Greek, for the same Lord of all is rich in all that inwardly call Him. For each man whoever shall inwardly call the name of the Lord, shall be safe. How then shall they inwardly call Him into whom they have not believed? Or how shall they believe to Him whom they have not heard? How shall they hear without a preacher? And how shall they preach, but they be sent? As it is written, How fair are the feet of them that preach peace, of them that preach good things?

But not all men obey to the gospel. For Isaiah says,

Lord, who believed to our hearing? For faith is of hear‑
ing, but hearing by the word of Christ. But I say,
Whether they heard not? Yes, soothly, the word of them
went out into all the earth, and their words into the ends
of the world. But I say, Whether Israel knew not? First
Moses says, I shall lead you to envy that ye are no folk,
that ye are an unwise folk. I shall send you into wrath.
And Isaiah is bold, and says, I am found of men that
seek Me not. Openly I appeared to them that asked not
Me. But to Israel, He says, All day I straught out Mine
hands to a people that believed not, but again‑said Me.

Chapter XI

Therefore I say, Whether God has put away His peo‑
ple? God forbid. For I am an Israelite, of the seed of
Abraham, of the lineage of Benjamin. God has not put
away His people which He before knew. Whether ye
wit not what the Scripture says in Elijah, how he prays
God against Israel, Lord, they have slain Thy prophets.
underdug, undermined   They have underdelved Thine altars, and I am left alone
and they seek my life? But what says God's answer to
him? I have left to Me seven thousands of men that have
not bowed their knees before Baal.

So therefore also in this time, the relifs have been
made safe by the choosing of the grace of God. And if it
be by the grace of God, it is not now of works, else grace
is not now grace. What then? Israel has not got this that
he sought, but election has got, and the others are
blinded. As it is written, God gave to them a spirit of
filled with remorse   compunction, eyes that they see not, and ears that they
hear not into this day. And David says, Be the board of
them made into a grin before them, and into catching
and into sclaunder, and into yielding to them. Be the
eyes of them made dark that they see not, and bow thou
down algates the back of them.

Therefore I say, Whether they offended so that they should fall down? God forbid. But by the guilt of them health is made to heathen men, that they sue them. That if the guilt of them are richesses of the world, and the making less of them are richesses of heathen men, how much more the plenty of them? But I say to you heathen men, for as long as I am an apostle of heathen men, I shall honour my ministry if in any manner I stir my flesh for to follow, and that I make some of them safe. For if the loss of them is the reconciling of the world, what is the taking up but life of dead men? For if a little part of that that is tasted is holy, the whole gobbet is holy. And if the root is holy, also the branches.

What if any of the branches are broken? When thou were a wild olive tree, are grafted among them, and are made fellow of the root and of the fatness of the olive tree, nil thou have glory against the branches. For if thou glorys, thou bears not the root, but the root thee. Therefore thou say, The branches are broken that I am grafted in.

Well, for unbelief the branches are broken. But thou stands by faith. Nil thou savour high thing, but dread thou, for if God spared not the kindly branches, lest per⁄adventure He spare not thee. Therefore see the goodness and the fierceness of God, yea, the fierceness into them that fell down, but the goodness of God into thee if thou dwells in goodness, else also thou shall be cut down. Yea, and they shall be set in if they dwell not in unbelief. For God is mighty to set them in eftsoon. For if thou art cut down of the kindly wild olive tree, and, against kind, art set into a good olive tree, how much more they that are by kind, shall be set in their olive tree?

But brethren, I will not that ye unknow this mystery, that ye be not wise to yourselves. For blindness has feld *befallen* a part in Israel till that the plenty of heathen men entered, and so all Israel should be made safe. As it is written, He shall come of Zion that shall deliver and turn away the wickedness of Jacob. And this testament to them of Me, when I shall do away their sins. After the gospel, they are enemies for you, but they are most dearworth by the election of the fathers.

And the gifts and the calling of God are without forthinking. And as sometime also ye believed not to God, but now ye have great mercy for the unbelief of them, so and these now believed not into your mercy, that also they get mercy. For God closed all things together in unbelief, that He have mercy on all.

Oh, the highness of the richesses of the wisdom and of the kunning of God! How incomprehensible are His dooms, and His ways are unsearchable! For why, who knew the wit of the Lord, or who was His counsellor? Or who former gave to Him, and it shall be quit to him? For of Him and by Him and in Him are all things! To Him be glory into worlds. Amen!

Chapter XII

Therefore, brethren, I beseech you by the mercy of God, that ye give your bodies a living sacrifice, holy, pleasing to God, and your service reasonable. And nil ye be conformed to this world, but be ye reformed in newness of your wit, that ye prove which is the will of God, good and well-pleasing, and perfect. For I say, by the grace that is given to me, to all that are among you, that ye savour no more that it behoves to savour, but for to savour to soberness, and to each man as God has departed the measure of faith. For as in one body, we have many members, but all the members have not the same deed, so we many are one body in Christ, and each are members one of another. Therefore, we that have gifts diversing, after the grace that is given to us, either

prophecy after the reason of faith, either service in minis⟨
tering, either he that teaches in teaching, he that stirs
softly in monesting, he that gives in simpleness, he that
is sovereign in business, he that has mercy in gladness.

Love without feigning, hating evil, drawing to good,
loving together the charity of brotherhood. Each come
before to worship others, not slow in business, fervent
in spirit, serving to the Lord, joying in hope, patient in
tribulation, busy in prayer, giving good to the needs of
the saints, keeping hospitality. Bless ye men that pursue
you. Bless ye, and nil ye curse, for to joy with men that
joy, for to weep with men that weep. Feel ye the same
thing together, not savouring high things, but consent⟨
ing to meek things. Nil ye be prudent anent yourselves,
to no man yielding evil for evil. But purvey ye good
things, not only before God, but also before all men.

If it may be done, that that is of you, have ye peace
with all men, ye most dear brethren, not defending your⟨
selves. But give ye place to wrath, for it is written, The
Lord says, To Me vengeance, and I shall yield. But if
thine enemy hungers, feed thou him. If he thirsts, give
thou drink to him. For thou, doing this thing, shall
gather together coals on his head. Nil ye be overcome of
evil, but overcome thou evil by good.

Chapter XIII

Every soul be subject to higher powers, for there is no
power but of God, and those things that are of God, are
ordained. Therefore, he that againstands power, again⟨
stands the ordinance of God, and they that againstand,
get to themselves damnation. For princes are not to the
dread of good work, but of evil. But will thou, that thou
dread not power? Do thou good thing, and thou shall
have praising of it, for he is the minister of God to thee
into good. But if thou does evil, dread thou, for not with⟨

out cause he bears the sword, for he is the minister of God, venger into wrath to him that does evil.

And therefore, by need, be ye subject, not only for wrath, but also for conscience. For therefore ye give tributes. They are the ministers of God, and serve for this same thing. Therefore yield ye to all men debts. To whom tribute, tribute. To whom toll, toll. To whom dread, dread. To whom honour, honour. To no man owe ye anything but that ye love together. For he that loves his neighbour, fulfilled the law. For thou shall do no lechery. Thou shall not slay. Thou shall not steal. Thou shall not say false witnessing. Thou shall not covet the thing of thy neighbour. And if there be any other commandment, it is instored into this word, Thou shall love thy neighbour as thyself. The love of neighbour works not evil. Therefore love is the fulfilling of the law.

And we know this time, that the hour is now that we rise from sleep, for now our health is nearer than when we believed. The night went before, but the day has nighed. Therefore cast we away the works of darknesses, and be we clothed in the arms of light. As in day wander we honestly, not in superfluous feasts and drunkenesses, not in beds and unchastities, not in strife and in envy. But be ye clothed in the Lord Jesus Christ, and do ye not the business of flesh in desires.

Chapter XIV

But take ye a sick man in belief, not in deemings of thoughts. For another man believes that he may eat all things. But he that is sick, eats worts. He that eats, despise not him that eats not. And he that eats not, deem not him that eats, for God has taken him to Him. Who art thou that deems another's servant? To his lord he stands, or falls from him. But he shall stand, for the

Lord is mighty to make him parfit. For why, one deems a day betwixt a day, another deems each day. Each man increase in his wit. He that understands the day, understands to the Lord. And he that eats, eats to the Lord, for he does thankings to God. And he that eats not, eats not to the Lord, and does thankings to God. For no man of us lives to himself, and no man dies to himself. For whether we live, we live to the Lord, and whether we die, we die to the Lord. Therefore, whether we live or die, we are of the Lord.

For why, for this thing Christ was dead and rose again, that He be Lord both of quick and of dead men. But what deems thou thy brother? Or why despises thou thy brother? For all we shall stand before the throne of Christ. For it is written, I live, says the Lord, for to Me each knee shall be bowed, and each tongue shall acknowledge to God. Therefore each of us shall yield reason to God for himself. Therefore no more deem we each other, but more deem ye this thing, that ye put not hurting or sclaunder to a brother.

I wot and trust in the Lord Jesus that nothing is unclean by Him. No, but to him that deems anything to be unclean, it is unclean. And if thy brother be made sorry in conscience for meat, now thou walks not after charity. Nil thou, through thy meat, leese him for whom Christ died. Therefore be not our good thing blasphemed. For why, the realm of God is not meat and drink, but rightwiseness and peace, and joy in the Holy Ghost. And he that in this thing serves Christ, pleases God and is proved to men.

Therefore sue we those things that are of peace, and keep we together those things that are of edification. Nil thou, for meat, destroy the work of God. For all things be clean, but it is evil to the man that eats by offending. It is good to not eat flesh, and to not drink wine, neither in what thing thy brother offends, or is sclaundered, or is made sick. Thou has faith anents thyself, have thou before God. Blessed is he that deems not himself in that thing that he proves. For he that deems, is damned if he eats, for it is not of faith. And all thing that is not of faith, is sin.

Chapter XV

more serious But we sadder men ought to sustain the feebleness of sick men, and not please to ourselves. Each of us please to his neighbour in good, to edification. For Christ pleased not to Himself, as it is written, The reproofs of men despising Thee, fell on Me. For whatever things are written, those are written to our teaching, that by patience and comfort of Scriptures we have hope. But God, of patience and of solace, give to you to under⁄ stand the same thing, each into other after Jesus Christ, that ye of one will, with one mouth, worship God and the Father of our Lord Jesus Christ.

For which thing, take ye together as also Christ took you into the honour of God. For I say that Jesus Christ was a minister of circumcision for the truth of God to confirm the behests of fathers. And heathen men ought to honour God for mercy, as it is written, Therefore, Lord, I shall acknowledge to Thee among heathen men, and I shall sing to Thy name. And eft He says, Ye heathen men, be ye glad with His people. And eft, All heathen men, hery ye the Lord, and all peoples, magnify ye Him. And eft Isaiah says, There shall be a root of Jesse that shall rise up to govern heathen men, and heathen men shall hope in Him. And God of hope fulfil you in all joy and peace in believing, that ye increase in hope and virtue of the Holy Ghost.

And brethren, I myself am certain of you that also ye are full of love, and ye are filled with all kunning, so that

ye moun monest each other. And, brethren, more
boldly I wrote to you apart, as bringing you into mind
for the grace that is given to me of God, that I be the
minister of Christ Jesus among heathen men. And I
hallow the gospel of God, that the offering of heathen
men be accepted and hallowed in the Holy Ghost.
Therefore I have glory in Christ Jesus to God. For I
dare not speak anything of those things which Christ
does not by me into obedience of heathen men, in word
and deeds, in virtue of tokens and great wonders, in virtue of the Holy Ghost, so that from Jerusalem by compass to the Illyric sea, I have fulfilled the gospel of
Christ. And so I have preached this gospel, not where
Christ was named, lest I build upon another's ground,
but as it is written, For to whom it is not told of Him,
they shall see, and they that heard not shall understand.
For which thing I was letted full much to come to you, *hindered, prevented*
and I am letted to this time.

And now I have not further place in these countries,
but I have desire to come to you of many years that are
passed. When I begin to pass into Spain, I hope that in
my going I shall see you, and of you I shall be lead
thither if I use you first in part. Therefore, now I shall
pass forth to Jerusalem to minister to saints. For
Macedonia and Achaia have assayed to make some gift
to poor men of saints that be in Jerusalem. For it pleased
to them and they be debtors of them. For heathen men
be made partners of their ghostly things, they ought also
in fleshly things to minister to them. Therefore, when I
have ended this thing, and have assigned to them this
fruit, I shall pass by you into Spain. And I wot that I,
coming to you, shall come into the abundance of the
blessing of Christ.

Therefore, brethren, I beseech you by our Lord Jesus
Christ, and by charity of the Holy Ghost, that ye help

me in your prayers to the Lord, that I be delivered from the unfaithful men that are in Judea, and that the offer^ ing of my service be accepted in Jerusalem to saints, that I come to you in joy by the will of God, and that I be refreshed with you. And God of peace be with you all. Amen.

Chapter XVI

And I commend to you Phoebe, our sister, which is in the service of the church at Cenchrea, that ye receive her in the Lord worthily to saints, and that ye help her in whatever cause she shall need of you. For she helped many men and myself. Greet ye Priscilla and Aquila, *put under, risked, subjected* mine helpers in Christ Jesus, which underput their necks for my life, to which not I alone do thankings, but also all the churches of heathen men. And greet ye well *domestic, homely* their menial church.

Greet well Epaenetus, loved to me, that is the first of Asia in Christ Jesus. Greet well Mary, the which has travailed much in us. Greet well Andronicus and Junia, my cousins and mine even prisoners, which are noble among the apostles and which were before me in Christ. Greet well Amplias, most dearworth to me in the Lord.

Greet well Urban, our helper in Christ Jesus, and Stachys, my darling. Greet well Apelles, the noble in Christ. Greet well them that are of Aristobulus' house. Greet well Herodion, my cousin. Greet well them that are of Narcissus' house that are in the Lord. Greet well Tryphena and Tryphosa, which women travail in the Lord. Greet well Persis, most dearworth woman that has travailed much in the Lord.

Greet well Rufus, chosen in the Lord, and his mother and mine. Greet well Asyncritus, Phlegon, Hermas, Patrobas, Hermes and brethren that are with them. Greet well Philologus and Julia, and Nereus and his sister, and Olympas, and all the saints that are with them. Greet ye well together in holy kiss. All the churches of Christ greet you well.

But brethren, I pray you that ye aspy them that make dissensions and hurtings beside the doctrine that ye have learned, and bow ye away from them. For such men serve not to the Lord Christ, but to their womb, and by sweet words and blessings deceive the hearts of innocent men. But your obedience is published into every place. Therefore I have joy in you. But I will that ye are wise in good thing, and simple in evil. And God of peace tread Satan under your feet swiftly. The grace of our Lord Jesus Christ be with you. Timothy, mine helper, greets you well, and also Lucius and Jason, and Sosipater, my cousins.

I, Tertius, greet you well that wrote this epistle in the Lord. Gaius, mine host, greets you well and all the church. Erastus, treasurer of the city, greets you well, and Quartus, brother.

The grace of our Lord Jesus Christ be with you all. Amen. And honour and glory be to Him that is mighty to confirm you by my gospel and preaching of Jesus Christ by the revelation of mystery held still in times everlasting, which mystery is now made open by Scriptures of prophets, by the commandment of God without beginning and ending, to the obedience of faith in all heathen men, the mystery known by Jesus Christ to God alone wise, to whom be honour and glory into worlds of worlds. Amen.

A Prologue on the first epistle to Corinthians

Corinthians are of Achaia, and they in like manner heard of the apostle the word of truth, and were perverted in many manners of false apostles. Some were perverted of eloquence, of philosophy full of words. Other men were led into the sect of law of Jews, that is, to hold it needful with the gospel. The apostle calls again these Corinthians to very faith and wisdom of the gospel, and writes to them from Ephesus by Timothy, his disciple. This says Jerome in his prologue on the first pistle to Corinthians.

Here begins the pistle to Corinthians I

Chapter I

Paul, called apostle of Jesus Christ by the will of God, and Sosthenes, brother, to the church of God that is at Corinth, to them that are hallowed in Christ Jesus and called saints, with all that inwardly call the name of our Lord Jesus Christ in each place of them and of ours, grace to you and peace of God our Father, and of the Lord Jesus Christ.

I do thankings to my God evermore for you, in the grace of God that is given to you in Christ Jesus. For in all things ye are made rich in Him, in each word and in each kunning, as the witnessing of Christ is confirmed in you, so that nothing fail to you in any grace, that abide the showing of our Lord Jesus Christ, which also shall confirm you into the end, without crime, in the day of the coming of our Lord Jesus Christ, a true God by whom ye are called into the fellowship of His Son, Jesus Christ our Lord.

But, brethren, I beseech you by the name of our Lord Jesus Christ, that ye all say the same thing, and that dissensions be not among you, but be ye perfect in the same wit and in the same kunning. For, my brethren, it is told to me of them that be at Chloe's, that strifes are among you. And I say that each of you says, For I am of Paul, and I am of Apollo, and I am of Cephas, but I am of

Christ. Whether Christ is departed? Whether Paul was crucified for you, either ye are baptized in the name of Paul? I do thankings to my God that I baptized none of you but Crispus and Gaius, lest any man say that ye are baptized in my name. And I baptized also the house of Stephanas. But I wot not that I baptized any other. For Christ sent me not to baptize, but to preach the gos-pel, not in wisdom of word, that the cross of Christ be not voided away. For the word of the cross is folly to them that perish. But to them that are made safe, that is to say, to us, it is the virtue of God. For it is written, I shall destroy the wisdom of wise men, and I shall reprove the prudence of prudent men.

Where is the wise man? Where is the wise lawyer? Where is the purchaser of this world? Whether God has not made the wisdom of this world fond? For the world in wisdom of God knew not God by wisdom, it pleased to God, by folly of preaching, to make them safe that believed. For Jews seek signs, and Greeks seek wis-dom. But we preach Christ crucified, to Jews sclaunder and to heathen men folly. But to those Jews and Greeks that are called, we preach Christ, the Virtue of God and the Wisdom of God. For that that is folly thing of God is wiser than men, and that that is the feeble thing of God, is stronger than men.

one who lives after the law

fond, foolish

But, brethren, see ye your calling, for not many wise men after the flesh, not many mighty, not many noble. But God chose those things that are fond of the world to confound wise men, and God chose the feeble things of the world to confound the strong things, and God chose the unnoble things and despisable things of the world, and those things that are not, to destroy those things that are, that each man have not glory in His sight. But of Him ye are in Christ Jesus, which is made of God to us wisdom, and rightwiseness, and holiness, and again-buying, that, as it is written, He that glories, have glory in the Lord.

Chapter II

And I, brethren, when I came to you, came not in the highness of word, either of wisdom, telling to you the witnessing of Christ. For I deemed not me to ken any‚ thing among you but Christ Jesus, and Him crucified. And I, in sickness and dread and much trembling, was among you, and my word and my preaching was not in subtly stirring words of man's wisdom, but in showing of spirit and of virtue, that your faith be not in the wis‚ dom of men, but in the virtue of God. For we speak wisdom among perfect men, but not wisdom of this world, neither of princes of this world that are destroyed. But we speak the wisdom of God in mystery, which wisdom is hidden. Which wisdom God before ordained before worlds into our glory, which none of the princes of this world knew. For if they had known, they should never have crucified the Lord of glory. But as it is written that, Eye saw not, ne ear heard, neither it styed into heart of man, what things God arrayed to them that love Him. But God showed to us by His Spirit.

For why, the Spirit searches all things, yea, the deep things of God. And who of men wot what things are of man, but the spirit of man that is in him? So what things are of God, no man knows but the Spirit of God. And we have not received the spirit of this world, but the Spirit that is of God, that we wit what things are given to us of God. Which things we speak also, not in wise words of man's wisdom, but in the doctrine of the Spirit, and make a likeness of spiritual things to ghostly men. For a beastly man perceives not those things that are of the Spirit of God, for it is folly to him and he may

not understand, for it is examined ghostly. But a spiritual man deems all things, and he is deemed of no man.
As it is written, And who knew the wit of the Lord, or
who taught Him? And we have the wit of Christ.

Chapter III

And I, brethren, might not speak to you as to spiritual
men, but as to fleshly men. As to little children in
Christ, I gave to you milk-drink, not meat, for ye might
not yet, neither ye moun now, for yet ye are fleshly. For
while strife is among you, whether ye are not fleshly,
and ye go after man? For when some says, I am of Paul,
another, But I am of Apollo, whether ye are not men?
What therefore is Apollo, and what Paul? They are
ministers of Him to whom ye have believed, and to each
man as God has given.

I planted, Apollo moistened, but God gave increasing. Therefore, neither he that plants is anything, neither
he that moistens, but God that gives increasing. And
he that plants and he that moistens, are one, and each
shall take his own meed after his travail. For we are the
helpers of God, ye are the earth-tilling of God.

Ye are the building of God. After the grace of God
that is given to me, I set the fundament, and another
builds above. But each see how he builds above. For no
man may set another fundament, out-taken that that is
set, which is Christ Jesus. For if any builds over this
fundament, gold, silver, precious stones, sticks, hay, or
stubble, every man's work shall be open. For the day of
the Lord shall declare, for it shall be shown in fire. The
fire shall prove the work of each man what manner work
it is. If the work of any man dwell still, which he built
above, he shall receive meed. If any man's work burn,
he shall suffer harm - but he shall be safe, so netheless as
by fire.

Wit ye not that ye are the Temple of God, and the Spirit of God dwells in you? And if any defouls the Temple of God, God shall leese him, for the Temple of God is holy, which ye are. No man deceive himself. If any man among you is seen to be wise in this world, be he made a fool that he be wise. For the wisdom of this world is folly anents God. For it is written, I shall catch *crafty* wise men in their fel wisdom. And eft, The Lord knows the thoughts of wise men, for those are vain. Therefore no man have glory in men. For all things are yours, either Paul, either Apollo, either Cephas, either the world, either life, either death, either things present, either things to coming. For all things are yours, and ye are of Christ, and Christ is of God.

Chapter IV

So a man guess us as ministers of Christ, and dispenders of the ministries of God. Now, it is sought here among the dispenders that a man be found true. And to me it is for the least thing that I be deemed of you, or of man's day. But neither I deem myself. For I am nothing over trowing to myself, but not in this thing I am justified, for He that deems me is the Lord. Therefore, nil ye deem before the time till that the Lord come, which shall lighten the hidden things of darknesses, and shall show the counsels of hearts. And then praising shall be to each man of God. And brethren, I have transfigured these things into me and into Apollo for you, that in us ye learn, lest over that it is written, One against another be blown with pride for another.

Who deems thee? And what has thou that thou has not received? And if thou has received, what glories thou as thou had not received? Now ye are filled, now ye are made rich. Ye reign without us, and I would that ye reign, that also we reign with you. And I guess that

God showed the last apostles as the ilk that are sent to the death, for we are made a spectacle to the world, and to angels, and to men ⁄ we, fools for Christ, but ye prudent in Christ. We, sick, but ye strong. Ye noble, but we unnoble.

Till into this hour, we hunger and thirst, and are naked, and are smitten with buffets. And we are unstable, and we travail, working with our hands. We are cursed, and we bless. We suffer persecution, and we abide long. We are blasphemed, and we beseech. As cleansings of this world, we are made the outcasting of all things till yet. I write not these things that I confound you, but I warn as my most dearworth sons. For why, if ye have ten thousand of under⁄masters in Christ, but not many fathers. For in Christ Jesus I have gendered you by the gospel.

Therefore, brethren, I pray you, be ye followers of me as I of Christ. Therefore I sent you Timothy, the which is my most dearworth son and faithful in the Lord, which shall teach you my ways that are in Christ Jesus, as I teach everywhere in each church. As though I should not come to you, so some are blown with pride. But I shall come to you soon, if God will, and I shall know not the word of them that are blown with pride, but the virtue. For the realm of God is not in word, but in virtue. What will ye? Shall I come to you in a yard, or in charity, and in spirit of mildness?

Chapter V

In all manner fornication is heard among you, and such fornication which is not among heathen men, so that some man have the wife of his father. And ye are bolned *ballooned, puffed up* with pride, and not more had wailing that he that did this work be taken away from the middle of you. And I, absent in body but present in spirit, now have deemed

as present him that has thus wrought, when ye are gath/
ered together in the name of our Lord Jesus Christ, and
my spirit, with the virtue of the Lord Jesus, to take such
a man to Satan into the perishing of flesh, that the spirit
be safe in the day of our Lord Jesus Christ.

impairs, sours

Your glorying is not good. Wit ye not that a little
sourdough apairs all the gobbet? Cleanse ye out the old
sourdough, that ye be new springing together as ye are
therf. For Christ offered, is our Pasch. Therefore eat we,
not in old sourdough, neither in sourdough of malice
and waywardness, but in therf things of clearness and of
truth.

mingled, mixed

I wrote to you in a pistle that ye be not meddled with
lechers, not with lechers of this world, ne covetous men,
ne raveners, ne with men serving to mawmets, else ye
shall have gone out of this world. But now I wrote to
you that ye be not meyned. But if he that is named a
brother among you, and is a lecher, or covetous, or ser/
ving to idols, or curser, of full of drunkenness, or rave/
ner, to take no meat with such. For what is it to me to
deem of them that are withoutforth? Whether ye deem
not of things that are withinforth? For God shall deem
them that are withoutforth. Do ye away evil from your/
selves.

Chapter VI

Dare any of you that has a cause against another, be
deemed at wicked men and not at holy men? Whether
ye wit not that saints shall deem of this world? And if
the world shall be deemed by you, be ye unworthy to
deem of the least things? Wit ye not that we shall deem
angels? How much more worldly things? Therefore, if
ye have worldly dooms, ordain ye those contemptible
men that are in the church to deem. I say to make you
ashamed. So there is not any wise man that may deem

betwixt a brother and his brother. But a brother with brother strives in doom, and that among unfaithful men.

And now trespass is algates in you, for ye have dooms among you. Why, rather, take ye no wrong? Why, rather, suffer ye not deceit? But and ye do wrong, and do fraud, and that to brethren. Whether ye wit not that wicked men shall not wield the kingdom of God? Nil ye err. Neither lechers, neither men that serve mawmets, neither advowterers, neither lechers against kind, neither they that do lechery with men, neither thieves, neither avarous men, neither full of drunkenness, *avaricious, greedy* neither cursers, neither raveners, shall wield the kingdom of God. And ye were sometime these things. But ye are washed. But ye are hallowed. But ye are justified in the name of our Lord Jesus Christ, and in the Spirit of our God.

All things are leaveful to me, but not all things are speedful. All things are leaveful to me, but I shall not be brought down under any man's power. Meat to the womb, and the womb to meats, and God shall destroy both this and that. And the body not to fornication, but to the Lord, and the Lord to the body. For God raised the Lord, and shall raise us by His virtue. Wit ye not that your bodies are members of Christ? Shall I then take the members of Christ, and shall I make the members of an whore? God forbid.

Whether ye wit not that he that cleaves to an whore, is made one body? For He says, There shall be twain in one flesh. And he that cleaves to the Lord, is one Spirit. Flee ye fornication. All sin whatever sin a man does, is without the body. But he that does fornication, sins against his body. Whether ye wit not that your members are the Temple of the Holy Ghost that is in you, whom ye have of God, and ye are not your own? For ye are bought with great price. Glorify ye, and bear ye God in your body.

Chapter VII

But of the ilk things that ye have written to me, it is good to a man to touch not a woman. But for fornication, each man have his own wife, and each woman have her own husband. The husband yield debt to the wife, and also the wife to the husband. The woman has not power of her body, but the husband. And the husband has not power of his body, but the woman.

attention Nil ye defraud each to other, but peradventure of consent to a time that ye give tent to prayer. And eft turn ye again to the same thing, lest Satan tempt you for your uncontinence. But I say this thing as giving leave, not by commandment. For I will that all men be as myself. But each man has his proper gift of God, one thus and another thus. But I say to them that are not wedded and to widows, it is good to them if they dwell so as I. That if they contain not themselves, be they wedded, for it is better to be wedded than to be burnt.

But to them that are joined in matrimony, I command, not I but the Lord, that the wife depart not from the husband. And that if she departs, that she dwell unwedded or be reconciled to her husband, and the husband forsake not the wife. But to others, I say, not the Lord, if any brother has an unfaithful wife, and she consents to dwell with him, leave he her not. And if any woman has an unfaithful husband, and this consents to dwell with her, leave she not the husband. For the unfaithful husband is hallowed by the faithful woman, and the unfaithful woman is hallowed by the faithful husband. Else your children were unclean, but now they are holy.

That if the unfaithful departs, depart he. For why,

the brother or sister is not subject in servage in such. For God has called us in peace. And whereof wist thou, woman, if thou shall make the man safe? Or whereof wist thou, man, if thou shall make the woman safe? But as the Lord has departed to each, and as God has called each man, so go he, as I teach in all churches.

A man circumcised is called, bring he not to the prepucy. A man called in prepucy, be he not circumcised. Circumcision is nought, and prepucy is nought, but the keeping of the commandments of God.

Each man, in what calling he is called, in that dwell he. Thou, servant, art called, be it no charge to thee. But if thou may be free, the rather use thou. He that is a servant, and is called in the Lord, is a freeman of the Lord. *one freed from slavery* Also, he that is a freeman and is called, is the servant of Christ. With price ye are bought. Nil ye be made servants of men. Therefore, each man, in what thing he is called a brother, dwell he in this anents God. But of virgins, I have no commandment of God, but I give counsel as he that has mercy of the Lord, that I be true.

Therefore I guess that this thing is good for the present need, for it is good to a man to be so. Thou art bound to a wife, nil thou seek unbinding. Thou art unbound from a wife, nil thou seek a wife. But if thou has taken a wife, thou has not sinned. And if a maiden is wedded, she sinned not. Netheless, such shall have tribulation of flesh.

But I spare you. Therefore, brethren, I say this thing, The time is short. Another is this, that they that have wives, be as though they had none, and they that weep as they wept not, and they that joy as they joyed not, and they that buy as they that had not, and they that use this world as they that use not. For why, the figure of this world passes. But I will that ye be without business, for he that is without wife is busy what things are of the

Lord, how he shall please God. But he that is with a wife, is busy what things are of the world, how he shall please the wife, and he is departed. And a woman unwedded and a maiden, thinks what things are of the Lord, that she be holy in body and spirit. But she that is wedded, thinks what things are of the world, how she shall please the husband.

And I say these things to your profit, not that I cast to you a snare, but to that that is honest and that gives easiness without letting, to make prayers to the Lord. If any man guesses himself to be seen foul on his virgin, that she is full waxed, and so it behoves to be done, do she that that she will. She sins not if she be wedded. For he that ordained stably in his heart, not having need, but having power of his will, and has deemed in his heart this thing to keep his virgin, does well. Therefore he that joins his virgin in matrimony, does well, and he that joins not, does better. The woman is bound to the law as long time as her husband lives. And if her husband is dead, she is delivered from the law of the husband, be she wedded to whom she will, only in the Lord. But she shall be more blessed if she dwells thus after my counsel. And I ween that I have the Spirit of God.

Chapter VIII

But of these things that are sacrificed to idols, we wit, for *puffs up with pride* all we have kunning. But kunning blows, charity edifies. But if any man guesses that he ken anything, he has not yet known how it behoves him to ken. And if any man loves God, this is known of Him. But of meats that are offered to idols, we wit that an idol is nothing in the world, and that there is no God but One. For though there are some that are said gods, either in heaven, either in earth, as there are many gods and many lords, netheless, to us is one God, the Father, of whom are all things and we in Him, and one Lord Jesus Christ, by whom are all things, and we by Him.

But not in all men is kunning. For some, with conscience of idol, till now ate as thing offered to idols, and their conscience is defouled, for it is sick. Meat commends us not to God, for neither we shall fail if we eat not, neither if we eat, we shall have plenty. But see ye, lest peradventure this your leave be made hurting to sick men. For if any man shall see him that has kunning, eating in a place where idols are worshipped, whether his conscience, since it is sick, shall not be edified to eat things offered to idols? And the sick brother, for whom Christ died, shall perish in thy kunning. For thus ye, sinning against brethren and smiting their sick conscience, sin against Christ. Wherefore, if meat sclaunders my brother, I shall never eat flesh, lest I sclaunder my brother.

Chapter IX

Whether I am not free? Am I not apostle? Whether I saw not Christ Jesus, our Lord? Whether ye are not my work in the Lord? And though to others I am not apostle, but netheless to you I am, for ye are the little sign of mine apostlehood in the Lord. My defence to them that *apostleship* ask me, that is. Whether we have not power to eat and drink? Whether we have not power to lead about a woman, a sister, as also other apostles and brethren of the Lord, and Cephas? Or I alone and Barnabas have not power to work these things?

Who travails any time with his own wages? Who plants a vineyard and eats not of his fruit? Who keeps a flock, and eats not of the milk of the flock? Whether, after man, I say these things? Whether also the law says not these things? For it is written in the law of Moses, Thou shall not bind the mouth of the ox threshing.

Whether of oxen is charge to God? Whether for us He says these things? For why, those are written for us, for *ploughs* he that eres, ought to ere in hope, and he that threshes, in hope to take fruits.

If we sow spiritual things to you, is it great if we reap your fleshly things? If others are partners of your power, why not rather we? But we use not this power, but we *evangel, gospel* suffer all things that we give no letting to the evangely of Christ. Wit ye not that they that work in the Temple, eat those things that are of the Temple? And they that serve to the altar, are partners of the altar? So the Lord ordained to them that tell the gospel, to live of the gospel. But I used none of these things. Soothly, I wrote not these things that those be done so in me, for it is good to me rather to die than that any man avoid my glory. For if I preach the gospel, glory is not to me, for needily I mote do it. For woe to me if I preach not the gospel. But if I do this thing wilfully, I have meed, but if against my will, dispending is betaken to me.

What, then, is my meed? That I, preaching the gospel, put the gospel without others' cost, that I use not my power in the gospel? For why, when I was free of all men, I made me servant to all men, to win the more men. And to Jews, I am made as a Jew to win the Jews. To them that are under the law, as I were under the law when I was not under the law, to win them that were under the law. To them that were without law, as I was without law when I was not without the law of God, but I was in the law of Christ, to win them that were without law. I am made sick to sick men, to win sick men. To all men I am made all things, to make all men safe. But I do all things for the gospel, that I be made partner of it.

Wit ye not that they that run in a furlong, all run, but one takes the prize? So run ye, that ye catch. Each man that strives in fight, abstains him from all things, and they, that they take a corruptible crown, but we an uncorrupt. Therefore I run so, not as into uncertain thing. Thus I fight, not as beating the air. But I chastise my body and bring it into servage, lest peradventure, when I preach to others, I myself be made reprovable.

Chapter X

Brethren, I nile that ye unknow that all our fathers were under cloud, and all passed the sea, and all were baptized in Moses, in the cloud and in the sea. And all ate the same spiritual meat, and all drank the same spiritual drink. They drank of the spiritual stone following them, and the stone was Christ. But not in full many of them it was well pleasant to God, for why, they were cast down in desert. But these things are done in figure of us, that we be not coveters of evil things, as they coveted. Neither be ye made idolaters as some of them. As it is written, The people sat to eat and drink, and they rise up to play. Neither do we fornication as some of them did fornication, and three and twenty thousands were dead in one day. Neither tempt we Christ as some of them tempted, and perished of serpents. Neither grouch ye, as some of them grouched, and they perished of a destroyer. And all these things fell to them in figure, but they are written to our amending, into which the ends of the worlds are come.

Therefore, he that guesses him that he stands, see he that he fall not. Temptation take not you but man's temptation, for God is true which shall not suffer you to be tempted above that that ye moun. But He shall make with temptation also purveyance, that ye moun suffer. Wherefore, ye most dearworth to me, flee ye from worshipping of mawmets. As to prudent men I speak. Deem ye yourselves that thing that I say.

Whether the cup of blessing which we bless, is not the communing of Christ's blood? And whether the bread which we break, is not the taking of the body of the Lord? For we many are one bread and one body, all we that take part of one bread and of one cup. See ye Israel after the flesh, whether they that eat sacrifices are not partners of the altar? What, therefore, say I? That the thing offered to idols is anything, or that the idol is anything? But those things that heathen men offer, they offer to devils and not to God. But I nile that ye are made fellows of fiends, for ye moun not drink the cup of the Lord and the cup of fiends. Ye moun not be partners of the board of the Lord and of the board of fiends.

Whether we have envy to the Lord? Whether we are stronger than He? All things are leaveful, but not all things are speedful. All things are leaveful to me, but not all things edify. No man seek that thing that is his own, but that thing that is of another. All thing that is sold in the butchery, eat ye, asking nothing for conscience. The earth and the plenty of it is the Lord's.

If any of heathen men calls you to supper, and ye will go, all thing that is set to you, eat ye, asking nothing for conscience. But if any man says, This thing is offered to idols, nil ye eat, for him that showed and for conscience. And I say not thy conscience, but of another. But whereto is my freedom deemed of another man's conscience? Therefore, if I take part with grace, what am I blasphemed for that that I do thankings? Therefore, whether ye eat or drink, or do any other thing, do ye all things into the glory of God. Be ye without sclaunder to Jews and to heathen men, and to the church of God, as I by all things please to all men, not seeking that that is profitable to me, but that that is profitable to many men, that they be made safe.

Chapter XI

Be ye my followers, as I am of Christ. And, brethren, I praise you that by all things ye are mindful of me, and as I betook to you my commandments, ye hold. But I will that ye wit that Christ is head of each man. But the head of the woman is the man, and the head of Christ is God. Each man praying and prophesying, when his head is hiled, defouls his head. But each woman praying or prophesying when her head is not hiled, defouls her head, for it is one as if she were polled. And if a woman be not *shaven* covered, be she polled. And if it is a foul thing to a woman to be polled or to be made bald, hile she her head.

But a man shall not hile his head, for he is the image and the glory of God. But a woman is the glory of man. For a man is not of the woman. And the man is not made for the woman, but the woman for the man. Therefore the woman shall have an hiling on her head, also for angels. Netheless, neither the man is without woman, neither the woman is without man in the Lord. For why, as the woman is of man, so the man is by the woman. But all things are of God. Deem ye yourselves. Beseems it a woman not hiled on the head to pray God? Neither the kind itself teaches us, for if a man nourish long hair, it is shenship to him. But if a woman nourish long hair, it is glory to her, for hairs be given to her for covering.

But if any man is seen to be full of strife, we have none such custom, neither the church of God. But this thing I command, not praising, that ye come together not into the better, but into the worse. First, for when ye come together into the church, I hear that dissensions are, and in part I believe. For it behoves heresies to be, that they that be proved, be openly known in you. Therefore, when ye come together into one, now it is not to eat the

Lord's Supper. For why, each man before takes his supper to eat, and one is hungry, and another is drunken. Whether ye have not houses to eat and drink, or ye despise the church of God and confound them that have none?

What shall I say to you? I praise you, but herein I praise you not. For I have taken of the Lord that thing which I have betaken to you. For the Lord Jesus, in what night He was betrayed, took bread and did thankings, and broke and said, Take ye and eat ye. This is My body which shall be betrayed for you. Do ye this thing into My mind. Also the cup, after that He had supped, and said, This cup is the New Testament in My blood. Do ye this thing as often as ye shall drink, into My mind. For as often as ye shall eat this bread and shall drink the cup, ye shall tell the death of the Lord till that He come.

Therefore, whoever eats the bread or drinks the cup of the Lord unworthily, he shall be guilty of the body and of the blood of the Lord. But prove a man himself, and so eat he of the ilk bread and drink of the cup. For he that eats and drinks unworthily, eats and drinks doom to him, not wisely deeming the body of the Lord. Therefore among you are many sick and feeble, and many sleep. And we deemed wisely ourselves, we should not be deemed. But while we are deemed of the Lord, we are chastised, that we be not damned with this world. Therefore, my brethren, when ye come together to eat, abide ye together. If any man hungers, eat he at home that ye come not together into doom. And I shall dispose other things when I come.

Chapter XII

But of spiritual things, brethren, I nile that ye unknow. For ye wit that when ye were heathen men, how ye were led, going to dumb mawmets. Therefore I make known to you that no man, speaking in the Spirit of God, says departing from Jesus. And no man may say the Lord Jesus, but in the Holy Ghost. And diverse graces there are, but it is all one Spirit. And diverse services there are, but it is all one Lord. And diverse workings there are, but all is one God that works all things in all things.

And to each man, the showing of Spirit is given to profit. The word of wisdom is given to one by Spirit. To another, the word of kunning by the same Spirit. Faith to another, in the same Spirit. To another, grace of healths in one Spirit. To another, the working of virtues. To another, prophecy. To another, very knowing of spirits. To another, kinds of languages. To another, expounding of words. And one and the same Spirit works all these things, departing to each by themselves as He will.

For as there is one body and has many members, and all the members of the body, when those are many, are one body, so also Christ. For in one Spirit all we are baptized into one body, either Jews, either heathen, either servants, either free, and all we are filled with drink in one Spirit. For the body is not one member, but many. If the foot says, For I am not the hand, I am not of the body, not therefore it is not of the body. And if the ear says, For I am not the eye, I am not of the body, not therefore it is not of the body. If all the body is the eye, where is hearing? And if all the body is hearing, where is smelling?

But now God has set members, and each of them in the body as He would. That if all were one member, where were the body? But now there be many members, but one body. And the eye may not say to the hand, I have no need to thy works. Or eft the head to the feet, Ye are not necessary to me. But much more those that are

seen to be the lower members of the body, are more need/
ful, and the ilk that we guess to be the unworthier mem/
bers of the body, we give more honour to them. And
those members that are unhonest, have more honesty.
For our honest members have need of none. But God
tempered the body, giving more worship to it, to whom
it failed that debate be not in the body, but that the mem/
bers be busy into the same thing each for other.

And if one member suffers anything, all members
suffer therewith. Either if one member joys, all members
joy together. And ye are the body of Christ, and mem/
bers of member. But God set some men in the church,
first apostles, the second time prophets, the third tea/
chers, afterward virtues, afterward graces of healings,
rudders helpings, governals, kinds of languages, interpretations
of words. Whether all apostles? Whether all prophets?
Whether all teachers? Whether all virtues? Whether all
men have grace of healings? Whether all speak with lan/
guages? Whether all expound? But sue ye the better
ghostly gifts. And yet I show you a more excellent way.

Chapter XIII

If I speak with tongues of men and of angels, and I have
not charity, I am made as brass sounding, or a cymbal
tinkling. And if I have prophecy and know all mys/
teries and all kunning, and if I have all faith so that I
move hills from their place, and I have not charity, I am
nought. And if I depart all my goods into the meats of
poor men, and if I betake my body so that I burn, and if
I have not charity, it profits me nothing.

Charity is patient. It is benign. Charity envies not. It
does not wickedly. It is not blown. It is not covetous. It
seeks not those things that are its own. It is not stirred to
wrath. It thinks not evil. It joys not on wickedness, but
it joys together to truth. It suffers all things. It believes all

things. It hopes all things. It sustains all things. Charity falls never down, whether prophecies shall be voided, either languages shall cease, either science shall be destroyed. For a part we know, and a part we prophesy. But when that shall come that is parfit, that thing that is of part shall be avoided.

When I was a little child, I spoke as a little child, I understood as a little child. But when I was made a man, I avoided those things that were of a little child. And we see now by a mirror in darkness, but then face to face. Now I know of part. But then I shall know as I am known. And now dwell faith, hope and charity. But the most of these is charity.

Chapter XIV

Sue ye charity. Love ye spiritual things, but more that ye prophesy. And he that speaks in tongues, speaks not to men, but to God, for no man hears. But the Spirit speaks mysteries. For he that prophesies, speaks to men to edification, and monesting and comforting. He that speaks in tongue, edifies himself, but he that prophesies, edifies the church of God. And I will that all ye speak in tongues, but more that ye prophesy. For he that prophesies, is more than he that speaks in languages. But peradventure he expound, that the church take edification.

But now, brethren, if I come to you and speak in languages, what shall I profit to you but if I speak to you either in revelation, either in science, either in prophecy, either in teaching? For those things that are without soul and give voices, either pipe, either harp, but those give distinction of soundings, how shall it be known that is sung, either that that is trumped? For if a trump give an uncertain sound, who shall make himself ready to battle? So but ye, given an open word by tongue, how shall

that that is said, be known? For ye shall be speaking in
vain.

There are many kinds of languages in this world,
and nothing is without voice. But if I know not the virtue of a voice, I shall be to him to whom I shall speak, a
barbarian barbaric, and he that speaks to me, shall be a barbaric.
So ye, for ye are lovers of spirits, seek ye that ye be plenteous to edification of the church. And therefore he that
speaks in language, pray, that he expound. For if I pray
in tongues, my spirit prays. Mine understanding is without fruit. What then? I shall pray in the Spirit. I shall
pray in mind. I shall say psalm in spirit. I shall say
psalm also in mind. For if thou bless in spirit who fills
the place of an idiot, how shall he say Amen on thy blessing, for he wot not what thou say? For thou does well
thankings, but another man is not edified.

I thank my God, for I speak in the language of all
you. But in the church I will speak five words in my wit
that also I teach other men, than ten thousand of words
in tongues. Brethren, nil ye be made children in wits,
but in malice be ye children. But in wits be ye parfit. For
in the law it is written that, In other tongues and other
lips I shall speak to this people, and neither so they shall
hear Me, says the Lord. Therefore languages are into
token, not to faithful men, but to men out of the faith.
But prophecies are not to men out of the faith, but to
faithful men. Therefore, if all the church come together
into one, and all men speak in tongues, if idiots either
men out of the faith enter, whether they shall not say,
mad What, are ye wood?

But if all men prophesy, if any unfaithful man or idiot
enter, he is convict of all. He is wisely deemed of all. For
the hidden things of his heart are known, and so he shall
fall down on the face and shall worship God, and show
verily that God is in you. What then, brethren? When

ye come together, each of you has a psalm. He has teach⁄ing. He has apocalypse. He has tongue. He has expounding. All things be they done to edification. Whether a man speaks in tongues by two men, either three at the most, and by parts, that one interpret. But if there be not an interpreter, be he still in the church, and speak he to himself and to God. Prophets, twain or three, say, and other wisely deem. But if anything be shown to a sitter, the former be still. For ye moun pro⁄phesy all, each by himself, that all men learn and all monest. And the spirits of prophets are subject to pro⁄phets. For why, God is not of dissension, but of peace, as in all churches of holy men I teach.

Women in churches be still, for it is not suffered to them to speak, but to be subject as the law says. But if they will anything learn, at home ask they their hus⁄bands. For it is foul thing to a woman to speak in church. Whether of you the word of God came forth, or to you alone it came? If any man is seen to be a prophet, or spiritual, know he those things that I write to you, for those are the commandments of the Lord. And if any man unknows, he shall be unknown. Therefore, breth⁄ren, love ye to prophesy, and nil ye forbid to speak in tongues. But be all things done honestly, and by due order in you.

Chapter XV

Soothly, brethren, I make the gospel known to you which I have preached to you, the which also ye have taken, in which ye stand, also by which ye shall be saved. By which reason I have preached to you, if ye hold, if ye have not believed idly. For I betook to you at the beginning that thing which also I have received, that Christ was dead for our sins by the Scriptures, and that He was buried, and that He rose again in the third day after Scriptures, and that He was seen to Cephas and after these things to eleven. Afterward, He was seen to more than five hundred brethren together, of which many live yet, but some are dead.

Afterward, He was seen to James, and afterward to all the apostles. And last of all, He was seen also to me, as to a dead-born child. For I am the least of apostles that am not worthy to be called apostle, for I pursued the church of God. But by the grace of God, I am that thing that I am, and His grace was not void in me. For I travailed more plenteously than all they, but not I, but the grace of God with me. But whether I or they, so we have preached and so ye have believed.

And if Christ is preached that He rose again from death, how say some among you that the again-rising of dead men is not? And if the again-rising of dead men is not, neither Christ rose again from death. And if Christ rose not, our preaching is vain, our faith is vain, and we have been found false witnesses of God, for we have said witnessing against God that He raised Christ, whom He raised not if dead men rise not again. For why, if dead men rise not again, neither Christ rose again. And if Christ rose not again, our faith is vain and yet ye are in your sins. And then they that have died in Christ, have perished.

If in this life only we have hoping in Christ, we are more wretches than all men. But now Christ rose again from death, the first fruit of dead men. For death was by a man, and by a man is again-rising from death. And as in Adam all men die, so in Christ all men shall be quickened. But each man in his order - the first fruit, Christ, afterward they that are of Christ, that believed in the coming of Christ. Afterward an end, when He shall betake the kingdom to God and to the Father, when He shall avoid all princehood and power and virtue. But it behoves Him to reign till He put all His ene⁄mies under His feet. And at the last, death, the enemy, shall be destroyed. For He has made subject all things under His feet.

And when He says all things are subject to Him, without doubt out⁄taken Him that subjected all things to Him. And when all things are subject to Him, then the Son Himself shall be subject to Him that made all things subject to Him, that God be all things in all things. Else what shall they do that are baptized for dead men? If in no wise dead men rise again, whereto are they baptized for them? And whereto are we in peril every hour? Each day I die for your glory, brethren, which glory I have in Christ Jesus our Lord. If, after man, I have fought to beasts at Ephesus, what profits it to me if dead men rise not again? Eat we, and drink we, for we shall die tomorrow.

Nil ye be deceived, for evil speeches destroy good thews. Awake ye, just men, and nil ye do sin, for some *manners, morals* have ignorance of God, but to reverence I speak to you. But some says, How shall dead men rise again, or in what manner body shall they come? Unwise man, that thing that thou sows is not quickened but it die first. And that thing that thou sows, thou sows not the body that is to come, but a naked corn as of wheat or of some other seeds. And God gives to it a body as He will, and to each of seeds a proper body.

Not each flesh is the same flesh. But one is of men, another is of beasts, another is of birds, another of fishes. And heavenly bodies are, and earthly bodies are. But one glory is of heavenly bodies, and another is of earthly. Another clearness is of the sun, another clear⁄ness is of the moon, and another clearness is of stars. And a star diverses from a star in clearness. And so the again⁄rising of dead men. It is sown in corruption. It *ignobleness* shall rise in uncorruption. It is sown in unnobley. It shall rise in glory. It is sown in infirmity. It shall rise in virtue. It is sown a beastly body. It shall rise a spiritual body.

If there is a beastly body, there is also a spiritual body. As it is written, The first man, Adam, was made into a soul living. The last Adam into a Spirit quickening. But the first is not that that is spiritual, but that that is beastly. Afterward, that that is spiritual. The first man of earth is earthly. The second Man of heaven is heavenly. Such as the earthly man is, such are the earthly men. And such as the heavenly Man is, such are also the heavenly men. Therefore, as we have borne the image of the earthly man, bear we also the image of the heavenly.

Brethren, I say this thing, that flesh and blood moun not wield the kingdom of God, neither corruption shall wield uncorruption. Lo, I say to you privity of holy things. And all we shall rise again, but not all we shall be changed. In a moment, in the twinkling of an eye, in the last trump, for the trump shall sound and dead men shall rise again without corruption, and we shall be changed. For it behoves this corruptible thing to clothe uncorruption, and this deadly thing to put away undeadliness. For when this deadly thing shall clothe undeadliness, then shall the word be done that is written, Death is supped up in victory. Death, where is thy victory? Death, where is thy prick? But the prick of death is sin, and the virtue of sin is the law. But do we thankings to God that gave to us victory by our Lord Jesus Christ. Therefore, my dearworth brethren, be ye steadfast and unmovable, being plenteous in work of the Lord, evermore witting that your travail is not idle in the Lord.

Chapter XVI

But of the gatherings of money that are made into saints as I ordained in the churches of Galatia, so also do ye one day of the week. Each of you keep at himself, keeping that that pleases to him, that when I come the gatherings are not made. And when I shall be present, which men ye prove, I shall send them by epistles to bear your grace into Jerusalem, that if it be worthy that also I go, they shall go with me. But I shall come to you when I shall pass by Macedonia, for why, I shall pass by Macedonia. But peradventure I shall dwell at you, or also dwell the winter, that and ye lead me whitherever I shall go.

And I will not now see you in my passing, for I hope to dwell with you a while if the Lord shall suffer. But I shall dwell at Ephesus till to Whitsuntide. For a great door and an open is opened to me, and many adversaries. And if Timothy come, see ye that he be without dread with you, for he works the work of the Lord as I. Therefore, no man despise him, but lead ye him forth in peace that he come to me, for I abide him with brethren.

But, brethren, I make known to you of Apollo, that I prayed him much that he should come to you with brethren. But it was not his will to come now. But he shall come, when he shall have leisure.

Walk ye, and stand ye in the faith. Do ye manly, and be ye comforted in the Lord, and be all your things done in charity. And brethren, I beseech you, ye know the house of Stephanus, and of Fortunatus, and Achaicus, for they are the first fruits of Achaia, and into ministry of saints they have ordained themselves, that also ye be subject to such, and to each, working together and travailing. For I have joy in the presence of Stephanus and of Fortunatus, and of Achaicus, for they filled that thing that failed to you, for they have refreshed both my spirit and yours. Therefore know ye them that are such manner men.

All the churches of Asia greet you well. Aquila and Priscilla, with their homely church, greet you much in the Lord, at the which also I am harboured. All brethren greet you well. Greet ye well together in holy kiss. My greeting by Paul's hand. If any man loves not our Lord Jesus Christ, be he cursed ⸴ Maranatha!

The grace of our Lord Jesus Christ be with you. My charity be with you all in Christ Jesus our Lord. Amen.

A Prologue on the second epistle to the Corinthians

After penance done, Paul writes to Corinthians a pistle of comfort from Troas by Titus, and he praises them and excites to better things, and shows that they were made sorry but amended.

Here begins the second epistle to the Corinthians

Chapter I

Paul, apostle of Jesus Christ by the will of God, and Timothy, brother, to the church that is at Corinth, with all saints that are in all Achaia, grace to you and peace of God our Father and of the Lord Jesus Christ. Blessed be God and the Father of our Lord Jesus Christ, Father of mercies and God of all comfort, which comforts us in all our tribulation, that also we moun comfort them that are in all disease by the monesting by which also we are monested of God. For as the passions of Christ are plenteous in us, so also by Christ

our comfort is plenteous. And whether we are in tribulation for your tribulation and health, either we are comforted for your comfort, either we are monested for your
monesting and health, which works in you the suffering
of the same passions which we also suffer, that our hope
be sad for you, witting for as ye are fellows of passions,
so ye shall be also of comfort.

For, brethren, we will that ye wit of our tribulation
that was done in Asia, for over manner we were grieved
over might, so that it annoyed us, yea, to live. But we in
ourselves had answer of death, that we trust not in us
but in God that raises dead men. Which delivered us
and delivers from so great perils, into whom we hope,
also yet He shall deliver while also ye help in prayer for
us, that of the persons of many faces of that giving that is
in us, thankings are done for us by many men to God.

For our glory is this, the witnessing of our conscience, that in simpleness and cleanness of God, and
not in fleshly wisdom, but in the grace of God we lived
in this world, but more plenteously to you. And we
write not other things to you that those that ye have read
and known, and I hope that into the end ye shall know,
as also ye have known us a part. For we are your glory,
as also ye are ours in the day of our Lord Jesus Christ.

And in this trusting I would first come to you, that ye
should have the second grace, and pass by you into
Macedonia, and eft from Macedonia come to you, and
of you be led into Judea. But when I would this thing,
whether I used unsteadfastness either those things that I
think, I think after the flesh that at me be, it is and it is
not? But God is true, for our word that was at you, is
and is not, is not therein but is in it. For why, Jesus
Christ, the Son of God, which is preached among you
by us ⁄ by me and Sylvanus and Timothy ⁄ there was
not in Him is and is not, but is was in Him. For why,

how many ever are behests of God, in the ilk is, that is, are filled. And therefore and by Him we say Amen to God, to our glory.

Soothly, it is God that confirms us with you in Christ, and the which God anointed us, and which marked us, and gave earnest of the Spirit in our hearts. For I called God to witness against my soul that I, sparing you, came not over to Corinth. Not that we are lords of your faith, but we are helpers of your joy, for through belief ye stand.

Chapter II

And I ordained this ilk thing at me, that I should not come eftsoon in heaviness to you. For if I make you sorry, who is he that glads me but he that is sorrowful of me? And this same thing I wrote to you that when I come, I have not sorrow on sorrow of the which it behoved me to have joy. And I trust in you all that my joy is of all you. For of much tribulation and anguish of heart I wrote to you by many tears, not that ye be sorry, but that ye wit what charity I have more plenteously in you. For if any man has made me sorrowful, he has not made me sorrowful but a part, that I charge not you all.

This blaming that is made of many, suffices to him that is such one, so that againward ye rather forgive and comfort lest peradventure he that is such a manner man, be supped up by more great heaviness. For which thing I beseech you, that ye confirm charity into him. For why, therefore I wrote this, that I know your proving whether in all things ye are obedient. For to whom ye have forgiven anything, also I have forgiven. For I, that that I forgave, if I forgave anything, have given for you in the person of Christ that we be not deceived of Satan, for we know his thoughts.

But when I was come to Troas for the gospel of

Christ, and a door was opened to me in the Lord, I had not rest to my spirit, for I found not my brother Titus. But I said to them farewell, and I passed into Macedonia. And I do thankings to God that evermore makes us to have victory in Christ Jesus, and shows by us the odour of His knowing in each place. For we are the good odour of Christ to God among these that are made safe, and among these that perish. To others, soothly, odour of death into death. But to others we are odour of life into life. And to these things, who is so able? For we are not as many that do advowtry by the word of God. But we speak of cleanness as of God, before God in Christ.

Chapter III

Begin we therefore eftsoon to praise ourselves? Or whether we need, as some, epistles of praising to you, or of you? Ye are our epistle, written in our hearts, which is known and read of all men and made open, for ye are the epistle of Christ ministered of us and written, not with ink, but by the Spirit of the living God. Not in stony tables, but in fleshly tables of heart. For we had such trust by Christ to God, not that we are sufficient to think anything of us, as of us, but our sufficiency is of God. Which also made us able ministers of the New Testament, not by letter, but by Spirit. For the letter slays, but the Spirit quickens.

And if the ministration of death, writ by letters in stones, was in glory, so that the children of Israel might not behold into the face of Moses for the glory of his cheer which is avoided, how shall not the ministration of the Spirit be more in glory? For if the ministration of damnation was in glory, much more the ministry of rightwiseness is plenteous in glory. For neither that that was clear was glorified in this part for the excellent glory.

And if that that is avoided was by glory, much more that that dwells still in glory.

Therefore, we that have such hope, use much trust, and not as Moses laid a veil on his face that the children of Israel should not behold into his face, which veil is avoided. But the wits of them are astonied, for into this day the same veil in reading of the Old Testament dwells not showed, for it is avoided in Christ. But into this day, when Moses is read, the veil is put on their hearts. But when Israel shall be converted to God, the veil shall be done away. And the Spirit is the Lord, and where the Spirit of the Lord is, there is freedom. And all we that, with open face, see the glory of the Lord, are transformed in the same image from clearness into clearness, as of the Spirit of the Lord.

Chapter IV

Therefore we that have this administration, after this that we have got mercy, fail we not. But do we away the privy things of shame, not walking in subtle guile, neither doing advowtry by the word of God, but in showing of the truth, commending ourselves to each conscience of men before God. For if also our gospel is covered, in these that perish it is covered, in which God *blinded* has blent the souls of unfaithful men of this world, that the lighting of the gospel of the glory of Christ, which is the image of God, shine not.

But we preach not ourselves, but our Lord Jesus Christ, and us your servants by Jesus. For God, that said light to shine of darknesses, He has given light in our hearts to the lighting of the science of the clearness of God, in the face of Jesus Christ. And we have this treasure in brittle vessels, that the worthiness be of God's virtue and not of us. In all things we suffer tribulation, but we are not anguished or annoyed. We are made poor, but we lack nothing. We suffer persecution, but we are not forsaken. We are made low, but we are not confounded. We are cast down, but we perish not. And evermore we bear about the slaying of Jesus in our body, that also the life of Jesus be shown in our bodies. For evermore we that live, are taken into death for Jesus, that the life of Jesus be shown in our deadly flesh.

Therefore death works in us, but life works in you. And we have the same Spirit of faith, as it is written, I have believed, I have spoken. And we believe, wherefore also we speak, witting that He that raised Jesus, shall raise also us with Jesus, and shall ordain with you and all things for you, that a plenteous grace by many thankings be plenteous into the glory of God. For which thing we fail not, for though our utter man be corrupted, netheless the inner man is renewed from day to day. But that light thing of our tribulation that lasts now, but as it were by a moment, works in us over measure an everlasting burthen into the highness of glory, while that we behold not those things that are seen, but those that are not seen. For those things that are seen, are but during for a short time. But those things that are not seen, are everlasting.

Chapter V

And we wit that if our earthly house of this dwelling be dissolved, that we have a building of God, an house not made by hands, everlasting into heavens. For why, in this thing we mourn, coveting to be clothed above with our dwelling which is of heaven ⁄ if netheless we are found clothed and not naked. For why, and we that are in this tabernacle, sorrow within and are heavied, for that we will not be spoiled but be clothed above, that the ilk thing that is deadly be supped up of life.

But who is it that makes us into this same thing?

God, that gave to us the earnest of the Spirit. Therefore, we are hardy algates, and wit that the while we are in this body, we go in pilgrimage from the Lord. For we walk by faith, and not by clear sight. But we are hardy and have good will more to be in pilgrimage from the body and to be present to God. And therefore we strive, whether absent, whether present, to please Him. For it behoves us all to be shown before the throne of Christ that every man tell the proper things of the body as he has done, either good, either evil.

Therefore we, witting the dread of the Lord, counsel men, for to God we are open, and, I hope, that we are open also in your consciences. We commend not ourselves eftsoon to you, but we give to you occasion to have glory for us, that ye have to them that glory in the face and not in the heart. For either we, by mind, pass to God, either we are sober to you. For the charity of Christ drives us, guessing this thing, that if One died for all, then all were dead. And Christ died for all that they that live, live not now to themselves, but to Him that died for them and rose again.

Therefore we, from this time, know no man after the flesh, though we know Christ after the flesh. But now we know not. Therefore, if any new creature is in Christ, the old things are passed. And lo, all things are of God, which reconciled us to Him by Christ, and gave to us the service of reconciling. And God was in *reckoning* Christ, reconciling to Him the world, not retting to them their guilts, and put in us the word of reconciling. Therefore we use message for Christ, as if God monests by us. We beseech for Christ, be ye reconciled to God. God the Father made Him sin for us which knew not sin, that we should be made rightwiseness of God in Him.

Chapter VI

But we, helping, monest, that ye receive not the grace of God in vain. For He says, In time well pleasing, I have heard thee, and in the day of health I have helped thee. Lo, now a time acceptable, now a day of health!

Give we to no man any offense, that our service be not reproved. But in all things give we ourselves as the ministers of God in much patience, in tribulations, in needs, in anguishes, in beatings, in prisons, in dissensions within, in travails, in wakings, in fastings, in chastity, in kunning, in long abiding, in sweetness, in the Holy Ghost, in charity not feigned, in the word of truth, in the virtue of God, by arms of rightwiseness on the right half and on the left half, by glory and unnobly, by evil fame and good fame, as deceivers and true men, as they that are unknown and known, as men dying and lo, we live, as chastised and not made dead, as sorrowful evermore joying, as having need but making many men rich, as nothing having and wielding all things.

Ah, ye Corinthians, our mouth is open to you, our heart is enlarged. Ye are not anguished in us, but ye are anguished in your inwardnesses. And I say as to sons, ye that have the same reward, be ye enlarged. Nil ye bear the yoke with unfaithful men. For what parting of rightwiseness with wickedness? Or what fellowship of light to darknesses? And what according of Christ to Belial? Or what part of a faithful with the unfaithful? And what consent to the Temple of God with mawmets? And ye are the Temple of the living God. As the Lord says, For I shall dwell in them and I shall walk among them, and I shall be God of them and they shall be a people to Me. For which thing, go ye out of the middle of them, and be ye departed, says the Lord, and touch ye not the unclean thing, and I shall receive you and shall be into you a Father, and ye shall be to Me into sons and daughters, says the Lord Almighty!

Chapter VII

Therefore, most dearworth brethren, we that have these behests, cleanse we us from all filth of the flesh and of the spirit, doing holiness in the dread of God. Take ye us. We have hurt no man, we have apaired no man. We have beguiled no man. I say not to your condemning, for I said before that ye are in your hearts to die together and to live together.

Much trust is to me anents you, much glorying is to me for you. I am filled with comfort. I am plenteous in joy in all our tribulation. For when we were come to Macedonia, our flesh had no rest. But we suffered all tribulation, withoutforth fightings and dreads within. But God, that comforts meek men, comforted us in the coming of Titus. And not only in the coming of him, but also in the comfort by which he was comforted in you, telling to us your desire, your weeping, your love for me, so that I joyed more. For though I made you sorry in an epistle, it rues me not, though it rued, seeing that though the ilk epistle made you sorry at an hour, now I have joy, not for ye were made sorrowful, but for ye were made sorrowful to repentance. For why, ye are made sorry after God, that in nothing ye suffer apairment of us. For the sorrow that is after God, works penance into steadfast health. But sorrow of the world works death. For lo, this same thing that ye are sorrowful after God, how much business it works in you, but defending, but indignation, but dread, but desire, but love, but vengeance.

In all things ye have given yourselves to be undefouled in the cause. Therefore I wrote to you. I wrote not for him that did the injury, neither for him that suf-

fered, but to show our business which we have for you
before God. Therefore we are comforted, but in your
comfort more plenteously we joyed more on the joy of
Titus, for his spirit is fulfilled of all you. And if I glor-
ied anything anents him of you, I am not confounded,
but as we have spoken to you all things, so also our
glory that was at Titus is made truth. And the inwardness of him be more plenteously in you which has in
mind the obedience of you all, how with dread and
trembling ye received him. I have joy that in all things
I trust in you.

Chapter VIII

But, brethren, we make known to you the grace of God
that is given in the churches of Macedonia, that in much
assaying of tribulation, the plenty of the joy of them was.
And the highest poverty of them was plenteous into the
richesses of the simpleness of them. For I bear witnessing to them, after might and above might, they were
wilful, with much monesting beseeching us the grace   *willing*
and the communing of ministering that is made to holy
men. And not as we hoped, but they gave themselves
first to the Lord, afterward to us by the will of God, so
that we prayed Titus that, as he began, so also he perform in you this grace.

But as ye abound in all things in faith and word and
kunning and all business, moreover in your charity into
us, that and in this grace ye abound. I say not as commanding, but by the business of other men approving
also the good wit of your charity. And ye wit the grace
of our Lord Jesus Christ, for He was made needy for
you when He was rich, that ye should be made rich by
His neediness. And I give counsel in this thing, for this
is profitable to you that not only have begun to do, but
also ye begin to have will from the former year.

But now perform ye in deed, that as the discretion of will is ready, so be it also of performing of that that ye have. For if the will be ready, it is accepted after that that it has, not after that that it has not. And not that it be remission to other men and to you tribulation, but of evenness in the present time your abundance fulfil the *distress, want* misease of them, that also the abundance of them be a fulfilling of your misease, that evenness be made. As it is written, He that gathered much was not increased, and he that gathered little had not less.

And I do thankings to God that gave the same busi-ness for you in the heart of Titus, for he received exhorta-tion. But when he was busier, by his will he went forth to you. And we sent with him a brother whose praising is in the gospel by all churches. And not only, but also he is ordained of churches the fellow of our pilgrimage into this grace that is ministered of us to the glory of the Lord and to our ordained will, eschewing this thing, that no man blame us in this plenty that is ministered of us to the glory of the Lord. For we purvey good things not only before God, but also before all men. For we sent with them also our brother whom we have proved in many things often, that he was busy but now much busier for much trust in you, either for Titus that is my fellow and helper in you, either for our brethren, apostles of the churches of the glory of Christ. Therefore, show ye into them in the face of churches that showing that is of your charity and of our glory for you.

Chapter IX

For of the ministry that is made to holy men, it is to me of plenty to write to you. For I know your will, for the which I have glory of you anents Macedonians, for also Achaia is ready from a year passed and your love has stirred full many. And we have sent brethren, that this thing that we glory of you be not avoided in this part, that, as I said, ye be ready, lest when Macedonians come with me and find you unready, we be shamed that we say you not in this substance. Therefore I guessed necessary to pray brethren that they come before to you, and make ready this behight blessing to be ready, so as blessing and not as avarice. For I say this thing, he that sows scarcely, shall also reap scarcely, and he that sows in blessings, shall reap also of blessings, each man as he cast in his heart, not of heaviness or of need, for God loves a glad giver.

And God is mighty to make all grace abound in you, that ye in all things evermore have all sufficiency and abound to all good work. As it is written, He dealt abroad. He gave to poor men. His rightwiseness dwells without end. And He that ministers seed to the sower, shall give also bread to eat, and He shall multiply your seed and make much the increasings of fruits of your rightwiseness, that in all things ye, made rich, wax plenteous into all simpleness, which works by us doing of thankings to God.

For the ministry of this office not only fills those things that fail to holy men, but also multiplies many thankings to God by the proving of this ministry, which glorify God in the obedience of your acknowledging in the gospel of Christ, and in simpleness of communication into them and into all, and in the beseeching of them for you, that desire you for the excellent grace of God in you. I do thankings to God of the gift of Him that may not be told.

Chapter X

And I myself, Paul, beseech you by the mildness and softness of Christ, which in the face am meek among you, and I, absent, trust in you. For I pray you that lest I,

present, be not bold by the trust in which I am guessed
to be bold into some that deem us as if we wander after
the flesh. For we, walking in flesh, fight not after the
flesh, for the arms of our knighthood are not fleshly, but
mighty by God to the destruction of strengths. And we
destroy counsels and all highness that highs itself
against the science of God, and drive into captivity all
understanding into the service of Christ. And we have
ready to venge all unobedience when your obedience
shall be filled.

See ye the things that are after the face. If any man
trusts to himself that he is of Christ, think he this thing
anents himself, for as he is Christ's, so also we. For if I
shall glory anything more of our power, which the Lord
gave to us into edifying and not into your destruction, I
shall not be shamed. But that I be not guessed as to fear
you by epistles, for they say that epistles are grievous and
strong, but the presence of the body is feeble and the word
worthy to be despised. He that is such one, think this, for
such as we, absent, are in word by epistles, such we are
present in deed. For we dare not put us among or compar͗
ison us to some that commend themselves. But we mea͗
sure us in ourselves and comparison us to ourselves.

For we shall not have glory over measure, but by the
measure of the rule which God measured to us, the mea͗
sure that stretches to you. For we overstretch not forth
us, as not stretching to you. For to you we came in the
gospel of Christ, not glorifying over measure in other
men's travails. For we have hope of your faith that
waxes in you to be magnified by our rule in abundance,
also to preach into those things that are beyond you, not
to have glory in other men's rule in these things that are
made ready. He that glories, have glory in the Lord. For
not he that commends himself is proven, but whom
God commends.

Chapter XI

I would that ye would suffer a little thing of mine unwisdom, but also support ye me, for I love you by the love of
God. For I have spoused to you one Husband, to yield a
chaste virgin to Christ. But I dread, lest as the serpent
deceived Eve with his subtle fraud, so your wits are corrupt and fallen down from the simpleness that is in
Christ. For if he that comes preaches another Christ,
whom we preached not, or of ye take another spirit
whom ye took not, or another gospel which ye received
not, rightly ye should suffer. For I ween that I have done
nothing less than the great apostles. For though I be
unlearned in word, but not in kunning. For in all things
I am open to you. Or whether I have done sin, meeking
myself that ye be enhanced, for freely I preached to you
the gospel of God? I made naked other churches, and I
took sowde to your service. And when I was among   *wages*
you and had need, I was chargeous to no man, for breth-   *burdensome*
ren that came from Macedonia fulfilled that that failed to
me. And in all things I have kept, and shall keep me,
without charge to you.

The truth of Christ is in me, for this glory shall not
be broken in me in the countries of Achaia. Why? For I
loved not you? God wot. For that that I do, and that I
shall do, is that I cut away the occasion of them that will
occasion, that in the thing in which they glory, they be
found as we. For such false apostles are treacherous
workmen, and transfigure them into apostles of Christ.
And no wonder, for Satan himself transfigures him into
an angel of light. Therefore it is not great if his ministers
are transfigured as the ministers of rightwiseness, whose
end shall be after their works.

Eft I say, lest any man guess me to be unwise, else
take me as unwise, that also I have glory a little what.

That that I speak, I speak not after God, but as in unwisdom in this substance of glory. For many men glory after
the flesh, and I shall glory. For ye suffer gladly unwise
men when yourselves are wise. For ye sustain if any man
drives you into servage, if any man devours, if any man
takes, if any man is enhanced, if any man smites you on
the face. By unnobly I say, as if we were sick in this part.

In what thing any man dare, in unwisdom I say, and
I dare. They are Hebrews, and I. They are Israelites,
and I. They are the seed of Abraham, and I. They are
the ministers of Christ, and I. As less wise I say, I more
in full many travails, in prisons more plenteously, in
wounds above manner, in deaths ofttimes. I received of
the Jews five siths forty strokes, one less. Thrice I was
beaten with yards, once I was stoned, thrice I was at
shipwreck shipbreech, a night and a day I was in the deepness of
the sea, in ways often, in perils of floods, in perils of
thieves, in perils of kin, in perils of heathen men, in
perils in city, in perils in desert, in perils in the sea, in
perils among false brethren, in travail and neediness, in
many wakings, in hunger, in thirst, in many fastings, in
cold and nakedness!

Without those things that are withoutforth, mine
each day's travailing is the business of all churches.
Who is sick, and I am not sick? Who is sclaundered,
and I am not burnt? If it behoves to glory, I shall glory
in those things that are of mine infirmity. God and the
Father of our Lord Jesus Christ, that is blessed into
worlds, wot that I lie not. The provost of Damascus, of
the king of the folk Aretas, kept the city of Damascenes
against me, and by a window in a leep I was let down
by the wall, and so I escaped his hands.

Chapter XII

If it behoves to have glory, it speeds not, but I shall come to the visions and to the revelations of the Lord. I wot a man in Christ that before fourteen year, whether in body, whether out of body I wot not ⁄ God wot ⁄ that such a man was ravished till to the third heaven. And I wot such a man, whether in body or out of body, I wot not ⁄ God wot ⁄ that he was ravished into paradise, and heard privy words which it is not leaveful to a man to speak. For such manner things shall I glory, but for me, nothing, nobbut in mine infirmities. For if I shall will to *except, no more than, only* glory, I shall not be unwise, for I shall say truth. But I spare, lest any man guess me over that thing that he sees in me or hears anything of me.

And lest the greatness of revelations enhance me in pride, the prick of my flesh, an angel of Satan, is given to me, that he buffet me. For which thing thrice I prayed the Lord that it should go away from me. And He said to me, My grace suffices to thee, for virtue is parfitly made in infirmity. Therefore gladly I shall glory in mine infirmities, that the virtue of Christ dwell in me. For which thing I am pleased in mine infirmities, in despis⁄ings, in needs, in persecutions, in anguishes, for Christ. For when I am sick, then I am mighty.

I am made unwitty. Ye constrained me. For I ought to be commended of you, for I did nothing less than they that are apostles above manner. Though I am nought, netheless the signs of mine apostlehood are made on you in all patience and signs, and great wonders and virtues. And what is it that ye had less than other churches, but that I myself grieved you not? Forgive ye to me this wrong. Lo, this third time I am ready to come to you, and I shall not be grievous to you. For I seek not those things that are yours, but you. For neither sons owe to treasure to father and mother, but the father and mother to the sons. For I shall give most wilfully, and I myself shall be given above for your souls, though I more love you and be less loved.

But be it, I grieved not you. But when I was subtle, I took you with guile. Whether I deceived you by any of them which I sent to you? I prayed Titus, and I sent him with a brother. Whether Titus beguiled you? Whether we went not in the same Spirit? Whether not in the same steps? Sometime ye ween that we shall excuse us anents you. Before God, in Christ we speak, and, most dear brethren, all things for your edifying. But I dread, lest when I come I shall find you not such as I will, and I shall be found of you such as ye will not, lest peradventure strivings, envies, sturdinesses, dissensions and detractions, privy speeches of discord, bolnings by pride, debates are among you. And lest eftsoon when I come, God make me low anents you and I bewail many of them that before sinned and did not penance of the uncleanness and fornication and unchastity that they have done.

Chapter XIII

Lo, this third time I come to you, and in the mouth of twain or of three witnesses every word shall stand. I said before, and say before, as present twice and now absent, to them that before have sinned and to all others, for if I come eftsoon I shall not spare. Whether ye seek the proof that is Christ that speaks in me, which is not feeble in you? For though He was crucified of infirmity, but He lives of the virtue of God. For also we are sick in Him, but we shall live with Him of the virtue of God in us.

Assay yourselves if ye are in the faith. Ye yourselves prove. Whether ye know not yourselves for Christ *chance* Jesus is in you? But in hap ye are reprovable. But I hope that ye know that we are not reprovable. And we pray the Lord that ye do nothing of evil. Not that we seem proven, but that ye do that that is good, and that we are as reprovable. For we moun nothing against the truth, but for the truth. For we joy when we are sick, but ye are mighty, and we pray this thing, your perfection. Therefore I, absent, write these things that I, present, do not harder by the power which the Lord gave to me into edification, and not into your destruction.

Brethren, henceforward joy ye, be ye parfit, excite ye. Understand ye the same thing. Have ye peace, and God of peace and of love shall be with you. Greet ye well together in holy kiss. All holy men greet you well. The grace of our Lord Jesus Christ and the charity of God, and the communing of the Holy Ghost, be with you all. Amen.

Prologue

Galatians are Greeks. They took first of the apostle the word of truth, but after his going away they were tempted of false apostles, that they were turned into the law and circumcision. The apostle again-calls them to the faith of truth and writes to them from Ephesus.

To Galatians

Chapter I

Paul the apostle, not of men nor by men, but by Jesus Christ and God the Father that raised Him from death, and all the brethren that are with me, to the churches of Galatia. Grace to you and peace of God the Father and of the Lord Jesus Christ that gave Himself for our sins to deliver us from the present wicked world by the will of God and of our Father, to whom is worship and glory into worlds of worlds. Amen.

I wonder that so soon ye be thus moved from Him that called you into the grace of Christ into another evangely, which is not another, but that there are some that *misrepresent, pervert* trouble you and will misturn the evangely of Christ. But though we or an angel of heaven preached to you beside that that we have preached to you, be he accursed. As I have said before, and now eftsoons I say, if any *received* preach to you beside that that ye have underfonged, be he cursed. For now, whether counsel I, men or God? Or whether I seek to please men?

If I pleased yet men, I were not Christ's servant. For, brethren, I make known to you the evangely that was preached of me, for it is not by man, nor I took it of man nor learned, but by revelation of Jesus Christ. For ye have heard my conversation sometime in the Jewry, and that I pursued passingly the church of God and fought against it. And I profited in the Jewry above many of *fellows of the same age* mine evenelds in my kindred, and was more abundantly a follower of my fathers' traditions. But when it pleased Him that departed me from my mother's womb, and called by His grace to show His Son in me that I should preach Him among the heathen, anon I drew me not to flesh and blood, nor I came to Jerusalem to the apostles that were tofore me, but I went into Araby and eftsoons I turned again into Damascus.

And sith three year after I came to Jerusalem to see Peter, and I dwelled with him fifteen days. But I saw none other of the apostles but James, our Lord's brother. And these things which I write to you, lo, tofore God I lie not. Afterward I came into the coasts of Syria and Cilicia. But I was unknown by face to the churches of Judea that were in Christ. And they had only an hearing that he that pursued us sometime preached now the faith, against which he fought sometime, and in me they glorified God.

Chapter II

And sith fourteen year after, eftsoons I went up to Jerusalem with Barnabas and took with me Titus. I went up by revelation and spoke with them the evangely which I preach among the heathen, and by themselves to these that seemed to be somewhat, lest I run or had run in vain. And neither Titus that had been with me, while he was heathen, was compelled to be circumcised, but for false brethren that were brought in which had entered to aspy our freedom which we have in Jesus Christ, to bring us into servage. But we give no place to subjection, that the truth of the gospel should dwell with you.

But of these that seemed to be somewhat, which they were sometime, it pertains not to me, for God takes not the person of man. For they that seemed to be somewhat, gave me nothing. But againward, when they had seen that the evangely of prepucy was given to me, as the evangely of circumcision was given to Peter, for He that wrought to Peter in apostlehood of circumcision, wrought also to me among the heathen. And when they had known the grace of God that was given to me, James and Peter, and John, which were seen to be the pillars, they gave right hand of fellowship to me and to Barnabas, that we among the heathen and they into circumcision, only that we had mind of poor men of Christ, the which thing I was full busy to do.

But when Peter was come to Antioch, I againststood him in the face, for he was worthy to be undernomed. *reproved* For before that there came some from James, he ate with the heathen men. But when they were come, he withdrew and departed him, dreading them that were of circumcision. And the other Jews assented to his feigning, so that Barnabas was drawn of them into that feigning.

But when I saw that they walked not rightly to the truth of the gospel, I said to Peter before all men, If thou that art a Jew lives heathenly, and not Jewly, how constrains thou heathen men to become Jews?

We Jews of kind, and not sinful men of the heathen, know that a man is not justified of the works of law, but by the faith of Jesus Christ. And we believe in Jesus Christ that we are justified of the faith of Christ and not of the works of law. Wherefore of the works of law each flesh shall not be justified. And if we seek to be justified in Christ, we ourselves are found sinful men, whether Christ be minister of sin? God forbid. And if I build again things that I have destroyed, I make myself a tres‑passer. For by the law I am dead to the law, and I am fixed to the cross, that I live to God with Christ. And now live not I, but Christ lives in me. But that I live now in flesh, I live in the faith of God's Son that loved me, and gave Himself for me. I cast not away the grace of God, for if rightwiseness be through law, then Christ died without cause.

Chapter III

Unwitty Galatians, tofore whose eyes Jesus Christ is exiled and is crucified in you, who has deceived you that ye should obey not to truth? This only I will to learn of you, whether ye have underfong the Spirit of works of the law, or of hearing of belief? So ye are fools that when ye have begun in Spirit, ye are ended in flesh. So great things ye have suffered without cause, if it be without cause. He that gives to you Spirit, and works virtues in you, whether of works of the law or of hearing of belief? As it is written, Abraham believed to God, and it was retted to him to rightfulness. And therefore know ye, that these that are of belief, are the sons of Abraham.

And the Scripture, seeing afar that God justifies the

heathen of belief, told tofore to Abraham that, In thee all the heathen shall be blessed. And therefore these that are of belief, shall be blessed with faithful Abraham. For all that are of the works of the law, are under curse, for it is written, Each man is cursed that abides not in all things that are written in the book of the law, to do those things. And that no man is justified in the law before God, it is open, for a rightful man lives of belief.

But the law is not of belief. But he that does those things of the law, shall live in them. But Christ again-bought us from the curse of the law, and was made accursed for us. For it is written, Each man is cursed that hangs in the tree ⁄ that among the heathen the bles-sing of Abraham were made in Christ Jesus, that we underfong the behest of Spirit through belief.

Brethren, I say after man, no man despises the testa-ment of a man that is confirmed or ordains above. The behests were said to Abraham and to his seed. He says not, In seeds as in many, but as in one, And to thy seed ⁄ that is, Christ. But I say, this testament is confirmed of God ⁄ the law that was made after four hundred and thirty year, makes not the testament vain to avoid away the behest. For if heritage were of the law, it were not now of behest, for God granted to Abraham through behest.

What then the law? It was set for trespassing, to the seed come, to whom He had made His behest. Which law was ordained by angels in the hand of a mediator. But a mediator is not of one. But God is One. Is then the law against the behests of God? God forbid. For if the law were given that might quicken, verily were right-fulness of law. But Scripture has concluded all things under sin, that the behest of the faith of Jesus Christ were given to them that believe. And tofore that belief came, they were kept under the law, enclosed into that belief that was to be shown. And so the law was our undermaster in Christ that we are justified of belief.

But after that belief came, we are not now under the undermaster. For all ye are the children of God through the belief of Jesus Christ. For all ye that are baptized, are clothed with Christ. There is no Jew, nor Greek, nor bondman, nor free, nor male, nor female, for all ye are one in Jesus Christ. And if ye are one in Jesus Christ, then ye are the seed of Abraham and heirs by behest.

Chapter IV

But I say, as long time as the heir is a little child, he diverses nothing from a servant when he is lord of all things. But he is under keepers and tutors into the time determined of the father. So we, when we were little children, we served under the elements of the world. But after that the fulfilling of time came, God sent His Son made of a woman, made under the law, that He should underfong the adoption of sons. And for ye are God's sons, God sent His Spirit into your hearts, crying, Abba-Father!

And so there is not now a servant, but a son, and if he is a son, he is an heir by God. But then ye, unknowing God, served to them that in kind were not gods. But now, when ye have known God, and are known of God, how are ye turned eftsoon to the feeble and needy elements to the which ye will eft serve? Ye take keep to days and months, and times and years. But I dread you, lest without cause I have travailed among you. Be ye as I, for I am as ye.

Brethren, I beseech you, ye have hurt me nothing. But ye know that by infirmity of flesh I have preached to you now before, and ye despised not, neither forsook your temptation in my flesh. But ye received me as an angel of God, as Christ Jesus. Where then is your blessing? For I bear you witness that if it might have been done, ye would have put out your eyes and have given them to me. Am I, then, made an enemy to you, saying to you the sooth?

They love not you well but they will exclude you, that ye sue them. But sue ye the good evermore in good, and not only when I am present with you. My small children, which I bear eftsoons till that Christ be formed in you, and I would now be at you and change my voice, for I am confounded among you. Say to me, ye that will be under the law, have ye not read the law? For it is written that Abraham had two sons, one of a servant and one of a free woman. But he that was of the servant, was born after the flesh. But he that was of the free woman, by a behest.

The which things are said by another understanding, for these are two testaments, one in the hill of Sinai gendering into servage, which is Hagar. For Sinai is an hill that is in Araby, which hill is joined to it that is now Jerusalem and serves with her children. But that Jerusalem that is above, is free, which is our mother. For it is written, Be glad, thou barren that bears not. Break out and cry that brings forth no children. For many sons are of her that is left of her husband, more than of her that has an husband. For brethren, we are sons of behest after Isaac, but now as this that was born after the flesh pursued him that was after the Spirit, so now. But what says the Scripture? Cast out the servant and her son, for the son of the servant shall not be heir with the son of the free wife. And so, brethren, we are not sons of the servant, but of the free wife, by which freedom Christ has made us free!

Chapter V

Stand ye therefore, and nil ye eftsoons be held in the yoke

of servage. Lo, I, Paul, say to you, that if ye are circumcised, Christ shall nothing profit to you. And I witness
eftsoons to each man that circumcises himself, that he is
debtor of all the law to be done, and ye are voided away
from Christ. And ye that are justified in the law, ye have
fallen away from grace. For we, through the Spirit of
belief, abide the hope of rightfulness. For in Jesus
Christ, neither circumcision is anything worth, neither
prepucy, but the belief that works by charity.

Ye ran well. Who letted you that ye obeyed not to
truth? Consent ye to no man, for this counsel is not of
Him that has called you. A little sourdough apairs all
the gobbet. I trust on you in our Lord that ye should
understand none other thing. And who that disturbles
you shall bear doom, whoever he be. And brethren, if I
preach yet circumcision, what suffer I yet persecution?
Than the sclaunder of the cross is avoided.

I would that they were cut away that disturble you,
for, brethren, ye are called into freedom. Only give ye
not freedom into occasion of flesh, but by charity of
Spirit serve ye together. For every law is fulfilled in one
word, Thou shall love thy neighbour as thyself. And if
ye bite and eat each other, see ye, lest ye are wasted each
from other.

And I say to you in Christ, walk ye in Spirit and ye
shall not perform the desires of the flesh. For the flesh
covets against the Spirit and the Spirit against the flesh,
for these are adversaries together, that ye do not all things
that ye will. That if ye are led by Spirit, ye are not under
the law.

And works of the flesh are open, which are fornication, uncleanness, unchastity, lechery, service of false
gods, witchcrafts, enmities, strivings, indignations,
wraths, chidings, dissensions, sects, envies, manslaugh-
ters, drunkennesses, unmeasurable eatings, and things

like to these, which, I say to you as I have told you tofore, for they that do such things shall not have the kingdom of God.

But the fruit of the Spirit is charity, joy, peace, patience, long abiding, benignity, goodness, mildness, faith, temperance, continence, chastity. Against such things is no law. And they that are of Christ have crucified their flesh with vices and covetings. If we live by Spirit, walk we by Spirit. Be we not made covetous of vainglory, stirring each other to wrath or having envy each to other.

Chapter VI

Brethren, if a man be occupied in any guilt, ye that are spiritual, inform ye such one in spirit of softness, beholding thyself lest that thou be tempted. Each bear other charges, and so ye shall fulfil the law of Christ. For who that trows that he be ought when he is nought, he beguiles himself. But each man prove his own work, and so he shall have glory in himself and not in another. For each man shall bear his own charge.

He that is taught by word, commune he with him that teaches him in all goods. Nil ye err. God is not scorned, for those things that a man sows, those things he shall reap. For he that sows in his flesh, of the flesh he shall reap corruption. But he that sows in the Spirit, of the Spirit he shall reap everlasting life. And doing good, fail we not, for in His time we shall reap, not failing. Therefore, while we have time, work we good to all men, but most to them that are homely of the faith.

See ye what manner letters I have written to you with mine own hand? For whoever will please in the flesh, this constrains you to be circumcised, only that they suffer not the persecution of Christ's cross. For neither they that are circumcised keep the law, but they will that ye are circumcised that they have glory in your flesh. But far be it from me to have glory, no, but in the cross of our Lord Jesus Christ, by whom the world is crucified to me and I to the world. For in Jesus Christ neither circumcision is anything worth nor prepucy, but a new creature. And whoever sue this rule, peace on them and mercy, and on Israel of God. And hereafter no man be heavy to me, for I bear in my body the tokens of our Lord Jesus Christ. The grace of our Lord Jesus Christ be with your spirit, brethren. Amen.

A Prologue on the epistle to the Ephesians

Ephesians are of Asia. These, when they had received the word of truth, abide steadfastly in the faith. The apostle praises them, writing to them from Rome out of prison, by Tychicus the deacon.

Chapter I

Paul, the apostle of Jesus Christ by the will of God, to all saints that are at Ephesus and to the faithful men of Jesus Christ. Grace be to you and peace, of God our Father and our Lord Jesus Christ.

Blessed be God and the Father of our Lord Jesus Christ, that has blessed us in all spiritual blessing in heavenly things in Christ, as He has chosen us in Himself before the making of the world, that we were *blemish* holy and without wem in His sight, in charity. Which has before ordained us into adoption of sons by Jesus Christ into Him by the purpose of His will into the herying of His grace in which He has glorified us in His dearworth Son. In whom we have redemption by His blood, forgiveness of sins after the richesses of His grace that abounded greatly in us in all wisdom and prudence, to make known to us the sacrament of His will by the good pleasure of Him. The which sacrament He purposed in Him in the dispensation of plenty of times to enstore all things in Christ, which are in heavens and which are in earth, in Him.

In whom we are called by sort, before ordained by the purpose of Him that works all things by the counsel of His will, that we are into the herying of His glory, we that have hoped before in Christ. In whom also ye were called when ye heard the word of truth, the gospel of your health, in whom ye, believing, are marked with the Holy Ghost of behest, which is the earnest of our heritage into the redemption of purchasing, into herying of His glory.

Therefore, and I hearing your faith that is in Christ Jesus, and the love into all saints, cease not to do thankings for you, making mind of you in my prayers that God of our Lord Jesus Christ, the Father of glory, give to you the Spirit of wisdom and revelation into the knowing of Him, and the eyes of your heart lightened that ye wit which is the hope of His calling, and which are the richesses of the glory of His heritage in saints, and which is the excellent greatness of His virtue into us that have believed by the working of the might of His virtue which He wrought in Christ, raising Him from death and setting Him on His right half in heavenly things above each principate and potentate and virtue *principality* and domination and above each name that is named, not only in this world but also in the world to coming, and made all things subject under His feet, and gave Him to be head over all the church that is the body of Him and the plenty of Him, which is all things in all things fulfilled.

Chapter II

And when ye were dead in your guilts and sins, in

which ye wandered sometime after the course of this world, after the prince of the power of this air, of the spirit that works now into the sons of unbelief, in which also we all lived sometime in the desires of our flesh, doing the wills of the flesh and of thoughts. And we were by kind the sons of wrath as other men. But God, that is rich in mercy, for His full much charity in which He loved us, yea, when we were dead in sins, quickened us together in Christ, by whose grace ye are saved, and again raised together and made together to sit in hea‑venly things in Christ Jesus, that He should show in the worlds above coming the plenteous richesses of His grace in goodness on us in Christ Jesus. For by grace ye are saved by faith, and this not of you, for it is the gift of God, not of works, that no man have glory.

For we are the making of Him, made of nought in Christ Jesus in good works which God has ordained, that we go in those works. For which thing be ye mind‑ful that sometime ye were heathen in flesh which were said prepucy, from that that is said circumcision made by hand in flesh. And ye were in that time without Christ, aliened from the living in Israel and guests of testaments, not having hope of behest and without God in this world. But now in Christ Jesus, ye that were sometime far, are made nigh by the blood of Christ. For He is our peace that made both one, and unbinding the middle wall of a wall without mortar, enmities in His flesh, and avoided the law of commandments by dooms, that He make twain in Himself into a new man, making peace to reconcile both in one body to God by the cross, slaying the enmities in Himself. And He, coming, preached peace to you that were far, and peace to them that were nigh, for by Him we both have nigh‑coming in one Spirit to the Father.

Therefore now, ye are not guests and strangers, but

ye are citizens of saints and household meyne of God, above built on the fundament of apostles and of pro-phets upon that highest cornerstone, Christ Jesus. In whom each building made, waxes into an holy Temple in the Lord. In whom also be ye built together into the habitacle of God in the Holy Ghost.   *dwelling place*

Chapter III

For the grace of this thing I, Paul, the bound of Christ Jesus for you heathen men, if netheless ye have heard the dispensation of God's grace that is given to me in you. For by revelation the sacrament is made known to me as I above wrote in short thing, as ye moun read and under-stand my prudence in the mystery of Christ. Which was not known to other generations to the sons of men as it is now shown to His holy apostles and prophets in the Spirit, that heathen men are even heirs and of one body, and partners together of His behest in Christ Jesus in the evangely, whose minister I am made by the gift of God's grace which is given to me by the working of His virtue.

To me, least of all saints, this grace is given to preach among heathen men the unsearchable richesses of Christ and to lighten all men, which is the dispensa-tion of the sacrament hidden from worlds in God that made all things of nought, that the muchfold wisdom   *manifold, multifarious* of God be known to princes and potestates in heavenly things by the church, by the before-ordinance of worlds which He made in Christ Jesus our Lord. In whom we have trust and nigh-coming in trusting by the faith of Him.

For which thing I ask that ye fail not in my tribula-tions for you, which is your glory. For grace of this thing, I bow my knees to the Father of our Lord Jesus Christ, of whom each fatherhood in heavens and in earth is named, that He give to you after the richesses of His glory, virtue to be strengthened by His Spirit in the inner man, that Christ dwell by faith in your hearts, that ye, rooted and grounded in charity, moun comprehend with all saints which is the breadth and the length and the highness and the deepness, also to wit the charity of Christ more excellent than science, that ye be filled with all the plenty of God. And to Him that is mighty to do all things more plenteously than we ask or understand, by the virtue that works in us, to Him be glory in the church and in Christ Jesus into all the generations of the world of worlds. Amen.

Chapter IV

Therefore I, bound for the Lord, beseech you that ye walk worthily in the calling in which ye have been called, with all meekness and mildness, with patience, supporting each other in charity, busy to keep unity of Spirit in the bond of peace. One body and one Spirit, as ye are called in one hope of your calling. One Lord, one faith, one baptism, one God and Father of all, which is above all men and by all things and in us all.

But to each of us grace is given by the measure of the giving of Christ, for which thing He says, He, stying on high, led captive captive ⁄ He gave gifts to men! But what is it, that He styed up? No, but that also He came down, first into the lower parts of the earth. He it is that came down and that styed on all heavens, that He should fill all things. And He gave some apostles, some prophets, other evangelists, other shepherds and tea⁄ chers, to the full ending of saints, into the work of minis⁄ try, into the edification of Christ's body, till we run all into unity of faith and of knowing of God's Son, into a parfit man after the measure of age and of the plenty of Christ, that we be not now little children, moving as

waves, and be not borne about with each wind of teach‑
ing in the waywardness of men, in subtle wit to the
deceiving of error.

But do we truth in charity and wax in Him by all
things, that is Christ our Head, of whom all the body,
set together and bound together by each jointure of
underserving, by working into the measure of each *helping by supplying*
member, makes increasing of the body into edification
of itself in charity. Therefore I say and witness this
thing in the Lord, that ye walk not now as heathen
men walk, in the vanity of their wit, that have under‑
standing darkened with darknesses, and are aliened
from the life of God by ignorance that is in them, for
the blindness of their heart. Which, despairing, beto‑
ken themselves to unchastity into the working of all
uncleanness in covetise. But ye have not so learned
Christ, if netheless ye heard Him and be taught in
Him, as is truth in Jesus.

Do ye away by the old, living the old man that is
corrupt by the desires of error, and be ye renewed in the
spirit of your soul, and clothe ye the new man which is
made after God in rightwiseness and holiness of truth.
For which thing ye put away leasing, and speak ye truth
each man with his neighbour, for we are members each
to other. Be ye wroth and nil ye do sin. The sun fall not
down on your wrath. Nil ye give stide to the devil. He *place*
that stole, steal he not. But more travail he in working
with his hands that that is good, that he have whereof he
shall give to the needy.

Each evil word go not of your mouth, but if any is
good to the edification of faith, that it give grace to men
that hear. And nil ye make the Holy Ghost sorry in
which ye are marked in the day of redemption. All bitter‑
ness and wrath and indignation and cry and blas‑
phemy, be taken away from you with all malice, and be

ye together benign, merciful, forgiving together, as also God forgave to you in Christ.

Chapter V

Therefore, be ye followers of God as most dearworth sons, and walk ye in love as Christ loved us and gave Himself for us, an offering and a sacrifice to God into the odour of sweetness. And fornication and all uncleanness or avarice be not named among you, as it becomes holy men, either filth or folly-speech, or harlotry, that pertains not to profit, but more doing of thankings. For wit ye this and understand, that each lecher or unclean man, or covetous that serves to mawmets, has not heritage in the kingdom of Christ and of God.

No man deceive you by vain words. For why, for these things the wrath of God came on the sons of unbelief. Therefore, nil ye be made partners of them, for ye were sometime darknesses. But now ye are light in the Lord, walk ye as the sons of light. For the fruit of light is in all goodness and rightwiseness and truth.

And prove ye what thing is well pleasing to God, *unfruitful* and nil ye commune to unfruitious works of darknesses. But more reprove ye. For what things are done of them in privy, it is foul, yea, to speak. And all things that are reproved of the light, are openly shown, for all thing that is shown is light. For which thing He says, Rise, thou that sleeps, and rise up from death, and Christ shall lighten thee.

Therefore brethren, see ye how warily ye shall go, not as unwise men, but as wise men, again-buying time for the days are evil. Therefore, nil ye be made unwise, but understanding which is the will of God. And nil ye be drunken of wine, in which is lechery. But be ye filled with the Holy Ghost, and speak ye to yourselves in psalms and hymns and spiritual songs, singing and say-

ing in your hearts to the Lord, evermore doing thank‑
ings for all things in the name of our Lord Jesus Christ
to God the Father.

Be ye subject together in the dread of Christ.
Women, be they subject to their husbands as to the
Lord, for the man is head of the woman, as Christ is
Head of the church. He is Saviour of His body. But as
the church is subject to Christ, so women to their hus‑
bands in all things.

Men, love ye your wives as Christ loved the church,
and gave Himself for it to make it holy, and cleansed it
with the washing of water in the word of life, to give the
church glorious to Himself, that it had no wem nor rivel‑ *wrinkle*
ing, or any such thing, but that it be holy and undefo‑
uled. So, and men shall love their wives as their own
bodies. He that loves his wife, loves himself, for no man
hated ever his own flesh, but nourishes and fosters it, as
Christ does the church. And we are members of His
body, of His flesh and of His bones. For this thing a
man shall forsake his father and mother, and he shall
draw to his wife, and they shall be twain in one flesh.
This sacrament is great. Yea, I say in Christ, and in the
church. Netheless, ye all, each man love his wife as him‑
self, and the wife dread her husband.

Chapter VI

Sons, obey ye to your father and mother in the Lord, for
this thing is rightful. Honour thou thy father and thy
mother ‑ that is the first commandment in behest ‑ that it
be well to thee and that thou be long living on the earth.
And fathers, nil ye terre your sons to wrath, but nourish *provoke, stir*
ye them in the teaching and chastising of the Lord.

Servants, obey ye to fleshly lords with dread and trem‑
bling, in simpleness of your heart, as to Christ, not ser‑
ving at the eye as pleasing to men, but as servants of

Christ, doing the will of God by discretion, with good will, serving as to the Lord and not as to men, witting that each man, whatever good thing he shall do, he shall receive this of the Lord, whether servant, whether free man.

And ye lords, do the same things to them, forgiving menaces, witting that both their Lord and yours is in heavens, and the taking of persons is not anents God.

Here afterward, brethren, be ye comforted in the Lord and in the might of His virtue. Clothe you with the armour of God, that ye moun stand against aspyings of the devil. For why, striving is not to us against flesh and blood, but against princes and potestates, against governors of the world of these darknesses, against spiritual things of wickedness in heavenly things. Therefore, take ye the armour of God, that ye moun againstand in the evil day, and in all things stand parfit. Therefore stand ye, and be girded about your loins in soothfastness, and clothed with the habergeon of rightwiseness, *breastplate, cuirass* and your feet shod in making ready of the gospel of peace. In all things, take ye the shield of faith in which ye moun quench all the fiery darts of the worst. And take ye the helm of health and the sword of the Ghost, that is the word of God.

By all prayer and beseeching, pray ye all time in Spirit, and in Him waking in all business and beseeching for all holy men. And for me, that word be given to me in opening of my mouth, with trust to make known the mystery of the gospel, for which I am sent in message in a chain, so that in it I be hardy to speak, as it behoves me. And ye wit what things are about me, what I do. Tychicus my most dear brother and true minister in the Lord, shall make all things known to you, whom I sent to you for this same thing, that ye know what things are about us, and that he comfort your hearts. Peace to breth-

ren and charity, with faith of God our Father and of the
Lord Jesus Christ. Grace with all men that love our
Lord Jesus Christ in uncorruption. Amen ⁄ that is, So
be it!

Philippians

*Philippians are of Macedonia. These, when they had received
the word of truth, stood steadfast in the faith, and they received
not false apostles. The apostle praises these, writing to them
from Rome out of prison by Epaphrodite.*

Chapter I

Paul and Timothy, servants of Jesus Christ, to all the
holy men in Christ Jesus that are at Philippi with
bishops and deacons. Grace and peace to you of God
our Father, and of the Lord Jesus Christ.

I do thankings to my God in all mind of you ever⁄
more in all my prayers for all you with joy, and make a
beseeching on your communing in the gospel of
Christ from the first day till now, trusting this ilk
thing, that He that began in you a good work, shall
perform it till into the day of Jesus Christ ⁄ as it is just
to me to feel this thing for all you for that I have you in
heart and in my bonds, and in defending and confirm⁄
ing of the gospel, that all ye be fellows of my joy. For
God is a witness to me how I covet all you in the
bowels of Jesus Christ. And this thing I pray, that
your charity be plenteous more and more in kunning
and in all wit, that ye prove the better things, that ye be
clean and without offence in the day of Christ, filled
with the fruit of rightwiseness by Jesus Christ into the
glory and the herying of God. For, brethren, I will that
ye wit that the things that are about me have come more
to the profit of the gospel, so that my bonds were made

known in Christ in each moot hall and in all other places, that more of brethren trusting in the Lord more plenteously for my bonds, dared without dread speak the word of God.

But some, for envy and strife, some for good will, preach Christ, and some of charity, witting that I am put in the defence of the gospel. But some of strife show Christ not cleanly, guessing them to raise tribulation to my bonds. But what? The while on all manner either by occasion, either by truth, Christ is shown, and in this thing I have joy. But also I shall have joy. And I wot that this thing shall come to me into health by your prayer and the underministering of the Spirit of Jesus Christ by mine abiding and hope. For in nothing I shall be ashamed, but in all trust as evermore and now, Christ shall be magnified in my body either by life, either by death. For me to live is Christ and to die is winning. That if to live in flesh is fruit of work to me, lo, what I shall choose I know not.

But I am constrained of two things. I have desire to be dissolved, and to be with Christ it is much better. But to dwell in flesh is needful for you. And I, trusting this thing, wot that I shall dwell and parfitly dwell to all you to your profit and joy of faith, that your thanking abound in Christ Jesus in me by my coming eftsoon to you. Only live ye worthily to the gospel of Christ, that whether when I come and see you, either absent I hear of you that ye stand in one Spirit of one will, travailing together to the faith of the gospel. And in nothing be ye afeared of adversaries, which is to them cause of perdition, but to you cause of health. And this thing is of God, for it is given to you for Christ, that not only ye believe in Him, but also that ye suffer for Him, having the same strife which ye saw in me, and now ye have heard of me.

Chapter II

Therefore, if any comfort is in Christ, if any solace of charity, if any fellowship of Spirit, if any inwardness of mercy-doing, fill ye my joy, that ye understand the same thing and have the same charity, of one will, and feel the same thing, nothing by strife, neither by vain-glory, but in meekness, deeming each other to be higher than himself, not beholding each by himself what things are his own, but those things that are of other men. And feel ye this thing in you which also is in Christ Jesus, that when He was in the form of God, deemed not raven that Himself were even to God. But He lowed Himself, taking the form of a servant, and was made into the likeness of men, and in habit was found as a man. He meeked Himself and was made obedient to the death, yea, to the death of the cross. For which thing God enhanced Him, and gave to Him a name that is above all name, that in the name of Jesus each knee be bowed of heavenly things, of earthly things and of hells, and each tongue acknowledge that the Lord Jesus Christ is in the glory of God the Father.

Therefore, my most dearworth brethren, as ever more ye have obeyed, not in my presence only but much more now in mine absence, work ye with dread and trembling your health. For it is God that works in you both to will and to perform for good will. And do ye all things without grouchings and doubtings, that ye be without plaint and simple as the sons of God, without reproof in the middle of a shrewd nation and a wayward, among which ye shine as givers of light in the world. And hold ye together the word of life to my glory in the day of Christ, for I have not run in vain, neither I have travailed in vain. But though I be offered or slain on the sacrifice and service of your faith, I have joy, and I thank you all.

And the same thing have ye joy, and thank ye me. And I hope in the Lord Jesus that I shall send Timothy soon to you, that I be of good comfort when those things are known that are about you. For I have no man so of one will that is busy for you with clean affection. For all men seek those things that are their own, not those that are of Christ Jesus. But know ye the assay of him, for as a son to the father he has served with me in the gospel. Therefore I hope that I shall send him to you anon as I see what things are about me.

And I trust in the Lord that also myself shall come to you soon. And I guessed it needful to send to you Epaphroditus, my brother and even worker⁄ and mine even knight! ⁄ but your apostle and the minister of my need. For he desired you all and he was sorrowful there⁄ fore that ye heard that he was sick. For he was sick to the death, but God had mercy on him, and not only on him but also on me, lest I had heaviness on heaviness. Therefore more hastily I sent him, that when ye have seen him, ye have joy eft, and I be without heaviness. Therefore receive ye him with all joy in the Lord, and have ye such with all honour. For the work of Christ he went to death, giving his life, that he should fulfil that that failed of you anents my service.

Chapter III

Henceforward, my brethren, have ye joy in the Lord. To write to you the same things to me it is not slow, and to you it is necessary. See ye hounds. See ye evil work⁄ men. See ye division. For we are circumcision which by Spirit serve to God and glory in Christ Jesus, and have not trust in the flesh, though I have trust, yea, in the flesh. If any other man is seen to trust in the flesh, I more, that was circumcised in the eighth day of the kin of Israel, of the lineage of Benjamin, an Hebrew of Hebrews, by the law a Pharisee, by love pursuing the church of God, by rightwiseness that is in the law living without plaint. But which things were to me winnings, I have deemed these apairings for Christ.

Netheless, I guess all things to be pairment for the clear science of Jesus Christ my Lord. For whom I made all things pairment and I deem as dirt, that I win Christ and that I be found in Him, not having my right-wiseness that is of the law, but that that is of the faith of Christ Jesus, that is of God the rightwiseness in faith, to know Him and the virtue of His rising again, and the fellowship of His passion and be made like to His death, if on any manner I come to the resurrection that is from death. Not that now I have taken, or now am par-fit. But I sue, if in any manner I comprehend in which thing also I am comprehended of Christ Jesus.

Brethren, I deem me not that I have comprehended but one thing, I forget those things that are behind, and stretch forth myself to those things that are before, and pursue to the ordained meed of the high calling of God in Christ Jesus. Therefore, whoever we are parfit, feel we this thing. And if ye understand in other manner anything, this thing God shall show to you. Netheless, to what thing we have come, that we understand the same thing, and that we parfitly dwell in the same rule.

Brethren, be ye my followers, and wait ye them that walk so, as ye have our form. For many walk, which I have said often to you. But now I, weeping, say, the ene-mies of Christ's cross, whose end is death, whose god is the womb and the glory in confusion of them that savour earthly things. But our living is in heavens, from whence also we abide the Saviour, our Lord Jesus Christ, which shall reform the body of our meekness that is made like to the body of His clearness by the working by which he may also make all things subject to Him.

Chapter IV

Therefore, my brethren, most dearworth and most desired, my joy and my crown, so stand ye in the Lord, most dear brethren. I pray Euodias and beseech Syntyche to understand the same thing in the Lord. *brother* Also I pray and thee, german fellow, help thou the ilk women that travailed with me in the gospel, with Clement and other mine helpers whose names are in the Book of Life. Joy ye in the Lord evermore, eft I say, joy ye. Be your patience known to all men. The Lord is nigh. Be ye nothing busy, but in all prayer and beseeching, with doing of thankings, be your askings known at God. And the peace of God that passes all wit, keep your hearts and understandings in Christ Jesus.

From henceforth, brethren, whatever things are sooth, whatever things chaste, whatever things just, whatever things holy, whatever things able to be loved, whatever things of good fame, if any virtue, if any praising of discipline, think ye these things, that also ye have learned and taken and heard and seen in me. Do ye these things, and God of peace shall be with you.

But I joyed greatly in the Lord that some time afterward *flourished* ward ye flowered again to feel for me, as also ye felt. But ye were occupied, I say not as for need, for I have learned to be sufficient in which things I am. And I can also be lowed. I can also have plenty. Everywhere and in all things I am taught to be filled and to hunger, and to abound and to suffer misease. I may all things in Him that comforts me.

Netheless, ye have done well, communing to my tribulation. For and ye, Philippians, wit that in the beginning of the gospel, when I went forth from Macedonia, no church communed with me in reason of thing given and taken, but ye alone, which sent to Thessalonica once and twice also into use to me. Not for I seek gift, but I require fruit abounding in your reason. For I have all things and abound. I am filled with those things taken of Epaphroditus which ye sent into the odour of sweetness, a covenable sacrifice pleasing to God. And my God fill all your desire by His richesses in glory in Christ Jesus. But to God and our Father be glory into worlds of worlds. Amen.

Greet ye well every holy man in Christ Jesus. Those brethren that are with me, greet you well. All holy men greet you well, most soothly they that are of the emperor's house. The grace of our Lord Jesus Christ be with your spirit. Amen.

Here ends the epistle to Philippians

Colossians

Colossians are also Laodiceans. These are of Asia, and they had been deceived by false apostles. The apostle himself came not to them, but he brings them again to correction by epistle, for they had heard the word of Archippus that had underfonged the ministry into them. Therefore the apostle, now bound, wrote to them from Ephesus by Tychicus the deacon and Onesimus the acolyte.

Chapter I

Paul, apostle of Christ Jesus by the will of God, and Timothy, brother, to them that are at Colossae, holy and faithful brethren in Christ Jesus, grace and peace to you of God our Father and of the Lord Jesus Christ.

We do thankings to God and to the Father of our Lord Jesus Christ, evermore praying for you, hearing your faith in Christ Jesus and the love that ye have to all holy men for the hope that is kept to you in heavens. Which ye heard in the word of truth of the gospel that came to you, as also it is in all the world and makes fruit and waxes, as in you, from that day in which ye heard and knew the grace of God in truth. As ye learned of Epaphras, our fellow most dearworth, which is a true minister of Jesus Christ for you, which also showed to us your loving in Spirit.

Therefore we, from the day in which we heard, cease not to pray for you and to ask that ye be filled with the knowing of His will in all wisdom and ghostly understanding, that ye walk worthily to God, pleasing by all things, and make fruit in all good work, and wax in the science of God and be comforted in all virtue by the might of His clearness, in all patience and long abiding with joy, that ye do thankings to God and to the Father which made you worthy into the part of heritage of holy men in light. Which delivered us from the power of darknesses, and translated into the kingdom of the Son of His loving, in whom we have again-buying and remission of sins. Which is the image of God unvisible, the first begotten of each crea-ture.

For in Him all things are made, in heavens and in earth, visible and unvisible, either thrones, either domi-nations, either princehoods, either powers. All things are made of nought by Him and in Him, and He is before all and all things are in Him. And He is head of the body of the church, which is the beginning and the first begotten of dead men, that He hold the first dignity in all things. For in Him it pleased all plenty to inhabit, and by Him all things to be reconciled into Him and made peace by the blood of His cross those things that are in earths, either that are in heavens.

And when ye were sometime aliened, and enemies by wit in evil works, now He has reconciled you in the body of His flesh by death, to have you holy and unwemmed and without reproof before Him. If nethe‐ *spotless, unblemished* less ye dwell in the faith, founded and stable and unmoveable from the hope of the gospel that ye have heard, which is preached into all creature that is under heaven, of which I, Paul, am made minister. And now I have joy in passion for you, and I fill those things that fail of the passions of Christ in my flesh for His body, which is the church. Of which I, Paul, am made minis‐ ter by the dispensation of God that is given to me in you, that I fill the word of God, the privity that was hidden from worlds and generations. But now it is shown to His saints, to which God would make known the richesses of the glory of this sacrament in heathen men, which is Christ in you, the hope of glory. Whom we show, reproving each man and teaching each man in all wisdom, that we offer each man parfit in Christ Jesus. In which thing also I travail by the working of Him, that He works in me in virtue.

Chapter II

But I will that ye wit what business I have for you, and for them that are at Laodicea, and which ever saw not my face in flesh, that their hearts are comforted and they are taught in charity into all the richesses of the plenty of the understanding, into the knowing of mystery of God, the Father of Jesus Christ, in whom all the treasures of wisdom and science are hidden. For this thing, I say, that no man deceive you in height of words. For though I be absent in body, by Spirit I am with you, joying and seeing your order and the sadness of your belief that is in Christ. Therefore, as ye have taken Jesus Christ our Lord, walk ye in Him, and be ye rooted and built above in Him and confirmed in the belief, as ye have learned, abounding in Him in doing of thankings.

See ye that no man deceive you by philosophy and vain fallacy after the tradition of men, after the elements of the world and not after Christ. For in Him dwells bodily all the fullness of the Godhead. And ye are filled in Him that is head of all principates and power. In whom also ye are circumcised in circumcision not made with hand in despoiling of the body of flesh, but in circumcision of Christ, and ye are buried together with Him in baptism in whom also ye have risen again by faith of the working of God that raised Him from death. And when ye were dead in guilts and in the prepucy of your flesh, He quickened together you with Him, forgiving to you all guilts, doing away that writing of decree that was against us, that was contrary to us. And He took away that from the middle, pitching it on the cross. And He spoiled principates and powers and led out trustily, openly overcoming them in Himself.

Therefore no man judge you in meat or in drink, or *feasts of new moon* in part of feast day, or of neomeny, or of Sabbaths, which are shadow of things to coming, for the body is of Christ. No man deceive you, willing to teach in meekness and religion of angels, those things which he has not seen, walking vainly, bolned with wit of his flesh, and not holding the head of which all the body, by hands and joinings together underministered and made, waxes into increasing of God. For if ye are dead with Christ from the elements of this world, what yet as men living to the world deem ye, that ye touch not, neither taste, neither treat with hands those things which all are into death by the ilk use after the commandments and the teachings of men ⁄ which have a reason of wisdom in vain religion and meekness, and not to spare the body, not in any honour to the fulfilling of the flesh?

Chapter III

Therefore, if ye have risen together with Christ, seek ye those things that are above, where Christ is sitting on the right half of God. Savour ye those things that are above, not those that are on the earth. For ye are dead, and your life is hidden with Christ in God. For when Christ shall appear, your life, then also ye shall appear with Him in glory. Therefore, slay ye your members which are on the earth, fornication, uncleanness, lechery, evil covetise and avarice, which is service of mawmets. For which things the wrath of God came on the sons of unbelief, in which ye walked sometime when ye lived in them.

But now put ye away all things, wrath, indignation, malice, blasphemy and foul word of your mouth. Nil ye lie together. Spoil ye you from the old man with his deeds, and clothe ye the new man that is made new again into the knowing of God, after the image of Him that made him, where is not male and female, heathen man and Jew, circumcision and prepucy, barbarous and Scythian, bondman and freeman, but all things and in all things, Christ.

Therefore ye, as the chosen of God, holy and loved, clothe you with the entrails of mercy, benignity and meekness, temperance, patience, and support ye each one other, and forgive to yourselves if any man against any has a quarrel. As the Lord forgave to you, so also ye. And upon all these things, have ye charity that is the bond of perfection. And the peace of Christ enjoy in your hearts, in which ye are called in one body. And be ye kind.

The word of Christ dwell in you plenteously in all wisdom, and teach and monest yourselves in psalms and hymns and spiritual songs, in grace singing in your hearts to the Lord. All thing, whatever thing ye do, in word or in deed, all things in the name of our Lord Jesus Christ, doing thankings to God and to the Father by Him.

Women, be ye subjects to your husbands, as it behoves in the Lord. Men, love ye your wives, and nil ye be bitter to them. Sons, obey ye to your father and mother by all things, for this is well pleasing in the Lord. Fathers, nil ye terre your sons to indignation, that they be not made feeble hearted. Servants, obey ye by all things to fleshly lords, not serving at eye as pleasing to men, but in simpleness of heart, dreading the Lord. Whatever ye do, work ye of will, as to the Lord and not to men, witting that of the Lord ye shall take yielding of heritage. Serve ye to the Lord Christ. For he that does injury, shall receive that that he did evil, and acception of persons is not anents God.

Chapter IV

Lords, give ye to servants that that is just and even, witting that also ye have a Lord in heaven. Be ye busy in prayer and wake in it in doing of thankings, and pray each for other and for us, that God open to us the door of word to speak the mystery of Christ, for which also I am bound, that I show it so as it behoves me to speak.

Walk ye in wisdom to them that are withoutforth, again-buying time. Your word be savoured in salt evermore in grace, that ye wit how it behoves you to answer to each man. Tychicus, most dear brother and faithful minister, and my fellow in the Lord, shall make all things known to you that are about me, whom I sent to you to this same thing, that he know what things are about you and comfort your hearts, with Onesimus, most dear and faithful brother, which is of you. Which shall make all things that are done here known to you.

Aristarchus, prisoner with me, greets you well, and Mark, cousin of Barnabas, of whom ye have taken commandments. If he come to you, receive ye him, and Jesus that is said Justus, which are of circumcision. They alone are mine helpers in the kingdom of God that were to me in solace.

Epaphras, that is of you, the servant of Jesus Christ, greets you well, ever busy for you in prayers that ye stand parfit and full in the will of God. And I bear witnessing to him that he has much travail for you and for them that are at Laodicea and that are at Heirapolis.

Luke, the leech most dear, and Demas greet you well. Greet ye well the brethren that are at Laodicea, and the woman Nymphas and the church that is in her house. And when this epistle is read among you, do ye that it be read in the church of Laodiceans. And read ye that pistle that is of Laodiceans. And say ye to Archippus, See the ministry that thou has taken in the Lord that thou fill it.

My salutation by the hand of Paul. Be ye mindful of my bonds. The grace of the Lord Jesus Christ be with you. Amen.

Here begins the Prologue on the Pistle to Laodiceans

Laodiceans are also Colossians, as two towns and one people in manners. These are of Asia, and among them had been false apostles and deceived many. Therefore the postle brings them to mind of his conversation and true preaching of the gospel, and excites them to be steadfast in the true wit and love of Christ, and to be of one will. But this epistle is not in common Latin books, and therefore it was but late translated into English tongue.

Thus ends the Prologue, and begins the epistle to Laodiceans

Here begins the epistle to the Laodiceans, which is not in the canon[4]

Paul, apostle, not of men nor by man, but by Jesus Christ, to the brethren that are at Laodicea, grace to you and peace, of God the Father and of the Lord Jesus Christ. I do thankings to my God by all my prayer that ye are dwelling and lasting in Him, abiding the behest in the day of doom. For neither the vain speaking of some unwise men has letted you, the which would turn you from the truth of the gospel that is preached of me. And now them that are of me to the profit of truth of the gospel, God shall make deserving and doing benignity of works and health of everlasting life. And now my bonds are open which I suffer in Christ Jesus, in which I glad and joy. And that is to me to everlasting health that this same thing be done by your prayers and minis⁄tering of the Holy Ghost, either by life, either by death. Forsooth, to me it is life to live in Christ, and to die joy. And His mercy shall do in you the same thing, that ye moun have the same love and that ye are of one will. Therefore, ye well beloved brethren, hold ye and do ye in the dread of God, as ye have heard [in] the presence of me, and life shall be to you without end. Soothly, it is God that works in you. And, my well beloved brethren, do ye without any withdrawing whatever things ye do. Joy ye in Christ, and eschew ye men defouled in lucre, either foul winning. Be all your askings open anents God, and be ye steadfast in the wit of Christ. And do ye those things that are holy and true, and chaste and just, and able to be loved. And keep ye in heart those things

4. See p.xiii.

that ye have heard and taken, and peace shall be to you. All holy men greet you well. The grace of our Lord Jesus Christ be with your spirit, and do ye that pistle of Colossians to be read to you.

Here ends the pistle to Laodiceans

I Thessalonians

Prologue

Thessalonians are Macedonians. In Jesus Christ, when they had received the word of truth, they stood steadfastly in the faith and also in persecution of their own citizens. Furthermore, they received not false apostles ne those things that were said of false apostles. These the apostle praises, writing to them from Athens by Tychicus and Onesimus.

Chapter I

Paul and Silvanus and Timothy, to the church of Thessalonians, in God the Father and in the Lord Jesus Christ, grace and peace to you.

We do thankings to God evermore for all you, and we make mind of you in our prayers without ceasing, having mind of the work of your faith and travail and charity, and abiding of the hope of our Lord Jesus Christ before God and our Father.

Ye loved brethren of God, we, witting your choosing, for our gospel was not at you in word only, but also in virtue and in the Holy Ghost and in much plenty, as ye wit, were among you for you. And ye are made followers of us and of the Lord, receiving the word in much tribulation with joy of the Holy Ghost, so that ye are made ensample to all men that believe in Macedonia

and in Achaia. For of you the word of the Lord is published not only in Macedonia and Achaia, but your
faith that is to God in each place is gone forth, so that it
is not need to us to speak anything. For they show of
you what manner entry we had to you, and how ye are
converted to God from mawmets, to serve the living
God and very, and to abide His Son from heavens
whom He raised from death ⁄ the Lord Jesus that delivered us from wrath to coming.

Chapter II

For, brethren, ye wit our entry to you, for it was not vain.
But first we suffered and were punished with wrongs, as
ye wit, in Philippi, and had trust in our Lord to speak
to you the gospel of God in much business. And our
exhortation is not of error, neither of uncleanness,
neither in guile, but as we are proven of God that the
gospel of God should be taken to us, so we speak, not as
pleasing to men, but to God that proves our hearts. For
flattering neither we were any time in word of glozing, as ye wit,
neither in occasion of avarice ⁄ God is witness ⁄ neither
asking glory of men, neither of you, neither of other,
when we, as Christ's apostles, might have been in
charge to you. But we were made little in the middle of
you, as if a nurse foster her sons. So we, desiring you
with great love, would have betaken to you not only the
gospel of God, but also our lives, for ye are made most
dearworth to us. For, brethren, ye are mindful of our
travail and weariness. We worked night and day that
we should not grieve any of you, and preached to you
the evangely of God.

God and ye are witnesses how holily and justly and
without plaint we were to you that believed ⁄ as ye wit ⁄
how we prayed you and comforted each of you, as the
father his sons. And we have witnessed that ye should

go worthily to God that called you into His kingdom
and glory.

Therefore we do thankings to God without ceasing.
For when ye had taken of us the word of the hearing of
God, ye took it not as the word of men, but as it is verily,
the word of God that works in you that have believed.
For, brethren, ye are made followers of the churches of
God that are in Judea in Christ Jesus, for ye have suffered the same things of your even lineages, as they of the
Jews which slew both the Lord Jesus and the prophets,
and pursued us. And they please not to God, and they
are adversaries to all men, forbidding us to speak to
heathen men that they be made safe, that they fill their
sins evermore. For the wrath of God came on them into
the end.

And, brethren, we, desolate from you for a time by
mouth and in beholding, but not in heart, have highed
more plenteously to see your face with great desire. For
we would come to you, yea, I Paul once and eftsoon. But
Satan letted us. For why, what is our hope, our joy or
crown of glory? Whether ye are not before our Lord
Jesus Christ in His coming? For ye are our glory and joy.

Chapter III

For which thing we suffered no longer, and it pleased to
us to dwell alone at Athens. And we sent Timothy, our
brother and minister of God in the evangely of Christ,
to you to be confirmed and to be taught for your faith,
that no man be moved in these tribulations. For yourselves wit that in this thing we are set. For when we were
at you, we before-said to you that we should suffer tribulations, as it is done and ye wit. Therefore I, Paul, no
longer abiding, sent to know your faith lest peradventure he that tempts tempt you, and your travail be made
vain. But now, when Timothy shall come to us from

you, and tell to us your faith and charity and that ye have good mind of us, ever desiring to see us as we also you, therefore, brethren, we are comforted in you in all our need and tribulation by your faith.

For now we live if ye stand in the Lord. For what doing of thankings moun we yield to God for you in all joy, in which we joy for you before our Lord? ⁄ night and day more plenteously praying that we see your face and fulfil those things that fail to your health. But God Himself and our Father, and the Lord Jesus Christ dress our way to you. And the Lord multiply you and make your charity to be plenteous of each to other and into all men, as also we in you, that your hearts are con⁄firmed without plaint in holiness before God and our Father, in the coming of our Lord Jesus Christ with all His saints. Amen.

Chapter IV

Therefore, brethren, from henceforward we pray you and beseech in the Lord Jesus, that as ye have received of us how it behoves you to go and to please to God, so walk ye, that ye abound the more. For ye wit what com⁄mandments I have given to you by the Lord Jesus. For this is the will of God, your holiness, that ye abstain you from fornication, that each of you can wield his vessel in holiness and honour, not in passion of lust as heathen men that know not God. And that no man overgo, neither deceive his brother in chaffaring. For the Lord is venger of all these things, as we before⁄said to you and have witnessed. For God called not us into uncleanness, but into holiness. Therefore, he that despises these things, despises not man but God that also gave His Holy Spirit in us.

But of the charity of brotherhood we had no need to write to you. Ye yourselves have learned of God that ye love together, for ye do that into all brethren in all Macedonia. And, brethren, we pray you that ye abound more and take keep, that ye be quiet and that ye do your need, and ye work with your hands as we have commanded to you, and that ye wander honestly to them that are withoutforth, and that of no man's ye desire anything.

For, brethren, we will not that ye unknow of men that die, that ye be not sorrowful as other that have not hope. For if we believe that Jesus was dead and rose again, so God shall lead with Him them that are dead by Jesus. And we say this thing to you in the word of the Lord, that we that live, that are left in the coming of the Lord, shall not come before them that are dead. For the Lord Himself shall come down from heaven in the commandment and in the voice of an archangel and in the trump of God, and the dead men that are in Christ shall rise again first. Afterward we that live, that are left, shall be ravished together with them in clouds, meeting Christ into the air, and so evermore we shall be with the Lord. Therefore, be ye comforted together in these words.

Chapter V

But, brethren, of times and moments ye need not that I write to you. For yourselves wit diligently that the day of the Lord shall come as a thief in the night. For when they shall say, Peace is and secureness, then sudden death shall come on them as sorrow to a woman that is with child, and they shall not scape. But, brethren, ye are not in darknesses that the ilk day as a thief catch you. For all ye are the sons of light and sons of day. We are not of night, neither of darknesses. Therefore sleep we not as others, but wake we and be we sober. For they that sleep, sleep in the night, and they that are drunken, are drunken in the night. But we that are of the day, are sober, clothed in the haburioun of faith and of charity, and in the helm of hope of health. For God put not us into wrath, but into the purchasing of health by our Lord Jesus Christ that was dead for us, that whether we wake, whether we sleep, we live together in Him.

For which thing, comfort ye together and edify ye each other, as ye do. And, brethren, we pray you that ye know them that travail among you and are sovereigns to you in the Lord and teach you, that ye have them more abundantly in charity. And for the work of them, have ye peace with them. And, brethren, we pray you, reprove ye unpeaceable men. Comfort ye men of little heart. Receive ye sick men. Be ye patient to all men. See ye that no man yield evil for evil to any man. But evermore sue ye that that is good, each to other and to all men. Evermore joy ye. Without ceasing, pray ye. In all things, do ye thankings. For this is the will of God in Christ Jesus in all you.

Nil ye quench the Spirit. Nil ye despise prophecies. But prove ye all things, and hold ye that thing that is good. Abstain you from all evil spice, and God Himself of peace shall make you holy by all things, that your spirit be kept whole, and soul and body without plaint, in the coming of our Lord Jesus Christ. God is true that called you, which also shall do.

Brethren, pray ye for us. Greet ye well all brethren in holy kiss. I conjure you by the Lord that this epistle be read to all holy brethren. The grace of our Lord Jesus Christ be with you. Amen.

The Prologue on the second epistle to Thessalonians

The apostle writes the second epistle to Thessalonians, and makes known to them of the last times and of the coming of the

adversary, and of the throwing down of him. He writes this epis-
tle from Athens by Tychicus the deacon and Onesimus the aco-
lyte.

Chapter I

Paul and Silvanus and Timothy, to the church of Thessalonians, in God our Father and in the Lord Jesus Christ. Grace to you and peace, of God our Father and of the Lord Jesus Christ.

We owe to do thankings evermore to God for you, brethren, so as it is worthy, for your faith overwaxes and the charity of each of you to other abounds. So that we selves glory in you in the churches of God for your patience and faith in all your persecutions and tribulations.

Which ye sustain into the ensample of the just doom of God, that ye be had worthy in the kingdom of God, for which ye suffer.

If, netheless, it is just tofore God to quite tribulation to them that trouble you, and to you that are troubled, rest with us in the showing of the Lord Jesus from heaven, with angels of His virtue, in the flame of fire that shall give vengeance to them that know not God and that obey not to the evangely of our Lord Jesus Christ. Which shall suffer everlasting pains in perishing from the face of the Lord and from the glory of His virtue when He shall come to be glorified in His saints and to be made wonderful in all men that believed. For our witnessing is believed on you in that day. In which also we pray evermore for you, that our God make you worthy of His calling and fill all the will of His goodness and the work of faith in virtue, that the name of our Lord Jesus Christ be clarified in you and ye in Him, by the grace of our Lord Jesus Christ.

Chapter II

But, brethren, we pray you by the coming of our Lord
Jesus Christ, and of our congregation into the same
coming, that ye be not moved soon from your wit,
neither be afeared, neither by spirit, neither by word,
neither by epistle as sent by us, as if the day of the Lord
be nigh. No man deceive you in any manner. For but
dissension come first and the Man of Sin be shown, the
son of perdition that is Adversary, and is enhanced over
all thing that is said God or that is worshipped, so that
he sit in the Temple of God and show himself as if he
were God. Whether ye hold not that yet when I was at
you, I said these things to you? And now what withhold ye wit, that he be shown in his time. For the privity
of wickedness works now, only that he that holds now,
hold till he be done away. And then the ilk wicked man
shall be shown, whom the Lord Jesus shall slay with
the Spirit of His mouth, and shall destroy with lightning of His coming him whose coming is by the working of Satan in all virtue and signs and great wonders,
false and in all deceit of wickedness to them that perish
for that they received not the charity of truth that they
should be made safe. And therefore God shall send
them a working of error, that they believe to leasing, that
all be deemed which believed not to truth, but consented
to wickedness.

But, brethren, loved of God, we owe to do thankings
evermore to God for you, that God chose us the first
fruits into health in hallowing of Spirit and in faith of
truth, in which also He called you by our gospel into
getting of the glory of our Lord Jesus Christ. Therefore,
brethren, stand ye and hold ye the traditions that ye have
learned, either by word, either by our epistle. And our
Lord Jesus Christ Himself, and God our Father which

loved us, and gave everlasting comfort and good hope in grace, stir your hearts and confirm in all good work and word.

Chapter III

Brethren, from henceforward pray ye for us, that the word of God run and be clarified, as it is anents you, and that we be delivered from noyous and evil men, for faith is not of all men. But the Lord is true that shall confirm you and shall keep from evil. And, brethren, we trust of you in the Lord for whatever things we command to you, both ye do and shall do. And the Lord dress your hearts in the charity of God and in the patience of Christ.

But, brethren, we denounce to you in the name of our Lord Jesus Christ that ye withdraw you from each brother that wanders out of order, and not after the teaching that they received of us. For yourselves wit how it behoves to sue us. For we were not unpeaceable among you, neither without our own travail we ate bread of any man, but in travail and weariness worked night and day, that we grieved none of you. Not as we had not power, but that we should give ourselves ensample to you to sue us. For also when we were among you, we denounced this thing to you that if any man would not *commanded* work, neither eat he. For we have heard that some among you go in rest and nothing work, but do curiously. But we denounce to them that are such men and beseech in the Lord Jesus Christ, that they work with silence and eat their own bread.

But nil ye, brethren, fail well doing. That if any man obey not to our word by epistle, mark ye him and commune ye not with him, that he be shamed. And nil ye guess him as an enemy, but reprove ye him as a brother, and God Himself of peace, give to you everlasting peace in all place. The Lord be with you all. My salutation by the hand of Paul which sign in each epistle I write thus. The grace of our Lord Jesus Christ be with all you. Amen.

The first to Timothy

He informs and teaches Timothy of the ordinance of bishop's office and of deacon's office and every discipline of holy church, writing to him from Macedonia by Tychicus the deacon.

Chapter I

Paul, apostle of Jesus Christ by the commandment of God our Saviour and of Jesus Christ our Hope, to Timothy, beloved son in the faith, grace and mercy and peace of God the Father and of Jesus Christ our Lord.

As I prayed thee that thou should dwell at Ephesus when I went into Macedonia, that thou should denounce to some men that they should not teach other way, neither give tent to fables and genealogies that are uncertain, which give questions more than edification of God that is in the faith. For the end of the command⁄ment is charity of clean heart and good conscience, and of faith not feigned. From which things some men have erred and are turned into vain speech, and will to be teachers of the law and understand not what things they speak, neither of what things they affirm. And we wit that the law is good, if any man use it lawfully. And witting this thing, that the law is not set to a just man, but to unjust men and not subject, to wicked men and to sinners, to cursed men and defouled, to slayers of father and slayers of mother, to men⁄slayers and lechers, *spreaders of lies* to them that do lechery with men, leasing⁄mongers and forsworn ⁄ and if any other thing is contrary to the whole⁄ some teaching that is after the evangely of the glory of blessed God which is betaken to me.

I do thankings to Him that comforted me in Christ Jesus our Lord, for He guessed me faithful and put me in ministry that first was a blasphemer and a pursuer and full of wrongs. But I have gotten the mercy of God, for I, unknowing, did in unbelief. But the grace of our Lord over abounded with faith and love that is in Christ Jesus ⁄ a true word and worthy of all receiving, for Christ Jesus came into this world to make sinful men safe, of which I am the first. But therefore I have gotten mercy, that Christ should show in me first all patience to the informing of them that shall believe to Him into everlasting life. And to the king of worlds, undeadly and unvisible God alone, be honour and *immortal* glory into worlds of worlds. Amen.

I betake this commandment to thee, thou son Timothy, after the prophecies that have been heretofore in thee, that thou travail in them a good travail, having faith and good conscience, which some cast away and perish about the faith. Of which is Hymenaeus and Alexander, which I betook to Satan that they learn not to blaspheme.

Chapter II

Therefore I beseech first of all things, that beseechings, prayers, askings, doings of thankings, are made for all men, for kings and all that are set in highness, that we lead a quiet and peaceable life, in all piety and chastity. For this thing is good and accepted before God our Saviour, that would all men are made safe and that they come to the knowing of truth. For one God, and a med⁄iator is of God and men, a man Christ Jesus, that gave Himself redemption for all men. Whose witnessing is confirmed in His times in which I am set a preacher and an apostle. For I say truth and I lie not, that am a teacher of heathen men in faith and in truth. Therefore I will that men pray in all place, lifting up clean hands without wrath and strife.

Also women, in covenable habit, with shamefastness and soberness arraying themselves, not in writhen hairs, either in gold, either pearls, either precious cloth. But that that becomes women, behighting piety by good works. A woman learn in silence with all subjection. But I suffer not a woman to teach, neither to have lordship on the husband, but to be in silence. For Adam was first formed, afterward Eve. And Adam was not deceived, but the woman was deceived in breaking of the law. But she shall be saved by generation of children if she dwells parfitly in faith and love, and holiness with soberness.

Chapter III

A faithful word. If any man desires a bishopric, he desires a good work. Therefore it behoves a bishop to be without reproof, the husband of one wife, sober, prudent, chaste, virtuous, holding hospitality, a teacher, not given much to wine, not a smiter. But temperate, not full of chiding, not covetous, well ruling his house, and have sons subject with all chastity ⁄ for if any man cannot govern his house, how shall he have diligence of the church of God? ⁄ not new converted to the faith, lest he be borne up into pride and fall into doom of the devil. For it behoves him to have also good witnessing of them that are withoutforth, that he fall not into reproof and into the snare of the devil.

Also it behoves deacons to be chaste, not double⁄ton⁄
of treacherous words gued, not given much to wine, not suing foul winning, that have the mystery of faith in clean conscience. But be they proved first and minister so, having no crime. Also it behoves women to be chaste, not backbiting, sober, faithful in all things. Deacons be husband of one wife,

which govern well their sons and their houses. For they that minister well shall get a good degree to themselves and much trust in the faith that is in Christ Jesus.

Son Timothy, I write to thee these things, hoping that I shall come soon to thee. But if I tarry, that thou wit how it behoves thee to live in the house of God, that is the church of living God, a pillar and sadness of truth. And openly it is a great sacrament of piety. That thing that was shown in flesh, it is justified in Spirit. It appeared to angels. It is preached to heathen men. It is believed in the world. It is taken up in glory.

Chapter IV

But the Spirit says openly that in the last times some men shall depart from the faith, giving tent to spirits of error and to teachings of devils, that speak leasing in hypocrisy and have their conscience corrupt, forbidding to be wedded, to abstain from meats which God made to take with doing of thankings to faithful men and them that have known the truth. For each creature of God is good, and nothing is to be cast away which is taken with doing of thankings, for it is hallowed by the word of God and by prayer.

Thou, putting forth these things to brethren, shall be a good minister of Christ Jesus, nourished with words of faith and of good doctrine which thou has gotten. But eschew thou uncovenable fables and old women's fables. Haunt thyself to piety, for bodily exercise is profitable to little thing. But piety is profitable to all things that has a behest of life that now is, and that is to come. A true word and worthy all acceptation. And in this thing we travail and be cursed, for we hope in living God, that is Saviour of all men, most of faithful men.

Command thou this thing and teach. No man despise thy youth, but be thou ensample of faithful men

in word, in living, in charity, in faith, in chastity. Till I
take heed come, take tent to reading, to exhortation and teaching.
Nil thou little charge the grace which is in thee, that is
given to thee by prophecy with putting on of the hands
of priesthood. Think thou these things, in these be thou,
that thy profiting be showed to all men. Take tent to
thyself and to doctrine. Be busy in them. For thou,
doing these things, shall make thyself safe and them that
hear thee.

Chapter V

Blame thou not an elder man, but beseech as a father,
young men as brethren, old women as mothers, young
women as sisters in all chastity. Honour thou widows
that are very widows. But if any widow has children of
sons, learn she first to govern her house and quite to
father and mother, for this thing is accepted before God.
And she that is a widow verily, and desolate, hope into
God and be busy in beseechings and prayers night and
day. For she that is living in delicies, is dead.

And command thou this thing, that they be without
reproof. For if any man has not cure of his own and most
of his household men, he has denied the faith and is
worse than an unfaithful man. A widow be chosen not
less than sixty year that was wife of one husband and
has witnessing in good works, if she nursed children, if
she received poor men to harbour, if she has washed the
feet of holy men, if she ministered to men that suffered
tribulation, if she followed all good work. But eschew
thou younger widows, for when they have done lechery,
they will be wedded to Christ having damnation, for
they have made void the first faith. Also they, idle, learn
to go about houses, not only idle but full of words and
curious, speaking things that behoves not. Therefore I
will that younger widows be wedded and bring forth

children, and be housewives, to give none occasion to
the adversary because of cursed thing. For now some are
turned aback after Satan.

If any faithful man has widows, minister he to them
that the church be not grieved, that it suffice to them that
are very widows. The priests that are well governors, be
they had worthy to double honour, most they that travail
in word and teaching. For Scripture says, Thou shall
not bridle the mouth of the ox threshing, and, A workman is worthy his hire. Nil thou receive accusing
against a priest, but under twain or three witnesses. But
reprove thou men that sin before all men, that also other
have dread.

I pray before God and Jesus Christ and His chosen
angels, that thou keep these things without prejudice,
and do nothing in bowing into the other side. Put thou
hands to no man, neither anon commune thou with
other men's sins. Keep thyself chaste. Nil thou yet drink
water, but use a little wine for thy stomach and for thine
oft-falling infirmities. Some men's sins are open before
going to doom. But of some they come after. And also
good deeds are open, and those that have them in other
manner, moun not be hidden.

Chapter VI

Whatever servants are under yoke, deem they their lords
worthy all honour, lest the name of the Lord and the
doctrine be blasphemed. And they that have faithful
lords, despise them not, for they are brethren. But more
serve they, for they are faithful and loved which are partners of benefice.

Teach thou these things and monest thou these
things. If any man teaches otherwise, and accords not to
the wholesome words of our Lord Jesus Christ and to
the teaching that is by piety, he is proud and kens noth-

ing, but languishes about questions and striving of words, of the which are brought forth envies, strifes, blasphemies, evil suspicions, fightings of men that are corrupt in soul and that be deprived from truth, that deem winning to be piety. But a great winning is piety with sufficiency. For we brought in nothing into this world, and no doubt that we moun not bear away anything. But we, having foods and with what things we shall be hiled, be we appayed with these things. For they that will be made rich, fall into temptation and into snare of the devil, and into many unprofitable desires and noyous which drench men into death and perdition. For the root of all evils is covetise, which some, coveting, erred from the faith and beset them with many sorrows.

But thou, man of God, flee these things. But sue thou rightwiseness, piety, faith, charity, patience, mildness. Strive thou a good strife of faith, catch everlasting life, into which thou art called and has knowledged a good acknowledging before many witnesses. I command to thee before God that quickens all things, and before Christ Jesus that yielded a witnessing under Pilate of Pontius a good confession, that thou keep the commandment without wem, without reproof, into the coming of our Lord Jesus Christ, whom the blessed and alone mighty King of Kings and Lord of Lords shall show in His times. Which alone has undeadliness and dwells in light to which no man may come, whom no man saw neither may see, to whom glory and honour and empire be without end. Amen.

Command thou to the rich men of this world that they understand not highly, neither that they hope in uncertainty of riches, but in the living God that gives to us all things plenteously to use, to do well, to be made rich in good works, lightly to give, to commune, to treasure to themselves a good fundament into time to com, ing, that they catch everlasting life.

Thou, Timothy, keep the thing betaken to thee, eschewing cursed novelties of voices and opinions of false name of kunning, which some, behighting about the faith, fell down. The grace of God be with thee. Amen.

He writes also to Timothy of exhortation into martyrdom and of every rule of truth, and what shall come in the last times and of his own passion, writing to him from the city of Rome.

The second epistle to Timothy

Chapter I

Paul, apostle of Jesus Christ by the will of God, by the behest of life that is in Christ Jesus, to Timothy his most dearworth son, grace, mercy and peace of God the Father and of Jesus Christ our Lord.

I do thankings to my God, to whom I serve from my progenitors in clean conscience, that without ceasing I have mind of thee in my prayers night and day, desiring to see thee, having mind of thy tears that I be filled with joy. And I bethink of that faith that is in thee, not feigned, which also dwelled first in thine aunt Lois, and in thy mother Eunice. And I am certain that also in thee. For which cause I monest thee that thou raise again the grace of God that is in thee by the setting on of mine hands. For why, God gave not to us the spirit of dread, but of virtue and of love, and of soberness.

Therefore nil thou shame the witnessing of our Lord Jesus Christ, neither me His prisoner. But travail thou together in the gospel by the virtue of God that delivered us and called with His holy calling, not after our works, but by His purpose and grace that is given in Christ Jesus before worldly times. But now it is open by the lightning of our Saviour Jesus Christ, which destroyed death and lightened life and uncorruption by the gospel. In which I am set a preacher and apostle, and master of heathen men. For which cause also I suffer these things. But I am not confounded. For I wot to whom I have believed, and I am certain that He is mighty for to keep, that is take to my keeping, into that day.

Have thou the form of wholesome words which thou heard of me in faith and love in Christ Jesus. Keep thou the good token to thy keeping by the Holy Ghost that dwells in us. Thou wost this, that all that are in Asia are turned away from me, of which is Phygellus and Hermogenes. The Lord give mercy to the house of Onesiphorus, for often he refreshed me and shamed not my chain. But when he came to Rome, he sought me busily and found. The Lord give to him to find mercy of God in that day. And how great things he ministered to me at Ephesus, thou knows better.

Chapter II

Therefore thou, my son, be comforted in grace that is in Christ Jesus. And what things thou has heard of me by many witnesses, betake thou these to faithful men which shall be also able to teach other men. Travail thou as a good knight of Christ Jesus. No man holding knighthood to God, laps himself with worldly needs, that he please to Him to whom he has proved himself. For he that fights in a battle shall not be crowned but he fight lawfully. It behoves an earthtiller to receive first of the fruits. Understand thou what things I say, for the Lord shall give to thee understanding in all things. Be thou mindful that the Lord Jesus Christ, of the seed of

David, has risen again from death after my gospel, in which I travail till to bonds as working evil, but the word of God is not bound. Therefore I suffer all things for the chosen, that also they get the health that is in Christ Jesus with heavenly glory.

A true word, that if we are dead together, also we shall live together. If we suffer, we shall reign together. If we deny, He shall deny us. If we believe not, He dwells faithful ⁄ He may not deny Himself. Teach thou these things, witnessing before God. Nil thou strive in words, for to nothing it is profitable but to the subvert⁄ ing of men that hear.

Busily keep to give thyself a proved, praisable work⁄ man to God, without shame, rightly treating the word of truth. But eschew thou unholy and vain speeches, for why, those profit much to unfaithfulness, and the word of them creeps as a canker. Of which Philetus is, and Hymenaeus, which fell down from the truth, saying that the rising again is now done, and they subverted the faith of some. But the sad fundament of God stands, having this mark, The Lord knows which are His, and, Each man that names the name of the Lord departs from wickedness.

But in a great house are not only vessels of gold and of silver, but also of tree and of earth. And so some are into honour, and some into despite. Therefore if any man cleanses himself from these, he shall be a vessel hal⁄ lowed into honour and profitable to the Lord, ready to all good work. And flee thou desires of yongth, but sue thou rightwiseness, faith, charity, peace, with them that inwardly call the Lord of a clean heart. And eschew thou foolish questions and without kunning, witting that those gender chidings. But it behoves the servant of the Lord to chide not, but to be mild to all men, able to teach patience with temperance, reproving them that againstand the truth, that sometime God give to them forthinking that they know the truth, and that they rise again from the snares of the devil, of whom they are held prisoners at his will.

Chapter III

But wit thou this thing, that in the last days perilous times shall nigh, and men shall be loving themselves, covetous, high of bearing, proud, blasphemers, not obe‑dient to father and mother, unkind, cursed, without affection, without peace, false blamers, uncontinent, *overmighty* unmild, without benignity, traitors, overthwart, bolned with proud thoughts, blind, lovers of lusts more than of God, having the likeness of piety but denying the virtue of it.

And eschew thou these men. Of these they are that pierce houses and lead women captives charged with sins, which are led with diverse desires, evermore learn‑ing and never parfitly coming to the science of truth. And as Jannes and Jambres againststood Moses, so these againstand truth, men corrupt in understanding, reproved about the faith. But further they shall not profit, for the unwisdom of them shall be known to all men, as theirs was.

But thou has got my teaching, ordinance, purposing, faith, long abiding, love, patience, persecutions, pas‑sions, which were made to me at Antioch, at Iconium, at Lystra, what manner persecutions I suffered. And the Lord has delivered me of all. And all men that will live faithfully in Christ Jesus, shall suffer persecution. But evil men and deceivers shall increase into worse, erring and sending into error. But dwell thou in these things that thou has learned, and that are betaken to thee, witting of whom thou has learned. For thou has known holy letters from thy youth which moun learn thee to health by faith that is in Christ Jesus. For all Scripture, inspired of God, is profitable to teach, to reprove, to chastise, to learn in rightwiseness, that the man of God be parfit, learned to all good work.

Chapter IV

I witness before God and Christ Jesus that shall deem the quick and the dead, and by the coming of Him and the kingdom of Him, preach the word. Be thou busy covenably, without rest. Reprove thou. Beseech thou. Blame thou in all patience and doctrine. For time shall be when men shall not suffer wholesome teaching, but at their desires they shall gather together to themselves masters itching to the ears. And truly they shall turn away the hearing from truth. But to fables they shall turn.

But wake thou. In all things travail thou. Do the work of an evangelist. Fulfil thy service. Be thou sober. For I am sacrificed now, and the time of my departing is nigh. I have striven a good strife. I have ended the course. I have kept the faith. In the t'other time a crown of rightwiseness is kept to me which the Lord, a just doomsman, shall yield to me in that day, and not only to me but also to these that love His coming.

Hye thou to come to me soon, for Demas, loving this world, has forsaken me and went to Thessalonika, Crescens into Galatia, Titus into Dalmatia. Luke alone is with me. Take thou Mark and bring with thee, for he is profitable to me in service. Forsooth, I sent Tychicus to Ephesus. The cloth which I left at Troas, at Carpus', when thou comes, bring with thee. And the books, but most parchment.

Alexander the treasurer showed to me much evil. The Lord shall yield to him after his works. Whom also thou eschew, for he againststood full greatly our words. In my first defence, no man helped me, but all forsook me. Be it not aretted to them. But the Lord helped me and comforted me, that the preaching be filled by me, and that all folks hear that I am delivered from the mouth of the lion. And the Lord delivered me from all evil work, and shall make me safe into His hea⁄venly kingdom. To whom be glory into worlds of worlds. Amen.

Greet well Prisca and Aquila, and the house of Onesiphorus. Erastus left at Corinth, and I left Trophimus sick at Miletus. Hye thou to come before winter. Eubulus and Pudens and Linus and Claudia, and all brethren, greet thee well. Our Lord Jesus Christ be with thy spirit. The grace of God be with you. Amen.

He warns Titus and informs him of the ordinance of priesthood and of spiritual conversation, and of heretics to be eschewed that believe in the Jews' writings, writing to him from Nicopolis.

Here begins the epistle to Titus

Chapter I

Paul, the servant of God and apostle of Jesus Christ, by the faith of the chosen of God and by the knowing of the truth which is after piety, into the hope of everlasting life, which life God, which lies not, behight before times of the world, but He has showed in these times His word in preaching that is betaken to me by the com⁄mandment of God our Saviour. To Titus, most dear⁄worth son by the common faith, grace and peace of God the Father and of Christ Jesus our Saviour.

For cause of this thing I left thee at Crete, that thou amend those things that fail, and ordain priests by cities, as also I disposed to thee. If any man is without crime,

an husband of one wife and has faithful sons, not in
accusation of lechery or not subject. For it behoves a
bishop to be without crime, a dispender of God, not
proud, not wrathful, not drunklew, not smiter, not cov- *given to drunkenness*
etous of foul winning, but holding hospitality, benign,
prudent, sober, just, holy, continent, taking that true
word that is after doctrine, that he be mighty to admonish in wholesome teaching and to reprove them that
againsay.

For there are many unobedient and vain speakers,
and deceivers, most they that are of circumcision, which
it behoves to be reproved, which subvert all houses,
teaching which things it behoves not for the love of foul
winning. And one of them ⸗ their proper prophet ⸗ said,
Men of Crete are evermore liars, evil beasts, of slow
womb. This witnessing is true. For what cause blame
them sore, that they are whole in faith, not giving tent to
fables of Jews and to commandments of men that turn
away them from truth. And all things are clean to clean
men. But to unclean men and to unfaithful, nothing is
clean, for the soul and conscience of them are made
unclean. They acknowledge that they know God, but
by deeds they deny when they are abominable and unbelieveful and reprovable to all good work.

Chapter II

But speak thou those things that beseem wholesome
teaching, that old men be sober, chaste, prudent, whole
in faith, in love and patience. Also old women in holy
habit, not sclaunderers, not serving much to wine, well
teaching, that they teach prudence. Monest thou young
women that they love their husbands, that they love their
children, and that they be prudent, chaste, sober, having
cure of the house, benign, subject to their husbands,
that the word of God be not blasphemed.

Also monest thou young men that they be sober. In all things give thyself ensample of good works, in teaching, in holiness, in sadness. An wholesome word and unreprovable, that he that is of the contrary side be ashamed, having none evil thing to say of you. Monest thou servants to be subject to their lords in all things, pleasing, not againsaying, not defrauding, but in all things showing good faith, that they honour in all things the doctrine of God our Saviour. For the grace of God our Saviour has appeared to all men and taught us, that we forsake wickedness and worldly desires, live soberly and justly and piteously in this world, abiding the blessed hope and the coming of the glory of the great God and of our Saviour Jesus Christ ⁄ that gave Himself for us to again⁄buy us from all wickedness and make clean to Himself a people acceptable and sure of good works. Speak thou these things and monest thou, and reprove thou with all commandment. No man despise thee.

Chapter III

Admonish them to be subject to princes and to powers, to obey to that that is said, and to be ready to all good work, to blaspheme no man, to be not full of chiding, but temperate, showing all mildness to all men. For we were sometime unwise, unbelieveful, erring and serving to desires and to diverse lusts, doing in malice and envy, worthy to be hated, hating each other. But when the benignity and the Manhood of our Saviour God appeared, not of works of rightwiseness that we did, but by His mercy He made us safe, by washing of again⁄ *regeneration* begetting and again⁄newing of the Holy Ghost, whom *renewing* He shed into us plenteously by Jesus Christ our Saviour, that we, justified by His grace, are heirs by hope of everlasting life.

A true word is, and of these things I will that thou confirm other, that they that believe to God, be busy to be above other in good works. These things are good and profitable to men. And eschew thou foolish questions and genealogies, and strifes and fightings of the law, for those are unprofitable and vain. Eschew thou a man heretic after one and the second correction, witting that he that is such a manner man, is subverted and trespasses, and is damned by his own doom.

When I send to thee Artemas or Tychicus, hye thou to come to me to Nicopolis, for I have purposed to dwell in winter there. Busily before, send Zenas, a wise man of law, and Apollos, that nothing fail to them. They that are of ours, learn to be governors in good works, to necessary uses, that they be not without fruit. All men that are with me greet thee well. Greet thou well them that love us in faith. The grace of God be with you all. Amen.

He makes homely letters to Philemon, for Onesimus, his servant, writing to him from the city of Rome out of prison by the foresaid Onesimus.

Philemon

Paul, the bound of Jesus Christ, and Timothy, brother, to Philemon, beloved and our helper, and to Apphia, most dear sister, and Archippus our even knight, and to the church that is in thine house, grace be to you and peace of God our Father, and of the Lord Jesus Christ.

I do thankings to my God, evermore making mind of thee in my prayers, hearing thy charity and faith that thou has in the Lord Jesus and to all holy men, that the communing of thy faith be made open in knowing of all good thing in Christ Jesus. And I had great joy and comfort in thy charity, for the entrails of holy men rested

by thee, brother. For which thing I, having much trust
in Christ Jesus, to command to thee that that pertains to
profit. But I beseech more for charity, since thou art such
as the old Paul and now the bound of Jesus Christ. I
beseech thee for my son, Onesimus, whom I in bonds
begat, which sometime was unprofitable to thee but
now profitable both to thee and to me, whom I sent
again to thee. And receive thou him as mine entrails,
whom I would withhold with me, that he should serve
for thee to me in bonds of the gospel. But without thy
counsel I would not do anything, that thy good should
not be as of need, but wilful. For peradventure, therefore, he departed from thee for a time, that thou should
receive him without end, now not as a servant, but for a
servant and a most dear brother - most to me! And how
much more to thee both in flesh and in the Lord?

Therefore if thou has me a fellow, receive him as me,
for if he has anything annoyed thee, either owes, arette
thou this thing to me. I, Paul, wrote with mine hand. I
shall yield. That I say not to thee, that also thou owes to
me thyself. So, brother, I shall use thee in the Lord. Fill
thou mine entrails in Christ. I, trusting of thine obedience, wrote to thee, witting that thou shall do over that
that I say. Also, make thou ready to me an house to
dwell in, for I hope that by your prayers I shall be given
to you.

Epaphras, prisoner with me in Christ Jesus, greets
thee well, and Mark, Aristarchus, Demas, Lucas,
mine helpers. The grace of our Lord Jesus Christ be
with your spirit. Amen.

A Prologue to the Hebrews

*First it is to say why Paul the apostle in this epistle, in writing
keeps his usage describing his name or the dignity of his order.*

This is the cause that he, writing to them that were of circumcision believed, wrote as the apostle of heathen men and not of Jews. And he, knowing their pride and showing his own humbleness, nold not put before the desert of his office. And in like manner also, John the apostle, for humbleness in his epistle, for the same skill set not his name tofore. As it is said, the apostle sent this epistle to the Hebrews writing in Hebrew tongue, and after the death of Paul the apostle, Luke the evangelist made it in Greek speech, holding the understanding and the order of it.

Chapter I

God, that spoke sometime by prophets in many manners to our fathers, at the last in these days He has spoke to us by the Son, whom He has ordained heir of all things, and by whom He made the worlds. Which, when also He is the brightness of glory and figure of His substance, and bears all things by word of His virtue, He makes purgation of sins, and sits on the right half of the Majesty in heavens, and so much is made better than angels by how much He has entered a more diverse name before them. For to which of the angels said God any time, Thou art My Son. I have gendered Thee today? And eftsoon, I shall be to Him into a Father, and He shall be to Me into a Son? And when, eftsoon, He brings in the first begotten Son into the world, He says, And all the angels of God worshipped Him.

But He says to angels, He that makes His angels spirits and His ministers flames of fire. But to the Son He says, Thy throne is into the world of world, a yard of equity is the yard of Thy realm. Thou has loved rightwiseness and hated wickedness. Therefore the God, Thy God, anointed Thee with oil of joy more than Thy fellows.

And Thou, Lord, in the beginning founded the earth, and heavens are the work of Thine hands. They shall perish, but Thou shall parfitly dwell. And all shall wax old as a cloth, and Thou shall change them as a cloth, and they shall be changed. But Thou art the same Thyself, and Thy years shall not fail.

But to which of the angels said God at any time, Sit Thou on My right half till I put Thine enemies a stool of Thy feet? Whether they all are not serving spirits, sent to serve for them that take the heritage of health?

Chapter II

Therefore more plenteously it behoves us to keep those things that we have heard, lest peradventure we float away. For if the ilk word that was said by angels was made sad, and each breaking of the law and unobedience took just retribution of meed, how shall we escape if we despise so great an health, which, when it had taken beginning to be told out by the Lord of them that heard, is confirmed into us? For God witnessed together by miracles and wonders and great marvels and diverse virtues, and departings of the Holy Ghost by His will.

But not to angels God subjected the world that is to coming, of which we speak. But some man witnessed in a place and said, What thing is man that Thou art mindful of him, or Man's Son for Thou visits Him? Thou has made Him a little less than angels. Thou has crowned Him with glory and honour. And Thou has ordained Him on the works of Thine hands. Thou has made all things subject under His feet. And in that that He subjected all things to Him, He left nothing unsubject to Him.

But now we see not yet all things subject to Him. But we see Him that was made a little less than angels Jesus, for the passion of death crowned with glory and honour, that He, through grace of God, should taste death for all men. For it beseemed Him, for whom all things, and by whom all things were made, which had brought many sons into glory and was Author of the health of them, that He had an end by passion. For He that hallows, and they that are hallowed, are all of one, for which cause He is not shamed to call them brethren, saying, I shall tell Thy name to My brethren. In the middle of the church I shall hery Thee! And eftsoon, I shall be trusting into Him. And eftsoon, Lo, I and My children which God gave to Me!

Therefore, for children communed to flesh and blood, and He also took part of the same, that by death He should destroy him that had lordship of death, that is to say, the devil, and that He should deliver them that by dread of death ⁄ by all life ⁄ were bound to servage. And He took never angels. But He took the seed of Abraham. Wherefore He ought to be likened to brethren by all things, that He should be made merciful and a faithful Bishop to God, that He should be merciful to the trespasses of the people. For in that thing in which He suffered and was tempted, He is mighty to help them that are tempted.

Chapter III

Therefore, holy brethren and partners of heavenly calling, behold ye the Apostle and the Bishop of our confession, Jesus, which is true to Him that made Him, as also Moses in all the house of Him. But this Bishop is had worthy of more glory than Moses by as much as He has more honour of the house that made the house. For each house is made of some man. He that made all things of nought, is God.

And Moses was true in all His house as a servant into witnessing of those things that were to be said, but Christ as a Son in His house. Which house we are if we

hold sad trust and glory of hope into the end.
Wherefore, as the Holy Ghost says, Today, if ye have
heard His voice, nil ye harden your hearts as in wrath⸗
provocation thing, like the day of temptation in desert, where your
fathers tempted Me and proved, and saw My works
forty years. Wherefore I was wroth to this generation,
and I said, Evermore they err in heart, for they know not
My ways. To which I swore in My wrath, they shall not
enter into my rest.

Brethren, see ye, lest peradventure in any of you be an
evil heart of unbelief to depart from the living God. But
monest yourselves by all days the while today is named,
that none of you be hardened by fallacy of sin. For we
are made partners of Christ if netheless we hold the
beginning of His substance sad into the end. While it is
said, Today if ye have heard the voice of Him, nil ye
harden your hearts as in that wraththing. For some, hear⸗
ing, wrathed, but not all they that went out of Egypt by
Moses. But to which was He wrathed forty years?
corpses Whether not to them that sinned, whose carrions were
cast down in desert? And to which swore He that they
should not enter into the rest of Him, not but to them
that were unbelieveful? As we see, that they might not
enter into the rest of Him for unbelief.

Chapter IV

Therefore dread we, lest peradventure while the behest
of entering into His rest is left, that any of us be guessed
to be away. For it is told to us as to them. And the word
that was heard, profited not to them, not mingled to faith
of those things that they heard. For we that have
believed, shall enter into rest. As He said, As I swore in
My wrath, they shall not enter into My rest! And when
the works were made parfit at the ordinance of the
world, He said thus in a place of the seventh day, And

God rested in the seventh day from all His works. And in this place eftsoon, They shall not enter into My rest. Therefore it sues that some shall enter into it, and they to which it was told tofore, entered not for their unbelief.

Eftsoon, He determines some day, and says in David, Today, after so much time of time, as it is beforesaid, Today if ye have heard His voice, nil ye harden your hearts. For if Jesus had given rest to them, He should never speak of other after this day. Therefore, the Sabbath is left to the people of God. For he that is entered into His rest, rested of his works as also God of His.

Therefore haste we to enter into that rest, that no man fall into the same ensample of unbelief. For the word of God is quick and speedy in working, and more able to pierce than any twain-edged sword, and stretches forth to the departing of the soul and of the spirit, and of the jointures and marrows, and deemer of thoughts and of *joints, junctures* intents and hearts. And no creature is unvisible in the sight of God. For all things are naked and open to His eyes, to whom a word to us. Therefore we that have a great Bishop that pierced heavens, Jesus the Son of God, hold we the acknowledging of our hope. For we have not a bishop that may not have compassion on our infirmities, but was tempted by all things by likeness ⁄ without sin! Therefore go we with trust to the throne of His grace, that we get mercy and find grace in covenable help.

Chapter V

For each bishop taken of men, is ordained for men in these things that are to God, that he offer gifts and sacrifices for sins. Which may together sorrow with them that are uncunning and err. For also he is environed with infirmity. And therefore he owes, as for the people so also for himself, to offer for sins. Neither any man takes to him honour but he that is called of God, as

Aaron was. So Christ clarified not Himself, that He were Bishop, but He that spoke to Him, Thou art My Son, today I gendered Thee. As in another place He says, Thou art a Priest without end, after the order of Melchizedek. Which in the days of his flesh offered, with great cry and tears, prayers and beseechings to Him that might make him safe from death, and was heard for his reverence.

And when He was God's Son, He learned obedience of these things that be suffered, and He, brought to the end, is made cause of everlasting health to all that obey to Him, and is called of God a Bishop by the order of Melchizedek. Of whom there is to us a great word for to say and able to be expounded, for ye are made feeble to hear. For when ye ought to be masters for time, eftsoon ye need that ye be taught which are the letters of the beginning of God's words. And ye are made the ilk to which is need of milk and not sad meat. For each that is partner of milk, is without part of the word of rightwiseness, for he is a little child. But of parfit men is sad meat, of them that for custom have wits exercised to discretion of good and of evil.

Chapter VI

Therefore we, bringing in a word of the beginning of Christ, be we born to the perfection of Him, not eftsoon laying the fundament of penance from dead works and of the faith to God, and of teaching of baptisms and of laying on of hands, and of rising again of dead men and of the everlasting doom. And this thing we shall do if God shall suffer. But it is impossible that they that are once lightened, and have tasted also an heavenly gift and are made partners of the Holy Ghost, and netheless have tasted the good word of God and the virtues of the world to coming, and are slid far away, that they are renewed eftsoon to penance. Which eftsoons crucify to themselves the Son of God and have to scorn. For the earth that drinks rain often coming on it, and brings forth covenable herbs to them of which it is tilled, takes blessing of God. But that that is bringing forth thorns and briars, is reproveable and next to curse, whose end⁄ing shall be into burning.

But ye, most dearworth, we trust of you better things and nearer to health, though we speak so. For God is not unjust that He forget your work and love which ye have shown in His name, for ye have ministered to saints and minister. And we covet that each of you show the same business to the filling of hope into the end, that ye be not made slow but also suers of them which by faith and patience shall inherit the behests.

For God, behighting so Abraham ⁄ for He had none greater by whom He should swear ⁄ swore by Himself and said, I, blessing, shall bless thee, and I, multiply⁄ing, shall multiply thee. And so he, long abiding, had the behest. For men swear by a greater than themselves, and the end of all their plea is an oath to confirmation. In which thing God, willing to show plenteouslier to the heirs of His behest the sadness of His counsel, put betwixt an oath, that by two things unmoveable ⁄ by which it is impossible that God lie ⁄ we have a strongest solace, we that flee together to hold the hope that is put forth to us. Which hope, as an anchor, we have secure to the soul and sad, and going into the inner things of hiding, where the before⁄goer, Jesus that is made Bishop without end by the order of Melchizedek, entered for us.

Chapter VII

And this Melchizedek, king of Salem and priest of the highest God, which met with Abraham as he turned again from the slaying of kings and blessed him, to whom also Abraham departed tithes of all things, first he is said king of rightwiseness and afterward king of Salem. That is to say, king of peace, without father, without mother, without genealogy, neither having beginning of days neither end of life. And he is likened to the Son of God and dwells priest without end.

But behold ye how great is this, to whom Abraham the patriarch gave tithes of the best things. For men of the sons of Levi, taking priesthood, have command‑ment to take tithes of the people by the law. That is to say, of their brethren, though also they went out of the loins of Abraham. But he whose generation is not num‑bered in them, took tithes to Abraham, and he blessed *promise* this Abraham which had repromissions. Without any againsaying, that that is less, is blessed of the better. *mortals* And here deadly men take tithes, but there he bears wit‑nessing that he lives. And that it be said so by Abraham, also Levi that took tithes, was tithed. And yet he was in his father's loins when Melchizedek met with him. Therefore, if perfection was by the priesthood of Levi, for under him the people took the law, what yet it was needful another Priest to rise by the order of Melchizedek, and not to be said by the order of Aaron? For why, when the priesthood is translated, it is need that also translation of the law be made.

But He in whom these things are said, is of another lineage, of which no man was priest to the altar. For it is open that our Lord was born of Judah, in which lineage Moses spoke nothing of priests. And more yet it is known, if by the order of Melchizedek another priest is risen up, which is not made by the law of fleshly com‑mandment but by virtue of life that may not be undone. For He witnesses that, Thou art a Priest without end by the order of Melchizedek ‑ that reproving of the com‑

mandment before going is made for the unsadness and unprofit of it. For why, the law brought nothing to perfection, but there is a bringing in of a better hope by which we nigh to God.

And how great it is, not without swearing, but the other are made priests without an oath, but this Priest with an oath by Him that said to Him, The Lord swore and it shall not rue Him, Thou art a Priest without end by the order of Melchizedek, insomuch Jesus is made behighter of the better Testament. And the other were made many priests therefore, for they were forbidden by death to dwell still. But this, for He dwells without end, has an everlasting Priesthood. Wherefore also He may save without end, coming nigh by Himself to God and evermore lives to pray for us.

For it beseemed that such a Man were Bishop to us, holy, innocent, undefouled, clean, departed from sinful men and made higher than heavens, which has not need each day, as priests, first for His own guilts to offer sacrifices, and afterward for the people. For He did this thing in offering Himself once. And the law ordained men priests having sickness, but the word of swearing which is after the law, ordained the Son parfit without end.

Chapter VIII

But a capital on those things that are said. We have such *short chapter, summary* a Bishop that sat in the right half of the seat of greatness in heavens, the Minister of saints and of the very Tabernacle that God made, and not man. For each bishop is ordained to offer gifts and sacrifices, wherefore it is need that also this Bishop have something that He shall offer. Therefore, if He were on earth, He were no priest when there were that should offer gifts by the law, which serve to the sampler and shadow of heavenly things. As it was answered to Moses when he should end the Tabernacle, See, He said, make thou all things by the sampler that is shown to thee in the mount.

But now He has got a better ministry by so much as He is mediator of a better Testament which is confirmed with better behests. For if the ilk first had lacked blame, the place of the second should not have been sought. For He, reproving them, says, Lo, days come, says the Lord, and I shall make parfit a New Testament on the house of Israel and on the house of Judah, not like the Testament that I made to their fathers in the day in which I caught their hand that I should lead them out of the land of Egypt. For they dwelled not parfitly in My Testament, and I have despised them, says the Lord. But this is the Testament which I shall dispose to the house of Israel after those days, says the Lord, in giving My laws into the souls of them, and into the hearts of them I shall above write them, and I shall be to them into a God, and they shall be to Me into a people. And each man shall not teach his neighbour and each man his brother, saying, Know thou the Lord. For I shall be merciful to the wickedness of them, and now I shall not bethink on the sins of them. But in saying a new, the former waxed old, and that that is of many days and waxes old, is nigh the death.

Chapter IX

And the former Testament had justifyings of worship and holy thing for a time. For the Tabernacle was made first in which were candlesticks and board, and setting forth of loaves which is said holy. And after the veil, the second Tabernacle that is said *Sancta Sanctorum* ⁄ that is, Holy of Holy Things ⁄ having a golden censer and the Ark of the Testament covered about on each side with gold, in which was a gold pot having manna and the yard of Aaron which flourished, and the Tables of the

Testament, on which things were cherubims of glory overshadowing the propitiatory ⁄ of which things it is not now to say by all.

But when these things were made thus together, priests entered evermore in the former Tabernacle, doing the offices of sacrifices. But in the second Tabernacle, the bishop entered once in the year, not without blood which he offered for his ignorance and the people's. For the Holy Ghost signified this thing, that not yet the way of saints was opened while the for⁄mer Tabernacle had stood. Which parable was of this present time, by which also gifts and sacrifices are offered which moun not make a man's serving parfit by conscience, only in meats, and drinks, and diverse washings, and rightwisenesses of flesh that were set to the time of correction.

But Christ, being a Bishop of God's to coming, entered by a larger and parfiter Tabernacle not made by hand, that is to say not of this making, neither by blood of goat bucks, or of calves, but by His own blood, entered once into the Holy Things that were found by an everlasting redemption. For if the blood of goat bucks and of bulls, and the ash of a cow sprinkled, hal⁄lows unclean men to the cleansing of flesh, how much more the blood of Christ, which by the Holy Ghost offered Himself unwemmed to God, shall cleanse our conscience from dead works to serve God that lives?

And therefore He is a Mediator of the New Testament, that by death falling betwixt, into redemp⁄tion of those trespassings that were under the former Testament, they that are called take the behest of everlast⁄ing heritage. For where a testament is, it is need that the death of the testament maker come betwixt. For a testa⁄ment is confirmed in dead men, else it is not worth while he lives that made the testament.

Wherefore neither the first Testament was hallowed without blood. For when each commandment of the law was read of Moses to all the people, he took the blood of calves and of bucks of goat, with water and red wool and hyssop, and besprinkled both the ilk book and all the people, and said, This is the blood of the Testament that God commanded to you. And he sprinkled with blood the Tabernacle and all the vessels of the service in like manner. And almost all things are cleansed in blood by the law, and without shedding of blood remission of sins is not made.

Therefore it is need that the samplers of heavenly things be cleansed with these things, but the ilk heavenly things with better sacrifices than these. For Jesus entered not into holy things made by hands that are samplers of very things, but into heaven itself, that He appear now to the cheer of God for us. Neither that He offer Himself often, as the bishop entered into holy things by all years in alien blood, else it behoved Him to suffer often from the beginning of the world. But now, once in the ending of worlds, to destruction of sin by His sacrifice He appeared. And as it is ordained to men once to die but after this the doom, so Christ was offered once to avoid the sins of many men. The second time He shall appear without sin to men that abide Him into health.

Chapter X

For the law, having a shadow of good things that are to come, not the ilk image of things, may never make men nighing parfit by the ilk same sacrifices, which they offer without ceasing by all years, else they should have ceased to be offered forasmuch as the worshippers, cleansed once, had not furthermore conscience of sin. But in them mind of sins is made by all years. For it is impossible that sins be done away by blood of bulls and of bucks of goat.

Therefore He, entering into the world, says, Thou would not sacrifice and offering, but Thou has shapen body to Me. Burnt sacrifices also for sin pleased not to Thee. Then I said, Lo, I come. In the beginning of the Book it is written of Me that I do Thy will, God. He, saying before that, Thou would not sacrifices and offer‚ings and burnt sacrifices for sin. Ne those things are plea‚sant to Thee which are offered by the law. Then I said, Lo, I come, that I do Thy will, God.

He does away the first, that He make steadfast the second. In which will we be hallowed by the offering of the body of Christ Jesus once. And each priest is ready, ministering each day, and ofttimes offering the same sacrifices which moun never do away sins. But this Man, offering for one sacrifice for sins, forevermore sits in the right half of God the Father, from thenceforth abiding till His enemies are put a stool of His feet. For by one offering, He made parfit forever hallowed men. And the Holy Ghost witnesses to us, for after that He said, This is the Testament which I shall witness to them after those days, the Lord says, in giving My laws in the hearts of them, and in the souls of them I shall above write them. And now I shall no more think on the sins and the wickednesses of them. And where remission of these is, now is there none offering for sin.

Therefore, brethren, having trust into the entering of holy things in the blood of Christ, which hallowed us a new way, and living by the hiling, that is to say, His flesh, and we having the Great Priest on the house of God, nigh we with very heart in the plenty of faith, and be our hearts sprinkled from an evil conscience and our bodies washed with clean water. And hold we the con‚fession of our hope, bowing to no side. For He is true that made the behest. And behold, we together, in the stirring of charity and of good works, not forsaking our gathering together as it is of custom to some men, but comforting, and by so much the more by how much ye see the day nighing. For why, now a sacrifice for sins is not left to us that sin wilfully after that we have taken the knowing of truth. For why, some abiding of the doom is dreadful, and the suing of fire which shall waste adversaries.

Who that breaks Moses' law, dies without mercy by twain or three witnesses. How much more, guess ye, that he deserves worse torments which defouls the Son of God and holds the blood of the Testament polluted in which he is hallowed, and does despite to the Spirit of grace? For we know Him that said, To Me vengeance, and I shall yield! And eft, For the Lord shall deem His people. It is fearful to fall into the hands of God living.

And have ye mind on the former days in which ye were lightened and suffered great strife of passions. And in the t'other ye were made a spectacle by shenships and tribulations. In another ye were made fellows of men living so. For also to bound men ye had compassion, and ye received with joy the robbing of your goods, knowing that ye have a better and a dwelling substance. Therefore, nil ye loose your trust, which has great rewarding. For patience is needful to you that ye do the will of God and bring again the behest. For yet a little, and He that is to coming, shall come and He shall not tarry. For My just man lives of faith, that if he withdraws himself he shall not please to My soul. But we are not the sons of withdrawing away into perdition, but of faith into getting of soul.

Chapter XI

But faith is the substance of things that are to be hoped, and an argument of things not appearing. And in this faith old men have great witnessing. By faith we understand that the worlds were made by God's word, that visible things were made of unvisible things. By faith Abel offered a much more sacrifice than Cain to God by which he got witnessing to be just, for God bore witnessing to his gifts, and by that faith he, dead, speaks yet.

By faith Enoch was translated that he should not see death. And he was not found, for the Lord translated him. For before translation, he had witnessing that he pleased God, and it is impossible to please God without faith. For it behoves that a man coming to God, believe that He is, and that He is rewarder to men that seek Him.

By faith Noah dreaded through answer taken of these things that yet were not seen, and shaped a ship into the health of his sons, by which he damned the world and is ordained heir of rightwiseness which is by faith.

By faith, he that is called Abraham obeyed to go out into a place which he should take into heritage. And he went out, not witting whither he should go. By faith he dwelt in the land of behest, as in an alien land, dwelling in little houses with Isaac and Jacob, even heirs of the same behest. For he abode a city having fundaments, whose Craftyman and Maker is God. By faith also, the ilk Sarah, barren, took virtue in conceiving of seed, yea, against the time of age, for she believed Him true that had behight. For which of one, and yet nigh dead, there are born as stars of heaven in multitude and as gravel that is at the seaside ⁄ out of number!

By faith all these are dead when the behests were not taken, but they beheld them afar and greeting them well, and acknowledged that they were pilgrims and harboured men on the earth. And they that saw these things, signify that they seek a country. If they had had mind of the ilk, of which they went out, they had time of turning again. But now they desire a better, that is to say, heavenly.

Therefore God is not confounded to be called the God of them, for He made ready to them a city. By faith Abraham offered Isaac when he was tempted, and he offered the one begotten which had taken the behests, to whom it was said, For in Isaac the seed shall be called to thee. For he deemed that God is mighty to raise him, yea, from death, wherefore he took him also into a parable.

By faith also of things to coming, Isaac blessed Jacob and Esau. By faith, Jacob, dying, blessed all the sons of Joseph and honoured the highness of his yard. By faith, Joseph, dying, had mind of the passing forth of the children of Israel and commanded of his bones. By faith, Moses, born, was hidden three months of his father and mother for that they saw the young child fair, and they dreaded not the commandment of the king. By faith, Moses was made great and denied that he was the son of Pharaoh's daughter, and chose more to be tormented with the people of God than to have mirth of temporal sin, deeming the reproof of Christ more richesses than the treasures of Egyptians, for he beheld into the rewarding.

By faith he forsook Egypt and dreaded not the hardiness of the king, for he abode as seeing Him that was unvisible. By faith he hallowed Pasch and the shedding out of blood, that He that destroyed the first things of Egyptians, should not touch them. By faith they passed the Red Sea as by dry land, which thing Egyptians, assaying, were devoured. By faith the walls of Jericho fell down by compassing of seven days. By faith Rahab, whore, received the aspiers with peace, and perished not with unbelieveful men.

And what yet shall I say? For time shall fail to me telling of Gideon, Barak, Samson, Jephthah, David and Samuel, and of other prophets, which by faith overcame realms, wrought rightwiseness, got repromissions. They stopped the mouths of lions. They quenched the fierceness of fire. They drived away the edge of sword. They covered of sickness. They were made strong in battle. They turned the hosts of aliens.

Women received their dead children from death to life. But other were held forth, not taking redemption that they should find a better again-rising. And other assayed scornings and beatings, moreover and bonds and prisons. They were stoned. They were sawn. They were tempted. They were dead in slaying of sword. They went about in brock skins and in skins of goat, *badger skins* needy, anguished, tormented, to which the world was not worthy. They erred in wildernesses, in mountains and dens and caves of the earth. And all these, proved by witnessing of faith, took not repromission. For God purveyed some better thing for us, that they should not be made parfit without us.

Chapter XII

Therefore, we that have so great a cloud of witnesses put to, do we away all charge and sin standing about us. And by patience run we to the battle purposed to us, beholding into the Maker of faith and the perfect Ender, Jesus, which, when joy was purposed to Him, He suffered the cross and despised confusion, and sits on the right half of the seat of God. And bethink ye on Him that suffered such againsaying of sinful men against Himself, that ye be not made weary, failing in your souls. For ye againstand not yet till to blood, fighting against sin. And ye have forgot the comfort that speaks to you as to sons, and says, My son, nil thou despise the teaching of the Lord, neither be thou made weary the while thou art chastised of Him. For the Lord chastises him that He loves. He beats every son that He receives.

Abide ye still in chastising. God proffers Him to you as to sons. For what son is it whom the Father chastises not? That if ye are out of chastising, whose partners are ye all made? Then ye are advowtrers and not sons. And afterward, we had fathers to our flesh, teachers, and we with reverence dreaded them. Whether not much more we shall obey to the Father of spirits, and we shall live?

And they in time of few days, taught us by their will. But this Father teaches to that thing that is profitable in receiving the hallowing of Him. And each chastising in present time seems to be not of joy, but of sorrow. But afterward it shall yield fruit of rightwiseness most peace-able to men exercised by it. For which thing, raise ye slow hands and knees unbound, and make ye rightful steps to your feet, that no man, halting, err, but more be healed.

Sue ye peace with all men, and holiness, without which no man shall see God. Behold ye that no man fail to the grace of God, that no root of bitterness burrowing upward let, and many are defouled by it. That no man be lecher, either unholy as Esau, which for one meat sold his first things. For wit ye that afterward he, covet-ing to inherit blessing, was reproved. For he found not place of penance though he sought it with tears.

But ye have not come to the fire able to be touched and able to come to, and to the whirlwind and mist and tempest, and sound of trump and voice of words. Which they that heard excused them, that the word should not be made to them. For they bore not that that was said. And if a beast touched the hill, it was stoned.

And so dreadful it was that Moses said, I am afeared and full of trembling.

But ye have come nigh to the hill, Zion, and to the city of God living, the heavenly Jerusalem, and to the multitude of many thousand angels, and to the church of the first men which are written in heavens, and to God, Doomsman of all and to the spirit of just, parfit men, and to Jesus, Mediator of the New Testament, and to the sprinkling of blood, better speaking than Abel.

See ye that ye forsake not the Speaker, for if they that forsook him that spoke on the earth escaped not, much more we that turn away from Him that speaks to us from heavens, whose voice then moved the earth. But now He again behights and says, Yet once and I shall move not earth only, but also heaven. And that He says, Yet once, He declares the translation of moveable things as of made things, that those things dwell that are unmoveable. Therefore we, receiving the kingdom unmoveable, have we grace, by which serve we pleasing to God with dread and reverence. For our God is fire that wastes.

Chapter XIII

The charity of brotherhood dwell in you, and nil ye forget hospitality. For by this, some pleased to angels that were received to harbour. Think ye on bound men, as ye were together bound, and of travailing men as yourselves dwelling in the body. Wedding is in all things honourable, and bed unwemmed. For God shall deem fornicators and advowtrers. Be your manners without covetise, appayed with present things, for He said, I shall not leave thee neither forsake. So that we say trustily, The Lord is an Helper to me. I shall not dread what a man shall do to me.

Have ye mind of your sovereigns that have spoken to you the word of God. Of which behold ye the going out of living and sue ye the faith of them ⁄ Jesus Christ, yesterday and today, He is also into worlds.

Nil ye be led away with diverse teachings and strange. For it is best to stable the heart with grace, not with meats which profit not to men wandering in them. We have an altar of which they that serve to the Tabernacle have not power to eat. For of which beasts the blood is borne in for sin into holy things by the bishop, the bodies of them are burnt without the castles. For which thing Jesus, that He should hallow the peo⁄ple by His blood, suffered without the gate. Therefore we go out to Him without the castles, bearing His reproof. For we have not here a city dwelling, but we seek a city to coming. Therefore by Him offer we a sacri⁄fice of herying evermore to God, that is to say, the fruit of lips acknowledging to His name.

And nil ye forget well⁄doing and communing, for *well served* by such sacrifices God is disserved. Obey ye to your sovereigns and be ye subject to them, for they parfitly wake as to yielding reason for your souls, that they do this thing with joy, not sorrowing, for this thing speeds not to you.

Pray ye for us, and we trust that we have good con⁄science in all things, willing to live well. Moreover I beseech you to do, that I be restored the sooner to you. And God of peace, that led out from death the Great Shepherd of sheep in the blood of everlasting Testament, our Lord Jesus Christ, shape you in all good thing, that ye do the will of Him. And He do in you that thing that shall please before Him, by Jesus Christ, to whom be glory into worlds of worlds. Amen.

And, brethren, I pray you that ye suffer a word of solace. For by full few things I have written to you.

Know ye our brother Timothy that is sent forth. With
whom, if he shall come more hastily, I shall see you.
Greet ye well all your sovereigns and all holy men. The
brethren of Italy greet you well. The grace of God be
with you all. Amen.

Here begins the Prologue on the Deeds of Apostles

*Luke of Antioch, of the nation of Syria, whose praising is told in
the gospel, at Antioch he was a worthy man of leech-craft and
afterward a disciple of Christ's apostles, and sued Paul the apostle. He served God in manhood without blame, and when he was
four score year old and four, he died in Bethany full of the Holy
Ghost. And he, through stirring of the Holy Ghost in the coasts
of Achaia, wrote the gospel to faithful Greeks, and showed the
incarnation of the Lord by a true telling, and showed also that He
was come of the kindred of David.*

    *To him, not without desert, was given power to write the
doings of the apostles in their ministry, that God, being full in
God, when the son of perdition was dead and the apostles had
made their prayer, through lot of the Lord's election the number
of the apostles were fulfilled, and also that Paul should end the
doings of apostles, whom the Lord had chosen that long time
winced against the prick. And to those that read and seek God, he
would show it by short telling rather than show forth anything
more longer to them that hate long things, knowing that it
behoves the tiller that works to eat of his own fruits. And he
found so much grace in God that not only his medicine profited to
bodies, but also to souls.*

Here begins the Deeds of Apostles

Chapter I

Theophilus, first I made a sermon of all things that Jesus began to do and to teach into the day of His ascension, in which He commanded by the Holy Ghost to His apostles which He had chosen. To which He showed Himself alive after His passion, by many arguments, appearing to them forty days and speaking of the realm of God. And He ate with them and commanded that they should not depart from Jerusalem, but abide the behest of the Father, ... which ye heard, He said, by My mouth. For John baptized in water, but ye shall be baptized in the Holy Ghost after these few days.

Therefore they that were come together, asked Him and said, Lord, whether in this time Thou shall restore the kingdom of Israel? And He said to them, It is not yours to know the times either moments which the Father has put in His power. But ye shall take the virtue of the Holy Ghost coming from above into you, and ye shall be My witnesses in Jerusalem, and in all Judea and Samaria, and to the utmost of the earth.

And when He had said these things, in their sight He was lifted up, and a cloud received Him from their eyes. And when they beheld Him going up into heaven, lo, two men stood beside them in white clothing, and said, Men of Galilee, what stand ye beholding into heaven? This Jesus, which is taken up from you into heaven, shall come as ye see Him going into heaven. Then they turned again to Jerusalem from the hill that is called the hill of Olivet, which is beside Jerusalem, an holiday's journey.

And when they were entered into the house where they dwelled, they went up into the solar, Peter and *an upper room* John, James and Andrew, Philip and Thomas, Bartholomew and Matthew, James of Alphaeus and Simon Zealotes, and Judas of James. All these were lastingly continuing with one will in prayer, with women and Mary, the mother of Jesus, and with His brethren.

In those days, Peter rose up in the middle of the brethren, and said ⁄ and there was a company of men together, almost an hundred and twenty ⁄ Brethren, it behoves that the Scripture be filled which the Holy Ghost before said by the mouth of David, of Judas that was leader of them that took Jesus and was num⁄ bered among us, and got a part of this service. And this Judas had a field of the hire of wickedness, and he was hanged and to⁄brast the middle, and all his *burst* entrails were shed abroad. And it was made known to all men that dwelt in Jerusalem, so that the ilk field was called Aceldama in the language of them, that is, the field of blood. And it is written in the book of Psalms, The habitation of them be made desert, and be there none that dwell in it, and another take his bish⁄ opric. Therefore it behoves of these men that are gath⁄ ered together with us in all the time in which the Lord Jesus entered and went out among us, and began from the baptism of John till into the day in which He was taken up from us, that one of these be made a witness of His resurrection with us.

And they ordained twain, Joseph that was called Barsabas, that was named Just, and Matthias. And they prayed and said, Thou, Lord, that knows the hearts of all men, show whom Thou has chosen of these twain, that one take the place of this service and apostle⁄ hood of which Judas trespassed, that he should go into his place. And they gave lots to them, and the lot fell on Matthias, and he was numbered with eleven apostles.

Chapter II

And when the days of Pentecost were filled, all the disciples were together in the same place. And suddenly there was made a sound from heaven as of a great wind coming, and it filled all the house where they sat. And diverse tongues, as fire, appeared to them, and it sat on each of them. And all were filled with the Holy Ghost, and they began to speak diverse languages as the Holy Ghost gave to them for to speak. And there were in Jerusalem dwelling Jews, religious men, of each nation that is under heaven. And when this voice was made, the multitude came together and they were astonied in thought, for each man heard them speaking in his language.

And all were astonied and wondered, and said together, Whether not all these that speak, are men of Galilee, and how heard we each man his language in which we are born? Parthians and Medes, and Elamites, and they that dwell at Mesopotamia, Judea and Cappadocia, and Pontus and Asia, Phrygia and Pamphylia, Egypt and the parts of Lybia that is above *foreigners, strangers* Cyrene, and comelings, Romans and Jews and proselytes, men of Crete and of Arabia. We have heard them speaking in our languages the great things of God! And all were astonied and wondered, and said together, What will this thing be? And other scorned and said, *new fermenting wine* For these men are full of must!

But Peter stood with the eleven and raised up his voice, and spoke to them, Ye Jews, and all that dwell at Jerusalem, be this known to you, and with ears perceive ye my words. For not as ye ween these are drunken when it is the third hour of the day. But this it is that was said by the prophet Joel, And it shall be in the last days, the Lord says, I shall held out My Spirit on each flesh, and your sons and your daughters shall prophesy, and your young men shall see visions, and your elders shall dream swevens. And on My servants and Mine handmaidens *dreams* in those days, I shall shed out of My Spirit, and they shall prophesy. And I shall give great wonders in heaven above and signs in earth beneath, blood and fire, and heat of smoke. The sun shall be turned into darknesses and the moon into blood before that the great and the open day of the Lord come. And it shall be, each man which ever shall call to help the name of the Lord, shall be safe!

Ye men of Israel, hear ye these words. Jesus of Nazareth, a Man proved of God before you by virtues and wonders and tokens, which God did by Him in the middle of you as ye wit, ye tormented and killed Him by the hands of wicked men, by counsel determined and betaken by the foreknowing of God. Whom God raised when sorrows of hell were unbound, by that that it was impossible that He were held of it. For David says of Him, I saw afar the Lord before me evermore, for He is on my right half that I be not moved. For this thing, mine heart joyed and my tongue made full out joy, and moreover my flesh shall rest in hope. For Thou shall not leave my soul in hell, neither Thou shall give Thine Holy to see corruption. Thou has made known to me the ways of life. Thou shall fill me in mirth with Thy face!

Brethren, be it leaveful boldly to say to you of the patriarch David, for he is dead and buried and his sepulchre is among us into this day. Therefore when he was a prophet, and wist that with a great oath God had sworn to him that of the fruit of his loins should One sit on his seat, he seeing afar spoke of the resurrection of Christ, for neither He was left in hell, neither His flesh saw corruption. God raised this Jesus, to whom we all are witnesses. Therefore He was enhanced by the right hand of God, and through the behest of the Holy Ghost that He took of the Father, He shed out this Spirit that ye see and hear. For David styed not into heaven, but he says, My Lord said to my Lord, Sit Thou on My right half till I put Thine enemies a stool of Thy feet. Therefore most certainly wit all the house of Israel that God made Him both Lord and Christ, this Jesus, whom ye crucified!

When they heard these things, they were compunct in heart, and they said to Peter and other apostles, Brethren, what shall we do? And Peter said to them, Do ye penance, and each of you be baptized in the name of Jesus Christ into remission of your sins, and ye shall take the gift of the Holy Ghost. For the behest is to you and to your sons, and to all that are far which ever our Lord God has called.

Also with other words full many he witnessed to them, and monested them and said, Be ye saved from this shrewd generation! Then they that received his word, were baptized, and in that day souls were increased about three thousand, and were lasting stably in the teaching of the apostles, and in coming of the breaking of bread and in prayers. And dread was made to each man, and many wonders and signs were done by the apostles in Jerusalem, and great dread was in all. And all that believed were together and had all things common. They sold possessions and cattle, and departed those things to all men as it was need to each. And each day they dwelled stably with one will in the Temple, and broke bread about houses, and took meat with full out joy and simpleness of heart, and heried together God and had grace to all folk. And the Lord increased them that were made safe, each day into the same thing.

Chapter III

And Peter and John went up into the Temple at the ninth hour of praying. And a man that was lame from the womb of his mother, was borne, and was laid each day at the gate of the Temple that is said Fair, to ask alms of men that entered into the Temple. This, when he saw Peter and John beginning to enter into the Temple, prayed that he should take alms. And Peter and John beheld on him and said, Behold thou into us. And he beheld into them and hoped that he should take somewhat of them. But Peter said, I have neither silver nor gold, but that that I have, I give to thee. In the name of Jesus Christ of Nazareth, rise thou up and go!

And he took him by the right hand and heaved him up, and anon his legs and his feet were sowded together, *strengthened* and he leaped and stood and wandered. And he entered with them into the Temple, and wandered and leaped, and heried God. And all the people saw him walking and herying God. And they knew him that he it was that sat at alms at the Fair Gate of the Temple. And they were filled with wondering and stonying in that thing that befell to him. But when they saw Peter and John, all the people ran to them at the porch that was called of Solomon, and wondered greatly.

And Peter saw, and answered to the people, Men of Israel, what wonder ye in this thing? Either what behold ye us, as by our virtue either power we made this man for to walk? God of Abraham, and God of Isaac, and God of Jacob, God of our fathers, has glorified His Son, Jesus, whom ye betrayed and denied before the face of Pilate when he deemed Him to be delivered. But ye denied the Holy and the Rightful, and asked a manslayer to be given to you. And ye slew the Maker of life, whom God raised from death, of whom we are witnesses. And in the faith of His name, He has confirmed this man whom ye see and know. The name of Him and the faith that is by Him gave to this man full health in the sight of all you. And now, brethren, I wot that by unwitting ye did, as also your princes. But God, that before told by the mouth of all prophets that His Christ should suffer, has filled so.

Therefore be ye repentant, and be ye converted, that your sins be done away, that when the times of refresh⁄ing shall come from the sight of the Lord, and He shall send the ilk Jesus Christ that is now preached to you. Whom it behoves heaven to receive into the times of res⁄titution of all things, which the Lord spoke by the mouth of His holy prophets from the world. For Moses said, For the Lord your God shall raise to you a Prophet of your brethren as me. Ye shall hear Him by all things whatever He shall speak to you. And it shall be that every man that shall not hear the ilk Prophet, shall be destroyed from the people. And all prophets, from Samuel and afterward, that spoke, told these days. But ye are the sons of prophets and of the Testament that God ordained to our fathers, and said to Abraham, In thy seed all the meynes of earth shall be blessed. God raised His Son first to you, and sent Him blessing you, that each man convert him from his wickedness.

Chapter IV

And while they spoke to the people, the priests and magistrates of the Temple, and the Sadducees, came upon them, and sorrowed that they taught the people and told in Jesus the again⁄rising from death. And they laid hands on them, and put them into ward into the morrow, for it was then eventide. But many of them that had heard the word, believed, and the number of men was made five thousands.

And amorrow it was done that the princes of them *in the morning*
and elder men and scribes, were gathered in Jerusalem,
and Annas, prince of priests, and Caiaphas, and John,
and Alexander, and how many ever were of the kind of
priests. And they set them in the middle and asked, In
what virtue, either in what name have ye done this
thing? Then Peter was filled with the Holy Ghost, and
said to them, Ye princes of the people, and ye elder men,
hear ye. If we today be deemed in the good deed of a sick
man, in whom this man is made safe, be it known to
you all and to all the people of Israel, that in the name of
Jesus Christ of Nazareth, whom ye crucified, whom
God raised from death, in This this man stands whole
before you. This is the Stone which was reproved of you
building, which is made into the head of the corner, and
health is not in any other! For neither other name under
heaven is given to men in which it behoves us to be
made safe.

And they saw the steadfastness of Peter and of John,
for it was found that they were men unlettered and lewd *common, unlearned*
men, and they wondered and knew them that they were
with Jesus. And they saw the man that was healed
standing with them, and they might nothing againsay.
But they commanded them to go forth without the council. And they spoke together and said, What shall we
do to these men? For the sign is made known by them to
all men that dwell at Jerusalem. It is open and we moun
not deny. But that it be no more published, menace we
to them that they speak no more in this name to any
man.

And they called them and denounced to them that
on no manner they should speak, neither teach, in the
name of Jesus. But Peter and John answered and said to
them, If it be rightful in the sight of God to hear you
rather than God, deem ye. For we must needs speak

those things that we have seen and heard. And they menaced and left them, and found not how they should punish them, for the people, for all men clarified that thing that was done in that that was befallen. For the man was more than of forty year in which this sign of health was made.

And when they were delivered, they came to their fellows and told to them how great things the princes of priests and the elder men had said to them. And when they heard, with one heart they raised voice to the Lord and said, Lord, Thou that made heaven and earth, sea, and all things that are in them, which said by the Holy Ghost, by the mouth of our father David, Thy child, Why heathen men gnashed with teeth together, and the peoples thought vain things? Kings of the earth stood nigh, and princes came together into one, against the Lord and against His Christ. For verily, Herod and Pontius Pilate, with heathen men and peoples of Israel, came together in this city against Thine holy Child, Jesus, whom Thou anointed to do the things that Thine hand and Thy counsel deemed to be done. And now, Lord, behold into the threatenings of them, and grant to Thy servants to speak Thy word with all trust in that thing, that Thou hold forth Thine hand, that healths and signs and wonders be made by the name of Thine holy Son, Jesus.

And when they had prayed, the place was moved in which they were gathered, and all were filled with the Holy Ghost, and spoke the word of God with trust. And of all the multitude of men believing was one heart and one will. Neither any man said any things of those things that he wielded to be his own, but all things were common to them. And with great virtue the apostles yielded witnessing of the again-rising of Jesus Christ our Lord, and great grace was in all them. For neither any needy man was among them, for how many ever were possessors of fields, either of houses, they sold and brought the prices of those things that they sold, and laid before the feet of the apostles. And it was departed to each as it was need to each. Forsooth, Joseph, that was named Barsabas of apostles, that is to say, the son of comfort, of the lineage of Levi, a man of Cyprus, when he had a field, sold it, and brought the price and laid it before the feet of apostles.

Chapter V

But a man, Ananias by name, with Sapphira, his wife, sold a field, and defrauded of the price of the field. And his wife was witting. And he brought a part and laid before the feet of the apostles. And Peter said to him, Ananias, why has Satan tempted thine heart that thou lie to the Holy Ghost, and to defraud of the price of the field? Whether it, unsold, was not thine? And when it was sold, it was in thy power? Why has thou put this thing in thine heart? Thou has not lied to men, but to God.

Ananias heard these words and fell down, and was dead. And great dread was made on all that heard. And young men rose and moved him away, and bore him out and buried. And there was made as a space of three hours, and his wife knew not that thing that was done, and entered. And Peter said to her, Woman, say to me whether ye sold the field for so much? And she said, Yea, for so much. And Peter said to her, What befell to you to tempt the Spirit of the Lord? Lo, the feet of them that have buried thine husband are at the door, and they shall bear thee out! Anon, she fell down at his feet and died. And the young men entered and found her dead, and they bore her out and buried to her husband. And great dread was made in all the church and into all that heard these things.

And by the hands of the apostles, signs and many wonders were made in the people. And all were of one accord in the porch of Solomon. But no man of other dared join himself with them, but the people magnified them. And the multitude of men and of women believ⸗ ing in the Lord was more increased, so that they brought out sick men into streets, and laid in little beds and couches, that when Peter came, namely the shadow of him should shadow each of them, and they should be delivered from their sicknesses. And the multitude of cities nigh to Jerusalem ran, bringing sick men and that were travailed of unclean spirits, which all were healed.

But the prince of priests rose up and all that were with him, that is the heresy of Sadducees, and were filled with envy, and laid hands on the apostles and put them in the common ward. But the angel of the Lord opened by night the gates of the prison and led them out, and said, Go ye, and stand ye, and speak in the Temple to the people all the words of this life. Whom, when they had heard, they entered early into the Temple and taught.

And the prince of priests came and they that were with him, and called together the council and all the elder men of the children of Israel, and sent to the prison that they should be brought forth. And when the minis⸗ ters came, found them not, and for the prison was opened they turned again, and told and said, We found the prison shut with all diligence and the keepers stand⸗ ing at the gates. But we opened, and found no man therein! And as the magistrates of the Temple and the princes of priests heard these words, they doubted of them what was done. But a man came and told to them, For lo, those men which ye have put into prison, are in the Temple, and stand and teach the people!

Then the magistrate went with the ministers, and brought them out with violence, for they dreaded the people lest they should be stoned. And when they had brought them, they set them in the council, and the princes of priests asked them and said, In command⁄ ment we commanded you that ye should not teach in this name, and lo, ye have filled Jerusalem with your teaching, and ye will bring on us the blood of this Man! And Peter answered, and the apostles, and said, It behoves to obey to God more than to men. God of our fathers raised Jesus, whom ye slew, hanging in a tree. God enhanced with His right hand this Prince and Saviour, that penance were given to Israel and remission of sins. And we are witnesses of these words, and the Holy Ghost, whom God gave to all obeying to Him!

When they heard these things, they were tormented, and thought to slay them. But a man rose in the council, a Pharisee, Gamaliel by name, a doctor of the law, a worshipful man to all the people, and commanded the men to be put withoutforth for a while. And he said to them, Ye men of Israel, take tent to yourselves on these men what ye shall do. For before these days, Theudas, that said himself to be some man, to whom a number of men consented about four hundred, which was slain, and all that believed to him were disparpled and brought to nought. After this, Judas of Galilee was in the days of profession, and turned away the people after him, and all how many ever consented to him, were scat⁄ tered, and he perished. And now therefore I say to you, depart ye from these men and suffer ye them. For if this counsel either work is of men, it shall be undone. But if it is of God, ye moun not undo them, lest peradventure ye be found to repugn God.

And they consented to him, and they called together the apostles and denounced to them that were beaten, that they should no more speak in the name of Jesus. And they let them go. And they went, joying, from the sight of the council, that they were had worthy to suffer despising for the name of Jesus. But each day they ceased not in the Temple and about houses to teach and to preach Jesus Christ.

Chapter VI

But in those days, when the number of disciples increased, the Greeks grouched against the Hebrews for that their widows were despised in every day's ministering. And the twelve called together the multitude of disciples, and said, It is not rightful that we leave the word of God and minister to boards. Therefore, brethren, behold ye men of you of good fame, full of the Holy Ghost and of wisdom, which we shall ordain on this work, for we shall be busy to prayer and preach the word of God.

And the word pleased before all the multitude, and they chose Stephen, a man full of faith and of the Holy Ghost, and Philip, and Prochorus, and Nicanor, and Timon, and Parmenas, and Nicholas, a proselyte of Antioch. They ordained these before the sight of apostles, and they prayed and laid hands on them. And the word of the Lord waxed, and the number of the disciples in Jerusalem was much multiplied. Also much company of priests obeyed to the faith.

And Stephen, full of grace and of strength, made wonders and great signs in the people. But some risen of the synagogue that was called of the Libertines, and Cyrenians and of men of Alexander, and of them that were of Cilicia and of Asia, and disputed with Stephen. And they might not withstand the wisdom and the Spirit that spoke. Then they privily sent men that should say that they heard him saying words of blasphemy against Moses and God. And so they moved together the people and the elder men and the scribes, and they ran together and took him, and brought into the council.

And they ordained false witnesses that said, This man ceases not to speak words against the holy place and the law. For we heard him saying that this Jesus of Nazareth shall destroy this place and shall change the traditions which Moses betook to us! And all men that sat in the council beheld him, and saw his face as the face of an angel.

Chapter VII

And the prince of priests said to Stephen, Whether these things have them so? Which said, Brethren and fathers, hear ye. God of glory appeared to our father, Abraham, when he was in Mesopotamia before he dwelt in Haran, and said to him, Go out of thy land and of thy kindred, and come into the land which I shall show to thee. Then he went out of the land of Chaldeans and dwelt in Haran. And from thence, after that his father was dead, he translated him into this land in which ye dwell now. And He gave not to him heritage in it, neither a pace of a foot. But He behight to give him it into possession, and to his seed after him when he had not a son. And God spoke to him that his seed should be comelings in an alien land, and they should make them subject to servage, and shall evil treat them four hundred years and thirty. And I shall judge the folk to which they shall serve, says the Lord. And after these things, they shall go out and they shall serve to Me in this place. And He gave to him the testament of circumcision, and so he gendered Isaac and circumcised him in the eighth day.

And Isaac gendered Jacob, and Jacob gendered the twelve patriarchs. And the patriarchs had envy to Joseph, and sold him into Egypt. And God was with

him, and delivered him of all his tribulations, and gave
to him grace and wisdom in the sight of Pharaoh, king
of Egypt. And He ordained him sovereign on Egypt
and on all his house. And hunger came into all Egypt
and Canaan, and great tribulation, and our fathers
found not meat. But when Jacob had heard that wheat
was in Egypt, he sent our fathers first. And in the second
time, Joseph was known of his brethren, and his kin
was made known to Pharaoh. And Joseph sent and
called Jacob, his father, and all his kindred, seventy and
five men. And Jacob came down into Egypt and was
dead, he and our fathers. And they were translated into
Sychem, and were laid in the sepulchre that Abraham
bought by price of silver of the sons of Emmor, the son
of Sychem.

And when the time of behest came nigh, which God
had acknowledged to Abraham, the people waxed and
multiplied in Egypt, till another king rose in Egypt
which knew not Joseph. This beguiled our kin and tormented our fathers, that they should put away their
young children, for they should not live. In the same
time, Moses was born, and he was loved of God. And
he was nourished three months in the house of his
father. And when he was put out in the river, the daughter of Pharaoh took him up and nourished him into her
son. And Moses was learned in all the wisdom of
Egyptians, and he was mighty in his words and works.

But when the time of forty year was filled to him, it
rose up into his heart that he should visit his brethren,
the sons of Israel. And when he saw a man suffering
wrong, he venged him and did vengeance for him that
suffered the wrong, and he killed the Egyptian. For he
guessed that his brethren should understand that God
should give to them health by the hand of him. But they
understood not. For in the day suing, he appeared to

them, chiding, and he accorded them in peace and said, Men, ye are brethren. Why noy ye each other? But he that did the wrong to his neighbour, put him away, and said, Who ordained thee prince and doomsman on us? Whether thou will slay me as yesterday thou killed the Egyptian? And in this word, Moses fled, and was made a comeling in the land of Midian, where he begat two sons.

And when he had filled forty year, an angel appeared to him in fire of flame of a bush in desert of the mount of Sinai. And Moses saw and wondered on the sight. And when he nighed to behold, the voice of the Lord was made to him, and said, I am God of your fathers, God of Abraham, God of Isaac, God of Jacob. Moses was made trembling and dared not behold. But God said to him, Do off the shoes off thy feet, for the place in which thou stands is holy earth. I, seeing, saw the tor⁄menting of My people that are in Egypt, and I heard the mourning of them, and I came down to deliver them. And now come thou, and I shall send thee into Egypt.

This Moses ⁄ whom they denied, saying, Who ordained thee prince and doomsman on us? ⁄ God sent this prince and again⁄buyer with the hand of the angel *one who redeems* that appeared to him in the bush. This Moses led them out, and did wonders and signs in the land of Egypt and in the Red Sea, and in desert forty years. This is Moses that said to the sons of Israel, God shall raise to you a Prophet of your brethren as me ye shall hear Him. This it is that was in the church in wilderness with the angel that spoke to him in the mount of Sinai, and with our fathers, which took words of life to give to us. To whom our fathers would not obey, but put him away and were turned away in hearts into Egypt, saying to Aaron, Make thou to us gods that shall go before us. For to this Moses that led us out of the land of Egypt, we wit not what is done to him. And they made a calf in those days, and offered a sacrifice to the mawmet, and they were glad in the works of their hands. And God turned and betook them to serve to the knighthood of heaven, as it is written in the book of prophets, Whether ye, house of Israel, offered to Me slain sacrifices forty years in desert? And ye have taken the tabernacle of Moloch and the star of your god, Remphan, figures that ye have made to worship them, and I shall translate you into Babylon.

The Tabernacle of Witnessing was with our fathers in desert as God disposed to them, and spoke to Moses that he should make it after the form that He say. Which also our fathers took with Joshua and brought into the possession of heathen men, which God put away from the face of our fathers till into the days of David that found grace anents God, and asked that he should find a tabernacle to God of Jacob. But Solomon built the house to Him. But the high God dwells not in things made by hand, as He says by the prophet, Heaven is a seat to Me, and the earth is the stool of My feet. What house shall ye build to Me, says the Lord, either what place is of My resting? Whether Mine hand *neck* made not all these things? With hard noll and uncir‚ cumcised hearts and ears ye withstand evermore the Holy Ghost. And as your fathers, so ye! Whom of the prophets have not your fathers pursued, and have slain them that before told of the coming of the Rightful Man, whose traitors and manslayers ye were now? Which took the law in ordinance of angels, and have not kept it?

And they heard these things and were diversely tor‚ *hissed* mented in their hearts, and grenned with teeth on him. But when Stephen was full of the Holy Ghost, he beheld into heaven and saw the glory of God, and Jesus standing on the right half of the virtue of God. And he said, Lo, I see heavens opened, and Man's Son stand⁄ing on the right half of the virtue of God! And they cried with a great voice and stopped their ears, and made with one will an assault into him. And they brought him out of the city and stoned. And the witnesses did off their clothes beside the feet of a young man that was called Saul. And they stoned Stephen that called to God to help, saying, Lord Jesus, receive my spirit! And he kneeled and cried with a great voice, and said, Lord, set not to them this sin! And when he had said this thing, he died.

Chapter VIII

But Saul was consenting to his death, and great persecu⁄tion was made in that day in the church that was in Jerusalem. And all men were scattered by the countries of Judea and Samaria, out⁄taken the apostles. But good men buried Stephen and made great mourning on him. But Saul greatly destroyed the church, and entered by houses and drew men and women, and betook them into prison. And they that were scattered, passed forth, preaching the word of God.

And Philip came down into a city of Samaria, and preached to them Christ. And the people gave tent to these things that were said of Philip, with one will hear⁄ing and seeing the signs that he did. For many of them that had unclean spirits cried with a great voice and went out. And many sick in the palsy and crooked, were healed. Therefore great joy was made in that city. But there was a man in that city whose name was Simon, a witch, that had deceived the folk of Samaria, saying that himself was some great man. Whom all hearkened, from the least to the most, and said, This is the virtue of God which is called Great! And they believed him, for long time he had madded them with his witchcrafts. But when they had believed to Philip that preached the kingdom of God, men and women were baptized in the name of Jesus Christ. And then also Simon himself believed. And when he was baptized, he drew to Philip, and he saw also that signs and great virtues were done. He was astonied and wondered.

But when the apostles that were at Jerusalem, had heard that Samaria had received the word of God, they sent to them Peter and John. And when they came, they prayed for them that they should receive the Holy Ghost. For He came not yet into any of them, but they were baptized only in the name of the Lord Jesus. Then they laid hands on them, and they received the Holy Ghost.

And when Simon had seen that the Holy Ghost was given by laying on of the hands of the apostles, and he proffered to them money, and said, Give ye also to me this power, that whomever I shall lay on mine hands, that he receive the Holy Ghost. But Peter said to him, Thy money be with thee into perdition, for thou guessed the gift of God should be had for money. There is no part nor sort to thee in this word, for thine heart is not rightful before God. Therefore, do thou penance for this wickedness of thee, and pray God if peradventure this thought of thine heart be forgiven to thee. For I see that thou art in the gall of bitterness and in the bond of wickedness. And Simon answered and said, Pray ye for me to the Lord, that nothing of these things that ye have said, come on me.

And they witnessed and spoke the word of the Lord, and went again to Jerusalem, and preached to many countries of Samaritans. And an angel of the Lord spoke to Philip and said, Rise thou, and go against the south to the way that goes down from Jerusalem into Gaza ⁄ this is desert. And he rose and went forth. And lo, a man of Ethiopia, a mighty manservant, a gelding of Candace, the queen of Ethiopians, which was on all her richesses, came to worship in Jerusalem. And he turned again, sitting on his chariot and reading Isaiah the prophet.

And the Spirit said to Philip, Nigh thou, and join thee to this chare. And Philip ran to, and heard him reading Isaiah the prophet. And he said, Guess thou whether thou understands what things thou reads? And he said, How may I, if no man show to me? And he prayed Philip that he should come up and sit with him. And the place of the Scripture that he read was this, As a sheep, He was led to slaying, and as a lamb before a man that shears him is dumb without voice, so He opened not His mouth. In meekness, His doom was taken up. Who shall tell out the generation of Him? For His life shall be taken away from the earth.

And the gelding answered to Philip, and said, I beseech thee, of what prophet says he this thing? Of himself, either of any other? And Philip opened his mouth and began at this Scripture, and preached to him Jesus. And the while they went by the way, they came to a water. And the gelding said, Lo, water! Who forbids me to be baptized? And Philip said, If thou believe of all the heart, it is leaveful. And he answered and said, I believe that Jesus Christ is the Son of God! And he commanded the chare to stand still. And they went down both to the water, Philip and the gelding, and Philip baptized him. And when they were come up of the water, the Spirit of the Lord ravished Philip, and the gelding saw him no more. And Philip was found in Azotus, and he passed forth and preached to all cities, till he came to Caesarea.

Chapter IX

But Saul, yet a blower of menaces and of beatings against the disciples of the Lord, came to the prince of priests and asked of him letters into Damascus, to the synagogues, that if he found any men and women of this life, he should lead them bound to Jerusalem. And when he made his journey, it befell that he came nigh to Damascus. And suddenly, a light from heaven shone about him. And he fell to the earth, and heard a voice saying to him, Saul, Saul, what pursues thou Me? And he said, Who art Thou, Lord? And He said, I am Jesus of Nazareth whom thou pursues. It is hard to thee to kick against the prick. And he trembled and wondered, and said, Lord, what will Thou that I do? And the Lord said to him, Rise up, and enter into the city, and it shall be said to thee what it behoves thee to do.

And those men that went with him, stood astonied, for they heard a voice, but they saw no man. And Saul rose from the earth, and when his eyes were opened, he saw nothing. And they drew him by the hands and led him into Damascus. And he was three days not seeing, and he ate not, neither drank.

And a disciple, Ananias by name, was at Damascus. And the Lord said to him in a vision, Ananias! And he said, Lo, I, Lord! And the Lord said to him, Rise thou, and go into a street that is called Rectus, and seek in the house of Judas, Saul by name, of Tarsus. For lo, he prays, and he saw a man, Ananias by name, entering and laying on him hands that he receive sight. And Ananias answered, Lord, I have heard of many of this man, how great evils he did to Thy saints in Jerusalem. And this has power of the princes of priests to bind all men that call Thy name to help. And the Lord said to him, Go thou, for this is to

Me a vessel of choosing, that he bear My name before heathen men and kings, and tofore the sons of Israel. For I shall show to him how great things it behoves him to suffer for My name.

And Ananias went and entered into the house, and laid on him his hands, and said, Saul, brother, the Lord Jesus sent me that appeared to thee in the way in which thou came, that thou see and be fulfilled with the Holy Ghost. And anon, as the scales fell from his eyes, he received sight. And he rose and was baptized, and when he had taken meat, he was comforted.

And he was by some days with the disciples that were at Damascus. And anon, he entered into the syna⁄ gogues and preached the Lord Jesus, for this is the Son of God. And all men that heard him, wondered and said, Whether this is not he that impugned in Jerusalem them that called to help this name? And hither he came for this thing, that he should lead them bound to the princes of priests! But Saul much more waxed strong, and confounded the Jews that dwelled at Damascus, and affirmed that this is Christ.

And when many days were filled, Jews made a coun⁄ sel that they should slay him, and the aspies of them were made known to Saul. And they kept the gates, day and night, that they should slay him. But his disciples took him by night and delivered him, and let him down in a leep by the wall.

And when he came into Jerusalem, he assayed to join him to the disciples, and all dreaded him, and believed not that he was a disciple. But Barnabas took and led him to the apostles, and told to them how in the way he had seen the Lord, and that He spoke to him, and how in Damascus he did trustily in the name of Jesus. And he was with them, and entered and went out in Jerusalem, and did trustily in the name of Jesus.

And he spoke with heathen men, and disputed with Greeks, and they sought to slay him. Which thing when the brethren had known, they led him by night to Caesarea, and let him go to Tarsus.

And the church, by all Judea and Galilee and Samaria, had peace and was edified, and walked in the dread of the Lord, and was filled with comfort of the Holy Ghost. And it befell that Peter, the while he passed about all, came to the holy men that dwelled at Lydda. And he found a man, Aeneas by name, that from eight year he had lain in bed, and he was sick in palsy. And Peter said to him, Aeneas, the Lord Jesus Christ heal thee! Rise thou, and array thee! And anon he rose, and all men that dwelt at Lydda and at Saron saw him, which were converted to the Lord.

And in Joppa was a discipless whose name was Tabitha, that is to say, Dorcas. This was full of good works and almsdeeds that she did. And it befell in those days that she was sick and died. And when they had washed her, they laid her in a solar. And for Lydda was nigh Joppa, the disciples heard that Peter was therein, and sent two men to him and prayed that, Thou tarry not to come to us. And Peter rose up and came with them. And when he was come, they led him into the solar. And all widows stood about him weeping and showing coats and clothes which Dorcas made to them. And when all men were put withoutforth, Peter kneeled and prayed. And he turned to the body and said, Tabitha, rise thou! And she opened her eyes, and when she saw Peter, she sat up again. And he took her by the hand and raised her. And when he had called the holy men and widows, he assigned her alive. And it was made known by all Joppa, and many believed in the Lord. And it was made that many days he dwelled *leatherworker or tanner* in Joppa at one Simon's, a currier.

Chapter X

A man was in Caesarea, Cornelius by name, a centur⁄
ion of the company of knights that is said of Italy, a reli⁄
gious man and dreading the Lord with all his meyne,
doing many alms to the people and praying the Lord
evermore. This saw in a vision, openly, as in the ninth
hour of the day, an angel of God entering into him, and
saying to him, Cornelius! And he beheld him and was
a dread, and said, Who art thou, Lord? And he said to
him, Thy prayers and thine almsdeeds have styed up
into mind in the sight of the Lord. And now, send thou
men into Joppa, and call one Simon that is named
Peter. This is harboured at a man, Simon, currier,
whose house is beside the sea. This shall say to thee
what it behoves thee to do. And when the angel that
spoke to him was gone away, he called two men of his
house, and a knight that dreaded the Lord, which were
at his bidding. And when he had told them all these
things, he sent them into Joppa.

And on the day suing, while they made journey and
nighed to the city, Peter went up into the highest place
of the house to pray, about the sixth hour. And when he
was hungered, he would have eaten. But while they
made ready, a ravishing of spirit fell on him, and he saw
heaven, opened, and a vessel coming down as a great
sheet with four corners, to be let down from heaven into
earth, in which were all four⁄footed beasts and creeping *creeping things*
of the earth, and volatiles of heaven. And a voice was
made to him, Rise thou, Peter, and slay and eat. And
Peter said, Lord, forbid! For I never eat any common
thing and unclean! And eft the second time the voice
was made to him, That thing that God has cleansed,
say thou not unclean. And this thing was done by
thrice, and anon the vessel was received again.

And while that Peter doubted within himself what the vision was that he saw, lo, the men that were sent from Cornelius, sought the house of Simon, and stood at the gate. And when they had called, they asked if Simon that is named Peter had there harbour. And while Peter thought on the vision, the Spirit said to him, Lo, three men seek thee. Therefore, rise thou and go down, and go with them, and doubt thou nothing, for I sent them.

And Peter came down to the men, and said, Lo, I am whom ye seek. What is the cause for which ye are come? And they said, Cornelius the centurion, a just man and dreading God, and has good witnessing of all the folk of Jews, took answer of an holy angel to call thee into his house, and to hear words of thee. Therefore he led them in and received in harbour, and that night they dwelled with him.

And in the day suing, he rose and went forth with them, and some of the brethren followed him from Joppa, that they be witnesses to Peter. And the other day, he entered into Caesarea. And Cornelius abided them and his cousins, and necessary friends that were called together. And it was done, when Peter was come in, Conelius came, meeting him, and fell down at his feet and worshipped him. But Peter raised him and said, Arise thou. Also I myself am a man, as thou. And he spoke with him and went in, and found many that were come together. And he said to them, Ye wit how abominable it is to a Jew to be joined either to come to an alien? But God showed to me that no man say a man common either unclean. For which thing I came when I was called, without doubting. Therefore I ask you, for what cause have ye called me?

And Cornelius said, Today, four days into this hour, I was praying and fasting in the ninth hour in mine house. And lo, a man stood before me in a white cloth, and said, Cornelius, thy prayer is heard and thine almsdeeds are in mind in the sight of God. Therefore send thou into Joppa, and call Simon that is named Peter. This is harboured in the house of Simon Currier, beside the sea. This, when he shall come, shall speak to thee. Therefore, anon I sent to thee, and thou did well in coming to us. Now therefore, we all are present in thy sight to hear the words whatever is commanded to thee of the Lord.

And Peter opened his mouth and said, In truth, I have found that God is no acceptor of persons. But in each folk, he that dreads God and works rightwiseness, is accept to Him. God sent a word to the children of Israel, showing peace by Jesus Christ ⁄ this is Lord of all things. Ye wit the word that is made through all Judea and began at Galilee after the baptism that John preached, Jesus of Nazareth, how God anointed Him with the Holy Ghost and virtue, which passed forth in doing well and healing all men oppressed of the devil, for God was with Him. And we are witnesses of all things which He did in the country of Jews and of Jerusalem, whom they slew, hanging in a tree. And God raised this in the third day, and gave Him to be made known not to all people, but to witnesses before⁄ ordained of God, to us that ate and drank with Him after that He rose again from death. And He com⁄ manded to us to preach to the people, and to witness that He it is that is ordained of God, Doomsman of the quick and of dead. To this all prophets bear witnessing, that all men that believe in Him should receive remis⁄ sion of sins by His name.

And yet, while that Peter spoke these words, the Holy Ghost fell on all that heard the word. And the faithful men of circumcision that came with Peter, won⁄

dered that also into nations the grace of the Holy Ghost is shed out. For they heard them speaking in languages and magnifying God. Then Peter answered, Whether any man may forbid water that these are not baptized that have also received the Holy Ghost as we? And he commanded them to be baptized in the name of the Lord Jesus Christ. Then they prayed him that he should dwell with them some days.

Chapter XI

And the apostles and the brethren that were in Judea, heard that also heathen men received the word of God, and they glorified God. But when Peter came to Jerusalem, they that were of circumcision disputed against him, and said, Why entered thou to men that *foreskin* have prepuce, and has eaten with them?

And Peter began and expounded to them by order, and said, I was in the city of Joppa, and prayed, and I saw in ravishing of my mind a vision that a vessel came down, as a great sheet with four cords, and was sent down from heaven, and it came to me. Into which I, looking, beheld and saw four-footed beasts of the earth, and beasts and creeping beasts, and volatiles of heaven. And I heard also a voice that said to me, Peter, rise thou, and slay and eat. But I said, Nay, Lord, for common thing either unclean entered never into my mouth. And the voice answered the second time from heaven, That thing that God has cleansed, say thou not unclean. And this was done by thrice, and all things were received again into heaven.

And lo, three men anon stood in the house in which I was, and they were sent from Caesarea to me. And the Spirit said to me that I should go with them and doubt nothing. Yea, and these six brethren came with me and we entered into the house of the man. And he told to us how he saw an angel in his house, standing and saying to him, Send thou into Joppa and call Simon that is named Peter, which shall speak to thee words in which thou shall be safe and all thine house. And when I had begun to speak, the Holy Ghost fell on them, as into us in the beginning. And I bethought on the word of the Lord as He said, For John baptized in water, but ye shall be baptized in the Holy Ghost. Therefore, if God gave to them the same grace as to us that believed in the Lord Jesus Christ, who was I that might forbid the Lord, that He give not the Holy Ghost to them that believed in the name of Jesus Christ? When these things were heard, they held peace and glorified God, and said, Therefore also to heathen men God has given penance to life.

And they that were scattered of the tribulation that was made under Stephen, walked forth to Phenice, and to Cyprus and to Antioch, and spoke the word to no man but to Jews alone. But some of them were men of Cyprus and of Cyrene, which, when they had entered into Antioch, they spoke to the Greeks and preached the Lord Jesus. And the hand of the Lord was with them, and much number of men, believing, was converted to the Lord.

And the word came to the ears of the church that was at Jerusalem on these things, and they sent Barnabas to Antioch. And when he was come and saw the grace of the Lord, he joyed and monested all men to dwell in the Lord in purpose of heart, for he was a good man and full of the Holy Ghost and of faith. And much people were increased to the Lord. And he went forth to Tarsus to seek Saul, and when he had found him, he led to Antioch. And all a year they lived there in the church and taught much people, so that the disciples were named first at Antioch, Christian men.

And in these days, prophets came over from Jerusalem to Antioch. And one of them rose up, Agabus by name, and signified by the Spirit a great hunger to coming in all the world, which hunger was made under Claudius. And all the disciples purposed, after that each had, for to send into ministry to brethren that dwelled in Judea. Which thing also they did, and sent it to the elder men by the hands of Barnabas and Saul.

Chapter XII

And in the same time, Herod the king sent power to torment some men of the church. And he slew by sword James, the brother of John. And he saw that it pleased to Jews, and cast to take also Peter. And the days of therf loaves were. And when he had caught Peter, he sent *groups of four men* him into prison, and betook to four quaternions of knights to keep him, and would, after Pasch, bring him forth to the people. And Peter was kept in prison. But prayer was made of the church without ceasing to God for him.

But when Herod should bring him forth, in that night Peter was sleeping betwixt two knights, and was bound with two chains. And the keepers before the door, kept the prison. And lo, an angel of the Lord stood nigh, and light shone in the prison house. And when he had smote the side of Peter, he raised him and said, Rise thou, swiftly! And anon the chains fell down from his hands. And the angel said to him, Gird thee, and do on thine hoses. And he did so. And he said to him, Do about thee thy clothes, and sue me. And he went out and sued him, and he wist not that it was sooth that was done by the angel, for he guessed himself to have seen a vision. And they passed the first and the second ward, and came to the iron gate that leads to the city, which anon was opened to them. And they went out and came into one street, and anon the angel passed away from him. And Peter turned again to himself, and said, Now I wot verily that the Lord sent His angel and delivered me from the hand of Herod, and from all the abiding of the people of Jews.

And he beheld and came to the house of Mary, mother of John that is named Mark, where many were gathered together and praying. And when he knocked at the door of the gate, a damsel, Rhoda by name, came forth to see. And when she knew the voice of Peter, for joy she opened not the gate but ran in, and told that Peter stood at the gate. And they said to her, Thou maddest! But she affirmed that it was so. And they said, It is his angel! But Peter abode still and knocked, and when they had opened the door, they saw him and wondered. And he beckoned to them with his hand to be still, and told how the Lord had led him out of the prison. And he said, Tell ye to James and to the brethren these things! And he went out and went into another place.

And when the day was come, there was not little troubling among the knights what was done of Peter. And when Herod had sought him and found not, after that he had made enquiring of the keepers, he commanded them to be brought to him. And he came down from Judea into Caesarea, and dwelled there. And he was wroth to men of Tyre and of Sidon. And they, of one accord, came to him when they had counselled with Blastus that was the king's chamberlain, they asked peace forasmuch as their countries were victualled of him. And in a day that was ordained, Herod was clothed with king's clothing, and sat for doomsman and spoke to them. And the people cried, The voices of God, and not of man! And anon an angel of the Lord smote him, for he had not given honour to God, and he was wasted of worms and died. And the word of the

Lord waxed, and was multiplied. And Barnabas and Saul turned again from Jerusalem when the ministry was filled, and took John that was named Mark.

Chapter XIII

And prophets and doctors were in the church that was at Antioch, in which Barnabas and Simon, that was called Black, and Lucius Cyrenensis, and Manaen that *sucking fellow, foster* was the sucking-fere of Herod Tetrarch, and Saul were. *brother* And when they ministered to the Lord and fasted, the Holy Ghost said to them, Depart ye to Me Saul and Barnabas into the work to which I have taken them. Then they fasted and prayed and laid hands on them, and let them go.

But they were sent of the Holy Ghost and went forth to Seleucia, and from thence they went by boat to Cyprus. And when they came to Salamis, they preached the word of God in the synagogues of Jews, and they had also John in ministry. And when they had walked by all the isle to Paphos, they found a man, a witch, a false prophet, a Jew, to whom the name was Barjesus, that was with the proconsul Sergius Paulus, a prudent man.

This called Barnabas and Paul, and desired to hear the word of God. But Elymas, witch, withstood them, for his name is expounded so, and he sought to turn away the proconsul from belief. But Saul, which is said also Paul, was filled with the Holy Ghost and beheld into him, and said, Ah, thou full of all guile and all falseness! Thou son of the devil! Thou enemy of all rightwiseness! Thou leaves not to turn upsedown the rightful ways of the Lord. And now lo, the hand of the Lord is on thee, and thou shall be blind, and not seeing the sun into a time. And anon, mist and darknesses fell down on him, and he went about and sought him that should give hand to him. Then the proconsul, when he had seen the deed, believed, wondering on the teaching of the Lord.

And when from Paphos, Paul had gone by boat and they that were with him, they came to Perga in Pamphylia. But John departed from them and turned again to Jerusalem. And they went to Perga and came to Antioch of Pisidia, and they entered into the synagogue in the day of Sabbaths, and sat. And after the reading of the law and of the prophets, the princes of the synagogue sent to them and said, Brethren, if any word of exhortation is in you, say ye.

And Paul rose, and with hand bade silence, and said, Men of Israel, and ye that dread God, hear ye. God of the people of Israel chose our fathers and enhanced the people when they were comelings in the land of Egypt, and in an high arm He led them out of it, and by the time of forty years He suffered their manners in desert. And He destroyed seven folks in the land of Canaan, and by sort departed to them their land as after four hundred and fifty years. And after these things, He gave doomsmen to Samuel the prophet. And from that time, they asked a king, and God gave to them Saul, the son of Kish, a man of the lineage of Benjamin, by forty years.

And when he was done away, He raised to them David king, to whom He bore witnessing and said, I have found David, the son of Jesse, a man after Mine heart, which shall do all My wills. Of whose seed, by the behest, God has led out to Israel a Saviour, Jesus, when John preached before the face of His coming the baptism of penance to all the people of Israel. But when John filled his course, he said, I am not He whom ye deem me to be, but lo, He comes after me, and I am not worthy to do off the shoes of His feet.

Brethren, and sons of the kind of Abraham, and which that in you dread God, to you the word of health is sent. For they that dwelled at Jerusalem, and princes of it, that knew not this Jesus and the voices of prophets that by every Sabbath are read, deemed and filled, and they found in Him no cause of death, and asked of Pilate that they should slay Him. And when they had ended all things that were written of Him, they took Him down off the tree and laid Him in a grave. And God raised Him from death in the third day, which was seen by many days to them that went up together with Him from Galilee into Jerusalem, which are till now His witnesses to the people. And we show to you the behest that was made to our fathers, for God has fulfilled this to their sons, and again-raised Jesus, as in the second Psalm it is written, Thou art My Son. Today I begat Thee!

And He again-raised Him from death, that He should not turn again into corruption, said thus, For I shall give to You the holy true things of David. And therefore, and on another stide, he says, Thou shall not give thine Holy to see corruption. But David, in his generation, when he had ministered to the will of God, died, and was laid with his fathers, and saw corruption. But He whom God raised from death, saw not corruption. Therefore, brethren, be it known to you that by Him remission of sins is told to you, from all sins, of which ye might not be justified in the law of Moses. In this, each man that believes is justified. Therefore see ye that it come not to you that is beforesaid in the prophets, Ye despisers, see ye and wonder ye, and be ye scattered abroad, for I work a work in your days, a work that ye shall not believe if any man shall tell it to you!

And when they went out, they prayed that in the Sabbath suing, they should speak to them these words.

And when the synagogue was left, many of Jews and of comelings worshipping God, sued Paul and Barnabas, that spoke and counselled them that they should dwell in the grace of God.

And in the Sabbath suing, almost all the city came together to hear the word of God. And Jews saw the people and were filled with envy, and againsaid these things that were said of Paul, and blasphemed. Then Paul and Barnabas steadfastly said, To you it behoved first to speak the word of God. But for ye put it away, and have deemed you unworthy to everlasting life, lo, we turn to heathen men. For so the Lord commanded us, I have set Thee into light to heathen men, that Thou be into health to the utmost of earth.

And heathen men heard and joyed, and glorified the word of the Lord, and believed, as many as were before ordained to everlasting life. And the word of the Lord was sown by all the country. But the Jews stirred religious women and honest, and the worthiest men of the city, and stirred persecution against Paul and Barnabas, and drove them out of their countries. And they shook away into them the dust off their feet and came to Iconium. And the disciples were filled with joy and the Holy Ghost.

Chapter XIV

But it befell at Iconium that they entered together into the synagogue of Jews and spoke, so that full great multitude of Jews and Greeks believed. But the Jews that were unbelieveful, raised persecution, and stirred to wrath the souls of heathen men against the brethren. But the Lord gave soon peace. Therefore they dwelled much time, and did trustily in the Lord, bearing witnessing to the word of His grace, giving signs and wonders to be made by the hands of them.

But the multitude of the city was departed, and some were with the Jews and some with the apostles. But when there was made an assault of the heathen men and the Jews with their princes, to torment and stone them, they understood, and fled together to the cities of Lycaonia, and Lystra and Derbe and into all the country about. And they preached there the gospel, and all the multitude was moved together in the teaching of them.

Paul and Barnabas dwelt at Lystra, and a man at Lystra was sick in the feet, and had set crooked from his mother's womb, which never had gone. This heard Paul speaking, and Paul beheld him and saw that he had faith that he should be made safe, and said with a great voice, Rise thou upright on thy feet. And he leaped and walked. And the people, when they had seen that that Paul did, raised their voice in Lycaonian tongue, and said, Gods made like to men are come down to us! And they called Barnabas, Jupiter, and Paul, Mercury, for he was leader of the word. And the priest of Jupiter brought bulls and crowns before the gates with peoples, and would have made sacrifice.

And when the apostles, Barnabas and Paul, heard this, they to-rent their coats, and they skipped out among the people, and cried and said, Men, what do ye this thing? and, We are deadly men like you, and show to you that ye be converted from these vain things to the living God that made heaven and earth and the sea, and all things that are in them, which in generations past suffered all folks to go into their own ways. And yet He left not Himself without witnessing in welldoing, for He gave rains from heaven and times bearing fruit, and fulfilled your hearts with meat and gladness!

assuaged, placated, quietened And they, seeing these things, unneth swaged the people that they offered not to them. But some Jews came over from Antioch and Iconium, and counselled the people, and stoned Paul, and drew out of the city and guessed that he was dead. But when disciples were come about him, he rose and went into the city, and in the day suing he went forth with Barnabas into Derbe.

And when they had preached to the ilk city and taught many, they turned again to Lystra and Iconium, and to Antioch, confirming the souls of disciples and monesting that they should dwell in faith, and said that, By many tribulations it behoves us to enter into the kingdom of heavens.

And when they had ordained priests to them by all cities, and had prayed with fastings, they betook them to the Lord in whom they believed. And they passed Pisidia and came to Pamphylia, and they spoke the word of the Lord in Perga and came down into Italy. And from thence they went by boat to Antioch, from whence they were taken to the grace of God into the work that they filled. And when they were come and had gathered the church, they told how great things God did with them, and that He had opened to heathen men the door of faith. And they dwelled not a little time with the disciples.

Chapter XV

And some came down from Judea and taught brethren that, But ye be circumcised after the law of Moses, ye moun not be made safe! Therefore, when there was made not a little dissension to Paul and Barnabas against them, they ordained that Paul and Barnabas, and some other of them, should go up to the apostles and priests in Jerusalem on this question. And so they were led forth of the church, and passed by Phenice and Samaria, and they told the conversation of heathen men, and they made great joy to all the brethren.

And when they came to Jerusalem, they were received of the church and of the apostles, and of the elder men, and told how great things God did with them. But some, of the heresy of Pharisees that believed, rose up and said that it behoves them to be circumcised and to command to keep also the law of Moses. And the apostles and elder men came together to see of this word. And when there was made a great seeking hereof, Peter rose and said to them, Brethren, ye wit that of old days in you, God chose by my mouth heathen to hear the word of the gospel and to believe, and God, that knew hearts, bore witnessing and gave to them the Holy Ghost as also to us, and nothing diversed betwixt us and them, and cleansed the hearts of them by faith. Now then, what tempt ye God, to put a yoke on the neck of the disciples which neither we, neither our fathers, might bear? But by the grace of our Lord Jesus Christ we believe to be saved, as also they!

And all the multitude held peace, and heard Barnabas and Paul telling how great signs and wonders God did by them in heathen men. And after that they held peace, James answered and said, Brethren, hear ye me. Simon told how God visited, first to take of heathen men a people to His name. And the words of prophets accord to him, as it is written, After this, I shall turn again and build the Tabernacle of David that fell down, and I shall build again the cast down things of it. And I shall raise it, that other men seek the Lord and all folks on which My name is called to help! ⸝ the Lord, doing this thing, says. From the world, the work of the Lord is known to the Lord. For which thing, I deem them that of heathen men are converted to God, to be not diseased, but to write to them that they abstain them from defoul‑ ings of mawmets and from fornication, and strangled things and blood. For Moses of old times has in all cities them that preach him in synagogues whereby each Sabbath he is read.

Then it pleased to the apostles, and to the elder men with all the church, to choose men of them, and send to Antioch with Paul and Barnabas, Judas that was name Barsabas, and Silas, the first men among brethren, and wrote by the hands of them, Apostles and elder breth⁄ ren, to them that are at Antioch and Syria, and Cilicia, brethren of heathen men, greeting. For we heard that some went out from us and troubled you with words, and turned upsedown your souls, to which men we commanded not. It pleased to us, gathered into one, to choose men and send to you, with our most dearworth Barnabas and Paul, men that gave their lives for the name of our Lord Jesus Christ. Therefore we sent Judas and Silas, and they shall tell the same things to you by words. For it is seen to the Holy Ghost and to us to put to you nothing more of charge than these needful things, that ye abstain you from the offered things of mawmets and blood strangled, and fornication. From which ye, keeping you, shall do well. Fare ye well.

Therefore they were let go and came down to Antioch. And when the multitude was gathered, they took the epistle which, when they had read, they joyed on the comfort. And Judas and Silas and they, for they were prophets, comforted brethren and confirmed, with full many words. But after that they had been there a little while, they were let go of brethren with peace, to them that had sent them. But it was seen to Silas to dwell there, and Judas went alone to Jerusalem.

And Paul and Barnabas dwelled at Antioch, teach⁄ ing and preaching the word of the Lord, with other many. But after some days, Paul said to Barnabas, Turn we again and visit brethren by all cities in which we have preached the word of the Lord, how they have them. And Barnabas would take with him John that was named Mark. But Paul prayed him that he that departed from them from Pamphylia, and went not with them into the work, should not be received. And *in two, separated* dissension was made, so that they departed a twinny. And Barnabas took Mark and came by boat to Cyprus. And Paul chose Silas, and went forth from the brethren and was betaken to the grace of God. And he went by Syria and Cilicia, and confirmed the church, commanding to keep the hests of the apostles and elder men.

Chapter XVI

And he came into Derbe and Lystra, and lo, a disciple was there, by name Timothy, the son of a Jewess Christian and of the father heathen. And brethren that were in Lystra and Iconium, yielded good witnessing to him. And Paul would that this man should go forth with him, and he took and circumcised him for Jews that were in the places. For all wist that his father was heathen.

When they passed by cities, they betook to them to keep the teachings that were deemed of apostles and elder men that were at Jerusalem. And the churches were confirmed in faith and increased in number each day. And they passed Phrygia and the country of Galatia, and were forbidden of the Holy Ghost to speak the word of God in Asia. And when they came into Mysia, they assayed to go into Bithynia, and the Spirit of Jesus suffered not them. But when they passed by Mysia, they came down to Troas, and a vision by night was shown to Paul. But a man of Macedonia that stood, prayed him and said, Go thou into Macedonia and help us! And as he had seen the vision, anon we sought to go forth into Macedonia, and were made certain that God had called us to preach to them.

And we went by ship from Troas, and came to Samothracia with straight course, and the day suing to Neapolis, and from thence to Philippi that is the first part of Macedonia, the city colony. And we were in this city some days, and spoke together.

And in the day of Sabbaths, we went forth without the gate beside the flood, where prayer seemed to be. And we sat and spoke to women that came together. And a woman, Lydia by name, a purpless of the city of *female seller of purple dye* Thyatira, worshipping God, heard, whose heart opened to give tent to these things that were said of Paul. And when she was baptized and her house, she prayed and said, If ye have deemed that I am faithful to the Lord, enter ye into mine house and dwell. And she constrained us.

And it was done when we went to prayer, that a damsel that had a spirit of divination, met us, which gave great winning to her lords in divining. This sued Paul and us, and cried and said, These men are servants of the high God that tell you the way of health! And this she did in many days. And Paul sorrowed and said to the spirit, I command thee in the name of Jesus Christ that thou go out of her! And he went out in the same hour. And the lords of her saw that the hope of her winning went away, and they took Paul and Silas, and led into the doom-place to the princes. And they brought *court of law* them to the magistrates and said, These men disturble our city, for they are Jews and show a custom which it is not leaveful to us to receive, neither do, since we are Romans. And the people and magistrates ran against them, and when they had to-rent the coats of them, they commanded them to be beaten with yards. And when they had given to them many wounds, they sent them into prison, and commanded to the keeper that he should keep them diligently.

And when he had taken such a precept, he put them into the inner prison, and strained the feet of them in a tree. And at midnight, Paul and Silas worshipped and heried God, and they that were in keeping, heard them. And suddenly a great earth‚moving was made, so that the fundaments of the prison were moved. And anon, all the doors were opened and the bonds of all were loosed. And the keeper of the prison was awakened and saw the gates of the prison opened, and with a sword drawn out, he would have slew himself, and guessed that the men that were bound had fled. But Paul cried with a great voice and said, Do thou none harm to thy‚ self, for all we are here! And he asked light and entered, and trembled and fell down to Paul and to Silas at their feet.

And he brought them withoutforth, and said, Lords, what behoves me to do that I be made safe? And they said, Believe thou in the Lord Jesus, and thou shall be safe and thine house. And they spoke to him the word of the Lord, with all that were in his house. And he took them in the ilk hour of the night and washed their wounds. And he was baptized and all his house anon. And when he had led them into his house, he set to them a board, and he was glad with all his house, and believed to God.

And when day was come, the magistrates sent catch‚
arresting officers poles and said, Deliver thou those men! And the keeper of the prison told these words to Paul that, The magis‚ trates have sent that ye be delivered. Now therefore, go ye out and go ye in peace. And Paul said to them, They sent us, men of Rome, into prison that were beaten
unconvicted of offence openly and undamned, and now privily they bring us out? Not so, but come they themselves and deliver us out! And the catchpoles told these words to the magis‚ trates, and they dreaded, for they heard that they were

Romans. And they came and beseeched them, and they brought them out and prayed that they should go out of the city. And they went out of the prison and entered into Lydia, and when they saw brethren, they comforted them and went forth.

Chapter XVII

And when they had passed by Amphipolis and Apollonia, they came to Thessalonica where was a synagogue of Jews. And by custom, Paul entered to them, and by three Sabbaths he declared to them of Scriptures, and opened and showed that it behoved Christ to suffer and rise again from death, and that, ... this is Jesus Christ whom I tell to you. And some of them believed and were joined to Paul and to Silas. And a great multitude of heathen men worshipped God, and noble women not a few.

But the Jews had envy and took of the common people some evil men, and when they had made a company, they moved the city. And they came to Jason's house and sought them to bring forth among the people. And when they found them not, they drew Jason and some brethren to the princes of the city, and cried that, These it is that move the world, and hither they came which Jason received. And these all do against the commandments of the emperor and say that Jesus is another king! And they moved the people and the princes of the city, hearing these things.

And when satisfaction was taken of Jason and of other, they let Paul and Silas go. And anon, by night brethren let Silas go into Berea. And when they came thither, they entered into the synagogue of the Jews. But these were the worthier of them that be at Thessalonica, which received the word with all desire, each day seeking Scriptures if these things had them so. And many of them believed, and of heathen women honest and men, not a few.

But when the Jews in Thessalonica had known that also at Berea the word of God was preached of Paul, they came thither, moving and disturbing the multitude. And those anon, brethren delivered Paul that he should go to the sea. But Silas and Timothy dwelt there. And they that led forth Paul, led him to Athens. And when they had taken commandment of him to Silas *hurriedly, quickly* and Timothy, that full hyingly they should come to him, they went forth.

And while Paul abode them at Athens, his spirit was moved in him, for he saw the city given to idolatry. Therefore he disputed in the synagogue with the Jews and with men that worshipped God, and in the doom/place by all days to them that heard. And some Epicureans and Stoics, and philosophers disputed with him. And some said, What will this sower of words say? And other said, He seems to be a teller of new fiends / for he told to them Jesus and the again/rising. And they took and led him to Areopagus and said, Moun we wit what is this new doctrine that is said of thee? For thou brings in some new things to our ears. Therefore we will wit what these things will be. For all men of Athens and comelings harboured, gave tent to none other thing but either to see either to hear some new thing.

And Paul stood in the middle of Areopagus, and said, Men of Athens, by all things I see you as vain wor/shippers. For I passed and saw your mawmets, and found an altar in which was written, To the unknown God. Therefore which thing ye, unknowing, worship this thing I show to you. God, that made the world and all things that are in it, this, for He is Lord of heaven and of earth, dwells not in temples made with hand, neither is worshipped by man's hands, neither has need of anything. For He gives life to all men, and breathing, and all things, and made of one all the kind of men to inhabit on all the face of the earth, determining times ordained and terms of the dwelling of them to seek God, if peradventure they feel Him, either find, though He be not far from each of you. For in Him we live, and move, and are. As also some of your poets said, And we are also the kind of Him. Therefore, since we are the kind of God, we shall not deem that godly thing is like gold and silver, either stone, either to graving of craft and thought of man. For God despises the times of this uncunning, and now shows to men that all everywhere do penance, for He has ordained a day in which He shall deem the world in equity, in a Man in which He ordained and gave faith to all men, and raised Him from death.

And when they had heard the again-rising of dead men, some scorned, and some said, We shall hear thee eft of this thing. So Paul went out of the middle of them. But some drew to him and believed, among which Dionysius Areopagite was, and a woman by name Damaris, and other men with them.

Chapter XVIII

After these things, Paul went out of Athens and came to Corinth. And he found a man, a Jew, Aquila by name, of Pontus by kind, that late came from Italy, and Priscilla his wife, for that Claudius commanded all Jews to depart from Rome. And he came to them. And for he was of the same craft, he dwelled with them and wrought, and they were of ropemakers' craft. And he disputed in the synagogue by each Sabbath, putting among the name of the Lord Jesus. And he counselled Jews and Greeks. And when Silas and Timothy came from Macedonia, Paul gave business to the word, and witnessed to the Jews that Jesus is Christ. But when they againsaid and blasphemed, he shook away his clothes and said to them, Your blood be on your head! I shall be clean from henceforth, and shall go to heathen men!

And he passed from thence, and entered into the house of a just man, Titus by name, that worshipped God. And Crispus, prince of the synagogue, believed to the Lord with all his house. And many of the Corinthians heard and believed, and were christened. And the Lord said by night to Paul, by a vision, Nil thou dread, but speak and be not still. For I am with thee, and no man shall be put to thee to noy thee, for much people is to Me in this city.

And he dwelled there a year and six months, teach-ing among them the word of God. But when Gallio was proconsul of Achaia, Jews rose up with one will against Paul, and led him to the doom, and said, Against the law this counsels men to worship God! And when Paul began to open his mouth, Gallio said to the Jews, If there were any wicked thing, either evil trespass, ye Jews, rightly I should suffer you. But if ques-tions are of the word and of names of your law, busy yourselves! I will not be doomsman of these things! And he drove them from the doom-place. And all took Sosthenes, prince of the synagogue, and smote him before the doom-place, and nothing of these was to charge to Gallio.

And when Paul had abided many days, he said fare-well to brethren, and by boat came to Syria. And Priscilla and Aquila came with him, which had clipped his head in Cenchrea, for he had a vow. And he came to Ephesus, and there he left them, and he went into the synagogue and disputed with Jews. And when

they prayed that he should dwell more time, he consented not, but he made farewell and said, Eft I shall
turn again to you, if God will. And he went forth from
Ephesus. And he came down to Caesarea, and he went
up and greeted the church, and came down to Antioch.
And when he had dwelled there somewhat of time, he
went forth, walking by row through the country of *in due order*
Galatia and Phrygia, and confirmed all the disciples.

But a Jew, Apollo by name, a man of Alexandria of
kind, a man eloquent, came to Ephesus, and he was
mighty in Scriptures. This man was taught the way of
the Lord and was fervent in spirit, and spoke and taught
diligently those things that were of Jesus, and knew only
the baptism of John. And this man began to do trustily
in the synagogue. Whom, when Priscilla and Aquila
heard, they took him and more diligently expounded to
him the way of the Lord. And when he would go to
Achaia, brethren excited, and wrote to the disciples that
they should receive him. Which, when he came, gave
much to them that believed. For he greatly overcame
Jews, and showed openly by Scriptures that Jesus is
Christ.

Chapter XIX

And it befell, when Apollo was at Corinth, that Paul,
when he had go the higher coasts, he came to Ephesus
and found some of disciples. And he said to them,
Whether ye that believe have received the Holy Ghost?
And they said to him, But neither have we heard if the
Holy Ghost is. And he said therefore, In what thing are
ye baptized? And they said, In the baptism of John.
And Paul said, John baptized the people in baptism of
penance, and taught that they should believe in Him
that was to coming after him, that is, in Jesus. When
they heard these things, they were baptized in the name

of the Lord Jesus. And when Paul had laid on them his hands, the Holy Ghost came in them, and they spoke with languages and prophesied. And all were almost twelve men.

And he went into the synagogue and spoke with trust, three months, disputing and treating of the kingdom of God. But when some were hardened and believed not, and cursed the way of the Lord before the multitude, he went away from them and departed the disciples, and disputed in the school of a mighty man each day. This was done by two years, so that all that dwelled in Asia heard the word of the Lord, Jews and heathen men. And God did virtues, not small, by the hand of Paul, so that on sick men the sudaries were borne from his body and sicknesses departed from them, and wicked spirits went out.

But also some of the Jew's exorcists went about and assayed to call the name of the Lord Jesus Christ on them that had evil spirits, and said, I conjure you by Jesus, whom Paul preaches! And there were seven sons of a Jew, Stephen, a prince of priests, that did this thing. But the evil spirit answered and said to them, I know Jesus, and I know Paul. But who are ye? And the man in which was the worst devil, leapt on them and had victory of both, and was strong against them that they, naked and wounded, fled away from that house! And this thing was made known to all the Jews and to heathen men that dwelled at Ephesus, and dread fell down on them all, and they magnified the name of the Lord Jesus.

And many believed and came, acknowledging and telling their deeds. And many of them that sued curious things, brought together books and burned them before all men. And when the prices of those were accounted, they found money of fifty thousand pence! ⁄ so strongly the word of God waxed and was confirmed.

And when these things were filled, Paul purposed in spirit, after that Macedonia was passed and Achaia, to go to Jerusalem, and said, For after that I shall be there, it behoves me to see also Rome. And he sent into Macedonia two men that ministered to him, Timothy and Erastus, and he dwelled for some time in Asia. And a great troubling was made in that day of the way of the Lord, for a man, Demetrius by name, a worker in silver, made silver houses to Diana, and gave to crafty *silver shrines* men much winning. Which he called together, them *craftsmen* that were such manner workmen, and said, Men, ye wit that of this craft, winning is to us. And ye see and hear that this Paul counsels and turns away much people, not only of Ephesus but almost of all Asia, and says that they are not gods that are made with hands. And not only this part shall be in peril to us to come into reproof, but also the temple of the great Diana shall be accounted into nought. Yea, and the majesty of her shall begin to be destroyed, whom all Asia and the world worship!

When these things were heard, they were filled with ire, and cried and said, Great is the Diana of Ephesians! And the city was filled with confusion, and they made an assault with one will into the theatre, and took Gaius and Aristarchus, men of Macedonia, fellows of Paul. And when Paul would have entered into the people, the disciples suffered not. And also, some of the princes of Asia that were his friends, sent to him and prayed that he should not give himself into the theatre. And other men cried other thing, for the church was confused and many wist not for what cause they were come together. But of the people, they drew away one Alexander, while Jews put him forth. And Alexander asked with his hand silence, and would give a reason to the people.

And as they knew that he was a Jew, one voice of all men was made, crying as by two hours, Great Diana of Ephesians! And when the scribe had ceased the people, he said, Men of Ephesus, what man is he that knows not that the city of Ephesians is the worshipper of great Diana and of the child of Jupiter? Therefore, when it may not be againsaid to these things, it behoves you to *foolishly* be ceased and to do nothing follily. For ye have brought these men neither sacriligers, neither blaspheming your goddess. That if Demetrius and the workmen that are with him, have cause against any man, there are courts and dooms and judges. Accuse they each other. If ye *absolved, resolved* seek aught of any other thing, it may be assoiled in the lawful church. For why, we are in peril to be reproved of this day's dissension, since no man is guilty of whom we moun yield reason of this running together! And when he had said this thing, he let the people go.

Chapter XX

And after the noise ceased, Paul called the disciples and monested them, and said farewell. And he went forth to go into Macedonia. And when he had walked by those coasts and had monested them by many words, he came to Greece, where, when he had been three months, the Jews laid aspies for him that was to sail into Syria, and he had counsel to turn again by Macedonia. And Sopater of Pyrrhus Bereansis followed him, of Thessalonica Aristarchus and Secundus, and Gaius Derbeus, and Timothy, and Asians Tychicus and Trophimus. These, for they went before, abode us at Troas, for we shipped after the days of therf loaves from Philippi, and came to them at Troas in five days, where we dwelled seven days.

And in the first day of the week when we came to break bread, Paul disputed with them and should go forth in the morrow, and he drew along the sermon into midnight. And many lamps were in the solar where we were gathered together. And a young man, Eutychus by name, sat on the window. When he was fallen into an heavy sleep while Paul disputed long, all sleeping he fell down from the third stage, and he was taken up and *storey* was brought dead. To whom, when Paul came down, he lay on him and beclipped, and said, Nil ye be troubled, for his soul is in him. And he went up and broke bread, and ate, and spoke enough unto the day. And so he went forth, and they brought the child alive, and they were comforted greatly.

And we went up into a ship and shipped into Assos to take Paul from thence, for so he had disposed to make journey by land. And when he found us in Assos, we took him and came to Mitylene. And from thence we shipped in the day suing, and we came against Chios. And another day we havened at Samos, and in the day suing we came to Miletus. And Paul purposed to ship over to Ephesus, lest any tarrying were made to him in Asia, for he hyed, if it were possible to him, that he should be in the day of Pentecost, at Jerusalem.

From Miletus, he sent to Ephesus and called the greatest men of birth of the church. And when they came to him and were together, he said to them, Ye wit from the first day in which I came into Asia how with you by each time I was, serving to the Lord with all meekness and mildness, and tears and temptations that fell to me of aspyings of Jews. How I withdrew not of profitable things to you that I told not to you, and taught you openly and by houses, and I witnessed to Jews and to heathen men penance into God, and faith into our Lord Jesus Christ. And now, lo, I am bound in spirit and go into Jerusalem. And I know not what things shall come to me in it, but that the Holy Ghost by all cities witnesses to me, and says that bonds and tribulations at Jerusalem abide me. But I dread nothing of these, neither I make my life preciouser than myself, so that I end my course and the ministry of the word, which I received of the Lord Jesus to witness the gospel of the grace of God. And now lo, I wot that ye shall no more see my face all ye by which I passed, preaching the kingdom of God. Wherefore I witness to you this day that I am clean of the blood of all men. For I flee not away, that I told not to you all the counsel of God.

Take ye tent to you, and to all the flock in which the Holy Ghost has set you bishops, to rule the church of God which He purchased with His blood. I wot that after my departing, ravishing wolves shall enter into you and spare not the flock, and men speaking shrewd things shall rise of yourselves, that they lead away disciples after them. For which thing wake ye, holding in mind that by three year, night and day, I ceased not with tears, monesting each of you. And now I betake you to God and to the word of His grace that is mighty to edify and give heritage in all that are made holy. And of no man I coveted silver and gold, either cloth, as yourselves wit, for to those things that were needful to me, and to these that are with me, these hands ministered. All these things I showed to you, for so it behoves men travailing to receive sick men, and to have mind of the word of the Lord Jesus. For He said, It is more blessful to give than to receive.

And when he had said these things, he kneeled and he prayed with all them. And great weeping of all men was made, and they fell on the neck of Paul and kissed him, and sorrowed most in the word that he said, for they shall no more see his face. And they led him to the ship.

Chapter XXI

And when it was done that we should sail, and were passed away from them, with straight course we came to Coos, and the day suing to Rhodes, and from thence to Patara, and from thence to Myra. And when we found a ship passing over to Phenice, we went up into it and sailed forth. And when we appeared to Cyprus, we left it at the left half and sailed into Syria and came to Tyre. For there the ship would be uncharged. *discharged, unloaded*

And when we found disciples, we dwelled there seven days, which said by spirit to Paul that he should not go up to Jerusalem. And when the days were filled, we went forth, and all men with wives and children led forth us without the city, and we kneeled in the sea brink and we prayed. And when we had made farewell together, we went up into the ship, and they turned again into their own places.

And when the ship, sailing, was filled from Tyre, we came down to Ptolemais, and when we had greeted well the brethren, we dwelled one day at them. And another day, we went forth and came to Caesarea, and we entered into the house of Philip Evangelist that was one of the seven, and dwelled at him. And to him were four daughters, virgins, that prophesied. And when we dwelled there by some days, a prophet, Agabus by name, came over from Judea.

This, when he came to us, took the girdle of Paul and bound together his feet and hands, and said, The Holy Ghost says these things, Thus Jews shall bind in Jerusalem the man whose is this girdle, and they shall betake into heathen men's hands. Which thing, when we heard, we prayed and they that were of that place, that he should not go up to Jerusalem. Then Paul answered and said, What do ye, weeping and torment ing mine heart? For I am ready not only to be bound, but also to die in Jerusalem for the name of the Lord Jesus. And when we might not counsel him, we were still, and said, The will of the Lord be done.

And after these days, we were made ready, and went up to Jerusalem. And some of the disciples came with us from Caesarea and led with them a man, Jason of Cyprus, an elder disciple at whom we should be harboured. And when we came to Jerusalem, brethren received us wilfully. And the day suing, Paul entered with us to James, and all the elder men were gathered. Which, when he had greeted, he told by all things what God had done in heathen men by the ministry of him. And when they heard, they magnified God and said to him, Brother, thou see how many thousands are in Jews that have believed to God, and all are lovers of the law. And they heard of thee that thou teaches departing from Moses of the ilk Jews that are by heathen men, that say that they owe not to circumcise their sons, neither owe to enter by custom. Therefore, what is? It behoves that the multitude come together, for they shall hear that thou art come. Therefore do thou this thing that we say to thee. There are to us four men that have a vow on them. Take thou these men and hallow thee with them. Hang on them, that they shave their heads, and that all men wit that the things that they heard of thee, are false, but that thou walks and thyself keeps the law. But of these that believed of heathen men, we write, deeming that they abstain them from things offered to idols and from blood, and also from strangled things and from fornication.

Then Paul took the men and in the day suing he was purified with them and entered into the Temple, and showed the filling of days of purifying, till the offering was offered for each of them. And when seven days were ended, the Jews that were of Asia, when they saw him in the Temple, stirred all the people and laid hands on him, and cried, Men of Israel, help ye us. This is the man that, against the people and the law, and this place, teaches everywhere all men, moreover and has led heathen men into the Temple, and has defouled this holy place! ✓ for they saw Trophimus of Ephesus in the city with him, whom they guessed that Paul had brought into the Temple.

And all the city was moved, and a running together of the people was made. And they took Paul and drew him out of the Temple, and anon the gates were closed. And when they sought to slay him, it was told to the tribune of the company of knights that all Jerusalem is confounded. Which anon took knights and centurions, and ran to them. And when they had seen the tribune and the knights, they ceased to smite Paul. Then the tribune came and caught him, and commanded that he were bound with two chains, and asked who he was and what he had done. But other cried other things among the people, and when he might know no certain thing for the noise, he commanded him to be led into the castles.

And when Paul came to the grees, it befell that he *steps* was borne of knights for strength of the people. For the multitude of the people sued him and cried, Take him away! And when Paul began to be led into the castles, he said to the tribune, Whether it is leaveful to me to speak anything to thee? And he said, Kenst thou Greek? Whether thou art not the Egyptian which before these days moved a noise and led out into desert four thousand men, manslayers? And Paul said to him, For I am a Jew, of Tarsus of Cilicia a citizen, which city is not unknown. And I pray thee, suffer me to speak to the people. And when he suffered, Paul stood in the grees and beckoned with the hand to the people. And when a great silence was made, he spoke in Hebrew tongue and said,

Chapter XXII

Brethren and fathers, hear ye what reason I yield now to you! And when some heard that in Hebrew tongue he spoke to them, they gave the more silence. And he said, I am a man, a Jew, born at Tarsus of Cilicia, nourished and in this city beside the feet of Gamaliel, taught by the truth of fathers' law, a lawyer of the law, as also ye all are today. And I pursued this way till to the death, binding *prisons* and betaking into holds men and women, as the prince of priests yields witnessing to me and all the greatest in birth. Of whom also I took pistles to brethren, and went to Damascus to bring from thence men bound into *punished* Jerusalem that they should be pained. And it was done, while I went and nighed to Damascus, at midday, suddenly from heaven a great plenty of light shone about me. And I fell down to the earth, and heard a voice from heaven saying to me, Saul, Saul, what pursues thou Me? It is hard to thee to kick against the prick. And I answered, Who art Thou, Lord? And He said to me, I am Jesus of Nazareth whom thou pursues.

And they that were with me saw but the light, but they heard not the voice of Him that spoke with me. And I said, Lord, what shall I do? And the Lord said to me, Rise thou and go to Damascus, and there it shall be said to thee of all things which it behoves thee to do. And when I saw not for the clarity of that light, I was led by the hand of fellows, and I came to Damascus. And a man, Ananias, that by the law had witnessing of all Jews dwelling in Damascus, came to me and stood nigh, and said to me, Saul, brother, behold. And I, in the same hour, beheld into him. And he said, God of

our fathers has before ordained thee that thou should
know the will of Him, and should see the Rightful Man
and hear the voice of His mouth. For thou shall be His
witness to all men of those things that thou has seen and
heard. And now, what dwells thou? Rise up and be
baptized, and wash away thy sins by the name Him
called to help.

And it was done to me, as I turned again into
Jerusalem and prayed in the Temple, that I was made in
ravishing of soul, and I saw Him saying to me, Hye
thou, and go out fast of Jerusalem, for they shall not
receive thy witnessing of Me. And I said, Lord, they wit
that I was closing together into prison and beating by
synagogues them that believed into Thee. And when
the blood of Stephen, Thy witness, was shed out, I
stood nigh and consented, and kept the clothes of men
that slew him. And He said to me, Go thou, for I shall
send thee far to nations.

And they heard him till this word. And they raised
their voice and said, Take away from the earth such a
manner man, for it is not leaveful that he live! And
when they cried and cast away their clothes and threw
dust into the air, the tribune commanded him to be led
into castles and to be beaten with scourges, and to be
tormented, that he wist for what cause they cried so to
him. And when they had bound him with cords, Paul
said to a centurion standing nigh to him, Whether it is
leaveful to you to scourge a Roman, and undamned?
And when this thing was heard, the centurion went to
the tribune and told to him, and said, What art thou to
doing? For this man is a citizen of Rome. And the tribune came nigh and said to him, Say thou to me
whether thou art a Roman! And he said, Yea. And the
tribune answered, I with much sum got this freedom.
And Paul said, And I was born a citizen of Rome.

Therefore anon, they that should have tormented him, departed away from him.

And the tribune dreaded after that he wist that he was a citizen of Rome, and for he had bound him. But in the day suing, he would wit more diligently for what cause he was accused of the Jews, and unbound him and commanded priests and all the council to come together. And he brought forth Paul and set him among them.

Chapter XXIII

And Paul beheld into the council and said, Brethren, I with all good conscience have lived before God till into this day. And Ananias, prince of priests, commanded to men that stood nigh him that they should smite his mouth. Then Paul said to him, Thou whited wall, God smite thee! Thou sits and deems me by the law, and against the law thou commands me to be smitten? And they that stood nigh said, Cursest thou the high priest of God? And Paul said, Brethren, I wist not that he is prince of priests, for it is written, Thou shall not curse the prince of thy people.

But Paul wist that one party was of Sadducees and the other of Pharisees, and he cried in the council, Brethren, I am a Pharisee, the son of Pharisees. I am deemed of the hope and of the again-rising of dead men! And when he had said this thing, dissension was made betwixt the Pharisees and the Sadducees, and the multi-tude was departed. For Sadducees say that no rising again of dead men is, neither angel, neither spirit. But Pharisees acknowledge ever either. And some Pharisees rose up and fought, saying, We find nothing of evil in this man! What if a spirit, either an angel, spoke to him? And when great dissension was made, the tribune dreaded lest Paul should be to-drawn of them. And he commanded knights to go down and to take him from the middle of them, and lead him into castles.

And in the night suing, the Lord stood nigh to him, and said, Be thou steadfast, for as thou has witnessed of Me in Jerusalem, so it behoves thee to witness also at Rome. And when the day was come, some of the Jews gathered them and made a vow, and said that they should neither eat nor drink till they slew Paul. And there were more than forty men that made this swearing together. And they went to the princes of priests and elder men, and said, With devotion we have avowed that we shall not taste anything till we slay Paul. Now therefore, make ye known to the tribune with the council that he bring him forth to you as if ye should know something more certainly of him, and we are ready to slay him before that he come.

And when the son of Paul's sister had heard the aspies, he came and entered into the castles and told to Paul. And Paul called to him one of the centurions and said, Lead this young man to the tribune, for he has something to show to him. And he took him and led to the tribune, and said, Paul, that is bound, prayed me to lead to thee this young man that has something to speak to thee. And the tribune took his hand and went with him asides half, and asked him, What thing is it that thou has to show me? And he said, The Jews are accorded to pray thee that tomorrow thou bring forth Paul into the council, as if they should enquire something more certainly of him. But believe thou not to them, for more than forty men of them aspied him which have avowed that they shall not eat neither drink till they slay him. And now they are ready, abiding thy behest.

Therefore the tribune left the young man, and commanded that he should speak to no man that he had made these things known to him. And he called together two centurions, and he said to them, Make ye ready two hundred knights that they go to Caesarea, *mounted soldiers* and horsemen seventy, and spearmen two hundred *lancers* from the third hour of the night. And make ye ready an horse for Paul to ride on, to lead him safe to Felix, the president. For the tribune dreaded lest the Jews would take him by the way and slay him, and afterward he might be challenged as he had taken money, and wrote him a pistle containing these things: Claudius Lysias, to the best Felix, president, greeting! This man that was taken of the Jews and began to be slain, I came upon them with mine host and delivered him from them when I knew that he was a Roman. And I would wit the cause which they put against him, and I led him to the council of them. And I found that he was accused of questions of their law, but he had no crime worthy the death either bonds. And when it was told me of the aspies that they arrayed for him, I sent him to thee, and I warned also the accusers that they say at thee. Farewell.

And so the knights, as they were commanded, took Paul and led him by night into Antipatris. And in the day suing, when the horsemen were left that should go with him, they turned again to the castles. And when they came to Caesarea, they took the pistle to the president, and they set also Paul before him. And when he had read and asked of what province he was, and knew that he was of Cilicia, I shall hear thee, he said, when thine accusers come. And he commanded him to be kept in the moot hall of Herod.

Chapter XXIV

And after five days, Ananias, prince of priests, came down with some elder men, and Tertullus, a fair speaker, which went to the president against Paul. And when Paul was summoned, Tertullus began to accuse him, and said, When in much peace we do by thee, and many things are amended by thy wisdom, evermore and everywhere, thou best Felix, we have received with all doing of thankings. But lest I tarry thee longer, I pray thee, shortly hear us for thy meekness. We have found this wicked man stirring dissension to all Jews in the world, and author of dissension of the sect of Nazarenus. And he also enforced to defoul the Temple, whom also we took and would deem after our law. But Lysias, the tribune, came with great strength above, and delivered him from our hands, and commanded his accusers to come to thee, of whom thou, deeming, may know of all these things of which we accuse him. And Jews put to and said that these things had them so.

And Paul answered, when the president granted him to say, Of many years I know thee, that thou art doomsman to this folk, and I shall do enough for me with good reason. For thou may know, for to me are not more than twelve days since I came up to worship in Jerusalem. And neither in the Temple they found me disputing with any man, neither making concourse of people, neither in synagogues, neither in city. Neither they moun prove to thee of the which things they now accuse me. But I acknowledge to thee this thing, that after the sect which they say heresy, so I serve to God the Father. And I believe to all things that are written in the law and prophets, and I have hope in God which also they themselves abide, the again-rising to coming of just men and wicked. In this thing I study without hurting, to have conscience to God and to men evermore. But after many years, I came to do almsdeeds to my folk, and offerings and avows, in which they found me puri-fied in the Temple, not with company, neither with noise. And they caught me, and they cried and said,

Take away our enemy! And some Jews of Asia, which it behoved to be now present at thee and accuse, if they had anything against me, either these themselves say if they found in me anything of wickedness since I stood in the council but only of this voice by which I cried, standing among them, For of the again-rising of dead men I am deemed this day of you!

Soothly, Felix delayed them and knew most certainly of the Way, and said, When Lysias, the tribune, shall come down, I shall hear you. And he commanded to a centurion to keep him and that he had rest, neither to forbid any man to minister of his own things to him. And after some days, Felix came, with Drusilla, his wife that was a Jewess, and called Paul, and heard of him the faith that is in Christ Jesus. And while he disputed of rightwiseness and chastity, and of doom to coming, Felix was made trembling and answered, That pertains now. Go. But in time covenable I shall call thee. Also he hoped that money should be given to him of Paul, for which thing eft he called him and spoke with him. And when two years were filled, Felix took a successor, Porcius Festus, and Felix would give grace to Jews and left Paul bound.

Chapter XXV

Therefore, when Festus came into the province, after the third day he went up to Jerusalem from Caesarea. And the princes of priests and the worthiest of the Jews went to him against Paul and prayed him, and asked grace against him that he should command him to be led to Jerusalem. And they set aspies to slay him in the way. But Festus answered that Paul should be kept in Caesarea, soothly that he himself should proceed more *cautiously, with prudence* advisedly. Therefore he said, They that in you are mighty, come down together, and if any crime is in the man, accuse they him. And he dwelled among them no more than eight either ten days, and came down to Caesarea. And the t'other day he sat for doomsman and commanded Paul to be brought.

And when he was brought forth, Jews stood about him which came down from Jerusalem, putting against him many and grievous causes which they might not prove. For Paul yielded reason in all things. That neither against the law of Jews, neither against the Temple, neither against the emperor I sinned anything. But Festus would do grace to the Jews, and answered to Paul and said, Will thou go up to Jerusalem and there be deemed of these things before me? And Paul said, At the doom-place of the emperor I stand, where it behoves me to be deemed. I have not noyed the Jews, as thou knows well. For if I have noyed, either done any-thing worthy death, I forsake not to die. But if nothing of those is that they accuse me, no man may give me to them. I appeal to the emperor! Then Festus spoke with the council and answered, To the emperor thou has appealed. To the emperor thou shall go.

And when some days were passed, Agrippa, king, and Berenice, came down to Caesarea to welcome Festus. And when they dwelled there many days, Festus showed to the king of Paul, and said, A man is left bound of Felix of which, when I was at Jerusalem, princes of priests and the elder men of Jews came to me, and asked damnation against him. To which I answered that it is not custom to Romans to damn any man before that he that is accused have his accusers pre-sent and take place of defending, to put away the crimes that be put against him. Therefore, when they came together hither, without delay in the day suing I sat for doomsman, and commanded the man to be brought. And when his accusers stood, they said no cause ⁄ of which things I had suspicion of evil. But they had against him some questions of their vain worshipping, and of one Jesus, dead, whom Paul affirmed to live. And I doubted of such manner question, and said whether he would go to Jerusalem and there be deemed of these things. But for Paul appealed that he should be kept to the knowing of the emperor, I commanded him to be kept till I send him to the emperor. And Agrippa said to Festus, I myself would hear the man. And he said, Tomorrow thou shall hear him.

And on the t'other day, when Agrippa and Berenice came with great desire and entered into the auditory with tribunes and the principal men of the city, when Festus bade, Paul was brought. And Festus said, King Agrippa, and all men that are with us, ye see this man of which all the multitude of Jews prayed me at Jerusalem, and asked and cried that he should live no longer. But I found that he had done nothing worthy of death, and I deem to send him to the emperor, for he appealed this thing. Of which man I have not certain what thing I shall write to the lord. For which thing I have brought him to you, and most to thee, thou king Agrippa, that when asking is made, I have what I shall write. For it is seen to me without reason to send a bound man and not to signify the cause of him.

Chapter XXVI

And Agrippa said to Paul, It is suffered to thee to speak for thyself. Then Paul held forth the hand and began to yield reason. Of all things in which I am accused of the Jews, thou king Agrippa, I guess me blessed at thee when I shall defend me this day, most for thou knows all things that are among Jews, customs and questions. For which thing, I beseech, hear me patiently. For all Jews that before knew me from the beginning, knew my life from yongth, that from the beginning was my folk in Jerusalem, if they will bear witnessing, that by the most certain sect of our religion, I lived a Pharisee. And now for the hope of repromission that is made to our fathers of God, I stand subject in doom, in which hope our twelve lineages, serving night and day, hope to come ⁄ of which hope, sir king, I am accused of the Jews!

What unbelieveful thing is deemed at you, if God raises dead men? And soothly I guessed that I ought do many contrary things against the name of Jesus Nazarene. Which thing also I did in Jerusalem, and I enclosed many of the saints in prison when I had taken power of the princes of priests. And when they were slain, I brought the sentence. And by all synagogues often I punished them, and constrained to blaspheme, and more I wax wood against them, and pursued into alien cities. In which, the while I went to Damascus with power and suffering of princes of priests, at midday in the way, I saw, sir king, that from heaven light shined about me, passing the shining of the sun, and about them that were together with me. And when we all had fallen down into the earth, I heard a voice saying to me in Hebrew tongue, Saul, Saul, what pursues thou Me? It is hard to thee to kick against the prick. And I said, Who art Thou, Lord? And the Lord said, I am Jesus whom thou pursues. But rise up and stand on thy feet. For why, to this thing I appeared to thee, that I ordain thee minister and witness of those things that thou has seen, and of those in which I shall show to thee. And I shall deliver thee from peoples and folks to which now I send thee, to open the eyes of them, that they are con⁄ verted from darknesses to light and from power of Satan to God, that they take remission of sins and part among saints, by faith that is in Me.

Wherefore, sir king Agrippa, I was not unbelieveful

to the heavenly vision, but I told to them that were at Damascus first, and at Jerusalem, and by all the country of Judea and to heathen men, that they should do penance and be converted to God, and do works worthy of penance. For this cause, Jews took me when I was in the Temple, to slay me. But I was helped by the help of God into this day, and stand, witnessing to less and to more. And I say nothing else than which things the prophets and Moses spoke that shall come if Christ is to suffer, if He is the first of the again-rising of dead men, that shall show light to the people and to heathen men!

When he spoke these things and yielded reason. Festus said with great voice, Paul, thou maddest! Many letters turn thee to woodness! And Paul said, I mad not, thou best Festus, but I speak out the words of truth and of soberness. For also the king, to whom I speak steadfastly, wot of these things. For I deem that nothing of these is hid from him, for neither in a corner was aught of these things done. Believe thou, king Agrippa, to prophets? I wot that thou believe.

And Agrippa said to Paul, In little thing thou counsels me to be made a Christian man. And Paul said, I desire anents God, both in little and in great, not only thee, but all these that hear today to be made such as I am - out-taken these bonds!

And the king rose up, and the president and Berenice and they that sat nigh to them. And when they went away, they spoke together and said that, This man has not done anything worthy death, neither bonds. And Agrippa said to Festus, This man might be delivered if he had not appealed to the emperor.

Chapter XXVII

But as it was deemed him to ship into Italy, they betook Paul with other keepers to a centurion, by name Julius, of the company of knights of the emperor. And we went up into the ship of Adramyttium and began to sail, and were borne about the places of Asia, while Aristarchus of Macedonia, Thessalonikan, dwelled still with us. And in the day suing, we came to Sidon. And Julius treated courteously Paul, and suffered to go to friends and do his needs.

And when we removed from thence, we undersailed *sailed beneath or close to* to Cyprus, for that winds were contrary. And we sailed into the sea of Cilicia and Pamphylia, and came to Lystra, that is Lycia. And there, the centurion found a ship of Alexandria sailing into Italy, and put us over into it. And when, in many days, we sailed slowly and unneth came against Cnidus, for the wind letted us, we sailed to Crete beside Salmone. And unneth we sailed beside, and came into a place that is called of Good Haven, to whom the city Lasea was nigh.

And when much time was passed, and when sailing then was not secure, for that fasting was passed Paul comforted them, and said to them, Men, I see that sailing begins to be wrong and much harm, not only of charge and of the ship, but also of our lives. But the centurion believed more to the governor and to the lord of the ship than to these things that were said of Paul. And when the haven was not able to dwell in winter, full many ordained counsel to sail from thence, if on any manner they might come to Phenice to dwell in winter at the haven of Crete, which beholds to Africa and to Corum. And when the south blew, they guessed them to hold purpose, and when they had removed from Assos, they sailed to Crete.

And not after much, the wind Typhonicus that is called North East, was against it. And when the ship was ravished, and might not enforce against the wind, when the ship was given to the blowings of the wind,

we were borne with course into an isle that is called
Clauda, and unneth we might get a little boat. And
when this was taken up, they used helps, girding
together the ship, and dreaded lest they should fall into
quicksands   sandy places. And when the vessel was underset, so
they were borne. And for we were thrown with strong
tempest, in the day suing they made casting out. And
the third day, with their hands, they cast away the instru⁄
accoutrements, ship's   ments of the ship. And when the sun, neither the stars,
tackle   were seen by many days, and tempest not a little nighed,
now all the hope of our health was done away.

And when much fasting had been, Paul stood in the
middle of them and said, Ah, men! It behoved when ye
heard me, not to have taken away the ship from Crete
and get this wrong and casting out. And now I counsel
you to be of good comfort, for loss of no person of you
shall be, out⁄taken of the ship. For an angel of God,
whose I am and to whom I serve, stood nigh to me in
this night and said, Paul, dread thou not. It behoves
thee to stand before the emperor. And lo, God has given
to thee all that are in the ship with thee. For which thing,
ye men, be ye of good comfort, for I believe to my God
that so it shall be as it is said to me, and it behoves us to
come into some isle!

But afterward, that in the fourteenth day the night
the Adriatic   came on us sailing in the Stony Sea, about midnight the
shipmen supposed some country to appear to them.
plumb line   And they cast down a plummet and found twenty paces
of deepness. And after a little, they were departed from
thence and found fifteen paces. And they dreaded lest
we should have fallen into sharp places, and from the
last part of the ship they sent four anchors, and desired
that the day had been come. And when the shipmen
sought to flee from the ship, when they had sent a little
boat into the sea under colour as they should begin to

stretch forth the anchors from the former part of the ship, Paul said to the centurion and to the knights, But these dwell in the ship, ye moun not be made safe! Then knights cut away the cords of the little boat and suffered it to fall away.

And when the day was come, Paul prayed all men to take meat, and said, The fourteenth day, this day, ye abide and dwell fasting, and take nothing. Wherefore I pray you to take meat for your health, for of none of you the hair of the head shall perish. And when he had said these things, Paul took bread and did thankings to God in the sight of all men. And when he had broken, he began to eat. And all were made of better comfort, and they took meat. And we were all men in the ship two hundred, seventy and six. And they were filled with meat and discharged the ship, and cast wheat into the sea.

And when the day was come, they knew no land, and they beheld a haven that had a water bank into which they thought, if they might, to bring up the ship. And when they had taken up the anchors, they betook them to the sea and shook together the jointures of the governals. And with a little sail lift up, by blowing of the wind they went to the bank. And when we fell into a place of gravel gone all about with the sea, they hurtled the ship. And when the former part was fitched, it dwelled unmoveable and the last part was broken of strength of the sea.

And counsel of the knights was to slay men that were in ward, lest any should escape when he had swum out. But the centurion would keep Paul and forbad it to be done. And he commanded them that might swim, to go into the sea and escape, and go out to the land. And they bore some other on boards, some on those things that were of the ship. And so it was done that all men escaped to the land.

Chapter XXVIII

And when we had escaped, then we knew that the isle was called Melita. And the heathen men did to us not little courtesy. And when a fire was kindled, they refreshed us all for the rain that came and the cold. But when Paul had gathered a quantity of cuttings of vines and laid on the fire, an adder she came forth from the heat and took him by the hand. And when the heathen men of the isle saw the beast hanging in his hand, they said together, For this man is a manqueller, and when he escaped from the sea, God's vengeance suffers him not to live in earth! But he shook away the beast into the fire and had none harm. And they guessed that he should be turned into swelling and fall down suddenly and die. But when they abided long, and saw that nothing of evil was done in him, they turned them together and said that he was God.

And in those places were manors of the prince of the isle, Publius by name, which received us by three days benignly and found us. And it befell that the father of Publius lay travailed with fevers and bloody flux. To whom Paul entered, and when he had prayed and laid his hands on him, he healed him. And when this thing was done, all that in the isle had sicknesses, came and were healed. Which also honoured us in many worships, and put what things were necessary to us when we shipped.

And after three months, we shipped in a ship of Alexandria that had wintered in the isle, to which was an excellent sign of Castors. And when we came to Syracuse, we dwelled there three days. From thence we sailed about and came to Rhegium, and after one day while the south wind blew, in the second day we came to Puteoli, where, when we found brethren, we were prayed to dwell there anents them seven days. And so we came to Rome.

And from thence, when brethren had heard, they came to us to the cheaping of Appius, and to the Three Taverns. And when Paul had seen them, he did thankings to God and took trust. And when we came to Rome, it was suffered to Paul to dwell by himself with a knight keeping him.

And after the third day, he called together the worthiest of the Jews. And when they came, he said to them, Brethren, I did nothing against the people either custom of fathers, and I was bound at Jerusalem and was betaken to the hands of Romans. And when they had asked of me, would have delivered me, for that no cause of death was in me. But for Jews againsaid, I was constrained to appeal to the emperor, not as having anything to accuse my people. Therefore for this cause I prayed to see you and speak to you, for for the hope of Israel I am gird about with this chain.

And they said to him, Neither we have received letters of thee from Judea, neither any of brethren coming showed either spoke any evil thing of thee. But we pray to hear of thee what things thou feels, for of this sect it is known to us that everywhere men againsay it. And when they had ordained a day to him, many men came to him into the inn. To which he expounded, witnessing the kingdom of God, and counselled them of Jesus, of the law of Moses and prophets from the morrow till to eventide.

And some believed to these things that were said of Paul, some believed not. And when they were not consenting together, they departed. And Paul said one word, For the Holy Ghost spoke well by Isaiah the prophet to our fathers, and said, Go thou to this people and say to them, With ear ye shall hear, and ye shall not understand. And ye, seeing, shall see, and ye shall not behold. For the heart of this people is greatly fatted, and with ears they heard heavily, and they closed together their eyes, lest peradventure they see with eyes and with ears hear, and by heart understand and be converted, and I heal them. Therefore, be it known to you that this health of God is sent to heathen men, and they shall hear!

And when he had said these things, Jews went out from him and had much question among themselves. And he dwelled full two year in his hired place, and he received all that entered to him and preached the kingdom of God, and taught those things that are of the Lord Jesus Christ with all trust, without forbidding. Amen.

Here begins the Prologue of the pistles of Christian faith that are seven in order

The order of the seven epistles which are called canonised, is not so among the Greeks that fully save the faith and sue the right order of the epistles as it is found in Latin books. For forasmuch as Peter is the first in the order of the apostles, his epistles are the first of them in order. But as we not long since corrected the evangelists to the life of truth, so we have set these through the help of God in their own order, for the first of them is an epistle of James, two of Peter's, three of John's, and one of Jude. The which epistles, if they had been truly turned of the translators into Latin speech, as they were made of the apostles, they should have made no doubt to the readers, ne the variance of words should not have impugned itself, namely in that place in the first epistle of John where we read of the onehood of the Trinity, where we find that there has been great error of untrue translators from the truth of the faith. While they set in their translations only the names of three things, that is of water, of blood and of the spirit, and leaves the witnessing of the Father and of the Son, and of the Spirit, in which witnessing our common belief is most strengthed, and it is proven that there is one substance of the Father and of the Son, and of the Holy Spirit. But other epistles, how much our transla-tion diverses from others, I leave to the prudence of the readers. But thou, while thou enquires busily of me the truth of scripture, thou puts out mine eld to be gnawed of envious men's teeth, which say that I am an apairer of holy scriptures. But I, in such a work, dread not the envy of mine enemies, ne I shall not deny to them that ask the truth of holy scripture. Jerome on this epistle, says all this.

Here begins the epistle of James

Chapter I

James, the servant of God and of our Lord Jesus Christ, to the twelve kindreds that are in scattering abroad, health!

My brethren, deem ye all joy when ye fall into diverse temptations, witting that the proving of your faith works patience. And patience has a parfit work, that ye be parfit and whole and fail in nothing. And if any of you need wisdom, ask he of God which gives to all men largely and upbraids not, and it shall be given to him. But ask he in faith and doubt nothing, for he that doubts is like to a wave of the sea, which is moved and borne about of wind. Therefore guess not the ilk man that he shall take anything of the Lord. A man, double in soul, is unstable in all his ways.

And a meek brother have glory in his enhancing, and a rich man in his lowness, for as the flower of grass he shall pass. The sun rose up with heat and dried the grass, and the flower of it fell down and the fairness of his cheer perished. And so a rich man wallows in his ways.

Blessed is the man that suffers temptation, for when he shall be proved he shall receive the crown of life which God behight to men that love Him. No man when he is tempted, say that he is tempted of God, for why, God is not a tempter of evil things, for He tempts no man. But each man is tempted, drawn and stirred of his own coveting. Afterward coveting, when it has conceived, brings forth sin. But sin, when it is filled, genders death. Therefore, my most dearworth brethren, nil ye err. Each good gift and each parfit gift is from above, and comes down from the Father of lights, anents whom is none other changing ne overshadowing of reward. For wilfully He begat us by the word of truth, that we be a beginning of His creature.

Wit ye, my brethren most loved, be each man swift to hear, be slow to speak, and slow to wrath. For the wrath of man works not the rightwiseness of God. For which thing, cast ye away all uncleanness and plenty of malice, and in mildness receive ye the word that is planted, that may save your souls. But be ye doers of the word and not hearers only, deceiving yourselves. For if any man is an hearer of the word and not a doer, this shall be likened to a man that beholds the cheer of his birth in a mirror. For he beheld himself and went away, and anon he forgot which he was.

But he that beholds in the law of parfit freedom, and dwells in it, and is not made a forgetful hearer but a doer of work, this shall be blessed in his deed. And if any man guesses himself to be religious and refrains not his tongue, but deceives his heart, the religion of him is vain. A clean religion and an unwemmed anents God and the Father is this, to visit fatherless and motherless children, and widows in their tribulation, and to keep himself undefouled from this world.

Chapter II

My brethren, nil ye have the faith of our Lord Jesus Christ of glory, in acception of persons. For if a man that has a golden ring and in a fair clothing, comes into your company, and a poor man enters in a foul clothing, and if ye are beholden into him that is clothed with clear clothing, and if ye say to him, Sit thou here well, but to the poor man ye say, Stand thou there, either sit under the stool of my feet, whether ye deem not anents yourselves and are made doomsmen of wicked thoughts? Hear ye, my most dearworth brethren, whether God chose not poor men in this world, rich in faith and heirs of the kingdom that God behight to men that love Him? Whether rich men oppress not you by power, and they draw you to dooms? Whether they blaspheme not the good name that is called to help on you? Netheless, if ye perform the King's law by Scriptures, Thou shall love thy neighbour as thyself, ye do well. But if ye take persons, ye work sin and are reproved of the law as trespassers.

And whoever keeps all the law but offends in one, he is made guilty of all. For He said, Thou shall do no lechery, said also, Thou shall not slay. That if thou do not lechery, but thou slays, thou art made trespasser of the law. Thus speak ye, and thus do ye, as beginning to be deemed by the law of freedom. For why, doom without mercy is to him that does no mercy. But mercy above raises doom.

My brethren, what shall it profit if any man say that he has faith, but he has not the works? Whether faith shall mow save him? And if a brother either sister be naked, and have need of each day's livelihood, and if any of you said to them, Go ye in peace, be ye made hot and be ye filled, but if ye give not to them those things that are necessary to body, what shall it profit? So also faith, if it has not works, is dead in itself. But some shall say, Thou has faith and I have works. Show thou to me thy faith without works, and I shall show to thee my faith of works.

Thou believe that one God is? Thou does well. And devils believe and tremble. But will thou wit man, vain man, that faith without works is idle? Whether Abraham our father was not justified of works, offering Isaac his son on the altar? Therefore thou see that faith wrought with his works, and his faith was filled of works. And the Scripture was filled, saying, Abraham believed to God and it was aretted to him to rightwise, ness, and he was called the friend of God. Ye see that a man is justified of works and not of faith only. In like manner and whether also, Rahab the whore was not justified of works and received the messengers and sent them out by another way? For as the body without spirit is dead, so also faith without works is dead.

Chapter III

My brethren, nil ye be made many masters, witting that ye take the more doom. For all we offend in many things. If any man offends not in word, this is a parfit man, for also he may lead about all the body with a bri, dle. For if we put bridles into horses' mouths for to con, sent to us, and we lead about all the body of them. And lo, ships, when they are great and are driven of strong winds, yet they are borne about of a little governal where the moving of the governor will. So also the tongue is but a little member and raises great things. Lo, how little fire burns a full great wood. And our tongue is fire, the university of wickedness.

The tongue is ordained in our members which defouls all the body, and it is enflamed of hell, and enflames the wheel of our birth. And all the kind of beasts and of fowls and of serpents and of other, is chastised, and those are made tame of man's kind. But no man may chastise the tongue, for it is an unpeaceable evil and full of deadly venom. In it we bless God the Father, and in it we curse men that are made to the likeness of God. Of the same mouth passes forth blessing and cursing. My brethren, it behoves not that these things are done so. Whether a well of the same hole brings forth sweet and salt water? My brethren, whether a fig tree may make grapes, either a vine figs? So neither salt water may make sweet water.

Who is wise and taught among you? Show he of good living his working, in mildness of his wisdom. That if ye have bitter envy, and strivings are in your hearts, nil ye have glory and be liars against the truth. For this wisdom is not from above coming down, but earthly and beastly, and fiendly. For where is envy and strife, there is unsteadfastness and all shrewd work. But wisdom that is from above, first it is chaste, afterward peaceable, mild, able to be counselled, consenting to good things, full of mercy and good fruits, deeming without feigning. And the fruit of rightwiseness is sown in peace to men that make peace.

Chapter IV

Wherefore be battles and cheests among you? Whether *chidings, strifes* not of your covetises that fight in your members? Ye covet and ye have not. Ye slay and ye have envy, and ye moun not get. Ye chide and make battle and ye have not, for ye ask not. Ye ask and ye receive not, for that ye ask evil, as ye show openly in your covetises. Advowtrers, wit not ye that the friendship of this world is enemy to God? Therefore, whoever will be friend of this world, is made the enemy of God.

Whether ye guess that the Scripture says vainly, The spirit that dwells in you covets to envy? But He gives the more grace, for which thing He says, God withstands proud men, but to meek men He gives grace. Therefore, be ye subject to God, but withstand ye the devil and he shall flee from you. Nigh ye to God, and He shall nigh to you.

Ye sinners, cleanse ye hands. And ye double in soul, purge ye the hearts. Be ye wretches and wail ye, your laughing turned into weeping and joy into sorrow of heart. Be ye meeked in the sight of the Lord, and He shall enhance you. My brethren, nil ye backbite each other. He that backbites his brother, either that deems his brother, backbites the law and deems the law. And if thou deems the law, thou art not a doer of the law, but a doomsman. But One is maker of the law and Judge, that may loose and deliver.

And who art thou that deems thy neighbour? Lo now, ye that say, Today either tomorrow we shall go into the ilk city and there we shall dwell a year, and we shall make merchandise and we shall make winning, which wit not what is to you in the morrow. For what is your life? A smoke appearing at a little, and afterward it shall be wasted. Therefore that ye say, If the Lord will, and if we live, we shall do this thing either that thing. And now ye make full out joy in your prides. Every such joy is wicked. Therefore it is sin to him that can do good, and does not.

Chapter V

Do now, ye rich men. Weep ye, yelling in your wretchednesses that shall come upon you. Your richesses are rotten and your clothes are eaten of moths. Your gold and silver has rusted, and the rust of them shall be to you into witnessing and shall eat your fleshes as fire. Ye have treasured to you wrath in the last days. Lo, the hire of your workmen that reaped your fields, which is frauded of you, cries, and the cry of them has entered into the ears of the Lord of Hosts. Ye have eaten on the earth, and in your lecheries ye have nourished your hearts. In the day of slaying ye brought and slew the just man, and he againststood not you.

Therefore, brethren, be ye patient till to the coming of the Lord. Lo, an earth-tiller abides precious fruit of the earth, patiently suffering till he receive timeful and lateful fruit. And be ye patient, and confirm ye your hearts, for the coming of the Lord shall nigh.

Brethren, nil ye be sorrowful each to other, that ye be not deemed. Lo, the Judge stands nigh before the gate.

Brethren, take ye ensample of evil going out, and of long abiding, and travail, and of patience, the prophets that speak to you in the name of the Lord. Lo, we bless them that suffered. Ye heard the suffering either patience of Job, and ye saw the end of the Lord, for the Lord is merciful and doing mercy.

Before all things, my brethren, nil ye swear, neither by heaven, neither by earth, neither by whatever other oath. But be your word, Yea, yea, Nay, nay, that ye fall not under doom. And if any of you is sorrowful, pray he with patient soul and say he a psalm.

If any of you is sick, lead he in priests of the church and pray they for him, and anoint with oil in the name of the Lord, and the prayer of faith shall save the sick man, and the Lord shall make him light. And if he be in sins, they shall be forgiven to him. Therefore, acknowledge ye each to other your sins, and pray ye each for other that ye be saved. For the continual prayer of a just man is much worth.

Elijah was a deadly man like us, and in prayer he prayed that it should not rain on the earth, and it rained

not three years and six months. And eftsoon he prayed,
and heaven gave rain and the earth gave his fruit. And,
brethren, if any of you errs from truth, and any converts
him, he owes to wit that he that makes a sinner to be
turned from the error of his way, shall save the soul of
him from death, and covers the multitude of sins.

Here begins the first of Peter

Chapter I

Peter, apostle of Jesus Christ, to the chosen men, to the
comelings of scattering abroad, of Pontus, of Galatia, of
Cappadocia, of Asia, and of Bithynia, by the before-
knowing of God the Father, in hallowing of Spirit by
obedience, and springing of the blood of Jesus Christ,
grace and peace be multiplied to you.

Blessed be God and the Father of our Lord Jesus
Christ, which by His great mercy begat us again into
living hope by the again-rising of Jesus Christ from
death into heritage uncorruptible and undefouled, and
that shall not fade, that is kept in heavens for you that in
the virtue of God are kept by the faith into health, and is
ready to be shown in the last time. In which ye shall
make joy, though it behoves now a little to be sorry in
diverse temptations, that the proving of your faith be
much more precious than gold that is proved by fire,
and be found into herying and glory and honour in the
revelation of Jesus Christ, whom, when ye have not
seen, ye love. Into whom also now ye not seeing, believe.

But ye that believe shall have joy and gladness that
may not be told out, and ye shall be glorified and have
the end of your faith, the health of your souls. Of which
health prophets sought and ensearched, that prophesied
of the grace to coming in you, and sought whichever

what manner time the Spirit of Christ signified in them, and before told those passions that are in Christ and the later glories. To which it was shown not to themselves, but to you they ministered those things that now are told to you by them that preached to you by the Holy Ghost sent from heaven, into whom angels desire to behold.

For which thing be ye gird the loins of your soul, sober, parfit, and hope ye in the ilk grace that is proffered to you by the showing of Jesus Christ, as sons of obedience, not made like to the former desires of your uncunningness, but like Him that has called you holy, that also yourselves be holy in all living. For it is written, Ye shall be holy, for I am holy. And if ye inwardly call Him Father, which deems without acception of persons by the work of each man, live ye in dread in the time of your pilgrimage, witting that not by corruptible gold either silver ye are bought again of your vain living of fathers' traditions, but by the precious blood as of the Lamb, undefouled and unspotted, Christ Jesus, that was known before the making of the world. But He is shown in the last times for you that by Him are faithful in God, that raised Him from death and gave to Him everlasting glory, that your faith and hope were in God.

And make ye chaste your souls in obedience of charity, in love of brotherhood. Of simple heart, love ye together more busily. And be ye born again, not of corruptible seed, but uncorruptible, by the word of living God, and dwelling into without end. For each flesh is hay and all the glory of it is as flower of hay. The hay dried up, and his flower fell down, but the word of the Lord dwells without end. And this is the word that is preached to you.

Chapter II

Therefore put ye away all malice and all guile, and feign-

ings and envies, and all backbitings. As newborn
young children, without guile, covet ye milk, that in it
ye wax into health, if netheless ye have tasted that the
Lord is sweet. And nigh ye to Him that is a living stone
and reproved of men ⸌ but chosen of God and honoured
⸌ and yourselves as quick stones be ye above built into
spiritual houses and an holy priesthood, to offer spiri⸌
tual sacrifices acceptable to God by Jesus Christ. For
which thing the Scripture says, Lo, I shall set in Zion
the highest corner stone, chosen and precious, and he
that shall believe in Him shall not be confounded.
Therefore honour to you that believe, but to men that
believe not, the stone whom the builders reproved, this
is made into the head of the corner, and the stone of hurt⸌
ing and stone of sclaunder to them that offend to the
word neither believe it, in which they be set.

But ye are a chosen kin, a kingly priesthood, holy
folk, a people of purchasing, that ye tell the virtues of
Him that called you from darknesses into His wonder⸌
ful light, which sometime were not a people of God.
But now ye are the people of God, which had not mercy,
but now ye have mercy.

Most dear, I beseech you as comelings and pilgrims,
to abstain you from fleshly desires that fight against the
soul. And have ye your conversation good among
heathen men, that in that thing that they backbite of you,
as of misdoers, they behold you of good works and glor⸌
ify God in the day of visitation. Be ye subject to each
creature ⸌ for God ⸌ either to the king as to him that is
higher in state, either to dukes as to the ilk that be sent of
him in the vengeance of misdoers and to the praising of
good men. For so is the will of God that ye do well, and
make the uncunningness of unprudent men to be
dumb, as free men, and not as having freedom the cover⸌
ing of malice, but as the servants of God.

Honour ye all men. Love ye brotherhood. Dread ye God. Honour ye the king. Servants, be ye subjects in all dread to lords, not only to good and to mild, but also to tyrants. For this is grace, if for conscience of God any man suffers heaviness, and suffers unjustly. For what grace is it if ye sin and be buffeted and suffer? But if ye do well and suffer patiently, this is grace anents God. For to this thing ye are called. For also Christ suffered for us, and left ensample to you that ye follow the steps of Him which did not sin, neither guile was found in His mouth. And when He was cursed, He cursed not. When He suffered, He menaced not. But He betook Himself to him that deemed Him unjustly. And He Himself bore our sins in His body on a tree, that we be dead to sins and live to rightwiseness, by whose wan wound ye are healed. For ye were as sheep, erring. But ye are now turned to the Shepherd and Bishop of your souls.

Chapter III

Also women, be they subject to their husbands, that if any man believe not to the word by the conversation of women, they be won without word. And behold ye in dread your holy conversation, of which there be not withoutforth curious ourning of hair, either doing about *adorning* of gold, either ourning of clothing. But the ilk that is the hidden man of heart, in uncorruption and of mild spirit which is rich in the sight of God. For so sometime holy women, hoping in God, ourned themselves and were subject to their own husbands. As Sarah obeyed to Abraham and called him lord, of whom ye are daughters well doing and not dreading any perturbation.

Also men, dwell together and by kunning give ye honour to the woman's frailty, as to the more feeble and as to even heirs of grace and of life, that your prayers be not letted. And in faith all of one will in prayer be ye each suffering with other, lovers of brotherhood, merciful, mild, meek, not yielding evil for evil, neither cursing for cursing, but againward blessing, for in this thing ye are called, that ye wield blessing by heritage. For he that will love life and see good days, constrain his tongue from evil and his lips that they speak not guile. And bow he from evil and do good. Seek he peace and parfitly sue it. For the eyes of the Lord are on just men, and His ears on the prayers of them. But the cheer of the Lord is on men that do evils.

And who is it that shall annoy you if ye are suers and lovers of goodness? But also if ye suffer anything for rightwiseness, ye are blessed. But dread ye not the dread of them, that ye be not disturbled. But hallow ye the Lord Christ in your hearts, and evermore be ye ready to satisfaction to each man asking you reason of that faith and hope that is in you, but with mildness and dread, having good conscience, that in that thing that they backbite of you, they are confounded which challenge falsely your good conversation in Christ. For it is better that ye do well and suffer if the will of God will, than doing evil. For also Christ once died for our sins, He just for unjust, that He should offer to God us made dead in flesh, but made quick in Spirit. For which thing He came in Spirit, and also to them that were closed together in prison preached, which were sometime unbelieveful when they abided the patience of Noah when the ship was made, in which a few, that is to say eight souls, were made safe by water.

And so baptism of like form makes us safe, not the putting away of the filths of flesh, but the asking of a good conscience in God by the again-rising of our Lord Jesus Christ that is in the right half of God and swallows death, that we should be made heirs of everlasting life. He went into heaven, and angels and powers and virtues are made subjects to Him.

Chapter IV

Therefore, for Christ suffered in flesh, be ye also armed by the same thinking. For he that suffered in flesh ceased from sins, that that is left now in flesh live not now to the desires of men, but to the will of God. For the time that is passed is enough to the will of heathen men to be ended, which walked in lecheries and lusts, in much drinking of wine, in unmeasurable eatings and drinkings, in unleaveful worshipping of mawmets. In which now they are astonied, in which thing they wonder, for ye run not together into the same confusion of lechery and blasphemy. And they shall give reason to Him that is ready to deem the quick and the dead.

For why, for this thing it is preached also to dead men, that they be deemed by men in flesh, and that they live by God in spirit. For the end of all things shall nigh. Therefore, be ye prudent and wake ye in prayers. Before all things, have ye charity each to other in yourselves algates lasting, for charity covers the multitude of sins. Hold ye hospitality together without grudging, each man as he has received grace, ministering it into each other as good dispenders of the manifold grace of God. If any man speaks, speak he as the words of God. If any man ministers, as of the virtue which God ministers, that God be honoured in all things by Jesus Christ our Lord, to whom is glory and lordship into worlds of worlds. Amen.

Most dear brethren, nil ye go in pilgrimage in fervour that is made to you to temptation, as if any new thing befall to you. But commune ye with the passions of Christ and have ye joy, that also ye be glad and have joy into the revelation of His glory. If ye are despised for the name of Christ, ye shall be blessed, for that that is of the honour and of the glory and of the virtue of God, and the Spirit that is His, shall rest on you.

But no man of you suffer as a manslayer, either a thief, either curser, either a desirer of other men's goods. But if as a Christian man, shame he not, but glorify he God in this name. For time is that doom begin at God's house, and if it begin first at us, what end shall be of them that believe not to the gospel? And if a just man unneth shall be saved, where shall the unfaithful man and the sinner appear? Therefore and they that suffer by the will of God, betake their souls to the faithful Maker of nought.

Chapter V

Therefore, I, an even elder man and a witness of Christ's passions, which also am a communer of that glory that shall be shown in time to coming, beseech ye, the elder men that are among you, feed ye the flock of God that is among you, and purvey ye, not as constrained, but wilfully, by God, not for love of foul winning but wilfully, neither as having lordship in the clergy, but that ye are made ensample of the flock, of will. And when the Prince of Shepherds shall appear, ye shall receive the crown of glory that may never fade.

Also ye, young men, be ye subject to elder men and all show ye together meekness, for the Lord withstands proud men. But He gives grace to meek men. Therefore, be ye meeked under the mighty hand of God, that He raise you in the time of visitation. And cast ye all your business into Him, for to Him is cure of you.

Be ye sober and wake ye, for your adversary the devil, as a roaring lion, goes about, seeking whom he shall devour. Whom againstand ye, strong in the faith, witting that the same passion is made to the ilk brotherhood of you that is in the world. And God of all grace, that

called you into His everlasting glory, you suffering a lit‚
tle, He shall perform and shall confirm, and shall make
sad. To Him be glory and lordship into worlds of
worlds. Amen.

By Silvanus, faithful brother to you as I deem, I
wrote shortly, beseeching and witnessing that this is the
very grace of God in which ye stand. The church that is
gathered at Babylon, and Marcus, my son, greets you
well. Greet ye well together in holy kiss. Grace be to you
all that be in Christ. Amen.

Here begins the second epistle of Peter

Chapter I

Simon Peter, servant and apostle of Jesus Christ, to
them that have taken with us the even faith in the right‚
wiseness of our God and Saviour Jesus Christ, grace
and peace be filled to you by the knowing of our Lord
Jesus Christ.

How all things of His godly virtue that are to life and
piety, be given to us by the knowing of Him that called
us for His own glory and virtue! By whom He gave to
us most precious behests, that by these things ye shall be
made fellows of God's kind and flee the corruption of
that covetise that is in the world. And bring ye in all
business and minister ye in your faith virtue, and in vir‚
tue kunning, in kunning abstinence, in abstinence
patience, in patience piety, in piety love of brotherhood,
and in love of brotherhood charity. For if these are in
you and overcome, they shall not make you void, neither
without fruit in the knowing of our Lord Jesus Christ.

But to whom these are not ready, he is blind and
gropes with his hand, and forgets the purging of his old
trespasses. Wherefore, brethren, be ye more busy, that
by good works ye make your calling and choosing cer‚

tain. For ye, doing these things, shall not do sin any time. For thus the entering into everlasting kingdom of our Lord and Saviour Jesus Christ, shall be ministered to you plenteously. For which thing I shall begin to monest you evermore of these things.

And I will that ye be cunning and confirmed in this present truth. Forsooth, I deem justly, as long as I am in this tabernacle, to raise you in monesting, and I am certain that the putting away of my tabernacle is swift by this that our Lord Jesus Christ has shown to me. But I shall give business, and often after my death ye have mind of these things. For we, not suing unwise tales, have made known to you the virtue and before-knowing of our Lord Jesus Christ. But we were made beholders of His greatness. For He took of God the Father honour and glory by such manner voice slid down to Him from the great glory, This is My loved Son in whom I have pleased to Me. Hear ye Him.

And we heard this voice brought from heaven when we were with Him in the holy hill. And we have a sadder word of prophecy to which ye, giving tent, do well, as to a lantern that gives light in a dark place till the day begin to give light, and the day star spring in your hearts. And first understand ye this thing, that each prophecy of Scripture is not made by proper interpretation, for prophecy was not brought any time by man's will, but the holy men of God, inspired with the Holy Ghost, spoke.

Chapter II

But also false prophets were in the people, as in you shall be masters, liars, that shall bring in sects of perdition, and they deny the ilk Lord that bought them, and bring on themselves hasty perdition. And many shall sue their lecheries, by which the way of truth shall be blasphemed. And they shall make merchandise of you in covetise by feigned words. To which doom, now a while ago, ceases not, and the perdition of them naps not. For if God spared not angels sinning, but betook them to be tormented and to be drawn down with bonds of hell into hell, to be kept into doom, and spared not the first world, but kept Noah, the eighth man, the before-goer of rightwiseness, and brought in the Great Flood to the world of unfaithful men, and He drove into powder the cities of men of Sodom and of men of Gomorrah, and damned by turning upsedown, and put them the ensample of them that were to doing evil, and delivered the just Lot, oppressed of the wrong and of the lecherous conversation of cursed men. For in sight and hearing he was just, and dwelled amongst them that from day into day tormented with wicked works a just soul. For the Lord can deliver piteous men from temptation, and keep wicked men into the day of doom to be tormented. But more them that walk after the flesh in coveting of uncleanness, and despise lordshipping, and are bold, pleasing themselves, and dread not to bring in sects, blaspheming where angels, when they are more in strength and virtue, bear not that was the execrable doom against them.

But these are as unreasonable beasts, kindly into taking and into death, blaspheming in these things that they know not, and shall perish in their corruption and receive the hire of unrightwiseness. And they guess delicies of defouling and of wem to be likings of day, flowing in their feasts with delicies, doing lechery with you and have eyes full of advowtry and unceasing trespass, deceiving unsteadfast souls, and have the heart exercised to covetise, the sons of cursing that forsake the right way, suing the way of Balaam of Bosor which loved the hire of wickedness. But he had reproving of his woodness, a dumb beast under yoke that spoke with voice of man, that forbad the unwisdom of the prophet.

These are wells without water and mists driven with whirling winds, to which the thick mist of darknesses is reserved. And they speak in pride of vanity, and deceive in desires of flesh of lechery them that scape a little. Which live in error and behight freedom to them when they are servants of corruption. For of whom any man is overcome, of him also he is servant. For if men forsake the uncleanness of the world by the knowing of our Lord and Saviour Jesus Christ, and eftsoon are lapped in these and are overcome, the latter things are made to them worse than the former. For it was better to them to not know the way of rightwiseness, than to turn again after the knowing, from that holy commandment that was betaken to them. For the ilk very proverb befell to them, The hound turned again to his casting, and a sow is washed in wallowing of sin.

Chapter III

Lo, ye most dearworth brethren, I write to you this second epistle in which I stir your clear soul by monesting together, that ye be mindful of those words that I before said of the holy prophets and of the commandments of the holy apostles of the Lord and Saviour. First, wit ye this thing, that in the last days deceivers shall come in deceit, going after their own covetings, saying, Where is the behest or the coming of Him? For since the fathers died, all things last from the beginning of creature.

But it is hidden from them willing this thing, that heavens were before, and the earth, of water, was standing by water, of God's word, by which that ilk world, cleansed, then by water perished. But the heavens that now are, and the earth, are kept by the same word and are reserved to fire into the day of doom and perdition of wicked men.

But, ye most dear, this one thing be not hidden to you, that one day anents God is as a thousand years, and a thousand years are as one day. The Lord tarries not His behest, as some guess, but He does patiently for you, and will not that any men perish, but that all turn again to penance. For the day of the Lord shall come as thief, in which heavens with great bire shall pass, and elements shall be dissolved by heat, and the earth and all the works that are in it, shall be burnt.

Therefore, when all these things shall be dissolved, what manner men behoves it you to be in holy livings and pieties, abiding and hying into the coming of the day of our Lord Jesus Christ, by whom heavens, burning, shall be dissolved and elements shall fail by burning of fire? Also we abide, by His behests, new heavens and new earth in which rightwiseness dwells. For which thing, ye most dear, abiding these things, be ye busy to be found to Him in peace, unspotted and undefouled.

And deem ye long abiding of our Lord Jesus Christ your health, as also our most dear brother Paul wrote to you by wisdom given to him, as and in all epistles he speaks in them of these things, in which are some hard things to understand, which unwise and unstable men deprave, as also they do other Scriptures to their own perdition. Therefore ye, brethren, before witting, keep yourselves, lest ye be deceived by error of unwise men and fall away from your own sadness. But wax ye in the grace and the knowing of our Lord Jesus Christ and our Saviour. To Him be glory, now and into the day of everlastingness. Amen.

Now begins the first epistle of John

Chapter I

That thing which was from the beginning, which we heard, which we saw with our eyes, which we beheld and our hands touched of the word of life, and the life is shown. And we saw and we witness and tell you the everlasting life that was anents the Father and appeared to us. Therefore we tell to you that thing that we saw and heard, that also ye have fellowship with us. And our fellowship be with the Father and with His Son, Jesus Christ. And we write this thing to you that ye have joy, and that your joy be full.

And this is the telling that we heard of Him and tell to you, that God is light, and there are no darknesses in Him. If we say that we have fellowship with Him and we wander in darknesses, we lie and do not truth. But if we walk in light, as also He is in light, we have fellowship together, and the blood of Jesus Christ, His Son, cleanses us from all sin.

If we say that we have no sin, we deceive ourselves and truth in not in us. If we acknowledge our sins, He is faithful and just that He forgive to us our sins, and cleanse us from all wickedness. And if we say we have not sinned, we make Him a liar, and His word is not in us.

Chapter II

My little sons, I write to you these things that ye sin not. But if any man sins, we have an Advocate anents the Father, Jesus Christ, and He is the forgiveness for our sins. And not only for our sins, but also for the sins of

all the world. And in this thing we wit that we know
Him, if we keep His commandments. He that says that
he knows God and keeps not His commandments, is a
liar, and truth is not in Him. But the charity of God is
parfit verily in him that keeps His word. In this thing
we wit that we are in Him, if we are parfit in Him. He
that says that he dwells in Him, he owes for to walk as
He walked.

Most dear brethren, I write to you not a new commandment, but the old commandment that ye had from
the beginning. The old commandment is the word that
ye heard. Eftsoon I write to you a new commandment
that is true both in Him and in you. For darknesses are
passed, and very light shines now. He that says that he
is in light and hates his brother, is in darkness yet. He
that loves his brother, dwells in light, and sclaunder is
not in him. But he that hates his brother, is in darknesses, and wanders in darknesses and wot not
whither he goes, for darknesses have blinded his eyes.

Little sons, I write to you that your sins are forgiven
to you for His name. Fathers, I write to you, for ye have
known Him that is from the beginning. Young men, I
write to you, for ye have overcome the wicked. I write to
you, young children, for ye have known the Father. I
write to you, brethren, for ye have known Him that is
from the beginning. I write to you, young men, for ye are
strong and the word of God dwells in you, and ye have
overcome the wicked.

Nil ye love the world, ne those things that are in the
world. If any man loves the world, the charity of the
Father is not in him. For all thing that is in the world, is
covetise of flesh and covetise of eyes, and pride of life,
which is not of the Father. But it is of the world. And
the world shall pass and the covetise of it, but he that
does the will of God, dwells without end.

My little sons, the last hour is, and as ye have heard that Antichrist comes, now many antichrists are made. Wherefore we wit that it is the last hour. They went forth from us, but they were not of us, for if they had been of us, they had dwelt with us, but that they be known that they are not of us. But ye have anointing of the Holy Ghost, and know all things.

I wrote not to you as to men that know not truth, but as to men that know it and for each leasing is not of truth. Who is a liar but this that denies that Jesus is not Christ? This is antichrist that denies the Father and the Son. So each that denies the Son has not the Father. But he that acknowledges the Son, has also the Father.

That thing that ye heard at the beginning, dwell it in you. For if that thing dwells in you which ye heard at the beginning, ye shall dwell in the Son and in the Father. And this is the behest, that He behight to us everlasting life. I wrote these things to you of them that deceive you, and that the anointing which ye received of Him dwell in you. And ye have not need that any man teach you. But as His anointing teaches you all things, and it is true and it is not leasing, and as He taught you, dwell ye in Him.

And now, ye little sons, dwell ye in Him, that when He shall appear, we have a trust and be not confounded of Him at His coming. If ye wit that He is just, wit ye that also each that does rightwiseness is born of Him.

Chapter III

See ye what manner charity the Father gave to us that we be named the sons of God, and are His sons. For this thing, the world knew not us, for it knew not Him. Most dear brethren, now we are the sons of God, and yet it appears not what we shall be. We wit that when He shall appear, we shall be like Him, for we shall see

Him as He is. And each man that has this hope in Him, makes himself holy as He is holy.

Each man that does sin, does also wickedness, and sin is wickedness. And ye wit that He appeared to do away sins, and sin is not in Him. Each man that dwells in Him, sins not, and each that sins, sees not Him neither knew Him. Little sons, no man deceive you. He that does rightwiseness is just, as also He is just. He that does sin is of the devil, for the devil sins from the beginning. In this thing, the Son of God appeared that He undo the works of the devil.

Each man that is born of God, does not sin, for the seed of God dwells in him and he may not do sin, for he is born of God. In this thing the sons of God are known, and the sons of the fiend. Each man that is not just, is not of God, and he that loves not his brother. For this is the telling that ye heard at the beginning, that ye love each other, not as Cain that was of the evil and slew his brother. And for what thing slew he him? For his works were evil, and his brother's just.

Brethren, nil ye wonder if the world hates you. We wit that we are translated from life to death, for we love brethren. He that loves not, dwells in death. Each man that hates his brother, is a manslayer, and ye wit that each manslayer has not everlasting life dwelling in him. In this thing we have known the charity of God, that He put His life for us, and we owe to put our lives for our brethren.

He that has the cattle of this world, and sees that his brother has need, and closes his entrails from him, how dwells the charity of God in him? My little sons, love we not in word, neither in tongue, but in work and truth. In this thing we know that we are of truth, and in His sight we monest our hearts. For if our heart reproves us, God is more than our heart, and knows all things.

Most dear brethren, if our heart reproves not us, we
have trust to God, and whatever we shall ask, we shall
receive of Him. For we keep His commandments, and
we do those things that are pleasant before Him. And
this is the commandment of God, that we believe in the
name of His Son, Jesus Christ, and that we love each
other, as He gave hest to us. And he that keeps His commandments, dwells in Him, and He in him. And in
this thing we wit that He dwells in us by the Spirit
whom He gave to us.

Chapter IV

Most dear brethren, nil ye believe to each spirit. But
prove ye spirits if they are of God, for many false prophets went out into the world. In this thing the Spirit of
God is known. Each spirit that acknowledges that
Jesus Christ has come in flesh, is of God, and each
destroys, undoes   spirit that fordoes Jesus, is not of God. And this is
Antichrist, of whom ye heard that he comes. And right
now he is in the world. Ye, little sons, are of God and ye
have overcome him, for He that is in you is more than he
that is in the world. They are of the world, therefore they
speak of the world and the world hears them. We are of
God. He that knows God, hears us. He that is not of
God, hears not us. In this thing we know the Spirit of
truth and the spirit of error.

Most dear brethren, love we together, for charity is of
God, and each that loves his brother is born of God,
and knows God. He that loves not, knows not God, for
God is charity. In this thing the charity of God
appeared in us, for God sent His one begotten Son into
the world, that we live by Him. In this thing is charity,
not as we had loved God, but for He first loved us, and
sent His Son ⸴ forgiveness for our sins.

Ye most dear brethren, if God loved us, we ought to

love each other. No man saw ever God. If we love together, God dwells in us, and the charity of Him is parfit in us. In this thing we know that we dwell in Him and He in us, for of His Spirit He gave to us. And we saw and witness that the Father sent His Son, Saviour of the world. Whoever acknowledges that Jesus is the Son of God, God dwells in him and he in God. And we have known and believe to the charity that God has in us. God is charity, and he that dwells in charity, dwells in God and God in him. In this thing is the parfit charity of God with us, that we have trust in the day of doom, for as He is, also we are in this world.

Dread is not in charity, but parfit charity puts out dread, for dread has pain. But he that dreads is not parfit in charity. Therefore love we God, for He loved us before. If any man says that I love God, and hates his brother, he is a liar. For he that loves not his brother which he sees, how may he love God whom he sees not? And we have this commandment of God, that he that loves God, love also his brother.

Chapter V

Each man that believes that Jesus is Christ, is born of God. And each man that loves Him that gendered, loves Him that is born of Him. In this we know that we love the children of God, when we love God and do His commandments. For this is the charity of God, that we keep His commandments, and His commandments are not heavy. For all thing that is born of God, overcomes the world, and this is the victory that overcomes the world, our faith. And who is he that overcomes the world but he that believes that Jesus is the Son of God?

This is Jesus Christ, that came by water and blood. Not in water only, but in water and blood. And the Spirit is He that witnesses that Christ is truth. For three are that give witnessing in heaven, the Father, the Son and the Holy Ghost. And these three are One. And three are that give witnessing in earth, the spirit, water and blood. And these three are one. If we receive the witnessing of men, the witnessing of God is more. For this is the witnessing of God that is more, for He witnessed of His Son.

He that believes in the Son of God, has the witnessing of God in him. He that believes not to the Son, makes Him a liar, for he believes not in the witnessing that God witnessed of His Son. And this is the witnessing, for God gave to you everlasting life, and this life is in His Son. He that has the Son of God, has also life. He that has not the Son of God, has not life.

I write to you these things, that ye wit that ye have everlasting life which believe in the name of God's Son. And this is the trust which we have to God, that whatever thing we ask after His will, He shall hear us. And we wit that He hears us. Whatever thing we ask, we wit that we have the askings which we ask of Him.

He that wot that his brother sins a sin not to death, ask he, and life shall be given to him that sins not to death. There is a sin to death. Not for it I say that any man pray. Each wickedness is sin, and there is sin to death. We wit that each man that is born of God, sins not. But the generation of God keeps him and the wicked touches him not. We wit that we are of God, and all the world is set in evil. And we wit that the Son of God came in flesh and gave to us wit, that we know very God and be in the very Son of Him. This is very God, and everlasting life. My little sons, keep ye you from mawmets.

The second epistle of John

The elder man to the chosen lady, and to her children which I love in truth. And not I alone, but also all men that know truth, for the truth that dwells in you and with you, shall be without end. Grace be with you, mercy and peace of God the Father and of Jesus Christ, the Son of the Father, in truth and charity.

I joyed full much, for I found thy sons going in truth as we received commandment of the Father. And now I pray thee, lady, not as writing a new commandment to thee, but that that we had from the beginning, that we love each other. And this is charity, that we walk after His commandments. For this is the commandment, that as ye heard at the beginning, walk ye in Him. For many deceivers went out into the world, which acknowledge not that Jesus Christ has come in flesh. This is a deceiver and antichrist. See ye yourselves, lest ye lose the things that ye have wrought, that ye receive full meed, witting that each man that goes before and dwells not in the teaching of Christ, has not God. He that dwells in the teaching, has both the Son and the Father.

If any man comes to you and brings not this teaching, nil ye receive him into house, neither say ye to him, Hail. For he that says to him, Hail, communes with his evil works. Lo, I before said to you that ye be not confounded in the day of our Lord Jesus Christ. I have more things to write to you, and I would not by parchment and ink, for I hope that I shall come to you and speak mouth to mouth, that your joy be full. The sons of thy chosen sister greet thee well. The grace of God be with thee. Amen.

The third epistle of John

The elder man to Gaius, most dear brother, whom I love in truth. Most dear brother, of all things I make prayer that thou enter and fare wealfully, as thy soul does wealfully. I joyed greatly, for brethren came and bore witnessing to thy truth, as thou walks in truth. I have not more grace of these things than that I hear that my sons walk in truth.

Most dear brother, thou does faithfully, whatever thou works in brethren and that into pilgrims, which yielded witnessing to thy charity in the sight of the church, which thou led forth and do well worthily to God. For they went forth for His name, and took nothing of heathen men. Therefore we ought to receive such, that we be even workers of truth. I had written, peradventure, to the church, but this Diotrephes, that loves to bear primacy in them, receives not us. For this thing, if I shall come, I shall monest his works which he does, chiding against us with evil words. And as if these things suffice not to him, neither he receives brethren and forbids them that receive, and puts out of the church.

Most dear brother, nil thou sue evil thing, but that that is good thing. He that does well, is of God. He that does evil, sees not God. Witnessing is yielded to Demetrius of all men and of truth itself. But also we bear witnessing, and thou knows that our witnessing is true. I had many things to write to thee, but I would not write to thee by ink and pen. For I hope soon to see thee, and we shall speak mouth to mouth. Peace be to thee. Friends greet thee well. Greet thou well friends by name.

This is the epistle of Jude

Jude, the servant of Jesus Christ and brother of James, to these that are loved, that are in God the Father, and to them that are called and kept of Jesus Christ. Mercy and peace and charity be filled to you.

Most dear brethren, I, doing all business to write to you of your common health, had need to write to you and pray to strive strongly for the faith that is once taken to saints. For some unfaithful men privily entered that sometime were before written into this doom, and overturn the grace of our God into lechery, and deny Him that is only a Lord, our Lord Jesus Christ. But I will monest you once that wit all things, that Jesus saved His people from the land of Egypt and the second time lost them that believed not. And He reserved under darkness angels that kept not their princehood, but forsook their house, into the doom of the great God into everlasting bonds ⁄ as Sodom and Gomorrah, and the nigh coasted cities that in like manner did fornication and went away after other flesh, and are made ensample, suffering pain of everlasting fire. In like manner also, these that defoul the flesh and despise lordship and blaspheme majesty.

When Michael, archangel, disputed with the devil and strove of Moses' body, he was not hardy to bring in doom of blasphemy, but said, The Lord command to thee. But these men blaspheme whatever things they know not. For whatever things they know kindly as dumb beasts, in these they are corrupt. Woe to them that went the way of Cain and that are shed out by error of Balaam for meed, and perished in the againsaying of

Core. These are in their meats, feasting together to filth, without dread feeding themselves. These are clouds without water, that are borne about of the winds, harvest trees without fruit, twice dead, drawn up by the root, waves of the wood sea, foaming out their confusions, erring stars to which the tempest of darknesses is kept without end. But Enoch, the seventh from Adam, prophesied of these, and said, Lo, the Lord comes with His holy thousands to do doom against all men, and to reprove all unfaithful men of all the works of the wickedness of them by which they did wickedly, and of all the hard words that wicked sinners spoke against God. These are grouchers, full of plaints, wandering after their desires. And the mouth of them speaks pride, worshipping persons by cause of winning.

And ye, most dear brethren, be mindful of the words which are before said of apostles of our Lord Jesus Christ, which said to you that in the last times there shall come guilers, wandering after their own desires, not in piety. These are which depart themselves, beastly men, not having spirit. But ye, most dear brethren, above build yourselves on your most holy faith, and pray ye in the Holy Ghost, and keep yourselves in the love of God, and abide ye the mercy of our Lord Jesus Christ into life everlasting. And reprove ye these men that are deemed, but save ye them and take ye them from the fire. And do ye mercy to other men in the dread of God, and hate ye also the ilk defouled coat which is fleshly.

But to Him that is mighty to keep you without sin, and to ordain before the sight of His glory you unwemmed in full out joy in the coming of our Lord Jesus Christ, to God alone our Saviour, by Jesus Christ our Lord, be glory and magnifying, empire and power before all worlds, and now and into all worlds of worlds. Amen.

Here begins a Prologue on the Apocalypse

All men that will live meekly in Christ, as the apostle says, suffer persecution after that. Thou son that nighes to the service of God, stand thou in rightwiseness and in dread, and make ready thy soul to temptation, for temptation is a man's life on the earth. But that faithful men fail not in them, the Lord comforts them and confirms, saying, I am with you unto the end of the world, and, Little flock, nil ye dread. Therefore God the Father, seeing the tribulations which holy church was to suffer, that was founded of the apostles on Christ the stone, disposed with the Son and the Holy Ghost to show that men dread them the less, and all the Trinity showed it, Christ in His Manhood, and Christ to John by an angel, and John to holy church, of which revelation John made his book. Wherefore this book is said Apocalypse, that is to say, Revelation, for here it is contained that God showed to John, and John to holy church, how great things holy church suffered in the first time, and now suffers, and shall suffer in the last times of Antichrist, when tribulation shall be so great that if it mow be, they that are chosen are moved, and which meeds she shall receive for these tribulations now and in time to come, that meeds that are behoved make them glad whom the tribulations that are told makes afeared.

Therefore this book, among other scriptures of the New Testament, is called by the name of prophecy, and it is more excellent than prophets, for as the New Testament is worthier than the Old, and the gospel than the law, so this prophecy passes the prophecies of the Old Testament, for it shows sacraments that are now a partly fulfilled of Christ and of holy church. Or else for to other is a manner prophecy, but to this is three manner prophecy given together. That is, of that that is past, and of that that is present, and of that that is to come, and to confirm the authority of it, there comes the authority of Him that sends and of him that bears, and of him that receives. He that sends is the Trinity. He that bears is the angel. He that receives is John. But when these things are shown to John in vision, and there are three kinds of visions, it is to be seen under which kind this be contained, for some vision is bodily, as when we see anything with bodily eyes. Some is spiritual or imaginary, as when we see sleeping or else waking. We behold the images of things by which some other thing is signified, as Pharaoh sleeping saw ears of corn, and Moses waking saw the bush burn. And other vision is of understanding, as when through revelation of the Holy Ghost. Through understanding of thought, we conceive the truth of mysteries, as John saw those things that are contained in this book, for not only he saw in spirit the figures, but also he understood in thought the things that were signified by them.

John saw and wrote in the Isle of Patmos when he was exiled of Domitian, the most wicked prince, and a cause compelled him to write. For while he was held in outlawry of Domitian in the Isle of Patmos, in the churches that he had governed, there were sprung many vices and diverse heresies, for there were some heretics there that said that Christ was not tofore Mary, forasmuch as He was in time born of her. Which heretics John, in the beginning of his gospel, undernomes and says, In the beginning was the Son, and in this book, when he says, I am Alpha and Omega, that is, the Beginning and the End.

Some also said that holy church should end tofore the end of the world for charge of tribulations, and that it should not underfong for her travail everlasting meed. Therefore John, willing to destroy the errors of these, shows that Christ was Beginning and End. Wherefore Isaiah says, Tofore Me was no god formed, and after Me there shall not be, and that holy church through exercise of tribulations, shall not be ended but shall profit, and for them receive an everlasting meed.

John writes to the seven churches of Asia and to their seven bishops of the foresaid things, informing and teaching by them all the general holy church. And so the matter of John in this work is specially of the church of Asia and of all holy church, what she shall suffer in this present time, and what she shall underfong in time to come. And his intent is to stir to patience which is to be kept, for the travail is short and the meed great. The manner of his treating is such, first he set before a Prologue and a salutation where he makes the hearers benign and taking well tent. And when he has set it tofore, he comes to the telling, but tofore his telling he shows that Christ is even without beginning and without end, rehearsing him that speaks, I am Alpha and Omega, Beginning and End.

Afterward he comes to his telling, and departs it into seven visions. And when they are ended, this book is ended. He sets tofore the Prologue and says, The Apocalypse of Jesus Christ. Understand that this is as it is in other, the vision of Isaiah, and also the parables of Solomon.

Chapter I

Apocalypse of Jesus Christ, which God gave to Him to make open to His servants, which things it behoves to be made soon. And He signified and sent by His angel to His servant John, which bore witnessing to the word of God and witnessing of Jesus Christ in these things, whatever things he saw. Blessed is he that reads and he that hears the words of this prophecy, and keeps those things that are written in it, for the time is nigh.

John, to the seven churches that are in Asia, grace and peace to you of Him that is, and that was, and that is to coming, and of the seven spirits that are in the sight of His throne, and of Jesus Christ that is a faithful witness, the first begotten of dead men and Prince of kings of the earth. Which loved us and washed us from our sins in His blood, and made us a kingdom and priests to God and to His Father. To Him be glory and empire into worlds of worlds. Amen.

Lo, He comes with clouds, and each eye shall see Him and they that pricked Him, and all the kindreds of the earth shall bewail themselves on Him. Yea, amen. I am Alpha and Omega, the Beginning and the End, says the Lord God that is, and that was, and that is to coming, Almighty.

I, John, your brother and partner in tribulation and kingdom and patience in Christ Jesus, was in an isle that is called Patmos for the word of God and for the witnessing of Jesus. I was in Spirit in the Lord's day, and I heard behind me a great voice as of a trump, saying to me, Write thou in a book that thing that thou see, and send to the seven churches that are in Asia. To Ephesus, to Smyrna, and to Pergamos, and to Thyatira, and to Sardis, and to Philadelphia, and to Laodicea.

And I turned that I should see the voice that spoke with me. And I turned and I saw seven candlesticks of gold, and in the middle of the seven golden candle⁄sticks, one like to the Son of Man, clothed with a long garment and girded about the teats with a golden girdle. And the head of Him and His hairs were white as white wool, and as snow, and the eyes of Him as flame of fire, *brass* and His feet like to latten as in a burning chimney, and the voice of Him as the voice of many waters. And He had in His right hand seven stars, and a sword, sharp on ever either side, went out of His mouth, and His face as the sun shines in his virtue.

And when I had seen Him, I fell down at His feet as dead. And He put His right hand on me, and said, Nil thou dread. I am the First and the Last, and I am alive and I was dead. And lo, I am living into worlds of worlds. And I have the keys of death and of hell. Therefore, write thou which things thou has seen, and which are, and which it behoves to be done after these things. The sacrament of the seven stars which thou saw in My right hand, and the seven golden candle-sticks: the seven stars are angels of the seven churches, and the seven candlesticks are seven churches.

Chapter II

And to the angel of the church of Ephesus write thou, These things says He that holds the seven stars in His right hand, which walks in the middle of the seven golden candlesticks. I wot thy works and travail, and thy patience, and that thou may not suffer evil men. And thou has assayed them that say that they are apostles, and are not, and thou has found them liars. And thou has patience, and thou has suffered for My name and failed not. But I have against thee a few things, that thou has left thy first charity. Therefore, be thou mindful from whence thou has fallen, and do penance and do the first works. Either else I come soon to thee, and I shall move thy candlestick from his place but thou does penance. But thou has this good thing, that thou hated the deeds of Nicolaitans, the which I also hate. He that has ears, hear he what the Spirit says to the churches. To him that overcomes, I shall give to eat of the Tree of Life that is in the paradise of My God.

And to the angel of the church of Smyrna write thou, These things says the First and the Last, that was dead and lives. I wot thy tribulation and thy poverty. But thou art rich, and thou art blasphemed of them that say that they are Jews, and are not, but are the synagogue of Satan. Dread thou nothing of these things which thou shall suffer. Lo, the devil shall send some of you into prison, that ye be tempted. And ye shall have tribulation ten days. Be thou faithful to the death, and I shall give to thee a crown of life. He that has ears, hear he what the Spirit says to the churches. He that overcomes, shall not be hurt of the second death.

And to the angel of the church of Pergamos write thou, These things says He that has the sword sharp on each side. I wot where thou dwells, where the seat of Satan is, and thou holds My name and denied not My faith. And in those days was Antipas, My faithful witness, that was slain at you where Satan dwells. But I have against thee a few things, for thou has there men holding the teaching of Balaam, which taught Balak for to send sclaunder before the sons of Israel, to eat of sacrifices of idols and to do fornication. So also thou has men holding the teaching of Nicolaitans also. Do thou penance. If anything less, I shall come soon to thee, and I shall fight with them with the sword of My mouth. He that has ears, hear he what the Spirit says to the churches. To him that overcomes, I shall give angel meat hid, and I shall give to him a white stone, and in the stone a new name written which no man knows but he that takes.

And to the angel of the church of Thyatira write thou, These things says the Son of God that has eyes as flame of fire, and His feet like latten. I know thy works and faith, and charity and thy service, and thy patience and thy last works mo than the former. But I have against thee a few things, for thou suffers the woman, Jezebel, which says that she is a prophetess, to teach and deceive My servants to do lechery, and to eat of things offered to idols. And I gave to her time that she should do penance, and she would not do penance of her fornication. And lo, I send her into a bed, and they that do lechery with her shall be in most tribulation but they do penance of their works. And I shall slay her sons into death, and all churches shall wit that I am searching *kidneys* reins and hearts, and I shall give to each man of you after his works. And I say to you and to other that are at Thyatira, whoever has not this teaching and that knew not the highness of Satan ⁄ how they say ⁄ I shall not send on you another charge. Netheless, hold ye that that ye have till I come. And to him that shall overcome, and that shall keep till into the end My works, I shall give power on folks, and he shall govern them in an iron yard. And they shall be broken together as a vessel of a potter, as also I received of My Father, and I shall give to him a morrow star. He that has ears, hear he what the Spirit says to the churches.

Chapter III

And to the angel of the church of Sardis write thou, These things says He that has the seven spirits of God and the seven stars. I wot thy works, for thou has a name that thou lives and thou art dead. Be thou waking, and confirm thou other things that were to dying. For I find not thy works full before My God. Therefore have thou in mind how thou received and heard, and keep and do penance. Therefore, if thou wake not, I shall come as a night thief to thee, and thou shall not wit in what hour I *one who steals by night* shall come to thee. But thou has a few names in Sardis which have not defouled their clothes, and they shall walk with Me in white clothes, for they are worthy. He that overcomes shall be clothed thus with white clothes, and I shall not do away his name from the Book of Life. And I shall acknowledge his name before My Father and before His angels. He that has ears, hear he what the Spirit says to the churches.

And to the angel of the church of Philadelphia write thou, These things says the Holy and True that has the key of David, which opens and no man closes, he closes and no man opens. I wot thy works, and lo, I gave before thee a door opened which no man may close, for thou has a little virtue and has kept My word, and denies not My name. Lo, I shall give to thee of the synagogue of Satan which say that they are Jews and are not, but lie.

Lo, I shall make them that they come and worship before thy feet, and they shall wit that I loved thee, for thou kept the word of My patience. And I shall keep thee from the hour of temptation that is to coming into all the world to tempt men that dwell in earth. Lo, I come soon. Hold thou that that thou has, that no man take thy crown. And him that shall overcome, I shall make a pillar in the Temple of My God, and he shall no more go out. And I shall write on him the name of My God and the name of the city of My God, of the new Jerusalem that comes down from heaven of My God, and My new name. He that has ears, hear he what the Spirit says to the churches.

And to the angel of the church of Laodicea write thou, These things says Amen, the Faithful Witness and True, which is beginning of God's creature. I wot thy works, for neither thou art cold, neither thou art hot. I would that thou were cold, either hot. But for thou art *warm* lew, and neither cold neither hot, I shall begin to cast thee out of My mouth. For thou say, I am rich and full of goods and I have need of nothing. And thou wost not that thou art a wretch and wretchful, and poor and blind and naked. I counsel thee to buy of Me burnt gold and proved, that thou be made rich and be clothed with white clothes, that the confusion of thy nakedness be *eye-salve* not seen, and anoint thine eyes with a collery, that thou see. I reprove and chastise whom I love. Therefore, sue thou good men and do penance. Lo, I stand at the door and knock. If any man hears My voice, and opens the gate to Me, I shall enter to him and sup with him, and he with Me. And I shall give to him that shall overcome to sit with Me in My throne, as also I overcame and sat with My Father in His throne. He that has ears, hear he what the Spirit says to the churches.

Chapter IV

After these things, I saw, and lo, a door was opened in heaven. And the first voice that I heard was as of a trump speaking with me, and said, Stye thou up hither and I shall show to thee which things it behoves to be done soon after these things. Anon I was in Spirit, and lo, a seat was set in heaven, and upon the seat One sitting. And He that sat was like the sight of a stone jaspis, and to sardine, and a rainbow was in compass _jasper_ of the seat, like the sight of a smaragdin. And in the _emerald_ compass of the seat were four and twenty small seats, and above the thrones four and twenty elder men sit⁄ ting, hiled about with white clothes, and in the heads of them, golden crowns. And lights and voices and thunderings came out of the throne, and seven lamps burning before the throne, which are the seven spirits of God.

And before the seat, as a sea of glass like a crystal, and in the middle of the seat and in the compass of the seat, four beasts, full of eyes before and behind. And the first beast like a lion. And the second beast like a calf. And the third beast having a face as of a man. And the fourth beast like an eagle flying. And the four beasts had every of them six wings, and all about and within they were full of eyes. And they had not rest day and night, saying, Holy, holy, holy, the Lord God Almighty, that was, and that is, and that is to coming.

And when the four beasts gave glory and honour and blessing to Him that sat on the throne, that lives into worlds of worlds, the four and twenty elder men fell down before Him that sat on the throne, and wor⁄ shipped Him that lives into worlds of worlds. And they cast their crowns before the throne, and said, Thou, Lord our God, art worthy to take glory and honour and virtue. For Thou made of nought all things, and for Thy will those were and are made of nought.

Chapter V

And I saw in the right hand of the Sitter on the throne, a book written within and without, and sealed with seven seals. And I saw a strong angel preaching with a great voice, Who is worthy to open the book and to undo the seals of it? And none in heaven, neither in earth, neither under earth, might open the book, neither behold it. And I wept much, for none was found worthy to open the book, neither to see it. And one of the elder men said to me, Weep thou not. Lo, a Lion of the lineage of Judah, the Root of David, has overcome to open the book and to undo the seven seals of it.

And I saw, and lo, in the middle of the throne and of the four beasts, and in the middle of the elder men, a Lamb standing, as slain, that had seven horns and seven eyes which are seven spirits of God sent into all the earth. And He came and took of the right hand of the Sitter in the throne, the book. And when He had opened the book, the four beasts and the four and twenty elder men fell down before the Lamb, and had each of them harps and golden vials full of odours which are the prayers of saints. And they sang a new song, and said, Lord our God, Thou art worthy to take the book and to open the seals of it. For Thou were slain and again bought us to God in Thy blood, of each lineage and tongue and people and nation, and made us a kingdom and priests to our God, and we shall reign on earth.

And I saw and heard the voice of many angels all about the throne, and of the beasts and of the elder men. And the number of them was thousands of thousands, saying with a great voice, The Lamb that was slain, is worthy to take virtue and Godhead and wisdom and strength, and honour and glory and blessing. And each creature that is in heaven and that is in earth, and under earth, and the sea and which things are in it, I heard all saying to Him that sat in the throne and to the Lamb, Blessing and honour and glory and power into worlds of worlds. And the four beasts said, Amen. And the four and twenty elder men fell down on their faces, and worshipped Him that lives into worlds of worlds.

Chapter VI

And I saw that the Lamb had opened one of the seven seals, and I heard one of the four beasts saying, as a voice of thunder, Come and see. And I saw, and lo, a white horse, and he that sat on him had a bow, and a crown was given to him. And he went out overcoming, that he should overcome.

And when He had opened the second seal, I heard the second beast saying, Come thou and see. And another, red, horse went out, and it was given to him that sat on him that he should take peace from the earth, and that they slay together themselves. And a great sword was given to him.

And when He had opened the third seal, I heard the third beast saying, Come thou and see. And lo, a black horse, and he that sat on him had a balance in his hand. And I heard a voice in the middle of the four beasts saying, A biliber of wheat for a penny, and three bilibers of *2lb weight* barley for a penny, and hurt thou not wine ne oil.

And when He had opened the fourth seal, I heard a voice of the four beasts saying, Come thou and see. And lo, a pale horse, and the name was Death to him that sat on him, and hell sued him. And power was given to him on four parts of the earth for to slay with sword and with hunger, and with death and with beasts of the earth.

And when He had opened the fifth seal, I saw under

the altar the souls of men slain for the word of God and for the witnessing that they had. And they cried with a great voice and said, How long Thou, Lord, that art holy and true, deems not and venges not our blood on these that dwell in the earth? And white stoles, for each soul a stole, were given to them, and it was said to them that they should rest yet a little time, till the number of their fellows and of their brethren are fulfilled that are to be slain, as also they.

And I saw, when He had opened the sixth seal, and lo, a great earth-moving was made, and the sun was made black as a sack of hair, and all the moon was made as blood. And the stars of heaven fell down on the earth, as a fig tree sends his unripe figs when it is moved of a great wind. And heaven went away as a book lapped in, and all mountains and isles were moved from their places. And kings of the earth, and princes and tri-bunes, and rich and strong, and each bondman and free-man hid them in dens and stones of hills. And they said to hills and to stones, Fall ye on us and hide ye us from the face of Him that sits on the throne and from the wrath of the Lamb, for the great day of Their wrath comes and who shall mow stand?

Chapter VII

After these things, I saw four angels standing on the four corners of the earth, holding four winds of the earth that they blew not on the earth, neither on the sea, neither on any tree. And I saw another angel stying from the rising of the sun, that had a sign of the living God. And he cried with a great voice to the four angels to which it was given to noy the earth and the sea, and said, Nil ye noy the earth and sea, neither trees, till we mark the ser-vants of our God in the foreheads of them. And I heard the number of men that were marked, an hundred thou-

sand and four and forty thousand marked, of every lineage of the sons of Israel.

Of the lineage of Judah, twelve thousand marked.
Of the lineage of Reuben, twelve thousand marked. Of
the lineage of Gad, twelve thousand marked. Of the
lineage of Aser, twelve thousand marked. Of the
lineage of Nephtalim, twelve thousand marked. Of the
lineage of Manasseh, twelve thousand marked. Of the
lineage of Simeon, twelve thousand marked. Of the
lineage of Levi, twelve thousand marked. Of the lineage
of Issachar, twelve thousand marked. Of the lineage
of Zebulun, twelve thousand marked. Of the lineage
of Joseph, twelve thousand marked. Of the lineage of
Benjamin, twelve thousand marked.

After these things, I saw a great people whom no
man might number, of all folks and peoples and languages, standing before the throne in the sight of the
Lamb. And they were clothed with white stoles, and
palms were in the hands of them. And they cried with
great voice, and said, Health to our God that sits on the
throne, and to the Lamb. And all angels stood all about
the throne, and the elder men and the four beasts. And
they fell down in the sight of the throne, on their faces,
and worshipped God and said, Amen. Blessing and
clearness and wisdom and doing of thankings, and honour and virtue and strength to our God into worlds of
worlds. Amen.

And one of the seniors answered and said to me,
Who are these that are clothed with white stoles? And
from whence came they? And I said to him, My lord,
thou wost. And he said to me, These are they that came
from great tribulations and washed their stoles, and
made them white in the blood of the Lamb. Therefore
they are before the throne of God, and serve to Him day
and night in His Temple. And He that sits in the

throne, dwells on them. They shall no more hunger neither thirst, neither sun shall fall on them ne any heat. For the Lamb that is in the middle of the throne, shall govern them and shall lead forth them to the wells of waters of life. And God shall wipe away each tear from the eyes of them.

Chapter VIII

And when He had opened the seventh seal, a silence was made in heaven as half an hour. And I saw seven angels standing in the sight of God, and seven trumps were given to them. And another angel came and stood before the altar, and had a golden censer. And many incenses were given to him, that he should give of the prayers of all saints on the golden altar that is before the throne of God. And the smoke of incenses of the prayers of the holy men, styed up from the angel's hand before God. And the angel took the censer and filled it of the fire of the altar, and cast into the earth. And thunders and voices and lightnings were made, and a great earth-moving. And the seven angels that had seven trumps, made them ready that they should trump.

And the first angel trumped and hail was made, and fire meyned together in blood, and it was sent into the earth. And the third part of the earth was burnt, and the third part of trees was burnt, and all the green grass was burnt.

And the second angel trumped, and as a great hill burning with fire was cast into the sea. And the third part of the sea was made blood, and the third part of creature was dead that had lives in the sea, and the third part of ships perished.

And the third angel trumped, and a great star, burning as a little brand, fell from heaven, and it fell into the third part of floods and into the wells of waters. And the name of the star is said, Wormwood. And the third part of waters was made into wormwood, and many men were dead of the waters, for those were made bitter.

And the fourth angel trumped, and the third part of the sun was smitten, and the third part of the moon, and the third part of stars, so that the third part of them was darked, and the third part of the day shined not, and also of the night. And I saw, and heard the voice of an eagle flying by the middle of heaven, and saying with a great voice, Woe, woe, woe to men that dwell in earth, of the voices of three angels that shall trump after.

Chapter IX

And the fifth angel trumped, and I saw that a star had fallen down from heaven into earth, and the key of the pit of deepness was given to it. And it opened the pit of deepness, and a smoke of the pit stied up as the smoke of a great furnace, and the sun was darked and the air, of the smoke of the pit. And locusts went out of the smoke of the pit into the earth, and power was given to them as scorpions of the earth has power. And it was commanded to them that they should not hurt the grass of earth neither any green thing, neither any tree, but only men that have not the sign of God in their foreheads. And it was given to them that they should not slay them, but that they should be tormented five months, and the tormenting of them as the tormenting of a scorpion when he smites a man. And in those days, men shall seek death and they shall not find it, and they shall desire to die, and death shall flee from them.

And the locusts are like horses made ready into battle, and on the heads of them as crowns like gold, and the faces of them as the faces of men. And they had hairs as hairs of women, and the teeth of them were as teeth of lions. And they had habergeons as iron habergeons, and the voice of their wings as the voice of chariots of many horses running into battle. And they had tails like scorpions, and pricks were in the tails of them, and the might of them was to noy men five months.

And they had on them a king, the angel of deepness, to whom the name by Hebrew is *Abbadon*, but by Greek, *Apollyon*. And by Latin he has the name *Exterminans*, that is, a destroyer. One woe is passed, and lo, yet come two woes.

After these things also the sixth angel trumped, and I heard a voice from four corners of the golden altar that is before the eyes of God, and said to the sixth angel that had a trump, Unbind thou four angels that are bound in the great flood Euphrates. And the four angels were unbound which were ready into hour and day and month and year, to slay the third part of men. And the number of the host of horsemen was twenty thousand siths ten thousand. I heard the number of them. And so I saw horses in vision, and they that sat on them had fiery habergeons, and of jacinth and of brimstone. And the heads of the horses were as heads of lions, and fire and smoke and brimstone comes forth of the mouth of them.

Of these three plagues the third part of men was slain, of the fire and of the smoke, and of the brimstone that came out of the mouth of them. For the power of the horses is in the mouth of them and in the tails of them, for the tails of them are like to serpents, having heads, and in them they noy.

And the t'other men that were not slain in these pla-gues, neither did penance of the works of their hands, *likenesses, similitudes* that they worshipped not devils and similacres of gold and of silver, and of brass and of stone and of tree, which neither moun see, neither hear, neither wander, and did not penance of their manslayings neither of their witch-crafts, neither of their fornication, neither of their thefts, were slain.

Chapter X

And I saw another strong angel coming down from heaven, clothed with a cloud and the rainbow on his head. And the face of him was as the sun, and the feet of him as a pillar of fire. And he had in his hand a little book opened, and he set his right foot on the sea and the left foot on the earth. And he cried with a great voice as a lion when he roars. And when he had cried, the seven thunders spoke their voices. And when the seven thunders had spoken their voices, I was to writing. And I heard a voice from heaven saying, Mark thou what things the seven thunders spoke, and nil thou write them.

And the angel whom I saw standing above the sea and above the earth, lift up his hand to heaven and swore by Him that lives into worlds of worlds, that made of nought heaven and those things which are in it, and the earth and those things that are in it, and the sea and those things that are in it, that time shall no more be. But in the days of the voice of the seventh angel, when he shall begin to trump, the mystery of God shall be ended, as He preached by His servants, prophets.

And I heard a voice from heaven eftsoon speaking with me, and saying, Go thou and take the book that is opened from the hand of the angel that stands above the sea and on the land. And I went to the angel and said to him that he should give me the book. And he said to me, Take the book and devour it, and it shall make thy womb to be bitter. But in thy mouth it shall be sweet as honey. And I took the book of the angel's hand and devoured it, and it was in my mouth as sweet honey, and when I had devoured it, my womb was bitter. And he said to me, It behoves thee eftsoon to prophesy to heathen men, and to peoples and languages and to many kings.

Chapter XI

And a reed like a yard was given to me, and it was said to me, Rise thou, and mete the Temple of God and the altar, and the men that worship in it. But cast thou out *forecourt* the foreyard that is without the Temple and mete not it, for it is given to heathen men and they shall defoul the holy city by forty months and twain. And I shall give to My two witnesses, and they shall prophesy a thousand days two hundred and sixty, and shall be clothed with sacks. These are twain olives and two candlesticks, and they stand in the sight of the Lord of the earth. And if any man will annoy them, fire shall go out of the mouth of them, and shall devour their enemies. And if any will hurt them, thus it behoves him to be slain. These have power to close heaven, that it rain not in the days of their prophecy. And they have power on waters to turn them into blood and to smite the earth with every plague and as often as they will.

And when they shall end their witnessing, the beast that styes up from deepness shall make battle against them and shall overcome them, and shall slay them. And the bodies of them shall lie in the streets of the great city that is called ghostly Sodom and Egypt, where the Lord of them was crucified. And some of lineages and of peoples and of languages, and of heathen men, shall see the bodies of them by three days and a half, and they shall not suffer the bodies of them to be put in burials. And men inhabiting the earth shall have joy on them, and they shall make merry and shall send gifts together, for these two prophets tormented them that dwell on the earth.

And after three days and a half, the Spirit of life of God entered into them, and they stood on their feet, and great dread fell on them that saw them. And they heard a great voice from heaven, saying to them, Come up hither. And they styed into heaven in a cloud, and the enemies of them saw them. And in that hour, a great earth‑moving was made and the tenth part of the city fell down, and the names of men, seven thousand, were slain in the earth‑moving. And the t'other were sent into dread and gave glory to God of heaven. The second woe is gone, and lo, the third woe shall come soon.

And the seventh angel trumped, and great voices were made in heaven, and said, The realm of this world is made our Lord's and of Christ, His Son. And He shall reign into worlds of worlds. Amen. And the four and twenty elder men that sat in their seats in the sight of the Lord, fell on their faces and worshipped God, and said, We do thankings to Thee, Lord God Almighty, which art, and which were, and which art to coming, which has taken Thy great virtue and has reigned. And folks are wroth, and Thy wrath came, and time of dead men to be deemed and to yield meed to Thy servants and prophets and hallows, and dreading Thy name, to small and to great, and to destroy them that corrupted the earth.

hallowed ones, saints

Chapter XII

And the Temple of God in heaven was opened, and the Ark of His Testament was seen in His Temple. And lightnings were made and voices and thunders, and earth‑moving and great hail. And a great sign appeared in heaven, a woman clothed with the sun, and the moon under her feet, and in the head of her a crown of twelve stars. And she had in womb and she cries, travailing of child, and is tormented that she bear child.

And another sign was seen in heaven, and lo, a great red dragon that had seven heads and ten horns, and in the heads of him, seven diadems. And the tail of him drew the third part of stars of heaven, and sent them into the earth. And the dragon stood before the woman that

was to bearing child, that when she had borne child, he
boy child, son should devour her Son. And she bore a knave child that
was to ruling all folks in an iron yerde. And her Son
was ravished to God and to His throne. And the
woman fled into wilderness where she has a place made
ready of God, that He fed her there a thousand days two
hundred and sixty.

And a great battle was made in heaven, and Michael
and his angels fought with the dragon. And the dragon
fought and his angels, and they had not might, neither
the place of them was found more in heaven. And the
ilk dragon was cast down, the great old serpent that is
called the devil and Satan that deceives all the world.
He was cast down into the earth, and his angels were
sent with him. And I heard a great voice in heaven, saying, Now is made health and virtue and kingdom of our
God and the power of His Christ. For the accuser of
our brethren is cast down which accused them before
the sight of our God day and night. And they overcame
him for the blood of the Lamb, and for the word of His
witnessing, and they loved not their lives till to death.
Therefore, ye heavens, be ye glad, and ye that dwell in
them. Woe to the earth and to the sea, for the fiend is
come down to you and has great wrath, witting that he
has little time.

And after that the dragon saw that he was cast down
to the earth, he pursued the woman that bore the knave
child. And two wings of a great eagle were given to the
woman that she should flee into desert, into her place
where she is fed by time and times and half a time, from
the face of the serpent. And the serpent sent out of his
mouth after the woman, water as a flood, that he should
make her to be drawn of the flood. And the earth helped
the woman, and the earth opened his mouth and supped
up the flood that the dragon sent of his mouth. And the

dragon was wroth against the woman, and he went to make battle with other of her seed that keep the commandments of God and have the witnessing of Jesus Christ. And he stood on the gravel of the sea.

Chapter XIII

And I saw a beast stying up of the sea, having seven heads and ten horns, and on his horns ten diadems, and on his heads the names of blasphemy. And the beast whom I saw, was like a leopard, and his feet as the feet of a bear, and his mouth as the mouth of a lion. And the dragon gave his virtue and great power to him.

And I saw one of his heads as slain into death, and the wound of his death was cured. And all earth wondered after the beast. And they worshipped the dragon that gave power to the beast, and they worshipped the beast and said, Who is like the beast, and who shall mow fight with it?

And a mouth speaking great things and blasphemies was given to it, and power was given to it to do two and forty months. And it opened his mouth into blasphemies to God, to blaspheme His name and His Tabernacle and them that dwell in heaven. And it was given to him to make battle with saints and to overcome them. And power was given to him into each lineage and people and language and folk. And all men worshipped it that dwell in earth, whose names are not written in the Book of Life of the Lamb that was slain from the beginning of the world. If any man has ears, hear he. He that leads into captivity, shall go into captivity. He that slays with sword, it behoves him to be slain with sword. This is the patience and the faith of saints.

And I saw another beast stying up from the earth, and it had two horns like the Lamb. And it spoke as the dragon and did all the power of the former beast in his sight. And it made the earth and men dwelling in it to worship the first beast, whose wound of death was cured. And it did great signs that also it made fire to come down from heaven into the earth in the sight of all men. And it deceives men that dwell in earth, for signs which are given to it to do in the sight of the beast, saying to men dwelling in earth, that they make an image of the beast that had the wound of sword and lived. And it was given to him that he should give spirit to the image of the beast and that the image of the beast speak. And he shall make that whoever honour not the image of the beast, be slain. And he shall make all, small and great and rich and poor, and freemen and bondmen, to have a character in their right hand, either in their foreheads, that no man may buy either sell but they have the character, either the name of the beast, either the number of his name. Here is wisdom. He that has understanding, account the number of the beast. For it is the number of man, and his number is six hundred sixty and six.

Chapter XIV

And I saw, and lo, a Lamb stood on the mount of Zion, and with Him an hundred thousand and four and forty thousand, having His name and the name of His Father written in their foreheads. And I heard a voice from heaven as the voice of many waters and as the voice of a great thunder, and the voice which is heard was as of many harpers harping in their harps. And they sung as a new song before the seat of God and before the four beasts and seniors. And no man might say the song but they, an hundred thousand and four and forty thousand that are bought from the earth. These it is that are not defouled with women, for they are virgins. These sue the Lamb whitherever He shall go. These are bought of all men, the first fruits to God and to the Lamb. And in the mouth of them, leasing is not found, for they are without wem before the throne of God.

And I saw another angel flying by the middle of heaven, having an everlasting gospel that he should preach to men sitting on earth, and of each folk and lineage and language and people, and said with a great voice, Dread ye the Lord and give ye to Him honour, for the hour of His doom comes. And worship ye Him that made heaven and earth, the sea and all things that are in them, and the wells of waters.

And another angel sued, saying, The ilk great Babylon fell down, fell down, which gave drink to all folks of the wine of wrath of her fornication.

And the third angel sued him, and said with a great voice, If any man worship the beast and the image of it, and takes the character in his forehead, either in his hand, this shall drink of the wine of God's wrath that is meyned with clear wine in the cup of His wrath, and shall be tormented with fire and brimstone in the sight of holy angels and before the sight of the Lamb. And the smoke of their torments shall stye up into the worlds of worlds. Neither they have rest day and night which worship the beast and his image, and if any man take the character of his name. Here is the patience of saints which keep the commandments of God and the faith of Jesus.

And I heard a voice from heaven saying to me, Write thou, Blessed are dead men that die in the Lord. From henceforth now, the Spirit says that they rest of their travails, for the works of them sue them.

And I saw, and lo, a white cloud, and above the cloud a Sitter like the Son of Man having in His head a golden crown, and in His hand a sharp sickle. And another angel went out of the Temple and cried with a great voice to Him that sat on the cloud, Send Thy sickle and reap, for the hour comes that it be reaped, for the corn of the earth is ripe. And He that sat on the cloud, sent His sickle into the earth, and reaped the earth.

And another angel went out of the Temple that is in heaven, and he also had a sharp sickle. And another angel went out from the altar that had power on fire and water. And he cried with a great voice to him that had the sharp sickle, and said, Send thy sharp sickle and cut away the clusters of the vineyard of the earth, for the grapes of it are ripe. And the angel sent his sickle into the earth and gathered grapes of the vineyard of the earth, and sent into the great lake of God's wrath. And the lake was trodden without the city, and the blood went out of the lake till to the bridles of horses, by furlongs a thousand and six hundred.

Chapter XV

And I saw another sign in heaven, great and wonderful, seven angels having seven the last vengeances, for the wrath of God is ended in them. And I saw as a glass sea meyned with fire, and them that overcame the beast and his image and the number of his name, standing above the glass sea, having the harps of God and singing the Song of Moses, the servant of God, and the Song of the Lamb, and said, Great and wonderful are Thy works, Lord God Almighty. Thy ways are just and true, Lord, King of worlds. Lord, who shall not dread Thee and magnify Thy name? For Thou art merciful, for all folks shall come and worship in Thy sight, for Thy dooms are open.

And after these things, I saw, and lo, the Temple of the Tabernacle of Witnessing was opened in heaven, and seven angels having seven plagues, went out of the Temple and were clothed with a stole clean and white, and were before girded with golden girdles about the breasts. And one of the four beasts gave to the seven angels seven golden vials full of the wrath of God that lives into worlds of worlds. And the Temple was filled with smoke of the majesty of God and of the virtue of Him, and no man might enter into the Temple till the seven plagues of seven angels were ended.

Chapter XVI

And I heard a great voice from heaven, saying to the seven angels, Go ye and shed out the seven vials of God's wrath into earth. And the first angel went and shed out his vial into the earth, and a wound, fierce and worst, was made on all that had the character of the beast, and on them that worshipped the beast and his image.

And the second angel shed out his vial into the sea, and the blood was made as of a dead thing, and each man living was dead in the sea.

And the third angel shed out his vial on the floods and on the wells of waters, and said, Just art Thou, Lord, that art and that were holy, that deems these things, for they shed out the blood of hallows and pro-phets, and Thou has given to them blood to drink, for they are worthy. And I heard another saying, Yea, Lord God Almighty, true and just be Thy dooms.

And the fourth angel shed out his vial into the sun, and it was given to him to torment men with heat and fire. And men swelled with great heat, and blasphemed the name of God having power on these plagues. Neither they did penance that they should give glory to Him.

And the fifth angel shed out his vial on the seat of the beast, and his kingdom was made dark. And they ate together their tongues for sorrow, and they blasphemed God of heaven for sorrows of their wounds, and they did not penance of their works.

And the sixth angel shed out his vial in that ilk great flood, Euphrates, and dried the water of it, that way were made ready to kings from the sunrising. And I saw three unclean spirits, by the manner of frogs, go out of the mouth of the dragon and of the mouth of the beast, and of the mouth of the false prophet. For they are spirits of devils making signs, and they go forth to kings of all earth to gather them into battle, to the great day of Almighty God. Lo, I come as a night thief. Blessed is he that wakes and keeps his clothes, that he wander not naked and that they see not the filthihood of him. And he shall gather them into a place that is called in Hebrew, Armageddon.

And the seventh angel shed out his vial into the air, and a great voice went out of heaven from the throne, and said, It is done. And lightnings were made and voices and thunders, and a great earth⁄moving was made which manner never was since men were on earth, such earth⁄moving so great. And the great city was made into three parts, and the cities of heathen men fell down. And great Babylon came into mind before God, to give to it the cup of wine of the indignation of His wrath. And each isle flew away, and hills are not found. And great hail, as a talent, came down from heaven into men, and men blasphemed God for the plague of hail, for it was made full great.

Chapter XVII

And one of the seven angels came that had seven vials, and spoke with me and said, Come thou, I shall show to thee the damnation of the great whore that sits on many waters, with which kings of earth did fornication. And they that dwell in the earth are made drunken of the wine of her lechery. And he took me in desert in spirit. And I saw a woman sitting on a red beast, full of names of blas⁄

phemy, having seven heads and ten horns. And the
woman was environed with purple and red, and overgilded with gold and precious stone, and pearls, having
a golden cup in her hand, full of abominations and
uncleanness of her fornication. And a name written in
the forehead of her, MYSTERY, BABYLON THE
GREAT, MOTHER OF FORNICATIONS
AND OF ABOMINATIONS OF EARTH.
And I saw a woman drunken of the blood of saints,
and of the blood of martyrs of Jesus. And when I saw
her, I wondered with great wondering.

And the angel said to me, Why wonders thou? I
shall say to thee the sacrament of the woman and of the
beast that bears her, that has seven heads and ten horns.
The beast which thou see, was and is not, and she shall
stye from deepness and she shall go into perishing. And
men dwelling in earth, shall wonder, whose names are
not written in the Book of Life from the making of the
world, seeing the beast that was and is not. And this is
the wit, who that has wisdom. The seven heads are
seven hills on which the woman sits, and kings seven
are. Five have fallen down, one is, and another comes
not yet. And when he shall come, it behoves him to
dwell a short time. And the beast that was and is not,
and she, is the eighth, and is of the seven and shall go
into perishing. And the ten horns which thou has seen,
be ten kings that yet have not taken kingdom. But they
shall take power as kings, one hour after the beast.
These have a counsel and shall betake their virtue and
power to the beast. These shall fight with the Lamb,
and the Lamb shall overcome them, for He is Lord of
Lords and King of Kings, and they that are with Him
are called chosen and faithful.

And he said to me, The waters which thou has seen,
where the whore sits, are peoples and folks and lan-

guages. And the ten horns that thou has seen in the beast, these shall make her desolate and naked, and shall eat the fleshes of her and shall burn together her with fire. For God gave into the hearts of them that they do that that is pleasant to Him, that they give their kingdom to the beast till the words of God are ended. And the woman whom thou has seen, is the great city that has kingdom on kings of the earth.

Chapter XVIII

And after these things, I saw another angel coming down from heaven, having great power. And the earth was lightened of his glory. And he cried with strong voice, and said, Great Babylon fell down, fell down, and is made the habitation of devils and the keeping of each unclean spirit, and the keeping of each unclean fowl and hateful. For all folks drank of the wrath of fornication of her, and kings of the earth and merchants of the earth did fornication with her, and they are made rich of the virtue of delices of her.

And I heard another voice of heaven saying, My people, go ye out of it and be ye not partners of the trespasses of it, and ye shall not receive of the wounds of it. For the sins of it came till to heaven, and the Lord had mind of the wickedness of it. Yield ye to it as she yielded to you, and double ye double things after her works. In the drink that she meddled to you, mingle ye double to her. As much as she glorified herself and was in delices, so much torment give to her and wailing. For in her heart she says, I sit a queen and I am not a widow, and I shall not see wailing. And therefore in one day her wounds shall come, death and mourning and hunger, and she shall be burnt in fire, for God is strong that shall deem her.

And the kings of the earth shall beweep and bewail themselves on her, which did fornication with her and lived in delices, when they shall see the smoke of the burning of it, standing far for dread of the torments of it, and saying, Woe, woe, woe. The ilk great city, Babylon, and the ilk strong city, for in one hour thy doom comes. And merchants of the earth shall weep on it and mourn, for no man shall buy more the merchandise of them, the merchandises of gold and of silver, and of precious stone and of pearl, and of bissen and of purple, and of silk and coctin, and each tree thyine, and all vessels of ivory, and all vessels of precious stone and of brass and of iron, and of marble and of canel and amony, and of sweet smelling things and ointments and incense, and of wine, and of oil, and of flour, and of wheat, and of work beasts and of sheep, and of horses and of carts, and of servants and other lives of men. And thine apples of the desire of thy life went away from thee, and all fat things and full clear, perished from thee. And merchants of these things shall no more find those things. They that are made rich of it, shall stand far for dread of torments of it, weeping and mourning and saying, Woe, woe, the ilk great city that was clothed with bissen and purple and red scarlet, and was overgilded with gold and precious stone and margarites, for in one hour so many richesses are destitute.

fine linen

fine scarlet cloth
thyine wood

cinnamon

And each governor, and all that sail by ship into place, and mariners and that work in the sea, stood far and cried, seeing the place of the burning of it, saying, What is like this great city? And they cast powder on their heads and cried, weeping and mourning, and saying, Woe, woe, the ilk great city, in which all that have ships in the sea are made rich of prices of it, for in one hour it is desolate. Heaven and holy apostles and prophets, make ye full out joy on it, for God has deemed your doom of it.

And one strong angel took up a stone, as a great millstone, and cast into the sea, and said, In this hire the ilk great city Babylon shall be burnt, and now it shall no more be found. And the voice of harps and of men of music, and singing with pipe and trump shall no more be heard in it. And each crafty man and each craft shall no more be found in it. And the voice of the millstone shall no more be heard in thee, and the light of lantern shall no more shine to thee, and the voice of the husband and of the wife shall no more yet be heard in thee, for thy merchants were princes of the earth. For in thy witch- crafts all folks erred. And the blood of prophets and saints is found in it, and of all men that are slain in earth.

Chapter XIX

After these things, I heard as a great voice of many trumps in heaven, saying, Hallelujah, herying and glory and virtue is to our God, for true and just are the dooms of Him which deemed of the great whore that defouled the earth in her lechery, and venged the blood of His servants of the hands of her. And eft they said, Hallelujah. And the smoke of it styes up into worlds of worlds. And the four and twenty seniors and four beasts fell down and worshipped God sitting on the throne, and said, Amen. Hallelujah.

And a voice went out of the throne, and said, All the servants of our God, say ye heryings to our God, and ye that dread God, small and great. And I heard a voice of a great trump, as the voice of many waters and as the voice of great thunders, saying, Hallelujah, for our Lord God Almighty has reigned. Joy we and make we mirth, and give glory to Him. For the weddings of the Lamb came, and the wife of Him made ready herself. And it is given to her that she cover her with white bis- sen shining, for why, bissen is justifyings of saints.

And he said to me, Write thou, Blessed are they that

are called to the supper of weddings of the Lamb. And he said to me, These words of God are true. And I fell down before his feet to worship him, and he said to me, See thou that thou do not. I am a servant with thee and of thy brethren, having the witnessing of Jesus. Worship thou God, for the witnessing of Jesus is Spirit of prophecy.

And I saw heaven opened, and lo, a white horse, and He that sat on him was called Faithful and Soothfast, and with rightwiseness He deems and fights. And the eyes of Him were as flame of fire, and in His head many diadems. And He had a name written which no man knew but He. And He was clothed in a cloth spreyned *sprinkled* with blood, and the name of Him was called, The Son of God. And the hosts that are in heaven sued Him on white horses, clothed with bissen, white and clean. And a sword, sharp on each side, came forth of His mouth that with it He smite folks, and He shall rule them with an iron yerde. And He treads the presser of wine of strong vengeance of the wrath of Almighty God. And He has written in His cloth and in the hem, King of Kings and Lord of Lords.

And I saw an angel standing in the sun, and he cried with great voice, and said to all birds that flew by the middle of heaven, Come ye, and be ye gathered to the great supper of God, that ye eat the flesh of kings and flesh of tribunes, and flesh of strong men and flesh of horses, and of those that sit on them, and the flesh of all freemen and bondmen and of small and of great.

And I saw the beast and the kings of the earth, and the hosts of them gathered to make battle with Him that sat on the horse and with His host. And the beast was caught, and with her the false prophet that made signs before her, in which he deceived them that took the character of the beast and that worship the image of it. These twain were sent quick into the pool of fire burning with brimstone. And the other were slain of sword of Him that sat on the horse, that comes forth of the mouth of Him, and all birds were filled with the flesh of them.

Chapter XX

And I saw an angel coming down from heaven, having the key of deepness and a great chain in his hand. And he caught the dragon, the old serpent that is the devil and Satan, and he bound him a thousand years. And he sent him into deepness and closed on him, that he deceive no more the folks till a thousand years be filled. After these things, it behoves him to be unbound a little time.

And I saw seats and they that sat on them, and doom was given to them. And the souls of men, beheaded for the witnessing of Jesus and for the word of God, and them that worship not the beast neither the image of it, neither took the character of it in their foreheads neither in their hands. And they lived and reigned with Christ a thousand years. Other of dead men lived not till a thousand years are ended. This is the first again-rising. Blessed and holy is he that has part in the first again-rising. In these men the second death has not power, but they shall be priests of God and of Christ, and they shall reign with Him a thousand years.

And when a thousand years shall be ended, Satan shall be unbound of his prison, and he shall go out and shall deceive folks that are on four corners of the earth, Gog and Magog. And he shall gather them into battle whose number is as the gravel of the sea. And they styed up on the broadness of earth and environed the castles of saints and the loved city. And fire came down of God from heaven and devoured them. And the devil that deceived them was sent into the pool of fire and of brimstone, where both the beast and false prophets shall be tormented day and night into worlds of worlds. Amen.

And I saw a great white throne, and One sitting on it from whose sight earth fled and heaven. And the place is not found of them. And I saw dead men, great and small, standing in the sight of the throne, and books were opened and dead men were deemed of these things that were written in the books after the works of them. And the sea gave his dead men that were in it, and death and hell gave their dead men that were in them. And it was deemed of each after the works of them. And hell and death were sent into a pool of fire. This is the second death, and he that was not found written in the Book of Life, was sent into the pool of fire.

Chapter XXI

And I saw new heaven and new earth, for the first heaven and the first earth went away, and the sea is not now. And I, John, saw the holy city Jerusalem, new, coming down from heaven, made ready of God as a wife adorned to her husband. And I heard a great voice from the throne, saying, Lo, the Tabernacle of God is with men, and He shall dwell with them and they shall be His people, and He, God, with them shall be their God. And God shall wipe away each tear from the eyes of them, and death shall no more be, neither mourning, neither crying, neither sorrow shall be over, which first things went away. And He said that sat in the throne, Lo, I make all things new.

And He said to me, Write thou, for these words are most faithful and true. And He said to me, It is done. I am Alpha and Omega, the Beginning and End. I shall give freely of the well of quick water to him that thirsts. He that shall overcome, shall wield these things, and I shall be God to him, and he shall be son to Me. But to fearful men and unbelieveful, and cursed, and manquel⁄

lers, and fornicators, and witches, and worshippers of idols, and to all liars, the part of them shall be in the pool burning with fire and brimstone that is the second death.

And one came of the seven angels having vials full of seven the last vengeances. And he spoke with me and said, Come thou, and I shall show to thee the spouse, the wife of the Lamb. And he took me up in spirit into a great hill and high, and he showed to me the holy city Jerusalem coming down from heaven of God, having the clarity of God. And the light of it like a precious stone, as the stone jasper, as crystal. And it had a wall great and high, having twelve gates, and in the gates of it twelve angels, and names written in that are the names of twelve lineages of the sons of Israel. From the east, three gates and from the north three gates, and from the south three gates and from the west three gates. And the wall of the city had twelve fundaments, and in them the twelve names of the twelve apostles and of the Lamb.

And he that spoke with me had a golden measure of a reed, that he should mete the city and the gates of it, and the wall. And the city was set in square, and the length of it is so much, as much as is the breadth. And he meted the city with the reed, by furlongs twelve thousands. And the height and the length and breadth of it are even. And he meted the walls of it, of an hundred and four and forty cubits by measure of man, that is, of an angel. And the building of the wall thereof was of the stone jasper. And the city itself was clean gold, like clean glass. And the fundaments of the wall were adorned with all precious stone. The first fundament, jasper. The second, sapphire. The third, chalcedony. The fourth, smaragdin. The fifth, sardonyx. The sixth, sardius. The seventh, chrysolite. The eighth, beryl. The ninth, topaz. The tenth, chrysoprasus. The eleventh, jacinth. The twelfth, amethyst. And twelve gates are twelve margarites by each. And each gate was of each margarite. And the streets of the city were clean gold, as of glass full shining.

And I saw no Temple in it, for the Lord God Almighty and the Lamb is Temple of it. And the city has no need of sun, neither moon that they shine in it, for the clarity of God shall lighten it, and the Lamb is the lantern of it. And folks shall walk in light of it, and the kings of the earth shall bring their glory and honour into it. And the gates of it shall not be closed by day, and night shall not be there. And they shall bring the glory and honour of folks into it. Neither any man defouled and doing abomination and leasing, shall enter into it, but they that are written in the Book of Life and of the Lamb.

Chapter XXII

And he showed to me a flood of quick water, shining as crystal, coming forth of the seat of God and of the Lamb in the middle of the street of it. And on each side of the flood, the Tree of Life, bringing forth twelve fruits, yielding his fruit by each month. And the leaves of the Tree are to health of folks. And each cursed thing shall no more be, but the seats of God and of the Lamb shall be in it. And the servants of Him shall serve to Him. And they shall see His face, and His name in their foreheads. And night shall no more be, and they shall not have need to the light of lantern, neither to light of sun, for the Lord God shall lighten them, and they shall reign into worlds of worlds.

And he said to me, These words are most faithful and true. And the Lord God of spirits of prophets sent His angel to show His servants what things it behoves to be done soon. And lo, I come swiftly. Blessed is he that keeps the words of prophecy of this book.

And I am John that heard and saw these things. And afterward that I had heard and seen, I fell down to worship before the feet of the angel that showed to me these things. And he said to me, See thou that thou do not, for I am servant with thee and of thy brethren, prophets, and of them that keep the words of prophecy of this book. Worship thou God. And he said to me, Sign either seal thou not the words of prophecy of this book, for the time is nigh. He that noyeth, noy he yet, and he that is in filths, wax foul yet. And a just man be justified yet, and the holy be hallowed yet.

Lo, I come soon, and My meed is with Me to yield to each man after his works. I am Alpha and Omega, the First and the Last, Beginning and End. Blessed be they that wash their stoles, that the power of them be in the Tree of Life, and enter by the gates into the city. For withoutforth hounds and witches and unchaste men, and manquellers and serving to idols, and each that loves and makes leasing. I, Jesus, sent Mine angel to witness to you these things in churches.

I am the Root and Kin of David, and the shining Morrow Star. And the Spirit and the spouse say, Come Thou. And he that hears say, Come Thou. And he that thirsts, come, and he that will, take he freely the Water of Life. And I witness to each man hearing the words of prophecy of this book, if any man shall put to these things, God shall put on him the vengeances written in this book. And if any man do away of the words of the book of this prophecy, God shall take away the part of him from the Book of Life and from the holy city and from these things that are written in this book. He says, that bears witnessing of these things, Yea, Amen. I come soon. Amen.

Come Thou, Lord Jesus. The grace of our Lord Jesus Christ be with you all. Amen.